SOCIAL ISSUES, JUSTICE AND STATUS

WORK-LIFE BALANCE IN THE 21ST CENTURY

PERSPECTIVES, PRACTICES, AND CHALLENGES

SOCIAL ISSUES, JUSTICE AND STATUS

Additional books in this series can be found on Nova's website
under the Series tab.

Additional e-books in this series can be found on Nova's website
under the e-book tab.

SOCIAL ISSUES, JUSTICE AND STATUS

WORK-LIFE BALANCE IN THE 21ST CENTURY

PERSPECTIVES, PRACTICES, AND CHALLENGES

JESSICA M. NICKLIN

EDITOR

nova
science publishers
New York

Library of Congress Cataloging-in-Publication Data

ISBN: 978-1-53612-526-9

Published by Nova Science Publishers, Inc. † New York

CONTENTS

ABOUT THE EDITOR

Jessica M. Nicklin, PhD
Associate Professor, Psychology
University of Hartford, Connecticut, US
Email: nicklin@hartford.edu

Jessica M. Nicklin is an Associate Professor of Psychology at the University of Hartford. She is also currently the Associate Dean for Student Academic Services and the Director of the Master of Science in Organizational Psychology Program Online. Her research interests include workplace motivation, the work-family interface, and how positive psychology constructs influence well-being and success. She is published in journals such as *Psychological Bulletin, Organizational Behavior and Human Decision Processes, Journal of Vocational Behavior,* and *Journal of Occupational Health Psychology.* She holds several leadership positions for the *Society of Industrial and Organizational Psychology,* and is currently the Belle K. Ribicoff Endowed Professor at the University of Hartford.

LIST OF CONTRIBUTORS

Dr. Cathleen Swody is Director of Assessment and Founding Partner of Thrive Leadership, a consulting firm dedicated to helping leaders find success, at work and beyond, by providing practical insights through education, coaching, networking, and original research. In her role as a consultant and researcher, Cathleen designs and delivers employee surveys, leadership development programs, and executive coaching engagements that incorporate self-awareness, interpersonal relations, employee engagement, and managing difficult conversations. Since earning her Ph.D. in Industrial/Organization Psychology from the University of Connecticut, Cathleen has served clients across industries, from non-profits to the Fortune 500. Her passion for championing leaders pursuing personally meaningful careers led her to co-found with Catherine Flavin the LeaderMom™ research panel, a high-performing cross-industry group of senior leaders and moms. A strong believer in passing along what she learns, Cathleen also serves as an adjunct professor for the University of Connecticut School of Business Graduate Programs.

Catherine Flavin, MA, has 20 years of experience in leadership, engagement and culture across industries (including financial and professional services, pharma, healthcare, insurance, hospitality, foundations, higher education). She helps the people with whom she works identify practical insights and behavioral ways forward. And she strives to do her work in a way that "lives" the research she loves. She also gives keynotes on topics related to diversity and inclusion, and positive psychology. Before she was Managing Partner and Co-Founder at Thrive Leadership, Catherine was a Principal with Leadership Research Institute. Her work in leadership began in the political sphere at the Roper Center for Public Opinion Research and at the national foundation, Everyday Democracy, which is dedicated to civic engagement and diversity. Catherine holds a BA from Franklin & Marshall College, and she completed an MA in political science with distinction and advanced doctoral work (ABD) at the University of Connecticut.

Maura J. Mills, PhD, is an Assistant Professor of Management at Culverhouse College of Commerce, University of Alabama. She earned her M.S. and Ph.D. degrees in Industrial/Organizational Psychology from Kansas State University after completing her undergraduate degrees at Massachusetts College of Liberal Arts. Her research focuses on positive organizational behavior, including primary attention to issues regarding employee attitudes and well-being, work engagement, and the work-life/work-family interface, particularly as it relates to employee gender. She is published in a number of premier journals, and is the editor of Gender and the Work-Family Experience: An Intersection of Two Domains (2015), which has received wide praise. She is also co-founder of the Work-Family Researchers' Network Special Interest Group 'Work-Family and Gender'

Adam Pervez is a doctoral student in the Department of Management at The University of Alabama. His research interests focus on positive organizational behaviour, particularly happiness at work.

Ashley M. Mandeville, PhD, is an Assistant Professor of Management at Lutgert College of Business, Florida Gulf Coast University. Her research interests include the work-family interface and gender considerations within the workplace.

Andrew A. Bennett, PhD, is an Assistant Professor of Management at Old Dominion University. He completed a post-doc at the University of Alabama, earned his Ph.D. from Virginia Commonwealth University, M.A. from Gonzaga University, and B.S. from Clemson University. His research focuses on how employees recover from work stress, employee engagement and burnout, and evidence-based management, and he has published in several leading academic journals including the *Journal of Applied Psychology, Journal of Management, Organizational Research Methods*, and *Academy of Management Learning and Education*. In addition, he has worked on projects for multiple Fortune 500 companies and national non-profits as both a researcher and consultant.

Stephen E. Lanivich, PhD, is an Assistant Professor of Entrepreneurship and Management at Old Dominion University. Dr. Lanivich received his PhD in Business Administration from the College of Business at Florida State University. Also, he holds a Master's degree in Economics and a Bachelor's degree in Finance from Walsh College of Business. His research interests include the entrepreneurial mindset and cognitions, entrepreneurs' perceptions of resources, and opportunity recognition and fit. Dr. Lanivich's work has appeared in such journals as *Entrepreneurship: Theory & Practice*, the *Journal of Management*, the *Journal of Applied Psychology*, the *Journal of Occupational and Organizational Psychology*, and the *Journal of Vocational Behavior*.

Also, Dr. Lanivich's work has been featured in the *Frontiers of Entrepreneurship*. Before entering academia, Dr. Lanivich successfully started and managed three different entrepreneurial ventures. He currently feeds his entrepreneurial spirit through outreach to the ODU community.

Yusuf Akbulut is a PhD student at Old Dominion University. He earned his MBA from Old Dominion University, and his B.S. from Turkish Military Academy. His research focusses on how institutions influence nascent entrepreneurs at the macro-level and how nascent entrepreneurs go international.

M Mahdi Moeini Gharagozloo is a PhD student at Old Dominion University. He completed a Master of Science degree at Edhec Business School and earned his MBA from University of Tehran. His research focuses on mergers and acquisitions, especially how different forms of corporate finance structures can influence the outcome of M&A transactions.

Rachel L. Williamson is a doctoral candidate in the Industrial and Organizational Psychology program at the University of Georgia. Her research interests include individual differences, well-being, research methods, and how the nature and measurement of workaholism impacts employee well-being. She is published in journals such as *Psychological Assessment, Journal of Personality Assessment, Journal of Personality*, and *Human Resource Management Review*.

Malissa Clark, PhD, is an Assistant Professor of Industrial/Organizational Psychology at the University of Georgia. Her research interests include workaholism, the work-family interface, emotions at work, and women in the workplace. She is published in journals such as *Journal of Applied Psychology, Journal of Management, Journal of Organizational Behavior,* and *Journal of Vocational Behavior,* and she serves on the editorial boards of *Journal of Business and Psychology* and *Journal of Vocational Behavior.*

Lauren O. Gilmer entered the Industrial-Organizational Psychology Master's program at Indiana University-Purdue University Indianapolis in the fall of 2016, after earning a B.S. in Psychology and English from the University of Alabama in the spring of 2016. Lauren's research broadly covers the spectrum of work-life balance concerns, and specifically centers on the effects of nonstandard/irregular work schedules and the importance of recovery processes. Additionally, Lauren's master's thesis explores the existence and implications of workplace chronotype bias.

Dr. Alex Lindsey joined the faculty of the Department of Psychology at Indiana University – Purdue University Indianapolis after earning his Ph.D. from George Mason University in 2016. Dr. Lindsey's program of research investigates fair and equitable solutions to mitigate diversity-related challenges such as prejudice and discrimination in the workplace. Because seemingly trivial instances of disadvantage can create substantial inequity over time in the workplace, it represents a ripe context in which to study manifestations of disadvantage and potential solutions to these serious problems. His research seeks to generate effective strategies that targets of prejudice, their allies, and organizations can use to reduce inequality and promote inclusion in the workplace. Specifically, Dr. Lindsey's work has addressed diversity training effectiveness, impression and identity management strategies, and diverse team dynamics. This work has been published in quality outlets such as *Journal of Applied Psychology* and *Journal of Business and Psychology*.

Dr. Kristen Jones is an Assistant Professor of Management at the University of Memphis. She earned her Ph.D. from George Mason University after completing her undergraduate work at the University of Virginia. In her faculty position at the University of Memphis, she teaches undergraduate and graduate level courses related to human resource management, conducts research on workforce diversity and inclusion, and mentors doctoral students in the Ph.D. program in Management. Her program of research focuses on identifying and remediating subtle bias that unfairly disadvantages diverse employees at work, particularly women and mothers. Her work has been published in premier outlets including Journal of Management, Harvard Business Review, Human Resource Management, Journal of Business and Psychology, and Journal of Occupational Health Psychology. Dr. Jones's research has also been recognized through grants from the Society of Human Resource Management (SHRM) Foundation, the Society for Industrial and Organizational Psychology (SIOP), the American Psychological Association (APA), and the Society for the Psychological Study of Social Issues (SPSSI).

Isabel S. Silva, PhD, is an Assistant Professor of Psychology at the University of Minho, Portugal. She has developed her academic activity – teaching, research and interaction with society – in the field of Psychology of Work, Organizations and Human Resources. The impact of working conditions on occupational health and safety, particularly shiftwork, has been one of the main areas of interest throughout her academic career. Another area of interest focuses on work-life balance (particularly work-family balance), namely on the study of organizational policies and practices that may influence and promote that interface. She is published in journals as *TÉKHNE - Review of Applied Management Studies, International Journal on Working Conditions, and Reports in Public Health,* a book about shiftwork and several chapters of books.

Daniela Costa, holds a Master's degree in Psychology from University of Minho, Portugal. Currently, she is dedicated to research in the area of Organizational and Work Psychology. Her major research concerns are work schedules, particularly shiftwork, work-life interface and occupational health and safety. She has participated in congresses such as *International Congress on Safety and Labor Market* and *International Symposium on Occupational Safety and Hygiene*. In addition to research, she has experience in the field of training, in particular in terms of needs assessment and evaluation of its effectiveness.

Kevin A. Byle, PhD, is a Personnel Research Psychologist at U.S. Customs and Border Protection (CBP), Department of Homeland Security (DHS). Prior to working at CBP, Kevin worked in personnel selection at GEICO. He has extensive experience in several areas of Industrial/Organizational Psychology, including the development and validation of a broad range of tests and assessments (e.g., in-baskets, role plays, cognitive ability tests, multitasking simulations, biodata inventories, structured interviews), large scale job analyses, and organizational surveys. His current research interests include integrity testing, mental abilities testing, and the use of organizational surveys. His research has been published in *Leadership Quarterly, Intelligence,* and *the Journal of Business and Psychology*. He received a M.A. in Clinical Psychology from Ball State University and a Ph.D. in Industrial/Organizational Psychology from Northern Illinois University.

Jeffrey M. Cucina, PhD, is a Personnel Research Psychologist at U.S. Customs Border Protection (CBP) where he develops and validates entry-level employment tests. He received his Ph.D. in industrial/organizational psychology from The George Washington University. His research interests include individual differences (e.g., mental abilities, personality), psychometrics, and research methodology. Dr. Cucina has published in journals such as *Personnel Psychology*, the *Journal of Applied Psychology*, the *Journal of Organizational Behavior*, *Intelligence*, the *International Journal of Selection and Assessment*, *Psychological Assessment*, and *Personnel Assessment and Decisions* (for which he is a member of the Editorial Board). He has previously served as the Historian of the Society for Industrial and Organizational Psychology (SIOP) and was the 2015 recipient of the SIOP Distinguished Early Career Contributions Award for Practice.

Laurel A. McNall, PhD, is an Associate Professor in the Department of Psychology at The College at Brockport, State University of New York. Her current research interests include employee attitudes, the work-life interface (with an emphasis on the benefits of multiple life roles) and worker well-being. She has published in journals such as *Organizational Behavior and Human Decision Processes, Journal of Vocational*

Behavior, Journal of Occupational Health Psychology, and *Journal of Business and Psychology.*

Anneliese Janssen, MS, graduated from the University of Hartford with a Master of Science in Organizational Psychology. Now, she currently works in the field of Human Resources. She is an active member amongst the Human Resources community with affiliations with the Society of Human Resources Management (SHRM) and Human Resources Association of Central Connecticut (HRACC). Her research interests included self-compassion, positive psychology, sympathy and empathy in the workplace, and work-life balance. This is her first published work.

YoungAh Park, PhD, Dr. Park is an Assistant Professor of the School of Labor and Employment Relations at the University of Illinois-Urbana-Champaign. Dr. Park earned her Ph.D. in Industrial–Organizational Psychology from Bowling Green State University. Her research examines psychological mechanisms of work stress, recovery, and work-life boundary management within various temporal (e.g., daily, weekly) and social contexts (e.g., couple dyads, work groups). Her research also focuses on identifying psychosocial factors that alleviate or aggravate these psychological mechanisms. Her research has been funded by the National Institute for Occupational Safety and Health and published in leading journals such as *Journal of Applied Psychology, Journal of Occupational Health Psychology, Journal of Management, and Journal of Organizational Behavior.*

Lucille Headrick, is a doctoral student in the School of Labor and Employment Relations at the University of Illinois at Urbana-Champaign. She graduated from Saint Louis University with a bachelor's degree in Psychology and Sociology in 2014. Her research interests include the work-nonwork interface and boundary management, recovery from work, employee health and well-being, and performance (counterproductive work behavior).

Elena Stepanova is an individual and organizational coach, researcher and lecturer at the Master of Systemic Coaching (Autonomous University of Barcelona, UAB) and member of the Panakía Project Platform. She holds a Master in Psychology of Intercultural Actions (University of Nancy 2, France), a Postgraduate degree in Systemic Coaching (UAB), and a Ph.D. in Social/Organizational Psychology (UAB). She graduated in psychology after studying in the Ukraine and the US. She has been involved in a number of consulting and training activities and collaborated with various academic and social institutions, particularly with IESE Business School, working in research and as a coach in executive programs. Elena's coaching practice and research focus on personal and professional well-being, work-life integration and positive organizational scholarship. She has co-authored various book chapters dedicated to these topics in scientific outlets like Cambridge University Press, Elsevier, Edward Elgar, Routledge, Palgrave MacMillan, Oxford University Press.

Lucia Ceja obtained her PhD in Work and Organizational Psychology from the University of Barcelona, and her MSc in Occupational Health Psychology from the University of Nottingham, UK. She is a research associate in the Family-Owned Business Chair in IESE Business School where she conducts research at the interface between the fields of Family-Owned Business and Positive Organizational Psychology. She is a family business consultant at the Family in Business Analysis Center (FIBAC) in areas related to happiness & well-being, intergenerational positive relationships and development of healthy psychological ownership. She has published numerous articles and book chapters in scientific outlets like Cambridge University Press, Journal of Organizational Behavior, European Journal of Work and Organizational Psychology, Human Relations, Applied Psychology: An International Review and the Journal of Happiness Studies.

Félix Castillo is the founder and director of the Master of Systemic Coaching of the Autonomous University of Barcelona. He is a clinical psychologist trained at the University of Barcelona. He holds a Master in Family Therapy and Master in Systemic Coaching from the Autonomous University of Barcelona. Félix is a supervisor of numerous teams of social work, child protection and mental health professionals. He serves as a psychotherapist and advisor of the PIAE Services (Therapeutic Attention to Families) at the Sant Joan de Déu Health Park. He is a member of Panakia Project Platform.

Tracy Brower, PhD, is a work sociologist and the author of *Bring Work to Life by Bringing Life to Work: A Guide for Leaders and Organizations.* Tracy has worked within the furniture and CPG industries and has also worked with many of the Fortune 500, as well as educational and health-care organizations. Tracy has taught university courses in management, HR, and organizational effectiveness. She is an award-winning speaker and executive advisor to the Michigan State University Professional Science Masters Industrial Mathematics Program and on the selection committee for the Rosabeth Moss Kanter award for excellence in work-family research. In addition to her PhD in sociology and MM in organizational culture, Tracy holds a Master of Corporate Real Estate. Tracy is a TEDx speaker and her work has been featured in *The Wall Street Journal, The Globe and Mail, Training Magazine, Facility Executive, Real Estate Review Journal, Fortune.com, Forbes.com, Inc. Magazine,* and more.

INTRODUCTION

The world of work is constantly evolving, as is the interplay between work and other life domains. As such, it is critical that practitioners and scholars recognize the complexities of balancing work and life in the 21st century. The goal of this book is therefore to meet the demand for knowledge and skills to help employees, employers and families successfully navigate work and life. The chapters address problems and propose solutions for diverse issues, ranging from classic, yet prevalent, topics (i.e., gender disparities) to novel ideas and new directions for research (i.e., chronotypes and recovery experience). To best serve the needs of the readers, both academic and applied, this volume includes empirical studies, practical reflections, review chapters, and research recommendations for the future.

The idea of work-family conflict is not a new one and has been of interest to scholars and organizational leaders for nearly five decades. Yet, we know now that balancing work and life goes beyond the needs of the "traditional family" and the "traditional nine-to-five job." We also know that in addition to the negative consequences associated with work-family conflict, there are indeed benefits associated with balancing multiple life roles. As such, the first section of this volume examines work-life balance in unique (and often, overlooked) populations of workers. The second section goes beyond the traditional idea of work-family conflict to explore innovative ways in which to conceptualize work-life balance for the future.

PART 1: BALANCE IN UNIQUE POPULATIONS

This section begins by discussing balance as it relates to gender. While gender is not a *unique* consideration, the authors in Chapters 1 and 2 introduce unique challenges faced by employees related to gender roles. We have made great strides in the quest for gender equality in the US workplace, yet women and men are still plagued by distinct challenges associated with balancing work and family roles. Drawing from a sample of "LeaderMoms" (women who are both high performers at work and mothers) in Chapter 1, Cathy Swody and Catherine Flavin address strategies that high-performing mothers can use to balance work and family roles. Their data suggest that it is important for women to know what is important, align their priorities, delegate, build a strong support system at work and home, and be present in their respective roles. They also share recommendations for managers of high-performing women to help LeaderMoms achieve personal and professional success. According to Swody and Flavin, women can successfully balance work and family while maintaining high-status careers, but they should rely on the strategies shared by other LeaderMoms.

Gender-related concerns surrounding work-life balance affect not only women professionals but men as well. In Chapter 2, Maura Mills, Adam Pervez, and Ashley Mandeville note that while the United States (slowly) makes advances in supporting a family-friendly workforce, it is doing so with a primary focus on female employees, missing the point of what it means to promote *gender-equitable work-family balance policies*. Men too feel intensified work-family conflict, as in today's egalitarian society they are now expected to provide more support for household and childcare responsibilities, yet most organizational cultures don't support men undertaking such home roles. Women, however, are still viewed as the primarily caretakers of children and suffer more from the consequences associated with gender-role stereotypes and flexibility bias. Furthermore, they argue that when initiatives such as maternity leaves are given in place of gender-equitable leaves, they can have the unintended side effect of stalling women's careers. Even gender-blind policies, treating men and women equally, limit women in many occupations (e.g., academia). The authors caution managers and policy makers of the unintended side effects of seeing work-family balance as primarily a women's issue and suggest that *everyone* benefits when precedence is given to family policies more generally.

Chapters 3–6 move beyond gender to explore more narrow segments of the working population who face diverse challenges with balancing work and life. In chapter 3, Andrew Bennett, Stephen Lanivich, Yusuf Akbulut, and M. Mahdi Moeini Gharagozloo highlight the challenges, identities, and characteristics of *entrepreneurs*, a growing segment of society, and show how these features differentially impact entrepreneurs' work-life balance. They discuss how a strong entrepreneurial identity may weaken the importance of other identities, hindering work-life balance. They also discuss how the permeable and flexible nature of entrepreneurs' boundaries can lead to more perceptions of imbalance as well as how the additional business stressors and lack of resources lead to increased stress for many entrepreneurs. To help minimize these challenges unique to entrepreneurs, they make recommendations for boundary management strategies and recovery experiences to achieve and maintain work-life balance. Furthermore, given that most adults spend a majority of their daily lives on work-related activities, Rachel

Williamson and Malissa Clark, in Chapter 4, discuss the experience of work-family conflict for workaholics (people who are addicted to work, feel internal pressures to work, persistently think about work, and work beyond expectations). They integrate *workaholism* into three theoretical perspectives utilized in the work-family literature: (1) resource and role-based theories, (2) boundary and boarder theories, and (3) spillover and crossover theories. Through a combination of theory and research they provide a thorough review of literature and make recommendations for future research. This is an important area for exploration, as their chapter illustrates the negative effects of workaholism on employees, that is, the chapter illustrates work-family conflict.

Following from the chapters on entrepreneurs and workaholics, in Chapter 5, Lauren Gilmer, Alex Lindsey, and Kristen Jones examine work-life balance through the lens of time. Using a biological approach, they explore how *chronotype, flexible scheduling*, and *recovery experiences* can hinder or support work-life balance. They draw attention to the fact that the demands of many occupations (e.g., shift work, night work, and nine-to-five schedules) do not fit individuals' internal clocks, thus creating negative psychological and physiological outcomes for many employees. They also discuss the need for more scheduling flexibility and recovery experiences for promoting work-life balance and other important organizational- and individual-level outcomes. They provide recommendations for employees and organizations to help maximize time to achieve work-life balance, and make suggestions for future programs research. Similarly, in Chapter 6, Isabel Silva and Daniela Costa also discuss the complexities associated with *nonstandard work schedules* for work-life balance. They specifically explore shift work, split-shift schedules, compressed workweeks, and part-time and flexible work hours. Like Swody and Flavin in Chapter 1, they call attention to the importance of flexible work hours for employees but do caution managers and employees of the dangers associated with flexible work arrangements. To wrap up Part 1, Kevin Byle, Jeffrey Cucina, Laurel McNall, and I review theoretical and empirical research on work-life enrichment as it specifically pertains to expatriates (employees who live and work outside of their native country). This is an important population for consideration as the workforce is becoming increasingly global and the need for expatriates is on the rise. Drawing on a model from Lazarova and colleagues (2010), we share research findings of a sample of federal agents working internationally at the US embassies and consulates around the world. We found that coworker support, individual differences, and work-life enrichment contribute directly to expatriate outcomes and that expatriation requires many personal sacrifices and considerations. We provide several recommendations for managers to support expatriate success.

PART 2: BEYOND WORK-FAMILY CONFLICT

The second section of this volume introduces forward-thinking approaches to conceptualizing work-life balance that look beyond the classic notion of "work-family conflict." In Chapter 8, Laurel McNall, Anneliese Janssen, and I draw attention to the positive side of the work-life interface by exploring how *positive psychological resources* (resilience, mindfulness, and self-compassion) can be used to enhance work-life enrichment and minimize work-life conflict, leading to higher levels of well-being, physical and psychological health, performance, and satisfaction with work and life, and lower levels of burnout and stress. We propose four agenda items for future research and practice to advance our understanding of how trainable resources can help generate and sustain work-life balance. My colleagues and I emphasize the importance of exploring domains outside of the traditional family, and following this in Chapter 9, YoungAh Park and Lucille Headrick discuss the complexities of achieving balance for the working student, a segment of society on the rise. As do my colleagues and I in Chapter 8, they examine both the negative and the positive sides of the *work-school interface*, by providing a detailed analysis of the work, nonwork, and individual difference variables that impact work-school conflict and facilitation. They also examine the consequences of work-school conflict and facilitation and offer future research directions to help promote balance for student workers.

The next two chapters take radical approaches to understanding work-life balance. In Chapter 10, Elena Stepanova, Lucía Ceja, and Félix Castillo provide a holistic model of *work-life integration* by exploring the "whole person" through the interactions among three dimensions: domain, identity, and temporal integration. They argue that by adopting a holistic view we can better understand the whole spectrum of resources and context-specific variables beyond work and family to life in general. Findings from an empirical study provide three themes that motivate and inspire people on their jobs: generative aspects, people-related sources, and work-related aspects. They conclude with recommendations for future research and practice regarding enhancing employee self-awareness, promoting high-quality connections, and fostering organizational support. In Chapter 11, Tracy Brower suggests that perhaps we have it all wrong by trying to achieve work-life balance. Through integration, fulfillment, and life-course perspectives, Brower offers that *work-life supports* should be used to bring work to life and life to work to achieve a more fulfilling and integrated life. Based on executive data she provides actionable recommendations for how to utilize work-life supports to create a more fulfilling whole person.

Throughout this volume, there are overarching and parallel themes among the chapters; however, each author or set of authors takes a novel approach to exploring work-life balance in the 21st century. There are a number of opportunities for practitioners and managers to implement initiatives promoting balance or a more integrative life, as well as many recommendations for future research. I hope this book serves as a catalyst for collaboration, research, and positive change for people balancing work and life in the 21st century.

PART 1. BALANCE IN UNIQUE POPULATIONS

In: Work-Life Balance in the 21st Century
Editor: Jessica M. Nicklin

ISBN: 978-1-53612-526-9
© 2018 Nova Science Publishers, Inc.

Chapter 1

LESSONS IN LEADERSHIP: INSIGHTS INTO HOW WOMEN THRIVE AT WORK WHILE RAISING FAMILIES

Cathleen Swody, PhD and Catherine Flavin*
Thrive Leadership, West Chester, PA, US

ABSTRACT

In popular media, we regularly hear messages about the challenges experienced by working mothers and the shortage of women in executive leadership positions. In companies, we have seen women turn down leadership roles purportedly because they have kids (or want to have kids), and struggle to find viable models for how to thrive at work and as a mother. In academia, researchers have well documented the negative outcomes of work-family conflict for individuals and organizations. The image of the challenging work-family interface can be discouraging for women who are considering their professional aspirations and for organizations that want to develop high-performing employees. In our research, we have observed a strong positive relationship between personal feelings of accomplishment in work and the belief that family responsibilities are compatible with advancing a career at an organization. In presenting the firsthand experiences of the women leaders who participated in our studies, our goal is to offer useful practices to individuals and their managers and to foster additional work-family research in organizations.

"How do other high-performing women approach the challenge of being a great mother and a top performer at work?" This question arose in an executive coaching session in which an up-and-coming vice president in a financial services firm spoke about

---
* Corresponding Author Email: cswody@thriveleadership.com.

the mixed sense of excitement and isolation she was experiencing at work. She was the only woman at her level in her group. She loved her job, enjoyed her work, and respected her colleagues. She had a new baby girl and was in the midst of re-creating her approach to her life at work and home, all with no role models in view. Variations of this theme have emerged in countless coaching discussions we have held with women leaders.

WORK-FAMILY CHALLENGES

In popular media, we regularly hear messages about the challenges of motherhood and the shortage of women in executive leadership positions (e.g., Fairchild, 2014; Slaughter, 2012; "Where are all?" 2011). In companies, we have seen women move away from leadership roles purportedly because they have kids (or want to have kids), and struggle to find viable models for how to thrive at work and as a mother. Successful fulfillment of one role often seems at odds with successful fulfillment of the other role (Ezzedeen & Ritchey, 2009; Knudsen, 2009), and having a family can be seen as a barrier for women's careers (Cross, 2010; Emslie and Hunt, 2009; Grady & McCarthy, 2008; Straub, 2007), especially for leaders who usually work long hours and experience responsibility-related demands (Knudsen, 2009).

In academia, researchers have well documented the negative outcomes of work-family conflict for both individuals and organizations (see Dorio, Bryant, & Allen, 2008; and Eby, Casper, Lockwood, Bordeaux, & Brinley, 2005). For example, work-family conflict is significantly related to lower work satisfaction and job satisfaction, lower psychological well-being, higher turnover intentions, and higher job stress (Amstad, Meier, Elfering, Fasel, & Semmer, 2011; Anderson, Coffey, & Byerly, 2002; Boyar, Maertz, Pearson, and Keough, 2003; Raghuram & Wiesenfeld, 2004; Shockley & Singla, 2011). With these known negative outcomes, work-family conflict can discourage women from pursuing professional aspirations and can prevent organizations from retaining a segment of talented employees.

In practice, we have heard from many talented junior-level women that they are looking upward for evidence that pursuing a career and a family is reasonable. As one manager explained, "I most often see senior women leaders without kids, and sometimes those with kids seem very stressed and at a disadvantage compared to their male counterparts who have stay-at-home wives supporting them." This young professional was wondering if she ought to lower her professional aspirations if she has children. The overall picture being painted can be daunting and disheartening—both for women who are considering their professional aspirations and for organizations that want to retain talented and high-performing employees.

However, not all women amend their professional aspirations to pursue career ambitions alongside family relationships. Some reject the notion that a choice needs to be made between work and family (i.e., fallacy of choice; Ezzedeen & Ritchey, 2009). For those who pursue leadership goals while raising children, a research question emerged about which strategies and tactics these women have found personally successful and what these women would recommend to others in similar situations as well as their managers. As noted by Major and Morganson (2011), the research literature has offered considerably less insight into how individuals can prevent, address, and cope with work-family conflict. In the following section, we share observations from our study of how women leaders navigate work and family challenges.

APPROACH TO UNDERSTANDING ADAPTIVE STRATEGIES

In response to the many requests from women who want to know specifically how high-achieving women leaders sustain their performance levels while managing family responsibilities, we assembled a cross-industry panel of high-performing leaders and mothers. Using a referral sampling technique, we sought accomplished women who were considered high performers at work and who were also seen as engaged with their families. Each participant had an opportunity to recommend additional women whom they considered high performers at work and who were also mothers. We eventually coined the term "LeaderMom" to offer common language for these women to discuss a shared experience.

In the first LeaderMom study, the sample included 76 leaders who had been identified as high performers in their careers in 11 industries and who were mothers; the second LeaderMom study grew to 120 leaders. In the first study, participants were invited to complete a confidential web-based survey, including open-ended questions of (1) their recommendations to *other mothers* to balance work and family based on their experiences, and (2) their recommendations to *managers* of other high-performing women to help them sustain performance and thrive in their roles. In addition, this first survey measured various aspects of participants' work environments, including manager support, job- and family-related attitudes, work-family balance, and ambition.

We agree with Carmeli (2003) that individual employees and their organizations each have responsibility for minimizing work-family conflict and effectively integrating work and family demands. To get as close as we could to offering practical suggestions within individuals' loci of control, we deliberately focused the field research on uncovering approaches and behaviors used by leaders. From women who were viewed as both excellent leaders and engaged mothers, we asked about their personal experiences and lessons, and gathered tactics that could be implemented by individuals and their managers. We applied quantitative and qualitative approaches to extract richer insights and to enable women to explain directly how they negotiated career and family demands.

We certainly do not advocate a "cookie cutter" approach to being a LeaderMom or applying the "Great Man" theory to their experiences. On the contrary, the women in the panel represent diverse life experiences, home situations, and cultural traditions. However, collective insights from other leaders can be a powerful source of ideas and guidance to help navigate the ambiguity and challenges that accompany leadership and motherhood. These examples may help more junior leaders who are looking for role models to confirm their own ambitions, release unhelpful doubts, take steps to support their success, and ultimately, inspire further dialogue.

Analyses included quantitative and qualitative approaches, including regression analyses, analysis of variance, and thematic analysis of participant responses to the open-ended questions. In analyzing the responses to the open-ended questions, themes were identified only if they met three criteria: (1) recurrence, (2) repetition, and (3) forcefulness (Owen, 1984). In the interest of brevity and unique value, this chapter focuses on the qualitative themes related to two research questions: (1) What strategies are used by *mothers* who are high performers at work to manage work and family responsibilities? and (2) What strategies do these high-performing mothers recommend for *managers* of people in similar situations?

Responses to these questions reveal the importance of leadership and professional growth. Teasing apart the skills that differentiate managers and women who are effectively navigating work-family challenges serves as a precursor to more effective leadership development. In the following sections, we will describe these findings in more detail.

STRATEGIES TO MANAGE WORK AND FAMILY RESPONSIBILITIES

Many leaders, irrespective of gender, feel overwhelmed at times. In our study, we heard from leaders who addressed being overwhelmed by being disciplined about priorities. The women who were most satisfied with their work and families had identified their essential priorities, made choices and set boundaries in alignment with those priorities, and refrained from worrying about tasks that matter less. These LeaderMoms report that much of their ability to thrive comes from working hard to identify what matters—both in their businesses and at home—and in developing habits to focus on these priorities, which we will discuss further in this section (see Table 1.1).

Table 1.1. Effective strategies used by *high-performing women leaders* to manage work and family responsibilities

Strategy
1. Know what really matters and return to these priorities often.
2. Ask for what you need, both personally and professionally.
3. Hone delegation skills.
4. Be mindful and limit multitasking.

Know What Really Matters and Return to These Priorities Often

This first piece of counsel from the LeaderMom study reflects a straightforward high-performer practice of doing what has the most value. Many respondents underscored the need to deliberately focus time and attention on the tasks and projects within an individual's area of influence that contribute most to the success of the organization or of the family. This disciplined focus allows people to make meaningful contributions that matter and to avoid being weighed down by less important tasks. Taking time upfront to clarify and define priorities helps leaders be less vulnerable to seemingly never-ending demands on their time and better prepared to make a series of moment-to-moment choices ("Which will I do?" versus "Can I do it all?"). When leaders deeply understand what is critical to them and make choices accordingly, they report experiencing less stress and less regret. Interestingly, knowing what personally matters appears to move the women in the panel off the defensive and saves them from a common pitfall: over-apologizing. Consider the following comments as representative of this theme:

When prioritizing at home, I focus on lifelong impact (i.e., "will it affect my child's or my own lifelong learning or health?"). If no, it goes on the "later" list. Eventually cleaning the house gets completed . . . when it seems a threat to someone's health!

There will always be another important meeting or conference call. There will never be another dance recital for a five-year-old dressed as a bluebird. Years from now, colleagues will not remember that you missed the meeting/call. You and your family will remember the bluebird.

Try to find a way not to miss the important things in your child's life. It helps you stay focused and in your career when you feel good about being able to be there for your kid when it really matters.

Schedule family events with the same (or higher) urgency as you do work tasks.

No apologies! Do what has to be done, make executive decisions, and don't make excuses (to your family or your work). It's all about owning your own choices and being responsible to both your clients and your family.

Cut yourself some slack. The house doesn't always have to be clean, you don't have to get to work at 8:00, and your kids don't have to take part in every single activity.

Ask for What You Need, both Personally and Professionally

A second theme we observed was that the most satisfied LeaderMoms were those who negotiated agreement with their families about their priorities. Leaders who did this very well were more than twice as likely to say their lives are close to ideal (100 percent versus 40 percent who responded Strongly Agree or Agree on a five-point Likert scale). Alignment with family on priorities is also a critical factor in women's engagement at work. The more a leader has alignment with her family about her personal priorities, the greater personal accomplishment she feels at work. Alignment involves open, two-way communication and negotiating priorities with other people (e.g., partner/spouse and children). Tactics such as asking children which events they most want you to attend and sharing work successes are mentioned as ways women create this alignment.

Moms will do what's important to their children and their families. To the degree that children and spouses articulate "*this* and not that" is important. My son will tell me, "I don't need you to go to the award ceremony where everyone gets an award; I really need you to come to my game . . . I'm pitching."

Communicate with your spouse/partner/family about what is important, and work to help each other stay true to those priorities.

The job will always want more and more of your time, so know your limits and be willing to speak up.

Ask for what you want. Ask for flexibility. If you deliver, then you can create what works for you.

Hone Delegation Skills

Participants in the study clearly and passionately convey the importance of building a strong team at work and at home. In fact, delegation is the most frequently identified skill by a large margin, a skill that participants had to develop to attain their current role (76 percent of participants have learned delegation skills compared to 46–61 percent for the next 10 most common skills; see Table 1.2). In sum, these accomplished women demonstrate that realism about their limitations serves them much more than any all-or-nothing idealization of an elusive perfect circumstance ("having it all"). At work and home, sharing the workload while developing others' skills along the way is a recommended approach for engaging others and achieving what needs to be accomplished. Self-sacrifice and heroic feats can meet short-term deadlines, but over time, they are not sustainable and are career limiting.

Build a strong team. Hire professionals who are smarter than you. Do not even think you are able to do it all yourself.

Delegate, delegate, delegate! It grows your staff's confidence and skills and improves your leadership abilities.

Delegating at home sets a good example for kids on what real life is all about. I constantly battle the "perfect mom" image in my head, but I have gotten much better at accepting that there is no universal standard of what that means, and my way seems to work for me and my family.

Be self-aware of your strengths and weaknesses and be okay with it. Surround yourself with people who complement your weaknesses.

I used to struggle with guilt for leaving my family and household to the care of another person. Over the years, my family and I have come to realize that my career is part of who I am and that my love and dedication to my family isn't tied to the amount of hours I spend physically with my kids or doing the housework.

I don't want to be superwoman! I want help. I tell my family all the time I want to be part of a team. Teamwork is how we roll.

I have delegated carelessly before, giving tasks/projects to team members who weren't ready for the level of work and needed more direction to accomplish it properly. You must know the people you are delegating to and know what their strengths are. You have to take the time to invest in and build a strong support team in order to have trustworthy employees who can carry the torch and execute projects that will be consistent to your standards. Be an encourager of those you delegate to; a little praise goes a long way!

Table 1.2. Skills that LeaderMoms report learning to advance to their current roles

Skill	Percentage of participants
Delegation/working more effectively through others	76
Saying no	61
Organizational skills; planning; time management	59
Executive presence	59
Networking; relationship-building	59
Financial acumen	58
Prioritizing	57
Efficiency of work processes/productivity	54
Assertiveness	53
Strategic thinking	51
Stress management/composure	46
Business development	34
Establishing boundaries	32

Note: Participants were asked to select all skills they had to learn and grow personally, as they advanced to their current roles.

Be Mindful and Limit Multitasking

By being present in the current domain, whether at work or with family, the LeaderMoms in our studies are better able to perform at their best. With more demands than hours, many participants advise other leaders to limit multitasking as well as the spillover of work into family time. While many women leaders struggle to protect family time from work intrusions, practicing mindfulness in the present moment is a useful skill rather than being physically present and mentally absent.

> Full, sequential focus works better than trying to multitask all the time. . . . You have to decide what is important to you and focus on it in the moment.

> It's important to be present during whatever function you are fulfilling, whether it is work or family. . . . When at work, 100 percent focus on work is critical. When at home, 100 percent focus on family is equally important—and the latter is likely harder for ambitious women.

> Identify specific times you can commit to being at home—for example, work late on weekdays if you can commit to being at home on weekends.

STRATEGIES RECOMMENDED FOR MANAGERS

In the research literature, consistent empirical support has emerged for how informal managerial support is negatively related to work-family conflict (i.e., more supportive manager, less work-family conflict for the employee; Anderson et al., 2002; Behson, 2002; Frye & Breaugh, 2004). When asked to advise more junior women cuing up the ranks, LeaderMoms recommend seeking managers who demonstrate the following skills better than other managers (and explicitly advise women to avoid managers who do not demonstrate these skills). The good news is that these skills are learnable for managers (see Table 1.3). With these skills, managers will be better able to engage and develop talented employees, including mothers.

Table 1.3. Effective strategies used by *leaders* of high-performing women

Strategy
1. Be flexible in when and where work occurs.
2. Develop and sponsor employees.
3. Allow employees latitude in decisions about work and family responsibilities.

Be Flexible in When and Where Work Occurs

We learned from participants that they want managers who are more focused on performance and achievement of results and *not* on how much time is spent in the office. LeaderMoms ask their managers to support flexibility in how work is completed and to show trust in their ability to complete work in their own way. When managers are overly prescriptive of when and where work is completed, they add artificial limits; with these high performers, energy is better focused on results than artificial limits. Participants provided these descriptions of especially effective managers:

> Giving me the flexibility to get the work done in perhaps less than conventional ways. To clarify, the leader has not been pedantic about "how" the work gets done but is willing to let me get things accomplished while I do the juggling of home versus work priorities.

> Use a results-only work philosophy, rather than worrying about how much time they spend at the office.

> Focus on what they deliver—not how.

Allow for flexibility, and encourage the creative thinking of mothers (who make it work somehow all the time).

Do not assume that you will get less out of a working mother. Give them the latitude to set a schedule that works and some flexibility within that, and be clear about job expectations. The working mother will Figure out how to get the job done well.

Let them have flexibility (while still requiring results, however). Work flexibility will actually result in higher productivity, dedication, and engagement.

Know that the work will get done. Laying on guilt of questioning ability or dedication when childcare issues arise (nannies don't show up; doctor's appointments, etc.) will only increase insecurity and anger that ultimately hurt the work product. Assume the mother can handle it until she shows you she can't.

Develop and Sponsor Employees

The second most frequent request that participants in the LeaderMom study have for their managers is to intentionally provide performance feedback and recognition (e.g., "here's where you are contributing" and "here's where you could contribute"). Many participants pointed out that when managers invest in their people and give them what they need to perform their responsibilities, they become motivated to perform even better. Helping LeaderMoms see where their value lays in the organization is essential to focusing their talents and enabling them to ask for what they need to perform. Furthermore, leaders need to develop and engage their own direct reports; and LeaderMoms, like any other leaders, are better positioned to do that with the benefit of having personally experienced effective leadership.

In addition, mentoring, developing, and investing in the long-term success of these women helps them cultivate and direct their ambitions. Our study supports that ambition is required to reach the levels these women have achieved; nearly the entire panel of women in this study described themselves as ambitious (98 percent). Better managers recognize the ambition of their people and deliberately help them focus on the right things for future success. One skill area in particular where leaders can offer support and perspective is prioritization. Participants' recommendations for managers related to growth and development include the following:

Determine the hi-po's [high-potential leader's] motivation—find them a mentor and continue to show interest. Use situational leadership so you don't cramp their style as they are learning and growing. Support them and give them good feedback so they can continue to develop.

Encourage, support, mentor women who are balancing family and work: if they are committed to the process while they are struggling with small children, imagine how dedicated and seasoned they will be in 10 years when the children don't demand as much time and attention. Invest in someone driven enough to make the difficult choice to manage a career and family at the same time, and don't make assumptions about her level of commitment or her willingness to take on tasks or roles or responsibilities based on some paternalistic idea of what she can handle or what she might want.

Encourage them. Guide them and give them consistent and constant feedback to help them advance.

Don't make assumptions about whether women who are mothers are able to take on certain assignments/functions/roles. Give credit to these women for having extraordinary organizational and leadership capability, and encourage and seek them out for bigger and better positions even if they don't raise their hand.

The most effective thing a leader has taught me is how to completely let go of those things that are not important—that is, not only do not prioritize them, but completely let go of them. In other words, quit worrying about (stressing over) things that can't be controlled or don't really matter anyway.

Everything doesn't have to be perfect. Focus more effort on the details of important things and . . . do not worry as much about the crossed t's and dotted i's if it wasn't as critical.

Allow Employees Latitude in Decisions about Work and Family Responsibilities

Effective managers act as a good example without expecting women to replicate precisely how they handle work and family challenges. This theme speaks to how alignment of words and behaviors shapes the culture of the organization. Note that this stands in stark contrast to leaders who overemphasize face time or who never attend or literally sneak out to their children's games or concerts. In those cases, no matter what the aspiration of the organization, the manager's verbal and nonverbal messages undermines confidence that one can balance work and family and still can get ahead.

Set a good example, by prioritizing family and getting *home* (not lingering in the office, not being in the office 24/7, although always available).

The former president of my company told her team that she expected that we would power down and spend time with our loved ones, so that we would be better on the job. She walked the walk and empowered the rest of us to do the same.

When you go home—be home! Set the expectation with you employees that you are not available 24/7.

Work with them to find best solutions for the employee and the company to allow them to finds ways [to] balance work and family while meeting the business imperatives. The willingness to adjust existing mindsets can result in tremendous output from these high-potential employees who are grateful for a chance to excel while meeting family obligations.

CLOSING THOUGHTS

Women who have benefited from development and mentoring were more than twice as likely to be confident in achieving a higher leadership position (47 percent High Confidence versus 22 percent). LeaderMoms indicated that "if you don't ask, you don't get"—and this advice applies to professional development. Being deliberate and focused in determining where to grow and how to develop one's professional skills is essential. Overall, the belief that women can balance work and family while advancing a career at their organization had a significant positive relationship with a personal feeling of accomplishment in work. In presenting the actual experiences of the women who participated in our studies, our goal is to offer useful practices to individuals and their managers and to foster further research into work-family balance in organizations.

REFERENCES

Amstad, F. T., Meier, L. L., Fasel, U., Elfering, A., & Semmer, N. K. (2011). A meta-analysis of work-family conflict and various outcomes with a special emphasis on cross-domain versus matching-domain relations. *Journal of Occupational Health Psychology, 16*(2), 151–169.

Anderson, S. E., Coffey, B. S., & Byerly, R. T. (2002). Formal organizational initiatives and informal workplace practices: Links to work-family conflict and job-related outcomes. *Journal of Management, 28*(6), 787–810.

Behson, S. J. (2002). Which dominates? The relative importance of work-family organizational support and general organizational context on employee outcomes. *Journal of Vocational Behavior, 61*(1), 53–72.

Boyar, S. L., Maertz, C. P., Pearson, A. W., & Keough, S. (2003). Work-family conflict: A model of linkages between work and family domain variables and turnover intentions. *Journal of Managerial Issues, 15*(2), 175–191.

Carmeli, A. (2003). The relationship between emotional intelligence and work attitudes, behavior and outcomes: An examination among senior managers. *Journal of Managerial Psychology, 18*(8), 788–813.

Cross, C. (2010). Barriers to the executive suite: Evidence from Ireland. *Leadership and Organization Development Journal, 31*(2), 104–119.

Dorio, J. M., Bryant, R. H., & Allen, T. D. (2008). Work-related outcomes of the work-family interface: Why organizations should care. In K. Korabik, D. S. Lero, & D. Whitehead (Eds.), *Handbook of work-family integration: Research, theory and best practices* (pp. 157–176). San Diego, CA: Elsevier.

Eby, L. T., Casper, W. J., Lockwood, A., Bordeaux, C., & Brinley, A. (2005). Work and family research in IO/OB: Content analysis and review of the literature (1980–2002). *Journal of Vocational Behavior, 66*(1), 124–197.

Emslie, C., & Hunt, K. (2009). "Live to work" or "work to live"? A qualitative study of gender and work-life balance among men and women in mid-life. *Gender, Work and Organization, 16*(1), 151–172.

Ezzedeen, S. R., & Richey, K. G. (2009). Career advancement and family balance strategies of executive women. *Gender in Management, 24*(6), 388–411.

Fairchild, C. (2014, June 3). Number of Fortune 500 women CEOs reaches historic high. *Fortune*. Retrieved from http://fortune.com/.

Frye, N. K., & Breaugh, J. A. (2004). Family-friendly policies, supervisor support, work-family conflict, family-work conflict, and satisfaction: A test of a conceptual model. *Journal of Business and Psychology, 19*(2), 197–220.

Grady, G., & McCarthy, A. (2008). Work-life integration: Experiences of mid-career professional working mothers. *Journal of Managerial Psychology, 23*(5), 599–622.

Knudsen, K. (2009). Striking a different balance: Work-family conflict for female and male managers in a Scandinavian context. *Gender in Management, 24*(4), 252–269.

Major, D. A., & Morganson, V. J. (2011). Coping with work-family conflict: A leader-member exchange perspective. *Journal of Occupational Health Psychology, 16*(1), 126–138.

Matthews, R. A., Wayne, J. H., & Ford, M. T. (2014). A work-family conflict/subjective well-being process model: A test of competing theories of longitudinal effects. *Journal of Applied Psychology, 99*(6), 1173–1187.

Owen, W. F. (1984). Interpretative themes in relational communication. *Quarterly Journal of Speech, 70*(3), 274–287.

Raghuram, S., & Wiesenfeld, B. (2004). Work-nonwork conflict and job stress among virtual workers. *Human Resource Management, 43*(2–3), 259–277.

Shockley, K. M., & Singla, N. (2011). Reconsidering work-family interactions and satisfaction: A meta-analysis. *Journal of Management, 37*(3), 861–886.

Slaughter, A. M. (2012, July/August). Why women still can't have it all. *Atlantic*.

Straub, C. (2007). A comparative analysis of the use of work-life balance practices in Europe: Do practices enhance females' career advancement? *Women in Management Review, 22*(4), 289–304.

Where are all the senior-level women? (2011, April 11). *Wall Street Journal*, p. R3.

In: Work-Life Balance in the 21st Century
Editor: Jessica M. Nicklin

ISBN: 978-1-53612-526-9
© 2018 Nova Science Publishers, Inc.

Chapter 2

WE'RE NOT THERE YET: GENDER AND THE WORK-FAMILY INTERFACE IN THE MODERN WORKSCAPE

Maura J. Mills[1,], Adam Pervez[1] and Ashley M. Mandeville[2]*

[1]University of Alabama, Culverhouse College of Commerce,
Department of Management, Tuscaloosa, AL, US
[2]Florida Gulf Coast University, Lutgert College of Business,
Department of Management, Fort Myers, FL, US

ABSTRACT

This chapter identifies and deconstructs some of the most notable ways in which gender intersects with the work-family interface in driving the employee experience. With the proportion of women in the workforce now comparable to that of men, issues of work-family balance and conflict have correspondingly gained traction. However, the continued existence of gendered role perceptions has meant that work-family considerations often function differentially depending on employee gender. This chapter examines some of the most pressing questions stemming from this, including issues related to family-friendly policies, gendered job types, gender role ideologies, and the importance of a gender-equitable division of household labor, among other considerations. Increased attention to these issues on levels of both research and practice will ultimately result in a more gender-equitable work-family interface for all. The zeitgeist is ripe for such progressive changes, and recognizing the far-reaching implications of differential work-family considerations by gender is the first step in realizing organizational practices that are better aligned with today's contemporary workforce.

---

* Corresponding Author Email: mjmills@culverhouse.ua.edu.

In today's increasingly international workscape, organizations worldwide are recognizing the importance of the work-family interface and are likewise coming face-to-face with what that means in a labor market comprised of comparable proportions of both male and female employees (Mills, 2015). At the time of this writing, the United States in particular lags behind almost all other nations in its attention (or lack thereof) to facilitating employees' effective management of these oft-competing life domains (Mills & Culbertson, 2017). Specifically, the International Labour Organization notes that the United States and New Guinea are the only nations failing to provide any financial benefits to women during the postpartum period (International Labour Organization, 2014). However, as the United States gradually advances to a slightly more progressive stance on these issues (via governmental policy-making as well as that of private corporations), it is doing so with a primary focus on female employees (e.g., maternity leaves)—thereby missing the proverbial boat on what work-family balance means in a progressive, gender-equitable 21st century.

As such, this chapter seeks to identify and deconstruct the many ways in which gender intersects with considerations of work-family balance, and does so with an eye toward redirecting the ship to a more egalitarian shoreline. This includes considerations of family-friendly policies, gendered job types (e.g., military, policing, and STEM [science, technology, engineering, and mathematics] careers), gender role ideologies of current and future employees, the limitations of the Family and Medical Leave Act, and the importance of gender-equitable responsibilities on the home front as well as in the workplace. As research recognizes and attends to these issues more fervently, we should see them translated into practice, resulting in a more gender-equitable work-family interface for all. The zeitgeist is ripe for such progressive movement, and this chapter serves as a call for such work, highlighting the most desperately warranted changes of immediate importance.

IMPLICATIONS OF GENDERED FAMILY-FRIENDLY POLICIES

With increased attention now given to the work-family interface, we have correspondingly seen amplified media attention to leaders' perspectives on family-friendly policies. In one of the most publicized instances, Marissa Mayer, CEO of Yahoo!, was widely criticized for putting an end to flexible schedules in 2013, as well as for more recently vowing to curtail her maternity leave after the birth of her twins. These examples struck a chord with many working parents, and while Mayer's policies are not as atypical as the media portrayed them to be (Mills, 2015), a large part of why they received such backlash was Mayer's gender (the implication being that, as a woman, she should "know better"). With female leaders' viewpoints on family-friendly policies being called into question more so than those of male leaders (see Mills, Tortez, & Gallego-

Pace, 2016), a close look at such policies in light of employee gender is both warranted and overdue.

The Benefits of Benefits

Despite increasing numbers of private companies implementing family-friendly policies beyond the 12 weeks of unpaid leave provided for by the Family and Medical Leave Act (FMLA, 1993), the United States—the only industrialized nation with no mandated paid maternity leave—still has a long way to go in supporting its talent in managing competing life domains, particularly when it comes to considering the gender of that talent (Mills, 2015). That said, objectively, this should not be a hard sell. It has been well established that employees' conflict between work and family domains results in a variety of negative consequences at the employee level (e.g., compromised job satisfaction and health) as well as the organizational level (e.g., compromised organizational commitment and job performance; Allen, Herst, Bruck, & Sutton, 2000; Hammer, Neal, Newsom, Brockwood, & Colton, 2005). As such, family-friendly policies benefit not only employees but also organizational functioning and performance. Indeed, various notable positive outcomes are known to arise from family-friendly initiatives (including, but not limited to, paid parental leave). These include benefits at the individual level (e.g., maternal health, breastfeeding rates, and improved childhood cognitive outcomes; e.g., Aitken, Garrett, Hewitt, Keogh, Hocking, & Kavanagh, 2015; Brooks-Gunn, Han, & Waldfogel, 2002; Guendelman, Kosa, Pearl, Graham, Goodman, & Kharrazi, 2009; Hill, Waldfogel, Brooks-Gunn, & Han, 2005; Huang and Yang, 2015) and the organizational level (e.g., employee satisfaction, well-being, engagement, commitment, retention, and performance; e.g., Bloom, Kretschmer, & Van Reenen, 2011; Breaugh and Frye, 2007; Matthews, Mills, Trout, & English, 2014; Wayne & Casper, 2012), as well as individual outcomes at a more macro societal level (e.g., lower infant mortality, improved infant access to health care, wide-ranging economic benefit, and more egalitarian division of household labor; e.g., Berger, Hill, & Waldfogel, 2005; Kotsadam & Finseraas, 2011; Levin-Epstein, 2006; Ruhm, 2000; Tanaka, 2005).

Given these wide-ranging and multifaceted benefits, it should be unsurprising that an organization's family-friendly reputation can also be beneficial at the recruiting stage, as companies offering family-friendly policies are more attractive to potential candidates (Bourhis & Mekkaoui, 2010; Wayne & Casper, 2012), thereby drawing more top talent. Moreover, equally as important as policies' existence are employees' perceptions that the policy is *usable* in line with company culture and informal expectations (Galinsky, Bond, & Sakai, 2008). Indeed, the stigma of policy utilization (Williams, 2010) translates into policies going un- or underutilized out of fear for the consequences of usage (Eaton, 2003), including compromised promotion opportunities (Dodson, 2013; Heilman &

Okimoto, 2008). While for male talent this stigma arises from breaking traditional gender norms, for female talent it arises from conforming to the stereotypical "risk" that women will bear more of the caretaking load (Sprung, Toumbeva, & Matthews, 2015). As such, the stigma is more readily attributable to female talent (where it aligns with traditional gender schemas) than it is to male talent (where it is counter to gender schemas; Williams, Blair-Loy, & Berdahl, 2013), although it nonetheless impacts policy utilization for both genders.

With this in mind, of foremost necessity moving forward is a greater push from the public and private sectors alike, whereby more organizations begin to implement gender-equitable paid leaves and corresponding policies that attract, retain, and sustain top talent. However, as organizations move throughout the development and implementation of new policies, it is crucial to ensure that they are not only equally applicable to men and women in letter but also equally as available to both in light of the organizational and societal cultures within which those policies exist. Indeed, it is these environmental contexts that are often greater determinants of whether employees will *feel able to utilize* the policies than are the policies themselves.

Family-Friendly Policies Support High-Potential Talent

Good people go to good places. High-potential employees are in sufficient enough demand that they can afford to expect—and receive—good benefits from employers. Key among these benefits are family-friendly policies. Top candidates can afford to "select out" of non-family-friendly organizations at the recruitment stage if a company's policies are not where they need to be (Mills, 2016). Correspondingly, if high-potential employees join a company without consideration of family-friendly policies (a possibility for young talent in particular) but find themselves in need of such benefits at a later stage, they may seek them out from a competing employer. That is, top talent has the leeway to "follow the policies." With turnover imposing substantial financial costs on companies (Hinkin & Tracey, 2000), failing to offer policies good enough to attract and retain top talent can amount to a costly error on the part of employers.

These policies take multiple forms. The most obvious, perhaps, is maternity leave. The benefits of maternity leaves are wide ranging. Beyond the aforementioned employee- and organizational-level benefits of family-friendly policies broadly defined, maternity leaves in particular are associated with decreased infant mortality (up to a plateau of 40 weeks paid leave, after which benefits drop off or even reverse; Ruhm, 2000). Although the United States currently mandates *no* paid leave, in today's increasingly globalized workforce it is important to consider the expectations of global talent in terms of family-friendly accommodations. With (paid) leaves in other nations lasting up to a year or longer (International Labour Organization, 2014), US companies will continue to fall short in recruiting global talent until they adjust their leave offerings to be more consistent with global norms.

However, as crucial as maternity leaves are, they are just the beginning of comprehensive family-friendly policies, which also facilitate creative work-family management via schedule flexibility (e.g., compressed workweeks, flextime, and telework) and childcare support (e.g., on-site childcare facilities, day care subsidies, and childcare support during required work travel). With indications pointing to the probability that top performers are not likely to be looking to remain on the home front indefinitely, instituting such supports in the workplace can be a crucial step in facilitating high-potential women's successful return to the workplace postpartum.

Such comprehensive support options should also accommodate women who have returned to work post-leave but are still supplying their babies with breast milk (Spitzmueller et al., 2016). Breastfeeding has consistently been found to offer health benefits for both baby (e.g., antibodies to stave off illnesses and reduced risk of asthma/allergies) and mother (e.g., decreased risk of breast/ovarian cancers; Department of Health and Human Services, 2011)—thereby serving an important preventative role relating to health-care costs for employers. Breastfeeding success is largely facilitated by longer maternity leaves (Huang & Yang, 2015), and lactation maintenance is often one of a new mother's primary concerns in returning to work postpartum. However, in the absence of extended leaves there are still supports that an organization can provide its female talent, including providing a designated lactation room, accommodating scheduling needs that may require two to three pumping sessions daily, and modifying travel requirements as needed (or expensing milk transport services such as MilkStork).

Gender-Differential Policies Widen the Talent Gap

Contrary to common misconception, women are not the only employees in need of family-friendly policies. Indeed, everyone (female *and* male talent) benefits when precedence is given to *parental* and *family* policies (e.g., leaves and schedule flexibility) more generally. Contextualize this ideal within today's increasingly egalitarian society, in which families are expecting more of men on the home front, but many organizations compromise that by limiting the family-friendly policies available to male employees. With men frequently serving as a new mother's only source of support after the birth of a child, their presence at home in the days and weeks postpartum is often critical. This is especially true considering that more so than ever before, families are widely geographically dispersed, meaning that postpartum familial support beyond one's partner is minimal (or nonexistent) for many women. Particularly in the (not infrequent) cases of childbirth complications or surgery, such support is essential. For instance, one-third of all births in the United States are via caesarean section (Centers for Disease Control and

Prevention, 2016), after which women are severely restricted with regard to physical activities as simple as driving, lifting, and climbing stairs. Further, if a family has one or more prior children still requiring care (a not unlikely circumstance, considering common sibling spacing of two to three years), a lack of paternity/partner policies often leaves a mother recovering from major abdominal surgery (and/or other postpartum complications) alone to care for herself, a toddler (potentially), and a newborn all without any support, under severe physical restrictions, and in a compromised state of health herself. It is therefore critical that paternity/partner leaves are not overlooked; indeed, they are indispensable to the overall well-being of the family and are often the only way to ensure necessary postpartum support for both mother and child(ren).

As such, men are feeling heightened work-family conflict because (insufficient) corporate policies as well as gender role–stereotypic organizational cultures often fail to support them in undertaking these home roles (Mills & Grotto, 2017). Correspondingly, when *maternity* leaves—while a good start—are instituted *in place of* gender-equitable leaves, they can have the unintended side effect of stalling women's careers or translating into female talent being overlooked for promotions as a result of being temporarily out-of-office—à la "out of sight, out of mind" (Heilman & Okimoto, 2008). One might argue that policies that marginalize female talent in this way—the implication being that children are primarily a woman's responsibility—are arguably manifest subterfuge, however unintentional it may be, when not similarly applied to men.

To some extent, differential policies are justifiable, given the physical complications presented by pregnancy and childbirth. However, organizational policies all too often use gender as a proxy for childbirth in framing policies (presuming any such policies exist). According to the (legitimate) childbirth justification, any such leave options should be specified to link to the physical needs of childbirth/postpartum, as opposed to blanketed to women across the board simply by virtue of gender; it is not a gender issue, per se—it is a childbirth issue. While the two frequently align, increasingly common family formations such as adoption, surrogacy, and the like are indicative of the fact that they often differ.

Nevertheless, we would be remiss were we not to recognize the other side of the proverbial coin. Indeed, some well-intentioned organizations have recently begun to offer gender-blind parental leaves. However, emerging research by economists (Antecol, Bedard, & Stearns, 2016) has found that leave policies treating mothers and fathers the same actually further disadvantages women in occupations with fluid and seemingly limitless work availability (e.g., research in academia). In this way, women's leaves are more likely to be usurped by true familial duties (e.g., childbirth recovery, breastfeeding, etc.), whereas given the same leave options, men are more likely to use that time to "get ahead" in work productivity. In academia, for example, Antecol and colleagues (2016) found that universities' "adoption of gender-neutral tenure clock stopping policies substantially *reduced female* tenure rates while substantially *increasing male* tenure rates" (p. 1; emphasis added). This, of course, cannot be the answer we seek, and speaks to the need for carefully constructed leave policies accounting for such considerations as occupational context.

Family-Supportive Organizations and Managers as Universally Beneficial

Inescapably, work-family considerations affect everyone. By virtue of the fact that this is a larger societal issue with widespread implications, we are all beneficiaries (or victims) of our society's work-family value system and corporations' corresponding actions and policies (or lack thereof). Detractors of family-friendly policies often claim that such initiatives favor parent-employees, thereby neglecting single/childless workers. However, recent research (Mills, Matthews, Henning, & Woo, 2014; Rosiello, Tortez, & Mills, 2016) indicates otherwise, finding that family-supportive supervisors positively impact subordinates' organizational commitment and job performance for childless employees just as they do for parent-employees. This is encouraging, indicating that family-supportive supervisors play a crucial role in enhancing not only the employee experience but also the extent to which those employees are positively contributing to their organizations.

Companies can take this to mean that when they allow their managers the flexibility to help employees balance work and family demands, they are not necessarily setting a precedent of preference for parent-employees, but rather are facilitating a resource that is beneficial to all employees, regardless of familial status, alongside supporting the company's "parent talent." It is imperative to underscore, however, that this is most likely to be the case when such policies are not restricted to childcare responsibilities (e.g., when they are equally applied to spousal care, eldercare, etc.), as doing so recognizes the importance of nonwork responsibilities in *all* employees' lives, regardless of their gender or parental status.

JOB TYPE MATTERS

Gendered Occupations

Although jobs are not inherently sexed, those dominated by a particular gender quickly come to be seen by society as gendered (Blackburn & Jarman, 2006; Pettinger, 2005). Many researchers believe that gendered occupations emerge out of gender role socialization beginning in childhood (Vervecken, Hannover, & Wolter, 2013; Wilbourn & Kee, 2010). Hakim's (2000) preference theory examines gendered occupations through a historical lens, postulating that the practical decisions women must make regarding work and family are guided by individual preferences regarding the type (and extent) of work in which a woman ultimately engages. On the other hand, social dominance theory explains societal-level gender stereotypes, leading to subtle gender-biased messaging in recruiting campaigns and job descriptions (Sidanius and Pratto, 1999; Wolin, 2003). Similarly, social cognitive career theory (Lent, Brown, & Hackett, 1994; 2002) and professional role confidence (Cech, Rubineau, Silbey, & Seron, 2011) represent individuals' beliefs in their ability to successfully exhibit the knowledge, skills, and abilities required of—and the identity characteristics stereotypically associated with (Cech et al., 2011)—a particular profession, which informs occupational interest and subsequent career choices. Thus, a woman may not recognize within herself the purported identity features of an engineer, for example, while a man may not identify with the stereotypical features of a nurse.

This is in line with social role theory (Eagly, 1987), which suggests that there exist common societal beliefs about the roles that men and women should fill and the types of tasks they should undertake. Historically, this has meant that men tended to fulfill breadwinning roles while women served predominantly in domestic and caretaking roles (Eagly, Wood, & Diekman, 2000; Franke, Crown, & Spake, 1997). In light of this theoretical backdrop, we examine gendered military, policing, and STEM occupations insofar as their (male) gendered nature contributes to additional work-family challenges. Indeed, literature suggests that in gendered occupations, the minority gender (here, women) experiences greater work-family conflict than does the majority gender (Cook & Minnotte, 2008). That is, by virtue of their inherent (male) gender association, these job types often unintentionally reinforce gendered stereotypes and are slower to adopt gender-equitable work-family policies and cultures, thereby limiting female employees' options in managing the work-family domain in a way that is not as limiting for male employees' options.

The Military

The US military is an overwhelmingly male workplace, with approximately 85 percent of its incumbents being male (Military Women in Service for America Foundation, 2011). Although women have contributed to the military in various ways since the American Revolution, it was not until 1901 that women were permitted to formally serve alongside men (McSally, 2011), and they were barred from combat roles until as recently as 2016 (Howell, 2016). Such stifled involvement results in perceptions of being unwelcome and/or serving as 'tokens', and highlights the systemic inequality embedded within the military as an institution (Huffman, Culbertson, & Barbour, 2015). Indeed, the idea that gendered jobs are engrained in children from an early age may be particularly relevant in regard to military jobs, given the strong traditions embedded within the military. In practice, not only does this result in an overrepresentation of male service members, but also those men who opt to serve in the military are more likely to possess gender-biased attitudes (Young & Nauta, 2013), including the belief that men and women belong in different types of occupational settings (Matthews, Ender, Laurence, & Rohall, 2009). Although this gendered culture in the military has been making slow but sure progress in recent years, the occupational culture of male dominance and gender inequality still largely abounds (Iverson, Seher, DiRamio, Jarvis, & Anderson, 2016; McSally, 2011), and can create an unwelcoming climate for women service members.

Compounding its gendered nature is the related consideration that the nature of military work presents unique work-family challenges (Mills & Tortez, in press). Today, more than half of the 2.1 million+ service members have dependents, far more than service members in past eras or civilians of comparable ages (Blaisure, Saathoff-Wells, Pereira, MacDermid Wadsworth, & Dombro, 2012). As a result, despite the military's gendered nature, work-life conflict is a reality for both male and female service members (Adams, Jex, & Cunningham, 2006). Meeting the demands of both the military and the family is challenging, particularly since, for many service members, the military is just as much of a lifestyle as it is an occupation (Huffman et al., 2015). Although the military has made improvements to make it more family friendly, it is still expected that the proverbial mission will supersede everything else when duty calls (Adams et al., 2006). As a result, service members often have limited schedule flexibility (or even predictability in certain circumstances), in addition to experiencing often-dangerous work that is sometimes accompanied by long periods away from family (during tours of duty and field training), or frequent moves to different installations (bases). Many of these issues have no comparison in civilian life, or at least not as many factors are concurrent. Correspondingly, children of military families are at increased risk of depression and poor academic performance compared to their counterparts from civilian families. In the long term, such risk factors may ultimately compromise well-being (Lucier-Greer, O'Neal, Arnold, Mancini, & Wickrama, 2014), as well as creating additional complications thwarting work-family balance.

These work-family balance considerations become more gendered when we consider issues such as pregnancy, postpartum recovery, and breastfeeding, all of which are largely incompatible with extreme service demands, such as deployments or extended field training assignments (Mills & Tortez, in press). On the other hand, male service members who want to be more involved in the home domain may find themselves up against increased resistance in such a masculine occupation. Adding further complexities to these considerations, perhaps, is women's recent opportunity to serve in combat roles, which will put them ever more at the center of the male-dominant culture that pervades this occupation. With research having found that combat impacts the well-being of military personnel and that exposure to combat increases conflict between work and family life (Vinokur, Pierce, Lewandowski-Romps, Hobfoll, & Galea, 2011; Vogt et al., 2011), it remains to be seen whether this effect will function differentially for male versus female service members. That said, exposure to trauma and work-family conflict leads to resource loss and stress, which can result in outcomes such as posttraumatic stress disorder (Hobfoll, Vinokur, Pierce, & Lewandowski-Romps, 2012). Lutwak (2012) suggested that women may be more susceptible to such emotional and mental strains of combat than are men. Although the recent combat-eligible changes within the military mean that such considerations have not yet had the opportunity for rigorous empirical testing, some have suggested that differential outcomes by gender thus far may be partly explained by women's increased likelihood of prior interpersonal victimization, their lessened perceptions of unit-level support and (in)sufficient predeployment training, and their greater concerns about how deployment may disrupt their family life (Kline et al., 2013; Polusny et al., 2014; Street, Vogt, & Dutra, 2009).

Policing

Much as in the military, gendered (masculine) characteristics such as competitiveness, assertiveness, aggression, physicality, and emotional detachment are often associated with the policing occupation (Martin & Jurik, 2007). Police work is also characterized by a variety of key stressors, including exposure to disturbing acts of violence, responsibility for the well-being of others, and a persistent sense of uncertainty and threat of physical harm (Spielberger, Westbury, Grier, & Greefield, 1981; Violanti and Aron, 1995). Together, these characteristics combine to make police work extremely mentally and emotionally demanding in addition to its obvious physical demands (Harpold & Feemster, 2002; Miller, 2008). Such work stress compromises officers' well-being (Mumford, Taylor, & Kubu, 2015) and contributes to depression (Gershon, Barocas, Canton, Li, & Vlahov, 2009), which may be further impacted by officers' need to withhold their true emotions to present themselves professionally (Wharton, 1999). This emotional labor, compounded with the aforementioned stressors, increases the likelihood of depersonalization and emotional exhaustion (Griffin, 2012; Hall, Dollard, Tuckey, Winefield, & Thompson, 2010), two important predictors of burnout (Burke, 1993; Loo, 2004), which often spills over into family life (Jackson & Maslach, 1982). Therefore, as a whole, this stressful work environment characteristic of policing has a tendency to negatively impact family and other nonwork relationships by virtue of leading to strain-based work-family conflict (Culbertson, Huffman, Mills, & Imhof, 2017; Howard, Donofrio, & Boles, 2004).

While such characteristics make the job inherently more stressful regardless of gender (Anshel, Robertson, & Caputi, 1997), some evidence suggests that policing may be more taxing for female officers, who in addition to the traditional job stressors, are also faced with being a minority gender in this highly masculine occupation. Consistent with this is some research reporting that female officers report higher levels of depression, stress, and strain than do male officers (He, Zhao, & Archbold, 2002; Kurtz, 2012; Silbert, 1982). Some have suggested that this may be related to female officers' increased risk of harassment, including sexual harassment, on the job, which can then spill over into the home domain (Somvadee & Morash, 2008). Similarly, early research found that female officers may be more prone to emotional exhaustion (Johnson, 1991), a key component in burnout, as well as at increased risk of burnout overall (Etzion, 1984; Schaufeli & Enzmann, 1998; Westman & Etzion, 1995). Other studies, however, found similar levels of burnout among male and female officers (Kop, Euwema, & Schaufeli, 1999), and no identifiable relationship between gender and stress among police officers, despite the unique challenges that women face in this occupation (Davis, 1984; Frye & Greenfield, 1980; Koenig, 1978; Morash & Haarr, 1995). Therefore, although there exist initial signs that strain-based work-family conflict may differ by officer gender, more research in this domain is clearly warranted.

Another consideration regarding how policing impacts work-family conflict differentially by gender is the issue of time-based conflict. By its very nature, policing is "round the clock" work in that it requires continual staffing. In addition to the nontraditional shifts that come with such a 24/7 staffing need, rotating shifts—whereby officers switch from working during daytime hours to nighttime hours, or have inconsistent days of the week off from work—are also relatively common in policing and are particularly detrimental to the work-family balance (Grosswald, 2003; Tausig & Fenwick, 2001; Williams, 2008; Willis, O'Connor, & Smith, 2008), including hindering family scheduling and planning (Rosiello & Mills, 2015). Chapters 5 and 6 of this volume further discuss the complexities of nonstandard work schedules. Regardless of gender, the difficulty imposed on officers' abilities to attend to family events (Fenwick & Tausig, 2001), as well as their day-to-day home lives (La Valle, Arthur, Millward, Scott, & Clayden, 2002), is palpable.

However, such nonstandard shifts may differentially affect work-family conflict considerations depending on gender (Rosiello & Mills, 2015). For instance, women are more likely to suffer negative health effects resulting from shiftwork—including compromised sleep, fatigue, irregular menstrual cycles, and increased risk of miscarrying pregnancies (Axelsson, Rylander, & Molin, 1989; Barthe, Messing, & Abbas, 2011; Costa, 1996). Collectively, this points to the possibility of female officers suffering increased strain-based work-family conflict as a result of policing's occupational characteristics, as compared to men. Gottzén and Kremer-Sadlik (2012), however, suggested that men may suffer more time-based conflict to the extent that, stereotypically, a substantial proportion of their involvement with their children is through extramural events and activities, which could be particularly affected by mandatory shiftwork, especially when it is on a rotational scheme. This, however, is changing as men adopt more varied household and childcare responsibilities, as evidenced by their rising levels of work-family conflict over recent decades (e.g., Mills & Grotto, 2017).

STEM

Characteristically different than the two abovementioned occupations—although still highly gendered—are STEM (science, technology, engineering, and mathematics) fields. Women have long been underrepresented in STEM professions (National Science Foundation, 2013), and despite comparable enrollments in STEM courses during grade school, college degrees in STEM fields are predominantly earned by men (Hill, Corbett, & St. Rose, 2010). This phenomenon is known as the "leaky pipeline," referring to the loss of women who enter the pipeline to STEM careers but do not emerge from it in equal proportions (Blickenstaff, 2005). It may be speculated that a major contributor to the "leaks" is gender-disparate work-family complications that are characteristic of many STEM professions.

With a notable proportion of STEM careers being within academia, one such challenge is the fact that semester/trimester academic schedules—coupled with the lack of paid maternity leave in the United States—can make timing a pregnancy/childbirth difficult, as it is often not feasible to take FMLA's six-week (unpaid) leave in the course of a 15–17-week semester. This has led to the remarkable phenomenon among female academics of "May babies" (Armenti, 2004), wherein professors attempt to time their childbirths to occur immediately after the close of a semester. Beyond the bounds of a teaching semester, however, a greater complication for female academics in STEM (and non-STEM) fields is that their childbearing prime often overlaps with their pre-tenure years—a time when research productivity is of critical importance in the ivory tower. As a result, childbearing and childrearing in this time period is often discouraged (either directly or indirectly), and certainly dampers the opportunity for research productivity as compared to male colleagues, who (despite increased childcare involvement) are not as limited by biological clocks or the unique responsibilities of (biological) motherhood (pregnancy, childbirth, breastfeeding, etc.). Such a career timeline often puts women at or past their mid-thirties by the time they earn tenure—well beyond the average age of reproduction (Sutton, Hamilton, & Mathews, 2011) and into the obstetric category of "advanced maternal age." The latter comes with decreased fertility (National Center for Biotechnology Information, 2013), as well as increased health risks for both mother and child (Cleary-Goldman et al., 2005). As such, delaying children until this career milestone can have notable and lasting implications for a woman's family life, including more miscarriages, the increased likelihood of raising a child with a chromosomal disorder, the risk of never being able to become a (biological) mother, and having fewer children than desired. Collectively, we refer to this as "career-limited family composition."

Although non-academic STEM jobs are not necessarily plagued by the complicating factor of tenure, it is nonetheless true that the late twenties and early thirties remain a prime time for both childbearing and key career milestones in these fields. An example is the field of information technology, in which career success is facilitated by rapid and ever-evolving acquisition of new knowledge and skills, which can be hampered by leave-taking from work (Menez, Munder, & Töpsch, 2001). Indeed, Simard and colleagues (2008) found that one-third of sampled women in the information technology (IT) sector reported that the decision to have children necessarily stalled their career. Similarly, Fouad and Singh (2011) more recently found that approximately one-quarter of female engineers who had left their careers had done so in order to spend more time with their family, citing the work-family complications inherent in the profession. This was in addition to the stereotypically masculine culture prevalent in such fields (Fouad, Fitzpatrick, & Liu, 2011) and a higher likelihood for women as targets of harassment within STEM fields (Clancy, Nelson, Rutherford, & Hinde, 2014)—both of which can be further alienating for women as the minority gender and can lead to work stress that spills over into the home domain.

Finally, other types of STEM fields include routine job tasks that are either precluded or inherently risky for women who are childbearing. For instance, many STEM professions (e.g., chemists) require contact with toxic substances or extensive fieldwork or frequent travel (e.g., anthropologists) that can be problematic for women during a pregnancy or postpartum period (Jean, Payne, & Thompson, 2015). Collectively, these challenges often force women to take a "step back" in STEM careers during their childbearing years. Doing so necessarily slows career progression and further contributes to the male-dominated culture that perpetuates women's visibility problems in STEM fields, including being invited less frequently to present their research or serve as speakers (Schroeder et al., 2013). Ultimately, this stalled career progression due to work-family conflict results in a lack of women in leadership roles in STEM fields (Valian, 1999). This, in turn, may become a circular problem such that there are then fewer women in the upper echelons of STEM occupations to advocate for work-family policies and considerations that promote gender equity within the field.

SOCIETAL CONSIDERATIONS AND THE PULSE OF THE FUTURE WORKFORCE

Beyond considerations of specific gendered professions, it is warranted to consider the broader societal perspective. A growing body of economic research finds a significant relationship between women's participation in the workforce and economic growth (IMF, 2013; World Bank, 2014). The ideologies for women at work appear to be egalitarian and thus support this growth; however, societal patterns and structures exist that do not appear to be in conjunction with that spirit. Today, 62 percent of Americans agree that both marital partners should contribute to the household income (Pew Research Center, 2010). However, it remains the case that even in dual-earner families, traditional roles tend to be upheld, where fathers devote more time to the role of breadwinner, while mothers devote more time to housework and childcare (Pew Research Center, 2013). This section discusses why this pattern exists, including the gender role ideologies and career plans of today's youth, (lack of) equitable responsibilities at home, increased likelihood of women being in poverty, and work-family guilt as differential by gender. Further, this section makes several suggestions for rectifying these patterns (e.g., via policy improvement) so society can move toward truly practicing gender equity in regard to the work-family interface, beyond simply believing it should exist.

Moving Forward or Moving Back? The Next Generation of Employed Parents

The next generation of young men and women seem to hold more egalitarian views than previous generations. This is likely due to a confluence of factors representing an increasingly progressive society, not the least of which is the increasing proportions of women in the workforce, as children's gender role beliefs typically align with their mother's employment status during their preschool and elementary school years (Cochran & Chambliss, 2009; D'Olio, 2009; Filipkowski & Chambliss, 2009; Goldberg, Kelly, Matthews, Kang, Li, & Sumaroka, 2012). As such, the shift toward more egalitarian views is evident in studies on young people's perceptions of their working parents. Over a decade ago, it was common for young men and women to assert that parental warmth and competence were dichotomous—that a parent could not possess both qualities simultaneously (Cuddy, Fiske, & Glick, 2004). However, today there are signs that young people no longer make such judgments on a continuous scale from worker to parent (e.g., home-based parents as warm but incompetent; worker-parents as cold but competent) but instead accept that such attributions are much more complex. In line with this, Coleman and Franiuk (2011) found that employed parents who took leave (12 weeks) following the birth of their child were judged to be equally as warm as stay-at-home parents (but warmer than parents who returned to work more immediately), while leave-taking parents were perceived to be just as competent as employed parents taking no leave (but still more competent than stay-at-home parents). Thus, while the attributions and stereotypes have evolved in recent years, they remain in a nascent stage. This is evident to the extent that, even though today's youth are showing signs of incremental changes in gender role beliefs, this may be truer of young women than it is of young men. For instance, the former tend to believe that the role of "caregiver" and "provider" can coexist within one person, regardless of gender; however, young men still support traditional gender roles when it comes to judgments of other men, and tend to have less favorable impressions of stay-at-home fathers than of working fathers (Coleman & Franiuk, 2011). Similarly, while young women perceive fewer costs and more benefits to maternal employment (especially if their mother worked while they were young), young men perceive greater costs and fewer benefits of maternal employment, regardless of their mother's employment history (Goldberg et al., 2012).

Further, while egalitarian beliefs are more widely held, intended behavior for both genders has not followed suit. Lucas-Thompson and Goldberg (2015) found that despite adolescent women espousing more egalitarian views than adolescent men, when asked to forward-think to their future familial and work goals, many reported intentions to work part-time (or not at all) in favor of taking on the majority of the childcare and household responsibilities. This calls into question the extent to which the increasingly espoused egalitarian views of this younger generation are ultimately translated (or not) into practice. Studies have found that while young women expect future employment (Goldin, Katz, & Kuziemko, 2006), typically both young men and women report the expectation of more traditional work-family arrangements once children are born (e.g., an expectation for women to reduce their work commitments in favor of childrearing; de Valk, 2008; Goldberg et al., 2012; Weinshenker, 2006). With this expectation, it is no wonder that by high school young women are already concerned with how they will manage their work and family lives, and thus give increased consideration to occupations that they perceive as facilitating work-family balance (McDonald, Pini, Bailey, & Price, 2011), even if those occupations do not align with their ideal professional interests. Notably, however, young men do not give the same consideration to future familial needs or conflicts when selecting a career path, instead doing so primarily based on personal skills and interests (Hardie & Hayford, 2012).

The Criticality of Equitable Responsibilities on the Home Front

It may be that young women are more prone to planning for work-family considerations due to the expectation that household responsibilities will be primarily theirs. In this vein, in recent years there has been a lot of consideration given to the issue of whether women can "have it all" (see Slaughter [2012] for a divisive article published in *The Atlantic*). Alluding to this, the label "superwomen" arose in the 1970s to describe women who maintain careers while simultaneously having primary responsibility for childcare and other domestic tasks (Shaevitz, 1984). Despite the seemingly flattering term, "superwomen" are said to be "double burdened" with the responsibilities of fulfilling both career and domestic obligations (Chen, Conconi, & Perroni, 2007)—the latter of which represents the "second shift" that is disproportionately levied upon women (Hochschild, 1989). These burdens have arguably lessened in recent years with fathers' increasing commitments to caregiving (Chesley, 2011; Goldberg et al., 2012; Kramer, Kelly, & McCulloch, 2015). However, despite moderately subsiding, they remain as a result of women's inequitably high responsibilities in the home domain (Bianchi, Milkie, Sayer, & Robinson, 2000; Himsel & Goldberg, 2003; Schiebinger & Gilmartin, 2010), which are particularly notable against the backdrop of an increase in women as primary breadwinners (e.g., 17 percent in 1987, 28.9 percent in 2009; Current Population Survey, 2011).

Notably, however, employed women's increased work commitments do not necessarily lead to a decrease in their time dedicated toward household responsibilities, and this pattern is not exclusive to couples with more traditional ideologies (Schiebinger & Gilmartin, 2010). While there is some evidence that wives with more egalitarian views tend to input reduced time toward household responsibilities as compared to wives with traditional views, husbands' time devoted to household responsibilities does not change based on gender ideologies (e.g., Bianchi et al., 2000; Himsel & Goldberg, 2003; Hochschild, 1989). This inequality is further exacerbated when couples have children, as the presence of children adds to housework requirements (Jacobs & Gerson, 2004), as well as the complexities of parental responsibilities (Doucet, 2015). The addition of children also brings an added layer of gendered norms and stereotypes (e.g., women as maternal and responsible for childrearing). Even in situations where both parents report wanting to spend more time with their children, wives disproportionately "scale back" their careers to attend to childrearing needs (Becker & Moen, 1999). At least in biological families, this begins as early as women's increased responsibilities during pregnancy (e.g., prenatal appointments), which we suspect can set the stage for postnatal expectations of primary childcare responsibilities.

Among the studies that aim to understand why households divide labor unequally, time- and resource-based reasoning appears to dominate. From a resource-based view (e.g., conservation of resources theory; Hobfoll, 1989—see also Chapters 4 and 8 in this volume), individuals who allocate more time to work will necessarily have less time to devote to household demands, and thus are likely to lean on their spouse to take over such responsibilities (Bianchi et al., 2000; Kalleberg & Rosenfeld, 1990). As such, resource-based perspectives describe certain dependencies that members of couples place on one another, and suggest that an accumulation of individual resources (e.g., income and education) gives one member of the partnership increased bargaining power in regard to roles and responsibilities (Brines, 1994; Bittman, England, Sayer, Folbre, & Matheson, 2003). This notion of resource dependencies is found in the tenets of exchange theory, suggesting that the partner possessing fewer resources (e.g., with a lower income or education level, or a less powerful job) will absorb the majority of the childcare responsibilities, up to and including sacrificing one's career to remain home with the children in the event that childcare expenses would surpass one's salary. Thus, the spouse who earns more, works more (Bennett, 2013; Casper & O'Connell, 1998; Kreager, Felson, Warner, & Wenger, 2013), and has more power in the relationship and less time to dedicate to household duties. However, there is some indication that higher incomes among women do not necessarily increase their partners' contributions to domestic labor, which suggests that factors other than income (e.g., societal power differentials and gender role ideologies and stereotypes) may be driving the relationship (see Gupta, 2006).

It is also important to consider partners' *perceptions of* the extent to which household responsibilities are (un)equal. As multiple studies have evidenced, although household work is typically unevenly distributed between partners, it may simultaneously be perceived as equal, and gender influences these perceptions (DeMaris & Longmore, 1996; Yavorsky, Kamp Dush, & Schoppe-Sullivan, 2015). Interestingly, men typically perceive the division of housework as equitable as long as they do approximately one-third of the housework, while women correspondingly perceive housework as equitable if they do no more than two-thirds of the housework (Lennon & Rosenfield, 1994). These fascinating results reinforce the aforementioned idea, arising from early gender ideologies and plans that women may enter into marriages and parenthood with the expectation of bearing a heavier brunt of the load. Men, however, do not typically report that expectation, and therefore may be less likely to adopt their fair share of housework (or have an accurate view of what their fair share is). Aligning with this, during the transition to parenthood specifically (and the corresponding increase in household responsibilities), men and women tend to perceive comparable increases in domestic workload, despite women's actual workload increase being substantially higher than that of men (Yavorsky et al., 2015).

The reasons for such (in)accurate perceptions may be due to what are considered gendered household chores. Indeed, most couples tend to divide household duties according to gender stereotypes. Stereotypically feminine chores, such as cleaning, cooking, and childcare, are typically allocated to women, while "masculine" chores such as financial planning and outdoor tasks are typically associated with and allocated to men (Mills, Culbertson, Huffman, & Connell, 2012). Moreover, even for similar household duties, the shifting standard model suggests that women and men are held to different standards, even for the same work (Biernat & Manis, 1994; Biernat & Wortman, 1991). These standards are based on role-based expectations for each gender, and upward deviation from expectation could be deemed favorable. For example, fathers who attend their children's doctor's appointments may be lauded for that degree of involvement, as this departs from expectations of their gender role. However, that degree of involvement is more often seen as a baseline expectation for women's involvement, so they are not lauded for it—or, worse, may be condemned if they are not the one to fulfill that role

(Fuegen, Biernal, Haines, & Deaux, 2004; Heilman & Okimoto, 2008). It follows then that when men contribute to household tasks that are typically consigned to women, women have a greater sense of fairness in regard to division of labor because it departs from expectations (Blair & Johnson, 1992; Kane & Sanchez, 1994). Further, fairness perceptions may be related to the quality of a couple's relationship, as marital problems have been shown to correlate with spousal perceptions of unfair division of household labor (Grote & Clark, 2001). Societal-level gender equality has also been shown to contribute to such perceptions, and women's actual shares of household labor have limited impact on their perceptions of fairness in the division of labor in nations with low gender equality, as compared to those with high gender equality (Frisco & Williams, 2003).

It is important to note the various negative consequences for individuals and organizations when household responsibilities fall heavily on only one partner. Increased household responsibilities can lead to increased work-family conflict, which on an individual level can lead to increased stress and burnout, compromised concentration and physical health, and decreased marital satisfaction (Allen et al., 2000; Anderson, Coffey, & Byerly, 2002; MacEwen & Barling, 1994; Wayne, Musisca, & Fleeson, 2004). For the organization, work-family conflict can lead to increased absenteeism and turnover, and decreased job satisfaction, job performance, and organizational commitment (Kossek & Ozeki, 1999; Wayne et al., 2004). Since work-family conflict has been shown to impact turnover, and since women tend to have increased work-family conflict due to shouldering more household responsibilities, the unequal distribution of household labor may be adding to the issue of women withdrawing from the workforce (Cleveland, Fisher, & Sawyer, 2015).

Household Poverty as Gendered

Following from the above, inequality in the household division of labor has also been linked to the disproportionate number of women in poverty. Pearce (1978) coined the phrase "the feminization of poverty" to describe women's increased likelihood of being in poverty as compared to men, despite their increased workforce participation and education levels in recent decades (Lichtenwalter, 2005). This is partly due to women disproportionately filling lower-wage jobs, an issue related to the gendered segregation of jobs as discussed earlier. Such segregation results from a number of factors, including societal norms driving considerations such as self-selection and organizational practices, the latter of which may contribute to occupational segregation either intentionally or unintentionally. For instance, men are more likely to be seen as an appropriate fit for a job with more societally compensable factors (e.g., physical exertion), while women are more likely to be viewed as a better fit for support roles (e.g., administration; Reskin &

Bielby, 2005). As such, even while maintaining legal hiring practices in accordance with the Equal Employment Opportunity Commission (EEOC), organizations may reinforce segregation of job roles through these internal structures (Odle-Dusseau, McFadden, & Britt, 2015).

Further complicating matters is the consideration that being entrenched in poverty presents a variety of challenges that thwart one's emergence into a higher socioeconomic status. For instance, employees in low-wage jobs are often hindered in searching for better employment opportunities due to limited job-related resources (e.g., education) compounded with increased restrictions insofar as job needs (e.g., requiring certain hours due to inability to afford quality childcare, and transportation limitations). In addition to limited direct compensation (e.g., pay), low-wage jobs also often have limited (or nonexistent) indirect compensation (e.g., health benefits), as well as relatively inflexible schedules (Richman, Johnson, & Buxbaum, 2006). This places a particular burden on employees with family demands; not only are individuals supporting dependents in greater need of benefits such as health care, but also resources and supports such as quality childcare are often not readily available (or affordable) in poor communities (Budig & Hodges, 2010). Further, while men and women are both subject to lower incomes when working in female-gendered jobs, women in these jobs are typically paid less than their male counterparts (Glauber, 2012). As such, poverty's high demands and limited resources are particularly relevant for working mothers.

Such a combination of job demands and (lack of) resources makes job flexibility particularly important for workers in low-wage jobs. However, these also tend to be the roles with the most limited flexibility—including defined shift hours, on-site work requirements, and no childcare provisions—and requesting such flexibility can further penalize parents (Dodson, 2013). While flexible work arrangements have the potential to reduce the gender inequality of work-family conflict, even when lower-wage jobs are able to offer such arrangements, a flexibility bias exists wherein employees who request schedule flexibility may be devalued and stigmatized (Glass, 2004; Wharton, Chivers, & Blair-Loy, 2008; Williams et al., 2013). While this bias applies to both genders (Cohen & Single, 2001), some research (Munsch, 2016) suggests that it may be disproportionally biased against women. Certainly, it discourages employees from requesting schedule flexibility even when it is available (Blair-Loy & Wharton, 2004; Williams et al., 2013), thereby contributing to further (perhaps unnecessary) work-family conflict.

Relatedly, however, it is worth noting that even in jobs that themselves are not necessarily low wage, mothers tend to be financially penalized for having children in a way that fathers are not. Specifically, women often find themselves up against a "motherhood wage penalty" post-children, while men are often rewarded with a "fatherhood bonus." These financial ramifications date back to a historical view that once men have children they will need to procure more financial resources in order to fulfill their stereotypical "provider" role for their families, whereas that assumption is not traditionally made of women. Regardless of the starting job wage, such gendered pay practices—intentional or not—further financially penalize working mothers.

However, resources exist beyond those offered by the organization itself. Most notably in the United States, the aforementioned Family and Medical Leave Act (FMLA, 1993) provides any qualified employee 12 weeks of leave during any twelve-month period for the birth or adoption of a child. However, in order to qualify for FMLA leave, employees must meet certain requirements, including working for an eligible company (e.g., 50 plus employees at that particular location for private-sector organizations) for a sufficiently long period of time (12 months), and with particular work input (1,250 hours in the 12 months prior to the requested leave). Often, low-wage jobs do not meet these requirements, as they tend to see comparatively frequent turnover and more part-time employees as compared to higher-wage jobs, in addition to often being within small companies (Cantor et al., 2001; Phillips, 2002). Further, considering that the leave is unpaid, even employees who are qualified to take it often cannot afford to go three months without any source of income—particularly at a time when expenses are rising with the introduction of a child. Therefore, it tends to be that precisely those employees most in need of the leave are also those for whom it is most restricted.

FMLA for the Future

In addition to secluding low-wage workers, policies such as FMLA have differential implications by gender and are insufficiently comprehensive for today's families. Although the semantics of FMLA allows for leave without direct reference to gender, underlying subtleties of the broader societal and workplace picture mean that its impact is often differential by employee gender. For instance, since few families can afford to forgo the income of both mother and father (since FMLA is unpaid), and since men continue to out-earn women (Bureau of Labor Statistics, 2016), there is a familial financial incentive for the mother to take the leave (if it is offered) as opposed to the father, as many households would see a smaller income loss in this circumstance. Thus, policies such as FMLA may inadvertently perpetuate the notion that the mother is the ideal primary caretaker of children. Not only does this limit female career advancement and growth, but it also puts men in a position where they are less able to participate in important family contributions, such as bonding with and developing a sense of care competency for their children (Rege & Solli, 2010; Stegelin & Frankel, 1997), which have positive effects on both children and parents alike (Allen & Daly, 2007; Han, Ruhm, & Waldfogel, 2009).

Moreover, FMLA and similar such policies, while well-intentioned, often fail to account for nontraditional families, including single parents (especially fathers) and those in the LGBTQ communities (Sawyer, Thoroughgood, & Cleveland, 2015). For instance, consider the circumstance wherein male same-sex couples find themselves not qualifying for *any* parental leave policies—for example, if a paternity leave is not offered and if formalized adoption proceedings are stalled, as is often the case. A single father might be similarly unable to take leave, particularly if he finds himself in one of the many organizations that is not held to honoring the FMLA. Such familial circumstances are far from uncommon but unfortunately are not sufficiently accounted for by the heteronormative and gender-biased assumptions inherent in existing policy – leaving many families without access to any parental leave coverage whatsoever.

Even in so-called traditional families, the net result of gendered policies is that even though women still tend to do the majority of childcare and housework (Bianchi et al., 2000; Himsel & Goldberg, 2003; Hochschild, 1989)—including in dual-earner and otherwise egalitarian partnerships (Schiebinger & Gilmartin, 2010)—men are now similarly suffering from considerable work-family conflict (Mills & Grotto, 2017) because organizational policies as well as societal gender role stereotypes often fail to support them in undertaking equitable childcare and other domestic responsibilities (Munn & Greer, 2015). To that end, while expanded maternity leave policies are an admirable goal toward which organizations should aim, without comparable consideration given toward paternity leave (including via generalized "parental" leaves), such policies have the unintended side effect of levying a majority of the childcare burden on women, as well as more of the burden of taking work leaves more broadly (e.g., compromised career progression opportunities and hampering inclusivity perceptions; Ryan & Kossek, 2008). Indeed, women are currently perceived as experiencing more family-to-work conflict as compared to men (regardless of their objective level of conflict; Hoobler, Wayne, & Lemmon, 2009). Should policies change to be more gender equitable, this perception (and the associated reality) may be reduced over time.

To serve this end, leave policies of the future must adapt to more thoroughly support "traditional" families, as well as being inclusionary to a far wider variety of familial configurations. US Senator Kirsten Gillibrand's proposed FAMILY Act (Gillibrand, 2016) takes a step in the right direction in this regard. Under US Senate consideration at the time of this writing, the FAMILY Act would provide up to 12 weeks of paid family leave for workers of either gender upon the birth or adoption of a child, as well as for the illness of an immediate family member needing the employee's care. While the FAMILY Act may still warrant additional provisions to be optimally practicable, its wider berth and explicit gender-invariant nature is a notable improvement over the current limited offerings.

The Guilt on Our Shoulders?

One final consideration of what may be perpetuating gender inequality in regard to balancing work and family is societally imposed guilt, which results in part from the double standards levied on women as compared to men (Banerjee, 2003), and ironically further engenders societal norms. Work-family guilt occurs when one's behavior violates the norms of how an individual believes he or she should balance work and family demands, thereby adversely affecting individuals' emotional lives (see also Chapter 1). In general, guilt has been associated with a variety of negative consequences, including decreased life satisfaction and increased likelihood of depression (Aycan & Eskin, 2005). While both genders are subject to work-family guilt (Aycan & Eskin, 2005; Hochwarter, Perrewé, Meurs, & Kacmar, 2007), mothers tend to report quantitatively more guilt, and the reasons for that guilt are qualitatively different from fathers' reasons. Specifically, mothers' guilt is more likely to be derived from fears of not being a "good" mother (or not *being perceived as* a "good" mother according to societal standards), while fathers' guilt is more related to the time- or strain-based conflict between their competing desires for parental involvement and workplace participation (Martínez, Carrasco, Aza, Blanco, & Espinar, 2011; Simon, 1995). Interestingly, individuals with egalitarian views tend to report more feelings of work-family guilt as compared to those with more traditional views, as the former are more likely to view their roles in both domains as important (Chappell, Korabik, & McElwain, 2005).

Overall, the intricacies of work-family guilt and its potential differential manifestation by gender is a relatively new consideration that is only recently gaining the attention of researchers (Korabik, 2015). As guilt poses an additional threat to gender inequality in the work-family interface, we contend that more research on work-family guilt is needed. One suggestion for this line of research is to examine the effects of "mom shaming" on women's work-related decisions through guilt. Although relatively limited to lay discourse at the time of this writing, mom shaming is said to occur as a result of women (mothers) attempting to "regulate" other women (mothers) to fit a societal norm (Zulkey, 2016). As such, judgment often results when women fail to behave in ways congruent with the societal norms. This judgment is a mechanism through which to inspire guilty feelings and change the behavior of the individual woman whose behavior has departed from the accepted norm. However, while mom shaming is a relatively new cultural term describing the process through which mothers judge other mothers for their parenting decisions, including their decision to participate in the paid workforce (Zulkey, 2016), the actual practice is not new. Nonetheless, it is now more frequently coming to the fore in modern cultural awareness, thanks in part to its referencing in pop culture, including the aptly-named 2016 film *Bad Moms*, wherein the main character is relentlessly judged by other mothers while trying to balance work and family commitments. It is clear that the zeitgeist is ripe for empirical research to examine this phenomenon, both in regard to its impact on employed mothers' guilt (and correspondingly their work-family conflict perceptions) as well as in regard to wider societal implications more generally.

CONCLUSION

Despite recent progress, the United States continues to lag behind other industrialized nations in its commitment to supporting employees of both genders in effectively managing multiple domains of responsibility, most notably those of work and family. This includes the nation's historical and persistent resistance to paid parental leaves. However, while some have pushed for paid maternity leaves to close this gap, such a solution in itself is largely insufficient, as it has the unintended side effect of identifying childcare as a predominantly female responsibility, thereby risking stalled career progress for female employees as compared to male employees. As Mills and Culbertson (2017) note, "As long as organizations see work-family considerations as a women's challenge, the issue will not only continue to exist, but its implications for organizations and diversity will worsen, and the equality gap will widen" (p. 30). Rather, an optimal solution must account for external considerations such as the gender role stereotypes and stigmas within which employees are entrenched, changing domestic and nondomestic responsibilities by gender, and an evolving picture of family composition: Overall, such a solution must be driven by a push toward a more egalitarian recognition of role responsibilities and opportunities. Ultimately, acceptance of the 21st-century reality that both men and women have responsibilities within the home—and correspondingly that both male and female talent is needed to drive an optimal workforce—is the key principle underlying implementation of effective work-family policy and considerations for the modern workplace.

REFERENCES

Adams, G. A., Jex, S. M. & Cunningham, C. J. L. (2006). Work-family conflict among military personnel. In C. A. Castro, A. B. Adler, & T. W. Britt (Eds.), *Military life: The psychology of serving in peace and combat,* (pp. 169–192). Westport, CT: Praeger.

Aitken, Z., Garrett, C. C., Hewitt, B., Keogh, L., Hocking, J. S. & Kavanagh, A. M. (2015). The maternal health outcomes of paid maternity leave: A systematic review. *Social Science and Medicine, 130,* 32–41.

Allen, S. M. & Daly, K. J. (2007). The effects of father involvement: An updated research summary of the evidence. Centre for Families, Work and Well-Being, University of Guelph, ON.

Allen, T. T., Herst, D. E. L., Bruck, C. S. & Sutton, M. (2000). Consequences associated with work-to-family conflict: A review and agenda for future research. *Journal of Occupational Health Psychology, 5,* 278–308.

Anderson, S. E., Coffey, B. S. & Byerly, R. T. (2002). Formal organizational initiatives and informal workplace practices: Links to work-family conflict and job-related outcomes. *Journal of Management, 28,* 787–810.

Anshel, M. H., Robertson, M. & Caputi, P. (1997). Sources of acute stress and their appraisals and reappraisals among Australian police as a function of previous experience. *Journal of Occupational and Organizational Psychology, 70,* 337–356.

Antecol, H., Bedard, K. & Stearns, J. (2016). Equal but inequitable: Who benefits from gender–neutral tenure clock stopping policies? IZA Discussion Paper, *9904.* Retrieved from: http://ftp.iza.org/dp9904.pdf.

Armenti, C. (2004). May babies and posttenure babies: Maternal decisions of women professors. *Review of Higher Education, 27,* 211–231.

Axelsson, G., Rylander, R. & Molin, I. (1989). Outcome of pregnancy in relation to irregular and incovenient work schedules. *British Journal of Industrial Medicine, 46,* 393–398.

Aycan, Z. & Eskin, M. (2005). Relative contributions of childcare, spousal support, and organizational support in reducing work-family conflict for men and women: The case of Turkey. *Sex Roles, 53,* 453–471.

Banerjee, S. (2003, November). Double standards. *Business Line,* 1–3.

Barthe, B., Messing, K. & Abbas, L. (2011). Strategies used by women workers to reconcile family responsibilities with atypical work schedules in the service sector. *Work, 40,* S47–S58.

Becker, P. E. & Moen, P. (1999). Scaling back: Dual-earner couples' work-family strategies. *Journal of Marriage and the Family, 61,* 995–1007.

Bennett, F. (2013). Researching within-household distribution: Overview, developments, debates, and methodological challenges. *Journal of Marriage and Family, 75,* 582–597.

Berger, L. M., Hill, J. & Waldfogel, J. (2005). Maternity leave, early maternal employment and child health and development in the U.S. *Economic Journal, 115,* F29–F47.

Bianchi, S. M., Milkie, M. A., Sayer, L. C. & Robinson, J. P. (2000). Is anyone doing the housework? Trends in the gender division of household labor. *Social Forces, 79,* 191–228.

Biernat, M. & Manis, M. (1994). Shifting standards and stereotype-based judgments. *Journal of Personality and Social Psychology, 66,* 5–20.

Biernat, M. & Wortman, C. B. (1991). Sharing of home responsibilities between professionally employed women and their husbands. *Journal of Personality and Social Psychology, 60,* 844–860.

Bittman, M., England, P., Sayer, L., Folbre, N. & Matheson, G. (2003). When does gender trump money? Bargaining and time in household work. *American Journal of Sociology, 109,* 186–214.

Blackburn, R. M. & Jarman, J. (2006). Gendered occupations. *International Sociology, 21,* 289–315.

Blair, S. L. & Johnson, M. P. (1992). Wives' perceptions of the fairness of the division of household labor: The intersection of housework and ideology. *Journal of Marriage and the Family, 54,* 570–581.

Blair-Loy, M. & Wharton, A. S. (2004). Organizational commitment and constraints on work-family policy use: Corporate flexibility policies in a global firm. *Sociological Perspectives, 47,* 243–267.

Blaisure, K. R., Saathoff-Wells, T., Pereira, A., MacDermid Wadsworth, S. & Dombro, A. L. (2012). *Serving military families in the 21st century.* New York, NY: Routledge.

Blickenstaff, J. C. (2005). Women and science careers: Leaky pipeline or gender filter? *Gender and Education, 17,* 369–386.

Bloom, N., Kretschmer, T. & Van Reenen, J. (2011). Are family-friendly workplace practices a valuable firm resource? *Strategic Management Journal, 32,* 343–367.

Bourhis, M. & Mekkaoui, R. (2010). Beyond work-family balance: Are family-friendly organizations more attractive? *Industrial Relations, 65,* 98–117.

Breaugh, J. A. & Frye, N. K. (2007). An examination of the antecedents and consequences of the use of family-friendly benefits. *Journal of Managerial Issues, 19,* 35–52.

Brooks-Gunn, J., Han, W. J. & Waldfogel, J. (2002). Maternal employment and child cognitive outcomes in the first three years of life: The NICHD study of early child care. *Child Development, 73,* 1052–1072.

Brines, J. (1994). Economic dependency, gender, and the division of labor at home. *American Journal of Sociology, 100,* 652–688.

Budig, M. J. & Hodges, M. J. (2010). Differences in disadvantage variation in the motherhood penalty across white women's earnings distribution. *American Sociological Review, 75,* 705–728.

Bull, R., Bustin, B., Evans, P. & Gahagan, D. (1983). *Psychology for police officers.* New York, NY: Wiley.

Bureau of Labor Statistics. (2016). *Highlights of women's earnings in 2015.* Retrieved from https://www.bls.gov/.

Burke, R. J. (1993). Work-family stress, conflict, coping and burnout in police officers. *Stress Medicine, 9,* 171–180.

Cantor, D., Waldfogel, J., Kerwin, J., Wright, M. M., Levin, K., Rauch, J. & Kudela, M. S. (2001). Balancing the needs of families and employers: Family and Medical Leave Surveys. US Department of Labor. Washington, DC: Westat.

Casper, L. M. & O'Connell, M. (1998). Work, income, the economy, and married fathers as child-care providers. *Demography*, *35*, 243–250.

Cech, E., Rubineau, B., Silbey, S. & Seron, C. (2011). Professional role confidence and gendered persistence in engineering. *American Sociological Review*, *76*, 641–666.

Centers for Disease Control and Prevention. (2016). Births: Method of delivery. *National Center for Health Statistics*. Retrieved from http://www.cdc.gov/.

Chappell, D., Korabik, K. & McElwain, A. (2005). The effects of gender-role attitudes on work-family conflict and work-family guilt. Poster presented at the Canadian Psychological Association, Montreal, QC.

Chen, N., Conconi, P. & Perroni, C. (2007). *Women's earning power and the "double burden" of market and household work*. Retrieved from https://ssrn.com/.

Chesley, N. (2011). Stay-at-home fathers and breadwinning mothers: Gender, couple dynamics, and social change. *Gender and Society*, *25*, 642–664.

Clancy, K. B. H., Nelson, R. G., Rutherford, J. N. & Hinde, K. (2014). Survey of Academic Field Experiences (SAFE): Trainees report harassment and assault. *PLoS One*, *9*. Retrieved from: http://journals.plos.org/plosone/ article?id=10.1371/ journal. pone.0102172.

Cleary-Goldman, J., Malone, F. D., Vidaver, J., Ball, R. H., Nyberg, D. A., Comstock, C. H. & D'Alton, M. (2005). Impact of maternal age on obstetric outcome. *Obstetrics and Gynecology*, *105*, 983–990.

Cleveland, J. N., Fisher, G. G. & Sawyer, K. B. (2015). Work-life equality: The importance of a level playing field at home. In M. J. Mills (Ed.), *Gender and the work-family experience: An intersection of two domains*, (pp. 177–200). New York, NY: Springer.

Cochran, S. & Chambliss, C. (2009). The relationship between full-time and part-time maternal employment during the preschool years and young adults' attitudes about maternal work status and career aspirations. In C. Chambliss (Ed.), *Maternal employment: Marvel or menace*, (pp. 61–92). New York, NY: Nova Science Publishers.

Cohen, J. R. & Single, L. E. (2001). An examination of the perceived impact of flexible work arrangements on professional opportunities in public accounting. *Journal of Business Ethics*, *32*, 317–328.

Coleman, J. M. & Franiuk, R. (2011). Perceptions of mothers and fathers who take temporary work leave. *Sex Roles*, *64*, 311–323.

Cook, A. & Minnotte, K. (2008). Occupational and industry sex segregation and the work-family interface. *Sex Roles*, *59*, 800–813.

Costa, G. (1996). The impact of shift and night work on health. *Applied Ergonomics, 27*, 9–16.

Cuddy, A. J., Fiske, S. T. & Glick, P. (2004). When professionals become mothers, warmth doesn't cut the ice. *Journal of Social Issues, 60*, 701–718.

Culbertson, S. S., Huffman, A. H., Mills, M. J. & Imhof, C. (2017). Balancing the badge: Work-family challenges within policing and recommended supports and initiatives. In R. J. Burke (Ed.), *Stress in policing: Sources, consequences, and interventions*, (pp. 66–80). London, UK: Routledge.

Current Population Survey. (2011). Labor force statistics from the current population survey. Retrieved from: http://www.bls.gov/cps/.

Davis, J. A. (1984). Perspectives on policewomen in Texas and Oklahoma. *Journal of Police Science and Administration, 12*, 395–403.

Department of Health and Human Services. (2011). *The surgeon general's call to action to support breastfeeding*. Retrieved from http://www.surgeongeneral.gov/.

DeMaris, A. & Longmore, M. A. (1996). Ideology, power, and equity: Testing competing explanations for the perception of fairness in household labor. *Social Forces, 74*, 1043–1071.

de Valk, H. A. (2008). Parental influence on work and family plans of adolescents of different ethnic background in the Netherlands. *Sex Roles, 59*, 739–751.

Dodson, L. (2013). Stereotyping low-wage mother who have work and family conflicts. *Journal of Social Issues, 69*, 257–278.

D'Olio, C. M. (2009). Male and female college students' perception of the costs and benefits associated with maternal employment during the preschool versus elementary school years. In C. Chambliss (Ed.), *Maternal employment: Marvel or menace*, (pp. 93–123). New York, NY: Nova Science Publishers.

Doucet, A. (2015). Parental responsibilities: Dilemmas of measurement and gender equality. *Journal of Marriage and Family, 77*, 224–242.

Eagly, A. H. (1987). *Sex differences in social behavior: A social-role interpretation*. Hillsdale, NJ: Erlbaum.

Eagly, A. H., Wood, W. & Diekman, A. B. (2000). Social role theory of sex differences and similarities: A current appraisal. In T. Eckes & H. M. Trautner (Eds.), *The developmental social psychology of gender*, (pp. 123–174). Mahwah, NJ: Erlbaum.

Eaton, S. C. (2003). If you can use them: Flexibility policies, organizational commitment, and perceived performance. *Industrial Relations, 42*, 145–167.

Etzion, D. (1984). Moderating effect of social support on the stress-burnout relationship. *Journal of Applied Psychology, 69*, 615–622.

Family and Medical Leave Act. (1993). *United States Department of Labor*. Retrieved from https://www.dol.gov/WHD/fmla.

Fenwick, R. & Tausig, M. (2001). Scheduling stress: Family and health outcomes of shift work and schedule control. *American Behavioral Scientist, 44*, 1179–1198.

Filipkowski, J. N. & Chambliss, C. (2009). College students' perceptions of the costs and benefits associated with maternal employment during preschool and their expectations for future spouse, self, and family. In C. Chambliss (Ed.), *Maternal employment: Marvel or menace,* (pp. 25–60). New York, NY: Nova Science Publishers.

Fouad, N., Fitzpatrick, M. & Liu, J. (2011). Persistence of women in engineering careers: A qualitative study of current and former female engineers. *Journal of Women and Minorities in Science and Engineering, 17,* 69–96.

Fouad, N. A. & Singh, R. (2011). Retention and attrition: The impact of workplace climate on women in the engineering field. *Marine Technology, 48,* 9–11.

Franke, G. R., Crown, D. F. & Spake, D. F. (1997). Gender differences in ethical perceptions of business practices: A social role theory perspective. *Journal of Applied Psychology, 82,* 920–934.

Frisco, M. L. & Williams, K. (2003). Perceived housework equity, marital happiness, and divorce in dual-earner households. *Journal of Family Issues, 24,* 51–73.

Frye, L. & Greenfield, S. (1980). An examination of attitudinal differences between policewomen and policemen. *Journal of Applied Psychology, 65,* 123–126.

Fuegen, K., Biernal, M., Haines, E. & Deaux, K. (2004). Stereotype accuracy: Do college women hit or miss the mark when estimating the "impact" of maternal employment on children's achievement and behavior? *Psychology of Women Quarterly, 38,* 1–13.

Galinsky, E., Bond, J. T. & Sakai, K. (2008). *2008 national study of employers.* New York, NY: Families and Work Institute.

Gershon, R. R., Barocas, B., Canton, A. N., Li, X. & Vlahov, D. (2009). Mental, physical, and behavioral outcomes associated with perceived work stress in police officers. *Criminal Justice and Behavior, 36,* 275–289.

Gillibrand, K. (2016). The American opportunity agenda: *Expand paid family and medical leave.* Retrieved from https://www.gillibrand.senate.gov/.

Glass, J. (2004). Blessing or curse? Work-family policies and mother's wage growth over time. *Work and Occupations, 31,* 367–394.

Glauber, R. (2012). Women's work and working conditions: Are mothers compensated for lost wages? *Work and Occupations, 39,* 115–138.

Goldberg, W. A., Kelly, E., Matthews, N. L., Kang, H., Li, W. & Sumaroka, M. (2012). The more things change, the more they stay the same: Gender, culture, and college students' views about work and family. *Journal of Social Issues, 68,* 814–837.

Goldin, C., Katz, L. F. & Kuziemko, I. (2006). The homecoming of American college women: The reversal of the college gender gap. *Journal of Economic Perspectives, 20,* 363–369.

Gottzén, L. & Kremer-Sadlik, T. (2012). Fatherhood and youth sports: A balancing act between care and expectations. *Gender and Society, 26,* 639–664.

Griffin, J. D. (2012). Are we protecting those who protect us? Stress and law enforcement in the 21st century. Unpublished doctoral dissertation, University of Delaware.

Grosswald, B. (2003). Shift work and negative work-to-family spillover. *Journal of Sociology and Social Welfare, 30,* 31–56.

Grote, N. K. & Clark, M. S. (2001). Perceiving unfairness in the family: Cause or consequence of marital distress? *Journal of Personality and Social Psychology, 80,* 281–293.

Guendelman, S., Kosa, J. L., Pearl, M., Graham, S., Goodman, J. & Kharrazi, M. (2009). Juggling work and breastfeeding: Effects of maternity leave and occupational characteristics. *Pediatrics, 123,* 38–46.

Gupta, S. (2006). The consequences of maternal employment during men's childhood for their adult housework performance. *Gender and Society, 20,* 60–86.

Hakim, C. (2000). *Work-lifestyle choices in the 21st century: Preference theory.* Oxford, UK: Oxford University Press.

Hall, G. B., Dollard, M. F., Tuckey, M. R., Winefield, A. H. & Thompson, B. M. (2010). Job demands, work-family conflict, and emotional exhaustion in police officers: A longitudinal test of competing theories. *Journal of Occupational and Organizational Psychology, 83,* 237–250.

Hammer, L. B., Neal, M. B., Newsom, J. T., Brockwood, K. J. & Colton, C. L. (2005). A longitudinal study of the effects of dual-earner couples' utilization of family-friendly workplace supports on work and family outcomes. *Journal of Applied Psychology, 90,* 799–810.

Han, W. J., Ruhm, C. & Waldfogel, J. (2009). Parental leave policies and parents' employment and leave-taking. *Journal of Policy Analysis and Management, 28,* 29–54.

Hardie, J. H. & Hayford, S. R. (2012). Opting in: Adolescent girls' work and family plans. Paper presented at the American Sociological Association Annual Meeting, Denver, CO.

Harpold, M. & Feemster, J. (2002). Negative influences of police stress. *FBI Law Enforcement Bulletin, 70,* 1–7.

He, N., Zhao, J. & Archbold, C. A. (2002). Gender and police stress: The convergent and divergent impact of work environment, work-family conflict, and stress coping mechanisms of female and male police officers. *Policing: An International Journal of Police Strategies and Management, 25,* 687–708.

Heilman, M. E. & Okimoto, T. G. (2008). Motherhood: A potential source of bias in employment decisions. *Journal of Applied Psychology, 93,* 189–198.

Hill, C., Corbett, C. & St. Rose, A. (2010). *Why so few? Women in science, technology, engineering, and math.* Washington, DC: AAUW.

Hill, J. L., Waldfogel, J., Brooks-Gunn, J. & Han, W. J. (2005). Maternal employment and child development: A fresh look using newer methods. *Development Psychology*, *41*, 833–850.

Himsel, A. J. & Goldberg, W. A. (2003). Social comparisons and satisfaction with the division of housework: Implications for men's and women's role strain. *Journal of Family Issues*, *24*, 843–866.

Hinkin, T. R. & Tracey, J. B. (2000). The cost of turnover. *Cornell Hospitality Quarterly*, *41*, 14–21.

Hobfoll, S. E. (1989). Conservation of resource: A new attempt at conceptualizing stress. *American Psychologist*, *44*, 513–524.

Hobfoll, S. E., Vinokur, A. D., Pierce, P. F. & Lewandowski-Romps, L. (2012). The combined stress of family life, work, and war in air force men and women: A test of conservation of resources theory. *International Journal of Stress Management*, *19*, 217–237.

Hochschild, A. R. (1989). *The second shift: Working parents and the revolution at home.* New York, NY: Viking.

Hochwarter, W. A., Perrewé, P. L., Meurs, J. A. & Kacmar, C. (2007). The interactive effects of work-induced guilt and ability to manage resources on job and life satisfaction. *Journal of Occupational Health Psychology*, *12*, 125–135.

Hoobler, J. M., Wayne, S. J. & Lemmon, G. (2009). Bosses' perceptions of family-work conflict and women's promotability: Glass ceiling effects. *Academy of Management Journal*, *52*, 939–957.

Howard, W. G., Donofrio, H. H. & Boles, J. S. (2004). Inter-domain work-family, family-work conflict and police work satisfaction. *Policing: An International Journal of Police Strategies and Management*, *27*, 380–395.

Howell, K. (2016, March 11). *Defense Secretary Ashton Carter OKs final strategy for women in combat.* Washington Times. Retrieved from http://www.washingtontimes. com/.

Huang, R. & Yang, M. (2015). Paid maternity leave and breastfeeding practice before and after California's implementation of the nation's first paid family leave program. *Economics and Human Biology*, *16*, 45–59.

Huffman, A. H., Culbertson, S. S. & Barbour, J. (2015). Gender roles in a masculine occupation: Military men and women's differential negotiation of the work-family interface. In M. J. Mills (Ed.), *Gender and the work-family experience: An intersection of two domains,* (pp. 271–290). New York, NY: Springer.

Huffman, A. H., Watrous-Rodriguez, K. & King, E. (2008). Supporting a diverse workforce: What type of support is most meaningful for lesbian and gay employees? *Human Resource Management*, *4*, 237–253.

International Labour Organization. (2014). Maternity and paternity at work: Law and practice across the world. Geneva, Switzerland: *International Labour Office*.

International Monetary Fund (IMF). (2013). Women, work, and the economy: Macroeconomic gains from gender equity. IMF Staff Discussion Note, SDN/13/10.

Iverson, S. V., Seher, C. L., DiRamio, D., Jarvis, K. & Anderson, R. (2016). Walking a gender tightrope: A qualitative study of female student veterans' experiences within military and campus cultures. *NASPA Journal about Women in Higher Education, 9,* 152–168.

Jackson, S. E. & Maslach, C. (1982). After-effects of job-related stress: Families as victims. *Journal of Organizational Behavior, 3,* 63–77.

Jacobs, J. A. & Gerson, K. (2004). *The time divide: Work, family, and gender inequality.* Cambridge, MA: Harvard University Press.

Jean, V. A., Payne, S. C. & Thompson, R. J. (2015). Women in STEM: Family-related challenges and initiatives. In M. J. Mills (Ed.), *Gender and the work-family experience: An intersection of two domains,* (pp. 291–312). New York, NY: Springer.

Johnson, L. B. (1991). Job strain among police officers: Gender comparison. *Police Studies, 14,* 12–16.

Kalleberg, A. L. & Rosenfeld, R. A. (1990). Work in the family and in the labor market: A cross-national, reciprocal analysis. *Journal of Marriage and the Family, 52,* 331–346.

Kane, E. W. & Sanchez, L. (1994). Family status and criticism of gender inequality at home and at work. *Social Forces, 72,* 1079–1102.

Kline, A., Ciccone, D. S., Weiner, M., Interian, A., St. Hill, L., Falca-Dodson, M., Black, C. M. & Losonczy, M. (2013). Gender differences in the risk and protective factors associated with PTSD: A prospective study of National Guard troops deployed to Iraq. *Psychiatry: Interpersonal and Biological Processes, 76,* 256–272.

Koenig, E. (1978). An overview of attitudes toward women in law enforcement. *Police Administration Review, 38,* 267–275.

Kop, N., Euwema, M. & Schaufeli, W. (1999). Burnout, job stress and violent behaviour among Dutch police officers. *Work and Stress, 13,* 326–340.

Korabik, K. (2015). The intersection of gender and work-family guilt. In M. J. Mills (Ed.), *Gender and the work-family experience: An intersection of two domains,* (pp. 141–158). New York, NY: Springer.

Kossek, E. E. & Ozeki, C. (1999). Bridging the work-family policy and productivity gap: A literature review. *Community, Work and Family, 2,* 7–32.

Kotsadam, A. & Finseraas, H. (2011). The state intervenes in the battle of the sexes: Causal effects of paternity leave. *Social Science Research, 40,* 1611–1622.

Kramer, K. Z., Kelly, E. L. & McCulloch, J. B. (2015). Stay-at-home fathers: Definition and characteristics based on 34 years of CPS data. *Journal of Family Issues, 36,* 1651–1673.

Kreager, D. A., Felson, R. B., Warner, C. & Wenger, M. R. (2013). Women's education, marital violence, and divorce: A social exchange perspective. *Journal of Marriage and Family, 75*, 565–581.

Kurtz, D. L. (2012). Roll call and the second shift: The influences of gender and family on police stress. *Police Practice and Research, 13*, 71-86.

La Valle, I., Arthur, S., Millward, C., Scott, J. & Clayden, M. (2002). *Happy families? Atypical work and its influence on family life*. Bristol, UK: Policy Press.

Lennon, M. C. & Rosenfield, S. (1994). Relative fairness and the division of housework: The importance of options. *American Journal of Sociology, 100*, 506–531.

Lent, R. W., Brown, S. D. & Hackett, G. (1994). Toward a unifying social cognitive theory of career and academic interest, choice, and performance. *Journal of Vocational Behavior, 45*, 79–122.

Lent, R. W., Brown, S. D. & Hackett, G. (2002). Social cognitive career model. In D. Brown (Ed.), *Career choice and development*, (pp. 255–311). San Francisco, CA: Jossey-Bass.

Levin-Epstein, J. (2006). *Getting punched: The job and family clock*. Washington, DC: Center for Law and Social Policy.

Lichtenwalter, S. (2005). Gender poverty disparity in US cities: Evidence exonerating female-headed families. *Journal of Sociology and Social Welfare, 32*, 75–96.

Lindsey, D. (2007). Police fatigue. *FBI Law Enforcement Bulletin, 76*, 1–8.

Loo, R. (2004). A typology of burnout types among police managers. *Policing: An International Journal of Police Strategies and Management, 27*, 156–165.

Lucas-Thompson, R. G. & Goldberg, W. A. (2015). Gender ideology and work-family plans of the next generation. In M. J. Mills (Ed.), *Gender and the work-family experience: An intersection of two domains*, (pp. 3–20). New York, NY: Springer.

Lucier-Greer, M., O'Neal, C. W., Arnold, A. L., Mancini, J. A. & Wickrama, K. K. (2014). Adolescent mental health and academic functioning: Empirical support for contrasting models of risk and vulnerability. *Military Medicine, 179*, 1279–1287.

Lutwak, N. (2012). The negative effects of MST and combat injuries among female soldiers: A major concern. *Journal of Psychiatric Research, 46*, 691–723.

MacEwen, K. E. & Barling, J. (1994). Daily consequences of work interference with family and family interference with work. *Work and Stress, 8*, 244–254.

Martin, S. E. & Jurik, N. C. (2007). *Doing justice, doing gender: Women in legal and criminal justice occupations*. Thousand Oaks, CA: Sage.

Martínez, P., Carrasco, M. J., Aza, G., Blanco, A. & Espinar, I. (2011). Family gender role and guilt in Spanish dual-earner families. *Sex Roles, 65*, 813–826.

Matthews, M. D., Ender, M. G., Laurence, J. H. & Rohall, D. E. (2009). Role of group affiliation and gender on attitudes toward women in the military. *Military Psychology, 21*, 241–251.

Matthews, R. A., Mills, M. J., Trout, R. & English, L. (2014). Family-supportive supervisor behaviors, employee engagement, and subjective well-being: A contextually-dependent mediated process. *Journal of Occupational Health Psychology*, *19*, 168–181.

McDonald, P., Pini, B., Bailey, J. & Price, R. (2011). Young people's aspirations for education, work, family and leisure. *Work, Employment and Society*, *25*, 68–84.

McSally, M. E. (2011). Defending America in mixed company: Gender in the U.S. armed forces. *Daedalus*, *140*, 148–164.

Menez, R., Munder, I. & Töpsch, K. (2001). Personnel recruitment and qualification in the IT sector: First results of the on-line study BIT-S. In Proceedings from Innovations for an E-society: Challenges for Technology Assessment, *ITAS* Karlsruhe. Berlin: Edition Sigma.

Military Women in Service for America Foundation. (2011). *Statistics on women in the military*. Retrieved from http://www.womensmemorial.org/.

Miller, L. (2008). Stress and resilience in law enforcement training and practice. *International Journal of Emergency Mental Health*, *10*, 109–124.

Mills, M. J. (2015). *Gender and the work-family experience: An intersection of two domains*. New York, NY: Springer.

Mills, M. J. (2016). The new rules of work-life balance: Paid maternity leave isn't enough; If you want to compete globally, you need to think bigger, broader, and better. *Talent Quarterly*, *12*, 21–23.

Mills, M. J. & Culbertson, S. S. (2017). The elephant in the family room: Work-family considerations as central to evolving HR and I-O. *Industrial and Organizational Psychology: Perspectives on Science and Practice*, *10*, 26–31.

Mills, M. J., Culbertson, S. S., Huffman, A. H. & Connell, A. R. (2012). Assessing gender biases: Development and initial validation of the gender role stereotypes scale. *Gender in Management: An International Journal*, *27*, 520–540.

Mills, M. J. & Grotto, A. R. (2017). Who can have it all and how? An empirical examination of gender and work-life considerations among senior executives. *Gender in Management: An International Journal*, *32*, 82–97.

Mills, M. J., Matthews, R. A., Henning, J. B. & Woo, V. A. (2014). Family-supportive organizations and supervisors: What difference do they make, and for whom? *International Journal of Human Resource Management*, *25*, 1763–1785.

Mills, M. J. & Tortez, L. M. (in press). Fighting for Family: Considerations of Work-Family Conflict in Military Service Member Parents. *Research in Occupational Stress and Well-Being*.

Mills, M. J., Tortez, L. M. & Gallego-Pace, M. E. (2016). Is she really into it? The media as misleading in its portrayals of female executives' work-family (im)balance. In C. J. Elliott (Ed.), *Gender, Media, and Organization: Challenging*

Mis(s)Representations of Women Leaders and Managers, (pp. 19–36). Charlotte, NC: Information Age.

Morash, M. & Haarr, R. N. (1995). Gender, workplace problems, and stress in policing. *Justice Quarterly, 12*, 113–140.

Mumford, E. A., Taylor, B. G. & Kubu, B. (2015). Law enforcement officer safety and wellness. *Police Quarterly, 18*, 111–133.

Munn, S. L. & Greer, T. W. (2015). Beyond the "ideal" worker: Including men in work-family discussions. In M. J. Mills (Ed.), *Gender and the work-family experience: An intersection of two domains*, (pp. 21–38). New York, NY: Springer.

Munsch, C. L. (2016). Gender, childcare, and type of request on the flexibility bias. *Social Forces, 94*, 1567–1591.

National Center for Biotechnology Information. (2013). *Infertility*. Retrieved from http://www.ncbi.nlm.nih.gov/.

National Science Foundation. (2013). Women, minorities, and persons with disabilities in science and engineering: 2013. Special Report *NSF* 13–304, Arlington, VA. Retrieved from http://www.nsf.gov/statistics/wmpd.

Odle-Dusseau, H., McFadden, A. C. & Britt, T. W. (2015). Gender, poverty, and the work-family interface. In M. J. Mills (Ed.), *Gender and the work-family experience: An intersection of two domains*, (pp. 39–56). New York, NY: Springer.

Øyane, N. M. F., Pallesen, S., Moen, B. E., Akerstedt, T. & Bjorvatn, B. (2013). Associations between night work and anxiety, depression, insomnia, sleepiness and fatigue in a sample of Norwegian nurses. *PLoS ONE, 8*, 1–7.

Pearce, D. (1978). The feminization of poverty: Women, work and welfare. *Urban and Social Change Review, 11*, 28–36.

Pettinger, L. (2005). Gendered work meets gendered goods: Selling and service in clothing retail. *Gender, Work and Organization, 12*, 460–478.

Pew Research Center. (2010). *The decline of marriage and rise of new families*. Washington, DC: Pew Research Center.

Pew Research Center. (2013). *On pay gap, millennial women near parity—for now*. Washington, DC: Pew Research Center.

Phillips, K. R. (2002). *Parent work and child well-being in low-income families*. Urban Institute. Retrieved from http://webarchive.urban.org/.

Polusny, M. A., Kumpula, M. J., Meis, L. A., Erbes, C. R., Arbisi, P. A., Murdoch, M., Thuras, P., Kehle-Forbes, S. & Johnson, A. K. (2014). Gender differences in the effects of deployment related stressors and pre-deployment risk factors on the development of PTSD symptoms in National Guard soldiers deployed to Iraq and Afghanistan. *Journal of Psychiatric Research, 49*, 1–9.

Rege, M. & Solli, I. F. (2010). The impact of paternity leave on long-term father involvement. Working Paper. Retrieved from https:// core.ac.uk/ download/ pdf/ 6238666.pdf.

Reskin, B. F. & Bielby, D. D. (2005). A sociological perspective on gender and career outcomes. *Journal of Economic Perspectives, 19,* 71–86.

Richman, A., Johnson, A. & Buxbaum, L. (2006). Workplace flexibility for lower-wage workers. Washington, DC: Corporate Voices for Working Families' Workplace Flexibility Project.

Rosiello, R. M. & Mills, M. J. (2015). Shiftwork as gendered and its impact on work-family balance. In M. J. Mills (Ed.), *Gender and the work-family experience: An intersection of two domains,* (pp. 251–270). New York, NY: Springer.

Rosiello, R. M., Tortez, L. & Mills, M. J. (2016, April). Equal opportunity support: Examining the work-family experience for single, childless employees. Paper presented at the Society for Industrial and Organizational Psychology Conference, Anaheim, California.

Ruhm, C. J. (2000). Parental leave and child health. *Journal of Health Economics, 19,* 931–960.

Ryan, A. M. & Kossek, E. E. (2008). Work-life policy implementation: Breaking down or creating barriers to inclusiveness? *Human Resource Management, 47,* 295–310.

Sawyer, K. B., Thoroughgood, C. N. & Cleveland, J. N. (2015). Challenging heteronormative and gendered assumptions in work-family research: An examination of LGB identity-based work-family conflict. In M. J. Mills (Ed.), *Gender and the work-family experience: An intersection of two domains,* (pp. 77–98). New York, NY: Springer.

Schaufeli, W. B. & Enzmann, D. (1998). *The burnout companion to study and practice: A critical analysis.* London, UK: Taylor & Francis.

Schiebinger, L. & Gilmartin, S. (2010). Housework is an academic issue. *Academe, 96,* 39–44.

Schroeder, J., Dugdale, H. L., Radersma, R., Hinsch, M., Buehler, D. M. & Horrocks, N. P. C. (2013). Fewer invited talks by women in evolutionary biology symposia. *Journal of Evolutionary Biology, 26,* 2063–2069.

Shaevitz, H. M. (1984). *The superwoman syndrome.* New York, NY: Warner Books.

Sidanius, J. & Pratto, F. (1999). *Social dominance: An intergroup theory of social hierarchy and oppression.* New York, NY: Cambridge University Press.

Silbert, M. H. (1982). Job stress and burnout and new police officers. *Police Chief, 49,* 46–68.

Simard, C., Henderson, A. D., Gilmartin, S. K., Schiebinger, L. & Whitney, T. (2008). *Climbing the technical ladder: Obstacles and solutions for mid-level women in technology.* Stanford, CA: Michelle R. Clayman Institute for Gender Research, Stanford University; Anita Borg Institute for Women and Technology.

Simon, R. W. (1995). Gender, multiple roles, role meaning, and mental health. *Journal of Health and Social Behaviour, 36,* 182–194.

Slaughter, A. M. (2012, July/August). Why women still can't have it all. *Atlantic*. http://www.theatlantic.com/.

Somvadee, C. & Morash, M. (2008). Dynamics of sexual harassment for policewomen working alongside men. *Policing: An International Journal of Police Strategies and Management, 31*, 485–498.

Spielberger, C., Westbury, L., Grier, K. & Greefield, G. (1981). *The police stress survey: Sources of stress in law enforcement*. Human Resources Institute, Tampa, FL.

Spitzmueller, C., Wang, Z., Matthews, R. A., Fisher, G. G., Perks, C., Zhang, J. & Strathearn, L. (2016). Got milk? Workplace factors related to breastfeeding among working mothers. *Journal of Organizational Behavior, 37*, 692–718.

Sprung, J. M., Toumbeva, T. H. & Matthews, R. A. (2015). Family-friendly organizational policies, practices, and benefits through the gender lens. In M. J. Mills (Ed.), *Gender and the work-family experience: An intersection of two domains*, (pp. 227–250). New York, NY: Springer.

Stegelin, D. A. & Frankel, J. (1997). Families of employed mothers in the United States. In J. Frankel (Ed.), *Families of employed mothers: An international perspective*, (pp. 237–260). New York, NY: Garland.

Street, A. E., Vogt, D. & Dutra, L. (2009). A new generation of women veterans: Stressors faced by women deployed to Iraq and Afghanistan. *Clinical Psychology Review, 29*, 685–694.

Sutton, P. D., Hamilton, B. E. & Mathews, T. J. (2011). Recent decline in births in the United States, 2007–2009 (*NCHS* data brief, no. 60). Hyattsville, MD: National Center for Health Statistics.

Tanaka, S. (2005). Parental leave and child health across OECD countries. *Economic Journal, 115*, F7–F28.

Tausig, M. & Fenwick, R. (2001). Unbinding time: Alternate work schedules and work-life balance. *Journal of Family and Economic Issues, 22*, 101–119.

Valian, V. (1999). *Why so slow? The advancement of women*. Cambridge, MA: MIT Press.

Vervecken, D., Hannover, B. & Wolter, I. (2013). Changing (s)expectations: How gender fair job descriptions impact children's perceptions and interest regarding traditionally male occupations. *Journal of Vocational Behavior, 82*, 208–220.

Vinokur, A. D., Pierce, P. F., Lewandowski-Romps, L., Hobfoll, S. E. & Galea, S. (2011). Effects of war exposure on air force personnel's mental health, job burnout and other organizational related outcomes. *Journal of Occupational Health Psychology, 16*, 3–17.

Violanti, J. M. & Aron, F. (1995). Police stressors: Variations in perception among police personnel. *Journal of Criminal Justice, 23*, 287–294.

Vogt, D., Smith, B., Elwy, R., Martin, J., Schultz, M., Drainoni, M. L. & Eisen, S. (2011). Predeployment, deployment, and postdeployment risk factors for posttraumatic stress symptomatology in female and male OEF/OIF veterans. *Journal of Abnormal Psychology, 120,* 819–831.

Wayne, J. H. & Casper, W. J. (2012). Why does firm reputation in human resource policies influence college students? The mechanisms underlying job pursuit intentions. *Human Resource Management, 51,* 121–142.

Wayne, J. H., Musisca, N. & Fleeson, W. (2004). Considering the role of personality in the work-family experience: Relationships of the big five to work-family conflict and facilitation. *Journal of Vocational Behavior, 64*(1), 108–130.

Weinshenker, M. N. (2006). Adolescents' expectations about mothers' employment: Life course patterns and parental influence. *Sex Roles, 54,* 845–857.

Westman, M. & Etzion, D. (1995). Crossover of stress, strain and resources from one spouse to another. *Journal of Organizational Behavior, 16,* 169–181.

Wharton, A. S. (1999). The psychosocial consequences of emotional labor. *Annals of the American Academy of Political and Social Science, 561,* 158–176.

Wharton, A. S., Chivers, S. & Blair-Loy, M. (2008). Use of formal and informal work-family policies on the digital assembly line. *Work and Occupations, 35,* 327–350.

Wilbourn, M. P. & Kee, D. W. (2010). Henry the nurse is a doctor too: Implicitly examining children's gender stereotypes for male and female occupational roles. *Sex Roles, 62,* 670–683.

Williams, C. (2008). Work-life balance of shift workers. *Perspectives on Labour and Income, 20,* 5–16.

Williams, J. (2010). *Reshaping the work-family debate: Why men and class matter.* Cambridge, MA: Harvard University Press.

Williams, J. C., Blair-Loy, M. & Berdahl, J. L. (2013). Cultural schemas, social class, and the flexibility stigma. *Journal of Social Issues, 69*(2), 209–234.

Willis, T. A., O'Connor, D. B. & Smith, L. (2008). Investigating effort-reward imbalance and work-family conflict in relation to morningness-eveningness and shift work. *Work and Stress, 22,* 125–137.

Wolin, L. D. (2003). Gender issues in advertising. *Journal of Advertising Research, 43,* 111–130.

World Bank. (2014). Gender at work: A companion to the World Development Report on Jobs. Washington, DC. Retrieved from https://openknowledge.worldbank.org/.

World Health Organization. (2007). Carcinogenicity of shift-work, painting, and fire-fighting. *Lancet Oncology, 8,* 1065–1066.

Yavorsky, J. E., Kamp Dush, C. M. & Schoppe-Sullivan, S. J. (2015). The production of inequality: The gender division of labor across the transition to parenthood. *Journal of Marriage and Family, 77,* 662–679.

Young, L. M. & Nauta, M. M. (2013). Sexism as a predictor of attitudes toward women in the military and in combat. *Military Psychology, 25,* 166–171.

Zhang, J., Zhu, Y., Zhan, G., Fenik, P., Panossian, L., Wang, M. M. & Veasey, S. (2014). Extended wakefulness: Compromised metabolics in and degeneration of locus ceruleus neurons. *Journal of Neuroscience*, *34*, 4418–4431.

Zulkey, C. (2006, August). *Why it's time for working mothers to stop apologizing.* Fast Company. Retrieved from https://www.fastcompany.com/.

In: Work-Life Balance in the 21st Century
Editor: Jessica M. Nicklin

ISBN: 978-1-53612-526-9
© 2018 Nova Science Publishers, Inc.

Chapter 3

THE BUSINESS OWNER BALANCING ACT: EXPLORING WORK-LIFE BALANCE IN ENTREPRENEURS

Andrew A. Bennett[*], Stephen E. Lanivich, Yusuf Akbulut and M. Mahdi Moeini Gharagozloo
Department of Management, Old Dominion University, Norfolk, VA, US

ABSTRACT

An entrepreneur is an individual who takes initiative to bundle resources in market-capturing ways and is willing to pursue his or her venture despite risk and uncertainty. Approximately 27 million working-age Americans are starting or running new ventures, yet not enough is known about how these individuals navigate their work and home lives. This chapter reviews what has been discovered about entrepreneurial work-life balance. In doing so, we focus on three influencing factors: identity as an entrepreneur, boundary preferences between life and work domains in an entrepreneurial context, and both the role and the business stress that entrepreneurs may feel. We then explore how entrepreneurs can use different boundary management tactics (e.g., behavioral, temporal, physical, and communicative) to better balance their work and home lives, as well as how being an entrepreneur may impact work respite and recovery from work stress. Finally, we conclude with future research directions for scholars to further develop the theoretical and practical ideas presented.

[*] Corresponding Author Email: aabennet@odu.edu.

Entrepreneurs are individuals engaged in the process of opportunity identification, evaluation, and exploitation wherein risk and uncertainty are assumed for the possibility of profit. Recently, Kelly, Singer, and Herrington (2016) found, through a survey of 60 nations, that as many as 21 percent of individuals intend to start a business in the next three years. It has been noted that research exploring the life of entrepreneurs, beyond their businesses, is lacking (Jennings & McDougald, 2007). The following discourse was inspired by a growing interest in work-life balance research (Ross, Intindola, & Boje, 2016), with our focus on individuals intending, or currently involved in, entrepreneurial activity. The purpose of this chapter is first to explore factors that may influence work-life balance of entrepreneurs, then examine mechanisms through which entrepreneurs can improve their work-life balance, and finally explore future research directions.

FACTORS INFLUENCING WORK-LIFE BALANCE IN ENTREPRENEURS

People start entrepreneurial ventures for many reasons, including the possibility of improved work-life balance (Jennings & McDougald, 2007; Kirkwood & Tootell, 2008). This is likely because entrepreneurs are perceived to have more control over their schedules, and having control over time off from work has a direct negative relationship with work-family interference (Geurts, Beckers, Taris, Kompier, & Smulders, 2009). In other words, people feel less conflict of work getting in the way of nonwork duties and desires when they believe they have more control over their time. However, creating a new venture may be a double-edged sword. For example, many social entrepreneurs enter a new venture to increase meaning within their life, yet they often sacrifice their own health and well-being to benefit others (Dempsey & Sanders, 2010).

In addition to starting a full-time business, individuals may engage in entrepreneurial activity on a part-time basis, especially as the independent contractor, freelance, or "gig" economy (e.g., Uber and Airbnb; Hathaway, 2015) becomes more prevalent in the 21st century. This part-time approach provides many benefits, including on-demand income and flexible working hours. However, the boundaries between home and work are blurred, and this may increase stress if lack of work structure detracts from nonwork activities. For instance, on-demand drivers (e.g., Uber or Lyft drivers) get higher rates during holidays and special occasions, and these are the days people most want to spend time with their family. In such cases, an individual must make a potentially difficult decision: spend time with family or friends and lose an income opportunity, or earn income and lose personal time. In this section, we explore three factors that influence work-life balance: identity, boundary preferences, and stress.

Entrepreneurial Identity

Identity, or who we are, is a long-studied phenomenon with roots in psychology and sociology. Stryker (1968) defined *identity* as internalized behavioral expectations that are thought to be derived from socially accepted role standards (see Burke, 2003). In this section, we explore the various ways an entrepreneurial identity can impact work-life balance. The focus on entrepreneurial identity stems from popular notions of entrepreneurship (which shape social role standards) that entrepreneurs have more control over their career and pursue meaning from their work, which can increase work-life balance (Direnzo, Greenhaus, & Weer, 2015).

As research into entrepreneurship has burgeoned, scholars have sought to define the identity of the individual who would become an entrepreneur (Schoon & Duckworth, 2012), the identity transition that occurs while in the process of entrepreneurship (Foss, 2009), and how identity affects entrepreneurial outcomes (Navis & Glynn, 2011; Shepherd & Haynie, 2009).

From an occupational perspective, as individuals experience their work life, a sense of identity is manifest by the activities and roles in which a person participates (Adamson, Doherty, & Viney, 1998). We can define occupational identity as the aspects of career engagement that influence a person's perceptions of self, intentions, behaviors, and work attributes (Hall, 1971). However, scholars have argued that identity cannot be removed from the other dimensions (e.g., family and leisure) of a person's life (Lewis, Ho, Harris, & Morrison, 2016). The literature regarding entrepreneurial identity suggests that an entrepreneur's identity is not easily separated from work-related aspects of life, perhaps because their work identity is more salient than a typical organizational employee.

Entrepreneurial identity is created through continual engagement in the entrepreneurial process and characterized by the individual being perceived by themselves and others as embodying, communicating, and representing the creation of value in a venture (Lundqvist, Williams-Middleton, & Nowell, 2015). Sexton and Bowman (1985) suggested that early in an entrepreneur's life he or she may be thought of as "unable to relate to family or peers . . . [and] unwilling and unable to submit to or work with authority"; they stressed that "an entrepreneur must be a capable executive and, in addition, must possess a number of psychological characteristics" that are different than others (p. 129). They go on to state that if the personal traits of entrepreneurs are ignored, there can be a negative influence on their venture and lifestyle. Below, we review some of the known characteristics of entrepreneurs in an effort to better understand why and how entrepreneurs can deal with the strain of managing a plethora of roles, including those outside of their business responsibilities. However, we note that separating work and other aspects of life may be difficult for entrepreneurs.

Characteristics of Entrepreneurs

Entrepreneurs' characteristics have been debated for predictive relevance (Gartner, 1989), yet they still represent the psychological profile of individuals behaving entrepreneurially. Early on, scholars recognized certain characteristics of entrepreneurs, including moderate risk-taking propensity (Sexton & Bowman, 1985), high ambiguity tolerance (Schere, 1982), internal locus of control (Brockhaus, 1982), and low needs for conformity, interpersonal affect, harm avoidance, support, sympathy, reassurance, or advice (Sexton & Bowman, 1985). More recently, van Ness and Seifert (2016) suggested that entrepreneurs could be identified by their work ethic, positive affect, and personality (conscientiousness and emotional stability).

An interesting inference from these known set of traits is that entrepreneurs' characteristics and environmental conditions make them susceptible to loneliness brought on by the absence of people in which they could confide, desires to project a strong image, achievement orientation, and conflicting values between themselves and family and friends (Boyd & Gumpert, 1984). Sexton and Bowman (1985) pointed out that entrepreneurs can become oblivious to the needs of friends and family because of their engrossment in their business. In turn, this can cause resentment that separates entrepreneurs from the friends and family that could otherwise alleviate their loneliness. This suggests that a typical entrepreneur, as defined by these characteristics, may have a different definition of what work-life balance means, perhaps with the balance more tilted toward work. In addition, achieving balance could be difficult for entrepreneurs with these characteristics.

However, the perspective that achieving work-life balance is more difficult for entrepreneurs may not be the most accurate. More recently, scholars have identified cognitive characteristics of entrepreneurs that can aid in coping with the inherent uncertainty and negative effects of their career on their personal life. Robert Baron's (1998) work presented cognitive characteristics as a way forward in individual-level entrepreneurship investigation. In essence, he thought there were important identifiers regarding the entrepreneurial identity that could help entrepreneurs navigate through the uncertainty and turmoil that arise during the process of business concept identification, exploitation, and management. Haynie, Shepherd, Mosakowski, and Earley (2010) proposed that cognitive adaptability in entrepreneurs is vital for navigating and adjusting to the dynamic entrepreneurial process. Their research suggests that entrepreneurial identity is, in part, based on a mindset for entrepreneurial activity and that such activity is aided by mental pliability and adaptation. This mental pliability can also help entrepreneurs in their quest for work-life balance if individuals utilize their adaptation skills in nonwork environments as well, such as changing life stages. Lanivich (2015) posited that a resource-induced coping heuristic assists entrepreneurs by inspiring the actions of resource conservation, specifically the attainment, protection, and development of resources that might attenuate unforeseen loss that can cause strain in business, as well as in life. In relation to work-life balance, recent research has shown that entrepreneurs who have higher levels of psychological capital (i.e., self-efficacy, hope, optimism, and resilience) felt less stress and greater life satisfaction, and these relationships were stronger in older entrepreneurs (Baron, Franklin, & Hmieleski, 2016). Overall, it seems likely that the coping skills and psychological capital gained by entrepreneurs can improve work-life balance, although the transfer of these skills from the work domain to the nonwork domain may take extra effort.

How Entrepreneurship Shapes Identity

Beginning in the nascent stages of the entrepreneurial process, individuals begin to learn to be entrepreneurs. In other words, individuals may *identify with* entrepreneurship before acting as an entrepreneur, but experience with the process of entrepreneurship is needed before individuals can really *identify as* entrepreneurs (Lundqvist et al., 2015). Gartner, Bird, and Starr (1992) suggest that as individuals begin to identify with entrepreneurship, and form intentions to become entrepreneurial, they must start acting as if they are entrepreneurs to fulfill the role. In essence, entrepreneurs sometimes need to fake it before they make it, or behave as if they know what and who they are until they really do know. Scholars suggest that entrepreneurs learn as they experience network and industry socialization, or the process by which entrepreneurs figure out the standards and normal behaviors perceived by others in society, and negotiate recognition that they have fulfilled the role of entrepreneur to acquire an entrepreneurial identity (Rae, 2006). In other words, entrepreneurs need to convince the people around them that they are indeed entrepreneurs.

While it is important to recognize that roles are distinct from identity, entrepreneurial identity is linked tightly with the experience of entrepreneurship roles (i.e., behaving entrepreneurially) because participating in these roles allow for social construction of the identity (Jones, Latham, & Betta, 2007). As such, entrepreneurs may feel pressured to always be in the process, especially in the initial stages of venture development, which may blur the lines between work and other aspects of life. For instance, an individual starting a new venture may have received start-up funding from friends and family, which could increase the need to always show to others that one is working hard on the new business. In this scenario, taking a vacation could be viewed as mismanagement of someone else's money, which could increase tensions around those individuals that typically provide meaning in the nonwork domain.

Transitioning into Entrepreneurship

Entrepreneurs often begin their journey into new venture creation by transitioning out of one work/career context and into their entrepreneurial roles. This change can cause major upheaval in a person's life and often requires assuming a new identity (Shepherd & Haynie, 2009). In fact, when overcoming the challenges of disengaging from old roles

(Ashforth, 2001), people contemplating entrepreneurship actively pursue their new identity through activities such as building new social relationships (Ibarra, 2003). Transitions from one work role to another, including making the change from employee to entrepreneur, have become a frequent occurrence for many people (Arthur & Rousseau, 1996). This type of disruptive change in individuals' lives can cause them to adjust their perspectives, attributes, orientation to time, and norms (Van Maanen & Schein, 1979). Hoang and Gimeno (2010) note that transitions to an entrepreneurship identity can be difficult and can cause conflict with broader self-concepts or personal and social identity. Individuals must go through social feedback loops wherein their new expectations of self are negotiated with others' perceptions of them to create congruence in identity (Lewis et al., 2016). It has also been suggested that women often have difficulty transitioning into entrepreneurship due to institutionalized masculinity (Lewis et al., 2016). They identified a cyclical process for mothers who left careers to have children and then returned to the workforce and transitioned their identity to entrepreneurs to fit their schedules and lifestyles. Warren (2004) highlighted ways that female entrepreneurs reduced the tensions of transition, such as negotiating their new identity by characterizing themselves as professionals. We make this specific note regarding gender because we recognize the roles outside of entrepreneurs' ventures may be different for women than for men. However, both must find a way to negotiate their identity while balancing their life outside of their venture.

Work-Life Boundaries of Entrepreneurs

Social roles imply different identities for different social domains and for different times (e.g., parent, spouse, sibling roles at home; coworker, supervisor, and subordinate roles at work). Historically, separation of these identities is aligned with social shifts. For example, as societies shifted from agricultural to industrial, the most relevant social change was the clear distinction between home and work for most individuals (Allen, Cho, & Meier, 2014). Thus, there was a need for separation of roles enacted at home and work. Societies and economies have again shifted, with blurred roles accelerating due to technological advancements and changes in mindsets to move the work to workers instead of workers to the work (Allen, Golden, & Shockley, 2015). Even though initially this idea was considered as a solution to traffic problems, it was later adopted by companies as an employee benefit. Therefore, with this increased flexibility for employees, the integration or segmentation of different social domains has become personal preference (Allen et al., 2014), and how one's behaviors match one's preference impacts perceptions of work-life balance.

Boundary theory refers to how people deal with the distinctiveness of their home and work environments (Ashforth, Kreiner, & Fugate, 2000) and is drawn upon to explain the cognitive, physical, and behavioral boundaries that people use to separate their work and home domains (see also chapter 4 of this volume). As an important phenomenon in sociology, boundary theory has been studied in regard to art, architecture, psychology, political science, anthropology, and organization theory. Boundary theory provides a framework for understanding management phenomena as well, including role transition (Ashforth et al., 2000) and conflict between organizational and individual identity (Kreiner, Hollensbe, & Sheep, 2006). The strength of these boundaries, and the similarities between work and home domains, can have an influence on individuals' sense of work-life balance (Clark, 2000). We explore boundary characteristics that impact all individuals and then how preferences for individuals may especially influence entrepreneurs.

Boundary Characteristics: Flexibility and Permeability

Theoretically, two dimensions characterize boundaries: permeability and flexibility. *Permeability* is related to overlap between roles that occur while physically being in one domain and behaviorally or psychologically dealing with tasks that belongs to another domain. For example, doing work-related tasks at home to meet a deadline represents a permeable work-home boundary. *Flexibility* refers to pliability of temporal and spatial boundaries. More flexible boundaries allow roles to be carried through in several settings and at varying times, in contrast to less flexible boundaries that dictate when or where a role can be carried through. Boundary flexibility may be useful to entrepreneurs, as those who perceive themselves as having more temporal flexibility also report less anxiety and tension (Bluedorn & Martin, 2008). Entrepreneurship and being in control of all the work produced, especially in a smaller venture, creates feelings of boundarylessness (Cohen & Mallon, 1999) and role blurring (Glavin & Schieman, 2012), which requires both high permeability and flexibility. One way a small business owner can manage these boundaries is to hire additional employees to help with the work, although this may hinder short-term monetary gains.

Boundary Preferences: Integration and Segmentation

As a product of both job characteristics and personal preference, individuals can experience different degrees of integration or segmentation between work and home domains. Integration and segmentation can be thought of as a continuum. In high *integration*, boundaries are more flexible and permeable between work and home roles. In full integration, boundaries do not exist between roles, and an individual may act the same with all interactions (e.g., supervisor and spouse; Nippert-Eng, 1996). As one example, consider a couple that works together at the same organization. They would work together, eat together, and do most of the things together. Eventually it will not matter where they are, at either home or work. In 1996, Nippert-Eng interviewed couples that worked together and interestingly found that not all individuals that worked together had high levels of work-life integration. As another example, consider the nascent entrepreneurs, or those who are in the very early stages of the entrepreneurial process. Again, many of these individuals will have high integrative behaviors with few work and nonwork boundaries.

In high *segmentation*, individuals prefer impermeable and inflexible boundaries between different domains. At the extreme end of the spectrum, full segmentation eliminates the overlap and sets a strict boundary between domains. For instance, people use different key rings and separate calendars for work and family activities (Nippert-Eng, 1996). Following this logic, entrepreneurs might create separate bank accounts for their business finances and personal finances. It is important to note that boundary preference is a limited personal choice, dependent on the job requirements. Context could impact what we prefer. For example, a social event organized by a firm after formal work hours could interfere with employees' segmentation preference. Additionally, the rules in an organization could prevent taking personal phone calls or bringing children into the workplace.

Entrepreneurs' boundary preference could be either voluntary or obligatory depending on their personality and their stage in the entrepreneurial process. The borders between entrepreneurship roles and nonwork roles can be highly permeable and flexible. Two different views exist in the literature to explain outcomes of such phenomena. The first view is the flexible resource perspective (Glavin & Schieman, 2012), which refers to flexibility that improves work-life balance. For example, entrepreneurs can hire agents that will allow them to attend to nonwork roles (Blair-Loy, 2009; Myrie & Daly, 2009). An example of this would be hiring an employee to manage a retail store in the afternoon while the business owner helps with childcare responsibilities. The second view is the greedy-role perspective (Glavin & Schieman, 2012), which entails borderlessness with the probability that work-related matters will appropriate nonwork matters and aggravate conflict between roles (Ashforth et al., 2000; Blair-Loy, 2009). Demanding jobs may require permeability that leads to allocation of resources from nonwork to work to alleviate the pressure of job demands (Glavin & Schieman, 2012; Olson-Buchanan & Boswell, 2006). Interviews with Canadian entrepreneurs found that individuals have both perspectives and use flexible resources to enhance work-life balance while also lamenting borderlessness (Ezzedeen & Zikic, 2015). From a practical perspective, we suggest that individuals find strategies to manage boundaries and discuss four specific tactics to use later in this chapter (see "Boundary Management" section).

Stress in Entrepreneurs

Stress is a physiological or psychological response to a demand (Selye, 1956) and is most commonly considered a state of higher arousal and tension that occurs in response to the threat or loss of something that has value (Hobfoll, 1989). An individual's perceived stress level is an important explanatory mechanism for better understanding why some individuals report higher work-life balance and quality of life (Greenhaus, Collins, & Shaw, 2003). The context of entrepreneurial work "can be characterized in terms of peaks and valleys, or periods of relatively high pressure, stress, uncertainty, and ambiguity and periods of relative stability and predictability" (Schindehutte, Morris, & Allen, 2006, p. 349). Thus, for an individual engaged in entrepreneurial activities, stress may be more likely to occur given the constantly changing nature of the role, which can create conflict between work and home domains. In addition, stress can negatively impact decision making (Starcke & Brand, 2012), which can hinder a business that requires making decisions for value creation. In this section, we explore different types of stress facing entrepreneurs and how this can also influence work-life balance.

Role Stress

In the context of work, occupational stress is that which is associated with a particular job (Marshall & Cooper, 1976) and is now often called *role stress*. Role stress takes a variety of forms in all working individuals and is most typically categorized as role conflict, role ambiguity, and role overload (Gilboa, Shirom, & Cooper, 2008). Role conflict occurs when there are incompatible expectations of different work demands (Rizzo, House, & Lirtzman, 1970). For entrepreneurs, role conflict may happen when there are too many contradicting expectations on them, such as when the stakeholders' requirements are opposed with the entrepreneur's own role (Wincent & Örtqvist, 2009). One example of this is when an entrepreneur tries to fulfill the customer's expectations, but is unable to find a supplier to provide necessary elements the entrepreneur needs to create value (Wincent & Örtqvist, 2006). Another example is how an entrepreneur may feel conflicted between providing short-term gains for shareholders versus long-term gains to strengthen the business. Role ambiguity is the lack of specificity and predictability for a person's job or role features and responsibility (Kahn, Wolfe, Quinn, Snoek, & Rosenthal, 1964). This is of vital interest to entrepreneurial activities, as role clarity (the opposite of role ambiguity) is positively related to innovation (Jansen & Chandler, 1994). Role ambiguity may be especially present in small ventures with only two or three people, when there is uncertainty as to which individual will conduct a new task. These small ventures require more sophisticated organizing than solo ventures, and we suggest that small businesses define individual work roles as much as possible to reduce how role ambiguity can negatively impact work-life balance. Role overload occurs in situations in which individuals have a sense that there are too many responsibilities or duties expected of them within a limited amount of time (Kahn et al., 1964). For example, entrepreneurs may feel rushed to complete a job task on time (Wincent & Örtqvist, 2006). When this occurs, entrepreneurs will spend more time on a work-related task, and less time on another aspect of their life (e.g., time with family or for self). In fact, within a sample of organizational employees, role overload and role conflict were strongly related to work-family conflict (Michel, Kotrba, Mitchelson, Clark, & Baltes, 2010). If the same is true for an entrepreneurial sample, individuals feeling higher role overload and role conflict could have their work tasks interfere with their home tasks in such a way that create a sense of work-life imbalance. One possible way that entrepreneurs can reduce these feelings of stress and improve work-life balance is to have a more routine (or fixed) work schedule, as this is related to lower role overload, role ambiguity, and overall felt stress (Jamal & Baba, 1992).

Business Stress

More unique to entrepreneurs, especially those starting a new venture on their own or with a very small team, is the additional stress coming from being responsible for the overall success or failure of a business. It has been proposed that improved work-life balance, through control over time and time flexibility, comes at the cost of increased business stress (Allen & Martin, 2017). For entrepreneurs, this may mean that the only way to achieve balance between work and nonwork domains is to feel greater levels of stress related to the business.

We suggest that business uncertainty and fear of failure are not just critical factors challenging entrepreneurial entry (Caliendo, Fossen, & Kritikos, 2009), but also two additional sources of stress for entrepreneurs that can have a negative impact on work-life balance. Uncertainty about business outcomes results from the limited availability of information for making decisions (Simon, 1955). Due to high levels of uncertainty, decision makers working in dynamic environments tend to suffer from greater information-processing burdens (Tushman, 1979). As a result, these individuals are likely to experience high levels of stress and anxiety (Waldman, Ramírez, House, & Puranam, 2001). Although the stress and anxiety of uncertainty can be reduced by distributing decision-making responsibilities among top managers (Hambrick & Mason, 1984), new ventures and start-ups usually lack members at the top level of the organization to share this burden. Thus, entrepreneurs will need to accept and cope with this increased business uncertainty so that stress and anxiety do not negatively influence their nonwork lives.

Fear of failure is conceptualized as the motivation to avoid failure (McClelland, Atkinson, Clark, & Lowell, 1953) and potentially as a trait-level disposition of an individual becoming anxious about entrepreneurial failure (e.g., Cacciotti, Hayton, Mitchell, & Giazitzoglu, 2016). Higher fear of failure is related to a reduced probability of starting a new venture (Arenius & Minniti, 2005). Nonetheless, some individuals start new ventures out of necessity (Margolis, 2014). These individuals who feel they must engage in entrepreneurial activities and have a high fear of failure may cope in a way that harms the balance between their work and home life. For example, fear of failure is related to Type A personality characteristics (e.g., ambitious and with sense of time urgency) and behaviors (e.g., competitive and aggressive), and these same individuals also report losing more friends and family (Burke & Deszca, 1982). The loss of close relationships with others during the entrepreneurial process can greatly hinder work-life balance, and we suggest that an entrepreneur work on relationship maintenance just as they would business maintenance.

Summary

In total, there are many factors that can influence an entrepreneur's work-life balance. One factor is having a strong entrepreneurial identity, as the salience of this identity may weaken the salience of other nonwork identities. This may prohibit work-life balance because the entrepreneur always feels the need to be acting in a business-related manner or on work tasks. A second, related factor is work-life boundaries. Entrepreneurs may have very permeable and flexible boundaries. This means they are more likely to let work cross over into nonwork time, which can lead to greater perceptions of imbalance. Stress can also influence work-life balance. Entrepreneurs have similar work-related role stressors to organizational employees (i.e., role ambiguity, role overload, and role conflict), along with additional business stressors. Without a team of employees and managers more typical in organizations, an entrepreneur may feel greater stress or find fewer resources to reduce stress, which can lead to increased conflict between work and nonwork. In the section below, we explore several ways in which entrepreneurs can improve their work-life balance, highlighting boundary management strategies and opportunities for recovery from work stress.

THE BALANCING ACT: EXPLORING HOW ENTREPRENEURS CAN IMPROVE WORK-LIFE BALANCE

In the previous section, we described how identity, boundary preferences, and stress can influence the work-life balance of entrepreneurs. In this section, we examine strategies that entrepreneurs can use to improve work-life balance. This is especially pertinent because self-employed individuals typically report higher work-family conflict and lower family satisfaction than organizational employees (Parasuraman & Simmers, 2001). We first utilize boundary theory to build potential ways that entrepreneurs can create boundaries and enhance their work-life balance. We then extend the literature on recovery from work stress to propose how entrepreneurs can use their nonwork time in a way to best obtain the benefits of work respite.

Boundary Management

Entrepreneurs typically work more hours than managers and often lack the level of separation between work and life that is very typical in managerial work (Dyer, 1994). Even though separation of work and life is a personal choice, and some prefer not to separate them, entrepreneurs may not have the luxury of making that choice. For example, in the early stages of entrepreneurial activities, individuals can be mentally consumed by their venture, dealing with the pressures of multiple roles, including accounting, marketing, and operation management. This makes it more difficult to maintain work-life balance.

Boundary work refers to the endeavor for constructing, dismantling, and sustaining the work-home border (Nippert-Eng, 1996). This boundary work includes mostly cognitive endeavors to separate one identity from mixing with another identity within a person. Boundary work consists of two elements that can be seen as the construction and maintenance of borders. Construction is the boundary development between different roles for different times and for different places. Maintenance involves tailoring boundaries according to contingencies and overlaps, and dealing with interventions.

Delving into more details regarding the separation of work and home, Kreiner, Hollensbe, and Sheep (2009) conducted interviews with Episcopal priests who experienced home-work boundary conflicts intensively. Advancing Nippert-Eng's work (1996), they came up with four distinct patterns, or *boundary tactics*. They propose that people utilize four boundary tactics to cope with the incongruence of different home and work roles: behavioral, physical, temporal, and communicative tactics. The use of these tactics to improve work-life balance depends on type (e.g., full-time or part-time) and phase (e.g., start-up or growth) of the entrepreneurial venture. We believe that entrepreneurs who are able to better manage their work-nonwork boundaries can achieve greater work-life balance.

Behavioral Tactics

People cope with boundary violations (i.e., overlap between different domains) and the associated work-home conflict with several social practices, which are referred to as behavioral tactics. One behavioral tactic is *using other people*, which is when an individual utilizes the support of someone else to help create a boundary. For example, business owners may use a secretary to take phone calls during specific time periods, relieving them of this role. A second behavioral tactic is *leveraging technology*, which can include using different email accounts for work and home or screening phone calls with caller ID or voicemail. Although it takes slightly more effort for an entrepreneur to create and use two separate e-mail accounts, this provides an easier opportunity to "turn off" one role. A third behavioral tactic, *invoking triage*, is a prioritizing tactic for handling simultaneously occurring conflicts. Entrepreneurs may know about some conflicts in advance and prepare accordingly. In the case of unplanned overlapping demands, individuals utilize intentional allocation decisions (Edwards & Rothbard, 2000) to deal with conflicts and decide how to best use resources. A fourth behavioral tactic is *allowing differential permeability*, which refers to the precise practices that people utilize in their segmentation or integration preferences. Some entrepreneurs allow certain types of demands to be integrated, yet not others. For example, they might work on a budget while at home, but not store inventory at home.

Temporal Tactics

Time is another consideration when managing the demands of home and work. Work-life balance has become more complicated due to advancing technology, elevating workloads, and changes in expectation on how we spend time (Milliken & Dunn-Jensen, 2005). Controlling when and how time is used can be a useful method for balancing work and home life. One temporal tactic for boundary development is *controlling work time*. For example, with flexible work hours, individuals can spend slack hours typically available for work tasks with family members instead, thus improving work-life balance. Another approach that has been observed is banking time, or working extra hours one day and allowing for that time to be used at home later. We know several successful entrepreneurs that track their work hours each day as a simple way to ensure that they know when a few hours are "banked" and can allocate their personal time accordingly. Creating a routine work time can also set a strong boundary. However, violations that occur outside this boundary during typical nonwork time are associated with increased work-family conflict and exhaustion (Golden, 2012). Another temporal tactic, *finding respite*, can improve work engagement and well-being (Sonnentag, 2003). We discuss this tactic more specifically in the "Recovery Experiences" section below. Overall, we suggest that entrepreneurs make an explicit effort to use several temporal tactics and assess which is most beneficial for them in achieving work-life balance.

Physical Tactics

Using physical tactics to create a stronger work-nonwork boundary may be especially useful for entrepreneurs and other individuals that work at home. Physical boundaries can be as simple as a door separating two rooms or a commute to another location. There are three categories of physical tactics: adapting physical boundaries, manipulating physical space, and managing physical artifacts. *Adapting physical boundaries* is related to creating a physical environment to encourage boundary work. Beyond their physical presence, some artifacts can intentionally be used to alter one's perceptions on something. For example, building a fence or a wall may help people to feel the presence of the different domains. *Manipulating physical space* is dependent on the preference of an individual regarding segmentation or integration. When possible, integrators tend to decrease the distance between home and work, and segmenters tend to increase this distance. Entrepreneurs that do not have a separate work location, but have a stronger segmentation preference, may find it useful to drive to a different location, such as a coffee shop. *Managing physical artifacts* entails using artifacts that specifically symbolize the home or work domain. For example, a banker may create a strong boundary by tying a necktie in the morning before work and removing it when he or she returns home after work. Entrepreneurs who desire to create a strong boundary can do so by adopting a uniform, which might be as simple as putting on a collared shirt before work, even at a home office. These routines help individuals create a physical work designation and can provide visual cues to others at home that work time is over, which help prevent conflicts between work and home lives. Several home-based small business owners we've talked with explain that having a separate room and a work uniform not only helps them separate work and nonwork domains, but it also signals to others when they are working and makes interruptions (and subsequent conflicts) less likely.

Communicative Tactics

Communication is another way to create and sustain work-nonwork boundaries, and we discuss two tactics: setting expectations and confronting violators. *Setting expectations* is one- or two-way communication with important stakeholders in each domain, such as coworkers, subordinates, spouse, and children. While one-way communication is simply the statement of an individual's expectations, two-way communication includes understanding and negotiating the demands of both parties. Setting expectations is especially useful for achieving greater work-life balance because it can take place before boundary violations occur (this is also discussed in chapter 1 of this volume). *Confronting violators* is a communication tactic that occurs after a boundary violation. When confronting violators, individuals clarify their boundary preference that was violated to reduce ambiguity in the future. Improving communication tactics, especially setting expectations and adapting as necessary, is very important for entrepreneurs as the new venture activities may quickly change nonwork boundaries. We suggest that communication tactics be used in conjunction with behavioral, temporal, and physical tactics. For example, clearly expressing a desire to create a temporal routine (e.g., being focused on work from 8:00 a.m. to 5:00 p.m.) can help others understand time requirements for work, and asking about the temporal needs of others (e.g., setting aside time for a meal together) can create a conversation so that all parties reach a shared agreement about the definition of work-life balance for their collective unit.

Recovery Experiences

Respites from work can have a beneficial effect for individuals by reducing the negative consequences of stressors and strain (Westman & Eden, 1997). These respites range in duration from a few minutes during a microbreak to several hours after a workday, as well as longer periods such as weekends and vacations (Sluiter, Frings-Dresen, Meijman, & van der Beek, 2000). In the work stress literature, recovery experiences are the underlying mechanisms that explain why a respite from work can be beneficial (Sonnentag & Fritz, 2007). In other words, rather than focus on what an individual does during the respite, recovery experiences are the attributes of the respite that can provide a recovery opportunity. For example, some individuals will find that meditation helps them relax, whereas other individuals read or watch television to feel relaxed. There are four primary recovery experiences (Sonnentag & Fritz, 2007): psychological detachment (i.e., not thinking about work during nonwork time), relaxation (i.e., taking time for leisure), mastery (i.e., experiencing something new or challenging), and control (i.e., deciding one's time use). Chapter 5 in this volume also discusses recovery experiences.

Recovery Experiences and Work-Life Balance

There is a robust literature relating recovery experiences, especially psychological detachment, with affective outcomes such as lower exhaustion and burnout (Sonnentag & Fritz, 2015). However, there is limited research thus far relating recovery experiences to work-life balance constructs. In addition, what has been found paints an unclear picture. For example, employees in Spain who reported greater levels of psychological detachment during time after work also report lower levels of both work-to-family conflict and family-to-work conflict (Moreno-Jiménez, Mayo, Sanz-Vergel, Geurts, Rodríguez-Muñoz, & Garrosa, 2009). However, in a study with North American students, higher psychological detachment was related to higher family-to-work conflict, but there was no statistical relationship with work-to-family conflict (Cheng & McCarthy, 2013). Furthermore, psychological detachment was negatively related to work-to-family conflict in a sample of university employees, and this relationship was true even with a spouse-reported work-to-family conflict measure (Demsky, Ellis, & Fritz, 2014). Beyond detachment, relaxation experiences during evenings and weekends are also linked to lower family interference with work (Lapierre, Hammer, Truxillo, & Murphy, 2012). Overall, there is initial evidence that psychological detachment and relaxation recovery experiences can reduce the conflict between work and home roles and potentially improve work-life balance.

Recovery Experiences and Entrepreneurs

In addition to a minimal amount of research exploring the relationship between recovery experiences and work-life balance, there is also very little research exploring recovery experiences in entrepreneurs (Sonnentag, Venz, & Casper, 2017). We believe that just as recovery experiences are beneficial for organizational employees, entrepreneurs can also use these strategies for enhanced well-being and improved work-life balance. In support of this idea, one recent study with a combined sample of organizational employees and self-employed individuals found that recovery experiences moderated the relationship between workload and work-family conflict (Molino, Cortese, Bakker, & Ghislieri, 2015). In other words, individuals (including entrepreneurs) who reported higher psychological detachment, relaxation, and control also reported less work-family conflict even with high workloads. However, many entrepreneurs find psychological detachment from work difficult. Drawing on research from a study of bed and breakfast innkeepers showing that some business owners prefer to take short daily or weekly breaks, whereas others prefer to take longer respites such as vacations (Shen, Miao, Lehto, & Zhao, 2015), we suggest that self-employed individuals utilize respite experiences and find time that fits best with their work schedule. In other words, some people require many small respites and others only need fewer, longer respites. We've seen these different respite patterns in our conversations with entrepreneurs as well, as some individuals prefer to take one day off each week, whereas others prefer one long (two- or three-week) vacation each year. We suggest that if an entrepreneur doesn't feel they have enough respite, they alter their current frequency and duration, and determine if a different respite schedule is more effective at providing recovery experiences.

FUTURE RESEARCH DIRECTIONS

As mentioned earlier in the chapter, there is less scholarly research about life outside of work for entrepreneurs, so we believe there are many fruitful opportunities for future research. Building on research showing that entrepreneurs have increased life satisfaction (e.g., Baron et al., 2016), future research can continue to explore whether individuals who select and stay in an entrepreneurial venture and have increased life satisfaction also have a perceived high work-life balance, or if their life satisfaction is mostly derived from their entrepreneurial identity and role. In other words, we wonder if a higher level of life satisfaction is because of improved work-life balance (through control and time flexibility), or if life satisfaction improves because one's role as an entrepreneur fits his or her ideal identity. Future research could also explore how entrepreneurial identity changes over time, and how these temporal dynamics influence other work-life balance dynamics.

Scholars focused on stress may also find entrepreneurs to be a useful (and understudied) sample. We expect that work-family conflict is high for entrepreneurs who also experience role overload or role conflict. However, in contrast to organizational employees, we believe role ambiguity is lower for entrepreneurs, as many entrepreneurs understand they are responsible for most or all decisions rather than being unsure of their role. An additional area for research will be gaining a better understanding of primary stress appraisals in entrepreneurs. For example, just the idea of starting a business will seem threatening to some individuals, but others will see the idea as a positive challenge.

The area of recovery experiences in entrepreneurs may also be insightful, especially considering that many entrepreneurs start a new venture to increase control over their time and work flexibility, potentially thinking they will have more time for respite. However, many entrepreneurs find themselves without much personal time (Bhide, 1996). Given these constraints, future research may be most useful by first exploring if and how entrepreneurs schedule their time off and then examining the impact of recovery experiences during this nonwork time. For example, some entrepreneurs choose to have only several, long time periods for recovery throughout the year (e.g., a week or two off), whereas others prefer to take small microbreaks to recover frequently. Given a potentially unconventional working schedule, the timing and preference for recovery experiences will likely be different in an entrepreneurial sample. Last, we invite consideration that some individuals perceive an entrepreneurial venture as a respite. For example, in what has been referred to as the *accidental entrepreneur* scenario, an organizational employee may have a hobby that leads to a new idea or part-time venture (Shah & Tripsas, 2007). Recall the old adage: *get paid to do what you love, and you will never work a day in your life.* It is possible that hobby-related new ventures will affect individuals as does the recovery experience of mastery, providing a positive challenge and welcomed learning experience.

CONCLUSION

As work continues to change in the 21st century, many individuals will be involved in an entrepreneurial venture to provide either a primary or a secondary income source. Beyond an economic perspective, individuals must be aware of changes in identity, boundaries, and stress that can occur. Entrepreneurs must manage their work and home lives in a way that achieves the best balance for them. In addition to maintaining their own personal wellness, reducing conflicts between work and home can improve business sustainability (Hsu, Wiklund, Anderson, & Coffey, 2016). We suggest that individuals engaged in entrepreneurial activities utilize tactics to achieve strong work-nonwork boundaries and engage in recovery experiences during nonwork time.

REFERENCES

Adamson, S. J., Doherty, N., & Viney, C. (1998). The meanings of career revisited: Implications for theory and practice. *British Journal of Management, 9,* 251–259. doi:10.1111/1467-8551.00096.

Allen, T. D., & Martin, A. (2017). The work-family interface: A retrospective look at 20 years of research in JOHP. *Journal of Occupational Health Psychology.* doi:10.1037/ocp0000065.

Allen, T. D., Cho, E., & Meier, L. L. (2014). Work-family boundary dynamics. *Annual Review of Organizational Psychology and Organizational Behavior, 1*, 99–121. doi:10.1146/annurev-orgpsych-031413-091330.

Allen, T. D., Golden, T. D., & Shockley, K. M. (2015). How effective is telecommuting? Assessing the status of our scientific findings. *Psychological Science in the Public Interest, 16*(2), 40–68. doi:10.1177/1529100615593273.

Arenius, P., & Minniti, M. (2005). Perceptual variables and nascent entrepreneurship. *Small Business Economics, 24*(3), 233–247. doi:10.1007/s11187-005-1984-x.

Arthur, M., & Rousseau, D. (1996). *The boundaryless career: A new employment for a new organizational era.* New York, NY: Oxford University Press.

Ashforth, B. E. (2001). *Role transitions in organizational life.* Mahwah, NJ: Erlbaum.

Ashforth, B. E., Kreiner, G. E., & Fugate, M. (2000). All in a day's work: Boundaries and micro role transitions. *Academy of Management Review, 25*, 472–491. doi:10.2307/259305.

Baron, R. A. (1998). Cognitive mechanisms in entrepreneurship: Why and when entrepreneurs think differently than other people. *Journal of Business Venturing, 13*, 275–294. doi:10.1016/S0883-9026(97)00031-1.

Baron, R. A., Franklin, R. J., & Hmieleski, K. M. (2016). Why entrepreneurs often experience low, not high, levels of stress: The joint effects of selection and psychological capital. *Journal of Management, 42*, 742–768. doi:10.1177/0149206313495411.

Bhide, A. (1996). The questions every entrepreneur must answer. *Harvard Business Review, 74*(6), 120–130.

Blair-Loy, M. (2009). Work without end? Scheduling flexibility and work-to-family conflict among stockbrokers. *Work and Occupations, 36*, 279–317. doi:10.1177/0730888409343912.

Bluedorn, A. C., & Martin, G. (2008). The time frames of entrepreneurs. *Journal of Business Venturing, 23*, 1–20. doi:10.1016/j.jbusvent.2006.05.005.

Boyd, D. P., & Gumpert, D. E. (1984). The loneliness of the start-up entrepreneur. In J. A. Hornaday, R. A. Tarpley, Jr., J. A. Timmons, & K. H. Vesper (Eds), *Frontiers of Entrepreneurship Research* (pp. 478-487). Wellesley, MA: Babson College.

Brockhaus, R. H. (1982). The psychology of the entrepreneur. In C. Kent, D. Sexton, & K. Vesper (Eds.), *Encyclopedia of Entrepreneurship* (pp. 39–57). Englewood Cliffs, NJ: Prentice-Hall.

Burke, P. J. (2003). Relationships among multiple identities. In *Advances in identity theory and research* (pp. 195–214). Boston, MA: Springer.

Burke, R. J., & Deszca, E. (1982). Career success and personal failure experiences and type A behaviour. *Journal of Occupational Behavior, 3*, 161–170.

Cacciotti, G., Hayton, J. C., Mitchell, J. R., & Giazitzoglu, A. (2016). A reconceptualization of fear of failure in entrepreneurship. *Journal of Business Venturing, 31*, 302–325.

Caliendo, M., Fossen, F. M., & Kritikos, A. S. (2009). Risk attitudes of nascent entrepreneurs: New evidence from an experimentally validated survey. *Small Business Economics, 32*(2), 153–167. doi:10.1007/s11187-007-9078-6.

Cheng, B. H., & McCarthy, J. M. (2013). Managing work, family, and school roles: Disengagement strategies can help and hinder. *Journal of Occupational Health Psychology, 18*, 241–251. doi:10.1037/a0032507.

Clark, S. C. (2000). Work/family border theory: A new theory of work/family balance. *Human Relations, 53*, 747–770. doi:10.1177/0018726700536001.

Cohen, L., & Mallon, M. (1999). The transition from organisational employment to portfolio working: The perceptions of "boundarylessness." *Work, Employment, and Society, 13*, 329–352.

Dempsey, S. E., & Sanders, M. L. (2010). Meaningful work? Nonprofit marketization and work/life imbalance in popular autobiographies of social entrepreneurship. *Organization, 17*, 437–459. doi:10.1177/1350508410364198.

Demsky, C. A., Ellis, A. M., & Fritz, C. (2014). Shrugging it off: Does psychological detachment from work mediate the relationship between workplace aggression and work-family conflict? *Journal of Occupational Health Psychology, 19*, 195–205. doi:10.1037/a0035448.

Direnzo, M. S., Greenhaus, J. H., & Weer, C. H. (2015). Relationship between protean career orientation and work-life balance: A resources perspective. *Journal of Organizational Behavior, 36*, 538–550. doi:10.1002/job.1996.

Dyer, W. G. (1994). Toward a theory of entrepreneurial careers. *Entrepreneurship: Theory and Practice, 19*, 7–21.

Edwards, J. R., & Rothbard, N. P. (2000). Mechanisms linking work and family: Clarifying the relationship between work and family constructs. *Academy of Management Review, 25*, 178–199. doi:10.5465/AMR.2000.2791609.

Ezzedeen, S. R., & Zikic, J. (2015). Finding balance amid boundarylessness: An interpretive study of entrepreneurial work-life balance and boundary management. *Journal of Family Issues*. doi:10.1177/0192513X15600731.

Foss, L. (2009). "Going against the grain . . .": Construction of entrepreneurial identity through narratives. University of Illinois at Urbana–Champaign's Academy for Entrepreneurial Leadership Historical Research Reference in Entrepreneurship. Available at SSRN: https://ssrn.com/abstract=1497284.

Gartner, W. B. (1989). "Who is an entrepreneur?" is the wrong question. *Entrepreneurship Theory and Practice, 13*, 47–68. doi:10.1210/jc.2003-031037.

Gartner, W. B., Bird, B. J., & Starr, J. A. (1992). Acting as if: Differentiating entrepreneurial from organizational behavior. *Entrepreneurship Theory and Practice, 16*(3), 13–31. doi:10.4337/9781783476947.00014.

Geurts, S. A. E., Beckers, D. G. J., Taris, T. W., Kompier, M. A. J., & Smulders, P. G. W. (2009). Worktime demands and work-family interference: Does worktime control buffer the adverse effects of high demands? *Journal of Business Ethics, 84*, 229–241. doi:10.1007/s10551-008-9699-y.

Gilboa, S., Shirom, A., & Cooper, C. (2008). A meta-analysis of work demand stressors and job performance: Examining main and moderating effects. *Personnel Psychology, 61*, 227–271.

Glavin, P., & Schieman, S. (2012). Work-family role blurring and work-family conflict: The moderating influence of job resources and job demands. *Work and Occupations, 39*, 71–98. doi:10.1177/0730888411406295.

Golden, T. D. (2012). Altering the effects of work and family conflict on exhaustion: Telework during traditional and nontraditional work hours. *Journal of Business and Psychology, 27*, 255–269. doi:10.1007/s10869-011-9247-0.

Greenhaus, J. H., Collins, K. M., & Shaw, J. D. (2003). The relation between work-family balance and quality of life. *Journal of Vocational Behavior, 63*, 510–531. doi:10.1016/S0001-8791(02)00042-8.

Hall, D. T. (1971). A theoretical model of career subidentity development in organizational settings. *Organizational Behavior and Human Performance, 6*, 50–76.

Hambrick, D. C., & Mason, P. A. (1984). Upper echelons: The organization as a reflection of its top managers. *Academy of Management Review, 9*, 193–206.

Hathaway, I. (2015). The gig economy is real if you know where to look. *Harvard Business Review*. Retrieved from: http://hbr.org/2015/08/the-gig-economy-is-real-if-you-know-where-to-look.

Haynie, J. M., Shepherd, D., Mosakowski, E., & Earley, P. C. (2010). A situated metacognitive model of the entrepreneurial mindset. *Journal of Business Venturing, 25*, 217–229. doi:10.1016/j.jbusvent.2008.10.001.

Hoang, H., & Gimeno, J. (2010). Becoming a founder: How founder role identity affects entrepreneurial transitions and persistence in founding. *Journal of Business Venturing, 25*, 41–53. doi:10.1016/j.jbusvent.2008.07.002.

Hobfoll, S. E. (1989). Conservation of resource: A new attempt at conceptualizing stress. *American Psychologist, 44*, 513–524.

Hsu, D. K., Wiklund, J., Anderson, S. E., & Coffey, B. S. (2016). Entrepreneurial exit intentions and the business-family interface. *Journal of Business Venturing, 31*, 613–627. doi:10.1016/j.jbusvent.2016.08.001.

Ibarra H. (2003). *Working identities: Uncovering strategies for reinventing your career*. Boston, MA: Harvard Business School Press.

Jamal, M., & Baba, V. V. (1992). Shiftwork and department-type related to job stress, work attitudes, and behavior intentions: A study of nurses. *Journal of Organizational Behavior, 13*, 449–462.

Jansen, E., & Chandler, G. N. (1994). Innovation and restrictive conformity among hospital employees: Individual outcomes and organizational considerations. *Journal of Healthcare Management, 39*, 63.

Jennings, J. E., & McDougald, M. S. (2007). Work-family interface experiences and coping strategies: Implications for entrepreneurship research and practice. *Academy of Management Review, 32*, 747–760.

Jones, R., Latham, J., & Betta, M. (2008). Narrative construction of the social entrepreneurial identity. *International Journal of Entrepreneurial Behavior & Research, 14*, 330-345. doi: 10.1108/13552550810897687

Kahn, R. L., Wolfe, D. M., Quinn, R. P., Snoek, J. D., & Rosenthal, R. A. (1964). *Organizational stress: Studies in role conflict and ambiguity.* Oxford, UK: Wiley.

Kelly, D., Singer, S., & Herrington, M. (2016). *Global Entrepreneurship Monitor: 2015/16 Global Report.* London, UK: GEM Consortium.

Kirkwood, J., & Tootell, B. (2008). Is entrepreneurship the answer to achieving work-family balance? *Journal of Management and Organization, 14*, 285–302.

Kreiner, G. E., Hollensbe, E. C., & Sheep, M. L. (2006). Where is the "me" among the "we"? Identity work and the search for optimal balance. *Academy of Management Journal, 49*, 1031–1057. doi:10.5465/AMJ.2006.22798186.

Kreiner, G. E., Hollensbe, E. C., & Sheep, M. L. (2009). Balancing borders and bridges: Negotiation the work-home interface via boundary work tactics. *Academy of Management Journal, 52*, 704–730. doi:10.5465/AMJ.2009.43669916.

Lanivich, S. E. (2015). The RICH entrepreneur: Using conservation of resources theory in contexts of uncertainty. *Entrepreneurship: Theory and Practice, 39*, 863–894. doi:10.1111/etap.12082.

Lapierre, L. M., Hammer, L. B., Truxillo, D. M., & Murphy, L. A. (2012). Family interference with work and workplace cognitive failure: The mitigating role of recovery experiences. *Journal of Vocational Behavior, 81*, 227–235. doi:10.1016/j.jvb.2012.07.007.

Lewis, K. V., Ho, M., Harris, C., Morrison, R. (2016). Becoming an entrepreneur: Opportunities and identity transitions. *International Journal of Gender and Entrepreneurship, 8*, 98–116.

Lundqvist, M., Williams-Middleton, K., & Nowell, P. (2015). Entrepreneurial identity and role expectations in nascent entrepreneurship. *Industry and Higher Education, 29*, 327–344. doi:10.5367/ihe.2015.0272.

Margolis, D. N. (2014). By choice and by necessity: Entrepreneurship and self-employment in the developing world. IZA Discussion Paper 8273. doi:10.1057/ejdr.2014.25.

Marshall, J., & Cooper, C. L. (1976). The mobile manager and his wife. *Management Decision, 14*, 179–224.

McClelland, D. C., Atkinson, J. W., Clark, R. A. & Lowell, E. L. (1953). *The achievement motive*. New York, NY: AppletonCentury-Crofts.

Michel, J. S., Kotrba, L. M., Mitchelson, J. K., Clark, M. A., & Baltes, B. B. (2010). Antecedents of work-family conflict: A meta-analytic review. *Journal of Organizational Behavior, 32*, 689–725. doi:10.1002/job.695.

Milliken, F. J., & Dunn-Jensen, L. M. (2005). The changing time demands of managerial and professional work: Implications for managing the work-life boundary. In E. E. Kossek & S. J. Lambert (Eds.), *Work and life integration: Organizational, cultural, and individual perspectives* (pp. 43–59). Mahwah, NJ: Erlbaum.

Molino, M., Cortese, C. G., Bakker, A. B., & Ghislieri, C. (2015). Do recovery experiences moderate the relationship between workload and work-family conflict? *Career Development International, 20*(7), 686–702. doi:10.1108/CDI-01-2015-0011.

Moreno-Jiménez, B., Mayo, M., Sanz-Vergel, A. I., Geurts, S., Rodríguez-Muñoz, A., & Garrosa, E. (2009). Effects of work-family conflict on employees' well-being: The moderating role of recovery strategies. *Journal of Occupational Health Psychology, 14*, 427–440. doi:10.1037/a0016739.

Myrie, J., & Daly, K. (2009). The use of boundaries by self-employed, home-based workers to manage work and family: A qualitative study in Canada. *Journal of Family and Economic Issues, 30*, 386–398. doi:10.1007/s10834-009-9166-7.

Navis, C., & Glynn, M. A. (2011). Legitimate distinctiveness and the entrepreneurial identity: Influence on investor judgments of new venture plausibility. *Academy of Management Review, 36*, 479–499.

Nippert-Eng, C. (1996). Calendars and keys: The classification of "home" and "work." *Sociological Forum, 11*, 563–582.

Olson-Buchanan, J. B., & Boswell, W. R. (2006). Blurring boundaries: Correlates of integration and segmentation between work and nonwork. *Journal of Vocational Behavior, 68*, 432–445. doi:10.1016/j.jvb.2005.10.006.

Parasuraman, S., & Simmers, C. A. (2001). Type of employment, work-family conflict and well-being: A comparative study. *Journal of Organizational Behavior, 22*, 551–568.

Rae, D. (2006). Entrepreneurial learning: A conceptual framework for technology-based enterprise. *Technology Analysis and Strategic Management, 18*, 39–56.

Rizzo, J. R., House, R. J., & Lirtzman, S. I. (1970). Role conflict and ambiguity in complex organizations. *Administrative Science Quarterly, 15*(2), 150–163. doi:10.2307/2391486.

Ross, J. P., Intindola, M. L., & Boje, D. M. (2016). It was the best of times; it was the worst of times: The expiration of work-life balance. *Journal of Management Inquiry*. doi:10.1177/1056492616675414.

Schere J. (1982). Tolerance of ambiguity as a discriminating variable between entrepreneurs and managers. *Academy of Management Proceedings*, New York, 406.

Schindehutte, M., Morris, M., & Allen, J. (2006). Beyond achievement: Entrepreneurship as extreme experience. *Small Business Economics, 27*, 349–368. doi:10.1007/s11187-005-0643-6.

Schoon, I., & Duckworth, K. (2012). Who becomes an entrepreneur? Early life experiences as predictors of entrepreneurship. *Developmental Psychology, 48*, 1719–1726. doi:10.1037/a0029168.

Selye, H. (1956). *The stress of life.* New York, NY: McGraw-Hill.

Sexton, D. L., & Bowman, N. (1985). The entrepreneur: A capable executive and more. *Journal of Business Venturing, 1*, 129–140. doi:10.1016/0883-9026(85)90012-6.

Shah, S. K., & Tripsas, M. (2007). The accidental entrepreneur: The emergency and collective process of user entrepreneurship. *Strategic Entrepreneurship Journal, 1*, 123–140. doi:10.1002/sej.15.

Shen, R., Miao, L., Lehto, X., & Zhao, X. (2015). Work or/and life? An exploratory study of respite experience of bed and breakfast innkeepers. *Journal of Hospitality and Tourism Research*, 1–24. doi:10.1177/1096348015597028.

Shepherd, D., & Haynie, J. M. (2009). Birds of a feather don't always flock together: Identity management in entrepreneurship. *Journal of Business Venturing, 24*, 316–337. doi:10.1016/j.jbusvent.2007.10.005.

Simon, H. A. (1955). A behavioral model of rational choice. *Quarterly Journal of Economics, 69*, 99–118.

Sluiter, J. K., Frings-Dresen, M. H., Meijman, T. F., & van der Beek, A. J. (2000). Reactivity and recovery from different types of work measured by catecholamines and cortisol: A systematic literature overview. *Occupational and Environmental Medicine, 57*, 298–315.

Sonnentag, S. (2003). Recovery, work engagement, and proactive behavior: A new look at the interface between nonwork and work. *Journal of Applied Psychology, 88*, 518–528. doi:10.1037/0021-9010.88.3.518.

Sonnentag, S., & Fritz, C. (2007). The Recovery Experience Questionnaire: Development and validation of a measure for assessing recuperation and unwinding from work. *Journal of Occupational Health Psychology, 12*(3), 204–221. doi:10.1037/1076-8998.12.3.204.

Sonnentag, S., & Fritz, C. (2015). Recovery from job stress: The stressor-detachment model as an integrative framework. *Journal of Organizational Behavior, 36*, S72–S103. doi:10.1002/job.1924.

Sonnentag, S., Venz, L., & Casper, A. (2017). Advances in recovery research: What have we learned? What should be done next? *Journal of Occupational Health Psychology.* doi:10.1037/ocp0000079.

Starcke, K., & Brand, M. (2012). Decision making under stress: A selective review. *Neuroscience and Biobehavioral Reviews, 36,* 1228–1248. doi:10.1016/ j.neubiorev.2012.02.003.

Stryker, S. (1968). Identity salience and role performance: The relevance of symbolic interaction theory for family research. *Journal of Marriage and Family, 30,* 558–564. doi:10.2307/349494.

Tushman, M. L. (1979). Work characteristics and subunit communication structure: A contingency analysis. *Administrative Science Quarterly, 24,* 82–98. doi:10.2307/2989877.

Van Maanen, J., & Schein, E. H. 1979. Toward a theory of organizational socialization. In B. M. Staw (Ed.), *Self and identity: Fundamental issues* (pp. 106–133). New York, NY: Oxford University Press.

Van Ness, R. K., & Seifert, C. F. (2016). A theoretical analysis of the role of characteristics in entrepreneurial propensity. *Strategic Entrepreneurship Journal, 10,* 89–96. doi:10.1002/sej.1205.

Waldman, D. A., Ramírez, G. G., House, R. J., & Puranam, P. (2001). Does leadership matter? CEO leadership attributes and profitability under conditions of perceived environmental uncertainty. *Academy of Management Journal, 44,* 134–143. doi:10.2307/3069341.

Warren, L. (2004). Negotiating entrepreneurial identity: Communities of practice and changing discourses. *International Journal of Entrepreneurship and Innovation, 5,* 25–35.

Westman, M., & Eden, D. (1997). Effects of a respite from work on burnout: Vacation relief and fade-out. *Journal of Applied Psychology, 82,* 516–27.

Wincent, J., & Örtqvist, D. (2006). Analyzing the structure of entrepreneur role stress. *Journal of Business and Entrepreneurship, 18,* 1.

Wincent, J., & Örtqvist, D. (2009). A comprehensive model of entrepreneur role stress antecedents and consequences. *Journal of Business and Psychology, 24,* 225–243. doi:10.1007/s10869-009-9102-8.

In: Work-Life Balance in the 21st Century
Editor: Jessica M. Nicklin

Chapter 4

WORKAHOLISM AND WORK-FAMILY CONFLICT: THEORETICAL PERSPECTIVES, EMPIRICAL FINDINGS, AND DIRECTIONS FOR FUTURE RESEARCH

*Rachel L. Williamson** and Malissa A. Clark, PhD*
Department of Psychology,
University of Georgia, Athens, GA, US

ABSTRACT

This chapter explores the literature on the intersection of workaholism and work-family conflict, focusing on theoretical perspectives, empirical findings, and suggestions for future research. From a theoretical perspective, we review three broad theories (resource and role–based theories, boundary and border theories, and spillover and crossover theory) that have been utilized to explain the relationship between workaholism and work-family conflict. We then review empirical research that has examined the relationship between workaholism and work-family conflict. Finally, we conclude with a review of what we perceive to be gaps in the current literature, and recommendations for future research on the relationship between workaholism and work-family conflict.

* Corresponding Author Email: rachelwilliamson2493@gmail.com.

Employees are spending more of their daily lives on work-related activities (US Department of Labor, 2016), both at work (Murphy & Sauter, 2003) and increasingly during time with their families (Ferguson, Carlson, Boswell, Whitten, Butts, & Kacmar, 2016). Technology advances (Towers, Duxbury, Higgins, & Thomas, 2006) and pressure to be constantly available (Barber & Santuzzi, 2015) only encourages the behavior of *workaholics* (someone who is addicted to work, feels internal pressures compelling them to work, persistently thinks about work when not working, and works beyond expectations; see Clark, Michel, Zhdanova, Pui, & Baltes, 2016), especially after work hours, and this overworking may influence other domains. Thus, while many workers and organizations are striving for balance and work detachment, there are a growing number of influences encouraging workaholic behavior, which may ultimately lead to conflict between the work and family domains.

The goal of the current chapter is to explore the intersection of workaholism and work-family conflict. Specifically, we integrate workaholism into the dominant theoretical perspectives of work-family conflict (resource and role-based theories, border and boundary theories, and spillover and crossover theory). We then summarize empirical findings of workaholism in relation to work-family conflict, and theoretical mechanisms of these relationships. Finally, we discuss gaps in the literature on workaholism and work-family conflict, suggesting future recommendations (e.g., how can workaholics try to prevent work-family conflict?).

WORKAHOLISM

Workaholism, first coined by Oates in 1971, can be defined as an addiction to work involving persistent thoughts about work when not working, feeling compelled to work because of internal pressures, and working beyond what is expected (Clark et al., 2016). Although workaholism is driven by an internal pressure, the literature argues that workaholics are driven by a compulsion that they "should" work rather than by passion or enjoyment of working (Clark et al., 2016). Furthermore, workaholism is conceptualized as a relatively stable trait (Bakker, Shimazu, Demerouti, Shimada, & Kawakami, 2014; Burke, Matthiesen, & Pallesen, 2006; Harpaz & Snir, 2003; Mazzetti, Schaufeli, & Guglielmi, 2014). For instance, workaholics will constantly think about work when they are not working, without much variation across time. Whether they are spending time away from work because they have "clocked out," have a day off work, or are on vacation, workaholics theoretically should still experience persistent thoughts drawing them back into thinking about work.

While organizations may promote a workaholic culture, hoping it may lead to employees accomplishing more and working harder, recent research suggests that possessing the trait of workaholism may not be so glamorous. A recent meta-analysis exploring the antecedents and outcomes of workaholism revealed there are certain individual characteristics that seem to be associated with workaholism tendencies, including perfectionism (ρ = .55), type A personality (ρ = .43), and negative affect (ρ = .31; Clark et al., 2016)—all of which could potentially be viewed as negative characteristics. Additionally, there are a multitude work characteristics that are associated with workaholic tendencies, such as time commitment to the job (ρ = .70), work-role conflict (ρ = .43), working overtime (ρ = .27), and managerial status (ρ = .14). Interestingly, the authors found that workaholism was not associated with work performance. Finally, workaholism is associated with undesirable outcomes across work (e.g., lower job satisfaction, ρ = −.11; higher job stress, ρ = .55), family (e.g., lower family satisfaction, ρ = −.16; higher work-life conflict, ρ = .47), and individual outcomes (e.g., higher burnout, ρ = .40; lower physical health, ρ = −.33; lower emotional health, ρ = −.39). In sum, workaholism appears to be unrelated to actual work performance yet results in a multitude of negative outcomes for the individual.

WORK-FAMILY CONFLICT

One of the most commonly studied correlates of workaholism is work-family conflict (WFC), which refers to interrole conflict in that the work and family domains elicit pressure on each other, leading to a sense of conflict (Carlson, Kacmar, & Williams, 2000; Greenhaus & Beutell, 1985). As workaholism involves constantly thinking about work when one is not working and working longer than what is expected, individuals with workaholic tendencies tend to experience greater work-family conflict than individuals who are not workaholics. Work-family conflict can exist in two different directions: work interfering with family (WIF) and family interfering with work (FIW). Furthermore, theory suggests three forms of work-family conflict: time-based conflict, strain-based conflict, and behavior-based conflict. Time-based work-family conflict occurs when something work related requiring time, such as after-hours electronic work communication, interferes with participation in the home domain. Strain-based work-family conflict occurs when stress of one domain, such as feeling stressed at work, carries over into the other domain, such as feelings of stress at home, and can ultimately hinder performance in the affected domain. Behavior-based work-family conflict occurs when specific behaviors required in one role are not conducive to performance in another role. For example, you may need to be authoritative at work to be successful, but behaving in an authoritative manner at home may not be conducive for family performance.

The forms of work-family conflict have several antecedents that aid in predictability (Michel, Kotrba, Mitchelson, Clark, & Baltes, 2011). Work-domain stressors tend to be more strongly associated with WIF, including job stressors (ρ = .50) and lack of organizational support (ρ = −.30). Likewise, family domain stressors tend to be more strongly associated with FIW, including family stressors (ρ = .40) and family climate (ρ = −.18). Additionally, the personality trait of negative affect/neuroticism is associated with both WIF (ρ = .38) and FIW (ρ = .33), as is internal locus of control (WIF: ρ = −.21; FIW: ρ = −.19). To date, workaholism and the forms of work-family conflict have not been examined in a meta-analysis. We will empirically review the literature on the relationship between these two constructs in a later section of this chapter.

THEORETICAL PERSPECTIVES ON WORK-FAMILY CONFLICT: THE INTEGRATION OF WORKAHOLISM

While the construct of workaholism is gaining increasing attention in the organizational literature, there has been more of a focus on the measurement of workaholism (e.g., Andreassen, Hetland, & Pallesen, 2014; Beiler-May, Williamson, Clark, & Carter, 2017; Burke, Richardsen, & Martinussen, 2002; Schaufeli, Shimazu, & Taris, 2009) and a lack of research on the theoretical underpinnings of workaholism (see Clark, Beiler, & Zimmerman, 2015, for an exception). To advance our understanding of the nature of workaholism, we seek to integrate workaholism into theories utilized to explain work-family conflict. In this section, we discuss three main theoretical perspectives utilized in the work-family literature and integrate the construct of workaholism into these theories. We examine (1) resource and role-based theories, (2) border and boundary theories, and (3) spillover and crossover theories.

Resource and Role-Based Theories

One of the most common theoretical perspectives utilized in the work-family literature is resource and role-based theories. A clear example of this is in an article by Grandey and Cropanzano (1999), which focuses on applying the conservation of resources model (Hobfoll, 1989) to work-family conflict. The conservation of resources model was originally conceptualized to model stress, resting on the central premise that individuals seek to retain current resources and gain new resources (for a review of the basic tenets of conservation of resources theory, see Halbesleben, Neveu, Paustian-Underdahl, & Westman, 2014). Although resources can take on a variety of definitions, Grandey and Cropanzano (1999) suggested the three categories of conditions (e.g., marital status), personal characteristics (e.g., self-esteem), and energies (e.g., time) were most relevant to the context of work-family.

Condition resources such as marital status and job tenure can apply to either the work or family domain, and are resources in the sense that they are sought after (Grandey & Cropanzano, 1999; Hobfoll, 1989). In the context of work-family, job tenure may be beneficial as it is associated with more resources, leading to lower WIF (Grandey & Cropanzano, 1999). Likewise, being married is valuable as individuals living with their spouse have more resources via the energy and finances brought in by their spouse. In the context of workaholism, we theorize that these condition resources may be differentially related.

In the original conceptualization of the conservation of resources model, conditions were defined as "resources to the extent that they are valued and sought after" (Hobfoll, 1989, p. 517). For instance, job tenure may be sought after by nonworkaholics as a resource from stress, as job tenure is associated with more control over work time and their experience and seniority may allow for more social capital. However, we suggest that job tenure is still valued by workaholics as a resource from stress but for different reasons. Past theory suggests that workaholism may be predicated by low self-esteem, seeking a positive self-view through an excessive workload (Ng, Sorensen, & Feldman, 2007). Thus, workaholics with lower job tenure may have lower levels of self-esteem and thus higher stress, and may feel a need to prove themselves through their work. In other words, workaholics may view job tenure as a resource against stress, in that regardless they will work excessively, but they may experience lower stress levels if they feel a higher level of self-confidence based on their job tenure. Likewise, the condition resource of marital status has theoretical implications in the context of workaholism. Workaholics spend excessive time working, meaning spousal support may be even more important for workaholics than nonworkaholics. At least one study on 168 dual-earner couples found that workaholics provided reduced support to their partner (Bakker, Demerouti, & Burke, 2009). In the context of conservation of resources theory, the condition resource of job tenure may be more important for workaholics due to potential self-confidence. Likewise, the condition resource of marital status may be more important in this population due to excessive work.

Regarding *personal characteristic* resources, Grandey and Cropanzano (1999) examined an individual's self-esteem as a potential buffer for alleviating work-family conflict. The authors did not find support for their prediction, instead finding that self-esteem is an important resource for the work environment but less impactful for the family environment. As workaholics are theorized to possess lower levels of self-esteem (Ng et al., 2007), this personal characteristic may not be a resource from stress for workaholics. However, we theorize that the personal characteristic of achievement striving, an antecedent of workaholism (Clark et al., 2016; Ng et al., 2007), could be an important personal characteristic in that it may serve as a buffer against stress. As workaholics continue to work excessively even at home, their focus on achievement reduces their concern of how much work-family conflict they are experiencing.

Finally, *energies* such as time or money were conceptualized as important resources for work-family conflict by Grandey and Cropanzano (1999). We posit that time is likely the most important energy resource for workaholics, as a need to work excessively is a key characteristic of any workaholic, and a threat to the time workaholics can allocate to work will likely cause intense stress. Money is not likely to be important to workaholics, as a defining feature of workaholism is that the compulsion to work is *not* due to external drivers such as finances (Clark et al., 2016). For instance, an employee may work excessive hours to try to earn additional income or to avoid an unhappy family situation, but working excessively due to these reasons would not be considered workaholism (see Snir & Harpaz, 2012). In sum, drawing on the conservation of resources model, time should be an especially important energy resource for workaholics, while money should not be a relevant resource for workaholics.

Figure 4.1. Resource drain conceptual model detailed in Clark et al. (2015).

At least one book chapter to date has discussed the incorporation of work-family conflict and workaholism into resource theory. Clark and colleagues (2015) utilize resource drain theory (Edwards & Rothbard, 2000), which suggests that the utilization of resources in one domain (e.g., work) drains resources available in the other domain (e.g., family; see Figure 4.1). Clark and colleagues explain that workaholics may experience work-family conflict due to the amount of resources they expend at work, such as cognitive energies completing work tasks and projects. This energy may lead to workaholics feeling exhausted when they get home, meaning they have less energy to help their partner with housework or their children with homework. Additionally, a study by Hakanen and Peeters (2015) attempted to integrate workaholism and work-family conflict using conservation of resources theory. Contrary to Clark and colleagues (2015), Hakanen and Peeters rely on resource substitution theory (Hobfoll, 2001), which suggests that a resource from another domain (e.g., family) can substitute for a lost resource (e.g., work). In the context of the current chapter, resource substitution would suggest that the loss of resources due to work-family conflict could be substituted by investment in work resources (see figure 4.2). This means that, over time, work-family conflict may also influence workaholism, which led Hakanen and Peeters to theorize a loss cycle may occur between workaholism and work-family conflict (2015). Hakanen and Peeters then tested this hypothesis and found that although workaholism does predict work-family conflict seven years later, there was not support for the notion of a loss cycle. Thus, in the context of conservation of resources theory, the findings of Hakanen and Peeters's (2015) study support the resource drain perspective proposed by Clark and colleagues (2015) but not the resource substitution and loss cycle proposed by Hakanen and Peeters.

Another theory frequently utilized in the work-family literature is role theory (Kahn, Wolfe, Quinn, Snoek, & Rosenthal, 1964). Role theory, and specifically the role scarcity hypothesis (Edwards & Rothbard, 2000; Goode, 1960), posits that competing pressures between work and family roles will result in personal conflict between these roles. Work-family conflict has largely been rooted in role theory (Dierdorff & Ellington, 2008), especially in terms of the differing forms of time-, strain-, and behavior-based conflict (Grandey & Cropanzano, 1999). In the context of work-family, role theory would suggest that engagement in one role (e.g., work) is complicated by participating in the other role (e.g., family; Greenhaus & Beutell, 1985; Kahn et al., 1964). This seems especially relevant for workaholics, as they spend excessive engagement in their work role, resulting in diminished engagement available for their family role.

Regarding time-based work-family conflict, having to spend large amounts of time at work can produce work-family conflict, or having to spend large amounts of time with family can produce family-work conflict (Greenhaus & Beutell, 1985). In line with the nature of workaholism, workaholics spend large amount of time working, likely producing time-based work-family conflict. Likewise, workaholics that are required to spend large amounts of time with their family (e.g., taking care of children or relatives) will be forced to spend less of their time working, resulting in higher levels of FIW. In either case (WIF or FIW), we theorize that workaholism will strengthen the amount of work-family conflict individuals experience, due to their compulsive nature.

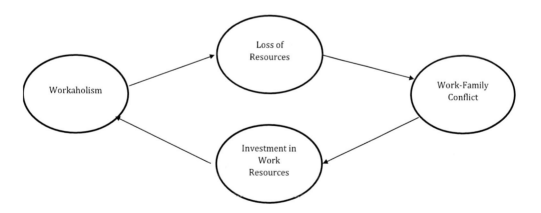

Figure 4.2. Resource substitution and loss cycle conceptual model details in Hakanen and Peeters (2015).

Work stressors or family stressors (e.g., anxiety and fatigue) are thought to produce strain-based work-family conflict. The demanding nature of workaholism can lead to many strain-related outcomes, including higher levels of burnout and lower levels of life satisfaction, physical health, and mental health (Clark et al., 2016). Due to the strain experienced by workaholics, they likely experience more strain-based work-family conflict than their nonworkaholic counterparts. Similarly, workaholics experience anger and agitation when they are prevented from working (Clark et al., 2016), thus even if they are physically home with their families, workaholics likely desire to continue working in any way they can. Although not intentional, when workaholics spend time with their families they may experience anger or agitation due to their compulsion to work, ultimately leading to strain-based FIW. In sum, possessing the trait of workaholism should lead to more WIF and FIW compared with nonworkaholics.

Although behavior-based work-family conflict has received far less attention in the literature, we theorize that certain behaviors of workaholics will not be conducive for family performance, resulting in work-family conflict. Workaholics have an obsessive and compulsive nature, explaining why workaholism is correlated with perfectionism (Clark et al., 2016). While perfectionism may be conducive at work, it is likely not conducive for family performance, as perfectionism is associated with lower levels of marital adjustment (Haring, Hewitt, & Flett, 2003). Furthermore, past research suggests that employed individuals with perfectionism tendencies may deplete more personal resources, particularly through poor recovery experiences that can lead to emotional exhaustion and fatigue (Flaxman, Menard, Bond, & Kinman, 2012). Thus, the behavioral tendencies of workaholics (i.e., perfectionism) may lead to higher levels of behavioral work-family conflict via lack of personal resources.

BOUNDARY AND BORDER THEORIES

Another theory commonly applied in the work-family literature is boundary theory (Nippert-Eng, 1996), which has been used to explain the boundaries individuals create between their work and family domains. Similar to boundary theory, border theory suggests there are daily fluctuations in the borders used between work and family (Clark, 2000), which ultimately impacts work-family balance. As noted by Desrochers and Sargent (2004), boundary theory and border theory share three main propositions: (1) work-family borders are easier to manage when work and family are kept separate; (2) when work and family are integrated, transitions are facilitated; and (3) integration or segmentation may improve employee well-being, depending on individual characteristics such as their preference for integration or segmentation.

One of the key tenants of boundary and border theory is the integration-segmentation continuum (Ashforth, Kreiner, & Fugate, 2000). Integrators tend to blend the domains of work and family (i.e., "thin" boundaries), while segmenters attempt to keep work and family separate (i.e., "thick" boundaries; Ashforth et al., 2000). Individuals are thought to operate on an integration-segmentation continuum, allowing for varying degrees of integration or segmentation across individuals. For instance, some individuals prefer to keep work and home somewhat separate—they try to refrain from engaging in work-related tasks while they are at home and refrain from engaging in home-related tasks at work. But these same individuals may still check work emails while they are at home and check their cell phone for home-related text messages and calls during their workday. Thus, they prefer to keep boundaries between work and home (i.e., prefer segmentation), but due to the nature of their job and/or family life, they must allow some level of integration. See also Chapters 3 and 11 in this volume.

Both ends of the integration-segmentation spectrum have their pros and cons (Ashforth et al., 2000). High segmentation is associated with lower role flexibility, meaning individuals have a harder time transitioning between roles. However, segmenters have less blurring between their roles, clarifying the transition. High integration reflects a blurring of boundaries, thus transitioning between roles is easier. Yet, this blurring between roles may be a downfall for individuals, as integrators have a harder time creating boundaries (Ashforth et al., 2000; Olson-Buchanan & Boswell, 2006). Regarding work-family conflict, research suggests that high integration is associated with more conflict ($\beta = .21$; Olson-Buchanan & Boswell, 2006). Furthermore, workaholics are likely integrators—they blur the boundaries of their roles by continuing to work excessively even when they are not physically at work, which has important implications for the work-family conflict of workaholics. Due to this preference, workaholics find certain jobs more appealing, especially if they are supportive of this preference. Research suggests that workaholics seek occupations that allow high levels of work and responsibility, including managers and high-level professionals (Harpaz & Snir, 2003; Taris, Van Beek, & Schaufeli, 2012), and thus require more work conducted even when they are not physically at work. Workaholics are also more likely to work in the private sector (Harpaz & Snir, 2003), which may allow for fluctuating work hours and more integration between work and home. As mentioned previously, integrators have a harder time creating boundaries, meaning the preference of workaholics to maintain a high level of integration likely leads to more work-family conflict.

SPILLOVER AND CROSSOVER

A third theoretical framework used to conceptualize work-family research in terms of stress contagion is spillover and crossover (Bolger, DeLongis, Kessler, & Wethington, 1989). Spillover occurs within an individual when stress experienced in one domain (e.g., work) spills over to stress experienced in the other domain (e.g., family). Crossover occurs across individuals when one individual's stress in the work domain crosses over to someone the individual is in close contact with (e.g., partner), leading to stress experienced by the individual's partner in the family domain. While the focus of the current chapter is on negative spillover and crossover (i.e., work-family conflict and workaholism), it is important to note that other research examines positive spillover and crossover, such as work-family enrichment (see Carlson, Kacmar, Wayne, & Grzywacz, 2006; see also Chapter 8) and work-family facilitation (see Grzywacz, Carlson, Kacmar, & Wayne, 2007).

A study conducted in 2000 by Grzywacz and Marks examined spillover from work to family and from family to work in a sample of 1,986 individuals. Some of the strongest correlates for negative spillover from work to family were pressure on the job, fewer work resources (i.e., less work support and less decision latitude at work), and working 45 hours or more a week. This last correlate is particularly interesting in the context of workaholism, as workaholics notoriously work longer than their nonworkaholic counterparts (Clark et al., 2016). On the other hand, some of the strongest correlates of negative spillover from family to work were low affectual (i.e., emotional) spousal support, pressure at work, and working 20 hours or more a week (Grzywacz & Marks, 2000).

At least one chapter (Clark et al., 2015) discusses workaholism and work-family conflict in the context of spillover theory. The authors suggest that negative emotions experienced at work (e.g., compulsive tendencies leading to feelings of anxiety) can spill over negatively at home. Likewise, negative emotions experienced at home (e.g., guilt experienced by workaholics when they are not working) may spill over negatively into the workplace. Utilizing spillover theory to understand workaholism and work-family conflict seems fruitful, and we encourage future research to draw upon this theoretical perspective to extend our understanding of this relationship.

Regarding crossover, theory and empirical evidence suggests there are three mechanisms accounting for the crossover process: (1) direct empathic crossover, in which stress is directly transferred from one partner to another due to empathic reasons, where partners share each other's emotional states; (2) indirect crossover of strain, in which strain is mediated through interactions or personal attributes between partners (e.g., coping strategies or interpersonal transactions); and (3) common stressors that jointly impact both partners (e.g., economic problems or death of a friend; Westman, 2002). While we know there are three main mechanisms of crossover, it is important to note that few studies test the mediating mechanism that accounts for this process; this is likely due to the complexity of capturing these mechanisms, which individuals may not even be aware are occurring.

Regarding the current chapter, only a handful of studies have empirically examined crossover effects for work-family conflict between spouses (e.g., Cinamon, Weisel, & Tzuk, 2007; Hammer, Allen, & Grigsby, 1997; Westman & Etzion, 2005). Hammer and colleagues (1997) and Westman and Etizon (2005) found that one partner's work-family conflict significantly predicted their spouse's work-family conflict. Cinamon and colleagues (2007) extended this finding, providing evidence in a sample of 60 married couples that work-family conflict of one spouse was correlated with family-work conflict of the other spouse. Thus, these studies provide initial evidence that one partner's work-family conflict may result in the other partner experiencing increased work-family conflict *and* family-work conflict.

Another study found evidence of direct crossover of work-relationship conflict (a form of work-family conflict reflecting work interfering with their relationship) in 113 dual-earner couples (Matthews, Del Priore, Acitelli, & Barnes-Farrell, 2006). While these studies previously mentioned had examined crossover effects of work-family conflict, there was still a need for theory to match these empirical findings. To address this, Bakker, Demerouti, and Dollard (2008) sought to integrate work-family conflict and crossover theory, specifically in terms of exhaustion. The authors intended to expand past studies of work-family conflict and crossover effects by attempting to explain the mediating processes between these two constructs. Bakker and colleagues' results suggested that work-family conflict mediates the relationship between job demands and social undermining, supporting the indirect crossover of strain. While this study provides direct evidence of the mediating mechanism between work-family conflict and crossover effects, which advances both theory and our empirical understanding of the nature of their relationship, there is much to be explored regarding work-family conflict, crossover effects, and the mediating mechanisms occurring regarding other outcomes of interest (e.g., workaholism).

To date, a handful of studies have begun to examine spillover and crossover of workaholism, with some integrating work-family conflict into the theoretical model. Bakker and colleagues (2014) examined a spillover-crossover model of workaholism and work engagement to differentiate between these two constructs in a sample of Japanese dual-earner couples. The authors theorized and found evidence that work-family conflict mediated the relationship between workaholism and family satisfaction. They concluded that workaholics spend more time working, leading to more WIF. In turn, workaholics have less energy and time to contribute to their household, leading to their partner experiencing lower levels of family satisfaction. In sum, workaholics possess reduced energy and resources due to their excessive working, which ultimately lead to negative consequences for both themselves (i.e., increased WIF) and their partner (i.e., lower family satisfaction).

Outside of work-family conflict, other research suggests that workaholism leads to poor relationship quality (Bakker et al., 2009) and family satisfaction (Bakker et al., 2014) for their spouse, through reduced resources available for family performance. Other research suggests that spouses of workaholics experience greater marital estrangement (Robinson, Carroll, & Flowers, 2001) and decreased well-being (Shimazu,

Demerouti, Bakker, Shimada, & Kawakami, 2011; Bakker et al., 2014). Taken together, the results of research to date seem to generally suggest that having a workaholic spouse may unfortunately come at a cost for the partner, specifically in terms of well-being.

EMPIRICAL FINDINGS: WORKAHOLISM AND WORK-FAMILY CONFLICT

Measurement of Workaholism

In order to understand the pattern of relationships that have been found between workaholism and work-family conflict, as well as the mediators and moderators of these relationships, it is important to first understand the myriad of ways workaholism has been conceptualized and measured in the literature. This is important because when a particular study concludes workaholism is related to work-family outcomes, this may mean something very different depending on how the construct of workaholism is conceptualized and measured.

One of the first ways organizational researchers have examined workaholism has been with the multidimensional WorkBat scale developed by Spence and Robbins (1992). According to Spence and Robbins, workaholism is conceptualized as the combination of having high work involvement and drive, and low work enjoyment (which they term the "workaholic triad"). Five studies used the full WorkBat to measure workaholism (Andreassen et al., 2014; Aziz, Wuensch, & Brandon, 2010b; Aziz & Zickar, 2006; Bonebright, Clay, & Ankenmann, 2000; Brady, Vodanovich, & Rotunda, 2008). Bonebright and colleagues (2000) examined differences between enthusiastic (high drive, high involvement, and high enjoyment) and unenthusiastic workaholics (high drive, high involvement, and low enjoyment) on a variety of outcomes, determining "high" and "low" values through mean splits. One study used only the enjoyment and drive subscales (Russo & Waters, 2006), where workaholics were conceptualized as having high scores on the drive subscale and low scores on the enjoyment subscale. Aziz and colleagues (2010b) created six profiles (similar to Spence & Robbins, 1992), using a composite approach rather than median or mean splits to categorize individuals into high and low on the subscales. As opposed to studies that created "types" of workaholics, other researchers (i.e., Andreassen et al., 2014; Brady et al., 2008) examined the subscales separately in relation to outcomes (e.g., drive is related to X; work enjoyment is related to Y).

We would like to point out several potential issues with the use of the WorkBat scale. First, it should be noted that there is disagreement about the inclusion of "work enjoyment" in the operationalization and measurement of workaholism (Baruch, 2011;

Mudrack, 2006; Ng et al., 2007; Schaufeli, Taris, & Bakker, 2008). Second, the work involvement subscale has been widely criticized for having low reliability and unreliable factor structure (e.g., McMillan, Brady, O'Driscoll, & Marsh, 2002). And third, researchers that divide individuals into "high" and "low" groups using mean or median splits are losing substantial power to detect effects. For these reasons, we do not advocate the use of this scale to assess workaholism.

Another early measure of workaholism is the Work Addiction Risk Test (WART; Robinson, 1999). The WART consists of five subscales: compulsive tendencies, control, impaired communication/self-absorption, inability to delegate, and self-worth (Robinson, 1999). Three of the articles we reviewed used the full WART (Aziz, Adkins, Walker, & Wuensch, 2010a; Brady et al., 2008;[1] Taris, Schaufeli, & Verhoeven, 2005). However, many of the subscales of the WART have been criticized for having limited overlap with current conceptualizations of workaholism (Mudrack, 2006). In light of this criticism, three articles we reviewed used only the nine-item compulsive-tendencies subscale of the WART to operationalize workaholism (Bakker et al., 2009; Clark, Michel, Stevens, Howell, & Scruggs, 2014; Hakanen & Peeters, 2015).

One commonly used measure of workaholism in recent years is the Dutch Work Addiction Scale (DUWAS; Schaufeli et al., 2009). The DUWAS contains two subscales—working excessively and working compulsively (Schaufeli et al., 2009), each of which reflect two subscales from the prior two scales we reviewed: the compulsive-tendencies scale of the WART was relabeled "working excessively," and the drive scale of the WorkBat was relabeled "working compulsively." Five of the articles we reviewed used the DUWAS to measure workaholism (Bakker, Demerouti, Oerlemans, & Sonnentag, 2013; Huyghebaert, Fouquereau, Lahiani, Baltou, Gimenes, & Gillet, in press; Kravina, Falco, De Carlo, Andreassen, & Pallesen, 2014; Schaufeli et al., 2009; Shimazu et al., 2011). Additionally, two studies did not use the three measures mentioned above to operationalize workaholism. Molino and colleagues (2016) used the Bergen Work Addiction Scale (BWAS; Andreassen, Griffiths, Hetland, & Pallesen, 2012), which was specifically developed to reflect the addictive nature of workaholism. Finally, Mudrack and Naughton (2001) conceptualized workaholism as a combination of nonrequired work and control of others, using a measure they developed themselves.

For the sake of clarity, if a particular research study used the WART, DUWAS, or the Bergen Work Addiction Scale to assess workaholism and did not separate out the particular dimensions of these scales, we refer to these simply as "workaholism." However, if the study authors used only one dimension of these scales, we refer specifically to this dimension (e.g., drive or compulsive tendencies) in our review. We also note specifically if the study authors used some other measure of workaholism.

---

[1] Brady et al. (2008) was the only article to use more than one measure to operationalize workaholism; the authors used both the DUWAS and the WorkBat.

Table 4.1. Summary of studies examining workaholism and work-family conflict

Author(s) (year)	Theory	Sample	Measure(s)	Key findings
Andreassen, Hetland, & Pallesen (2013)	None	Norwegian cross-occupational employees	WorkBat	• Drive positively related to family-to-work negative spillover • Work involvement and enjoyment of work significantly related to greater family-to-work positive spillover • Work involvement and drive positively related to negative work-to-family spillover • Drive negatively related to positive work-to-family spillover • Enjoyment positively related to positive work-to-family spillover
Aziz, Adkins, Walker, & Wuensch (2010a)	Relative deprivation theory	Employees in variety of fields in United States	WART	• Workaholism and work-life imbalance were significantly correlated.
Aziz, Wuensch, & Brandon (2010b)	None	Employees in a range of professional organizations in United States	WorkBat	• Workaholics and disenchanted workers (low involvement and enjoyment, high drive) had higher work-life imbalance than the other six types.
Aziz & Zickar (2006)	None	White-collar professionals in Canada (78%) and United States (22%)	WorkBat	• Workaholics (cluster having high involvement and drive, low enjoyment) had greater work-life imbalance than unengaged workers and positively engaged workers.
Bakker, Demerouti, & Burke (2009)	Crossover theory	Dual-earner parents in the Netherlands	Dutch version of WART	• Workaholism led to greater WFC. • WFC mediated relationship between workaholism and social report received by the partner, which led to the partner experiencing lower relationship satisfaction.
Bakker, Shimazu, Demerouti, Shimada, & Kawakami (2014)	Spillover-crossover, COR, role scarcity hypothesis	Dual-earner couples from Tokyo	DUWAS	• Workaholism was positively related to WFC, which was negatively related to one's own family satisfaction (and partner's family satisfaction).

Author(s) (year)	Theory	Sample	Measure(s)	Key findings
Bonebright, Clay, & Ankenmann (2000)	None	Employees in a large technology corporation in the US Midwest	WorkBat	• Nonenthusiastic and enthusiastic workaholics (high on all three dimensions) had higher work-life conflict scores than nonworkaholics. • Nonenthusiastic and enthusiastic workaholics did not differ.
Brady, Vodanovich, & Rotunda (2008)	None	Working professionals who were members of SHRM (S1) and faculty and staff members from a public university in southeastern United States (S2)	Both WorkBat and WART	• Both S1 and S2: drive subscale, work enjoyment subscale, and total WART score predicted WFC.
Clark, Michel, Stevens, Howell, & Scruggs (2014)	Personality theory, broaden and build theory	US workers in a variety of industries	Compulsive tendencies subscale of WART	• Workaholism predicted WIF and FIW. • Workaholism indirectly related to FIW through home anger and home disappointment.
Hakanen & Peeters (2015)	COR	Finnish dentists	Compulsive tendencies subscale of WART	• Workaholism predicted future WFC, not vice versa.
Huyghebaert, Fouquereau, Lahiani, Baltou, Gimenes, & Gillet (in press)	COR, effort-recovery theory	French managers in health-care setting	DUWAS	• Working excessively positively related to WFC. • Working compulsively was not. • Working excessively mediated the effects of workload on WFC and lack of psychological detachment.
Kravina, Falco, De Carlo, Andreassen, & Pallesen (2014)	Modeling and dysfunctional family systems	Undergrads at University of Padua and their parents	DUWAS	• Work excessively (for fathers) positively related to work excessively for adult children. • Neither dimension in mothers was related to workaholism for adult children.
Molino, Bakker, & Ghislieri (2016)	Job demands-resources model	Italian workers in a variety of occupations	BWAS	• Workaholism positively and directly related to WFC and exhaustion • Workaholism indirectly related to intentions to change jobs through exhaustion.

Table 4.1. (Continued)

Author(s) (year)	Theory	Sample	Measure(s)	Key findings
Mudrack & Naughton (2001)	None	Full time employees in variety of industries that attended evening MBA program in major metropolitan area in United States	*Nonrequired work* (time and energy spent thinking about ways to improve their work), and *control of others* (time and energy spent controlling others at work	• Nonrequired work correlated with work-nonwork conflict. • Control of others correlated with work-nonwork conflict.
Russo & Waters (2006)	None	Australian employees working in legal industry	WorkBat	• Workaholics experienced higher levels of WFC than uninvolved workers or relaxed workers (didn't differ significantly from enthusiastic workers). • Worker type did not moderate relationship with supervisor support. • Workaholics, uninvolved, and relaxed workers did not experience a decrease in WFC if they could change their schedule on a weekly basis, but enthusiastic workers did.
Schaufeli, Bakker, Van der Heyden, & Prins (2009)	None	Dutch medical residents	DUWAS	• Work-home conflict was highest in the cluster called "workaholic" (the group with high scores on working excessively and working compulsively).
Shimazu, Demerouti, Bakker, Shimada, & Kawakami (2011)	Scarcity hypothesis, spillover-crossover	Dual-earner couples with preschool children in Japan	DUWAS	• Both men's and women's working excessively and working compulsively were positively correlated to their own WFC and psychological distress, respectively. • Women's working compulsively was positively correlated to their partners' (i.e., men's) WFC and psychological distress. • Men's working excessively and working compulsively were unrelated to women's WFC and psychological distress. • Husbands of workaholic women were more likely to report WFC after adjusting for demographic variables.

Author(s) (year)	Theory	Sample	Measure(s)	Key findings
Taris, Schaufeli, & Verhoeven (2005)	None	S1: Dutch workers from a variety of occupations S2: Dutch white-collar personnel S3: Dutch outpatient clinic patients diagnosed with burnout	WART	S1: Confirmed five factors in WART S2: Creating shorter measure of workaholism (compulsive tendencies subscale of WART). Both long and short version of WART positively related to WFC. S3: Workaholism positively related to WFC directly and indirectly. Indirect pathways: experiencing high perceived job demands and higher exhaustion.

Note: WFC = work-family conflict; WIF = work interfering with family; FIW = family interfering with work. WART = Work Addiction Risk Test (Robinson, 1999); DUWAS = Dutch Work Addiction Scale (Schaufeli, Shimazu, & Taris, 2009); WorkBat = Workaholism Battery (Spence & Robbins, 1992).

Workaholism and Work-Family Conflict

Many of the studies we reviewed examined the relationship between workaholism and either overall WFC or general work-life imbalance. In a couple of studies, Aziz and colleagues (Aziz et al., 2010b; Aziz & Zickar, 2006) created clusters of workers, finding that the workaholic cluster (those with high work involvement and drive, and low work enjoyment) reported greater work-life imbalance than the other worker types. In another study, Aziz and colleagues hypothesized that for white workers, there would be a positive correlation between workaholism and work-life balance, but this relationship would be nonsignificant for black workers; however, they found a significant correlation between workaholism and work-life imbalance for both groups (Aziz et al., 2010a). Brady and colleagues (2008) surveyed university employees and Society for Human Resource Management (SHRM) members in the United States and found positive relationships between workaholism (as measured by the WART) and general work-family conflict, and between the drive subscale of the Spence and Robbins's WorkBat (1992) and general work-family conflict. Thus, workaholism has been consistently found to relate to overall WFC, and this does not appear to differ by race.

A number of studies have examined the relationship between workaholism and directional work-to-family conflict. For example, Andreassen and colleagues (2013) surveyed Norwegian employees and across two studies found a positive relationship between the subscales of drive and work involvement with WIF. Bakker and colleagues (2009) surveyed dual-earner parents in the Netherlands and found that workaholism was positively related to that person's WIF, and these results did not differ by the gender of the parent. Also finding no difference between men and women, Shimazu and colleagues (2011) found that both men and women workaholics (characterized by high scores on working compulsively and excessively) reported greater WIF and psychological distress, respectively. Also examining types of workers, several studies have found that the workaholic cluster (high work involvement and drive, low work enjoyment) reported higher WIF than other clusters of workers (i.e., Bonebright et al., 2000; Russo & Waters, 2006; Schaufeli, Bakker, Van der Heyden, & Prins, 2009). Several other studies found positive relationships between overall workaholism and WIF (Molino, Bakker, & Ghislieri, 2016; Taris et al., 2005), and between the compulsive-tendencies subscale of the WART and WIF (Taris et al., 2005). Clark and colleagues (2014) surveyed US workers across two time points and found that those reporting more compulsive tendencies (subscale of the WART) had greater WIF one month later. Using a much longer time lag, Hakanen and Peeters (2015) found that workaholism was positively related to WIF seven years later (but the reverse was not true; WIF did not predict future workaholism). Interestingly, Huyghebaert and colleagues (in press) surveyed a sample of French managers on working excessively and working compulsively and found that although each was independently related to WIF three months later, when these were entered into the same structural model, the relationship between working compulsively and WIF became nonsignificant. Finally, Mudrack and Naughton (2001) found that workaholism subscales of nonrequired work and control of others positively related to WIF. Overall, using both cross-sectional and longitudinal designs, workaholism and its dimensions have been consistently linked to WIF. Moreover, these effects do not appear to differ by gender.

Several studies have begun to explore the mechanisms through which workaholism is related to WIF (and other family outcomes). For example, Bakker and colleagues (2009) surveyed dual-income partners in the Netherlands and found that WIF mediated the relationship between the compulsive-tendencies workaholism dimension and social support received by the partner. In turn, social support received by the partner mediated the relationship between the original partner's WIF and the partner's relationship satisfaction. In another study of dual-earner couples in Japan, Bakker and colleagues found that WIF mediated the relationship between workaholism and one's own as well as partner's family satisfaction. Clark and colleagues (2014) examined the emotional mechanisms underlying the relationship between workaholism and WIF, finding that feeling anxiety and disappointment at work mediated the relationship between the compulsive-tendencies dimension of workaholism and WIF. Taris and colleagues (2005) found support that perceptions of high job demands and feeling greater exhaustion mediated the relationship between the compulsive-tendencies dimension of workaholism and WIF. The working-excessively dimension of workaholism has also been found to mediate the effects of workload on WIF and lack of psychological detachment (Huyghebaert et al., in press).

To date, not many studies have found support for moderators of the relationship between workaholism and either overall work-family conflict or WIF. As mentioned previously, both race and gender have been examined as potential moderators, but thus far these have not been shown to significantly moderate the relationship between workaholism and work-family conflict (i.e., Aziz et al., 2010a; Bakker et al., 2009; Shimazu et al., 2011). One study examined workaholic types as a moderator of the relationship between schedule flexibility and WIF (Russo & Waters, 2006). In their study, workaholics (high drive and low work enjoyment)—in contrast with enthusiastic workaholics (high drive and high work enjoyment)—did not experience a decrease in WIF if they could change their schedule.

Far fewer studies have examined the relationship between workaholism and FIW. Of these studies, those workers reporting higher drive, work involvement (Andreassen et al., 2014), and compulsive tendencies (Clark et al., 2014) also experience greater FIW. One study examined mediators of this relationship, finding that feeling anger and disappointment at home mediated the relationship between the compulsive-tendencies dimension of workaholism and FIW. One study examined gender as a moderator of the relationship between workaholism dimensions and FIW (Shimazu et al., 2011). In their study of dual-earner couples, women's working compulsively was positively related to their male partners' FIW and psychological distress. However, men's working excessively and compulsively was unrelated to their female partners' FIW and psychological distress. Thus, in contrast to the lack of gender differences found in relation to WIF, there is preliminary evidence of gender as an important moderator of the relationship between workaholism and FIW.

GAPS IN THE LITERATURE AND RECOMMENDATIONS FOR FUTURE RESEARCH

The goal of this chapter was to review the state of the literature on workaholism and work-family conflict, which has led us to point out some important areas that may be especially fruitful for future research to examine. First, while we know workaholism is associated with a plethora of negative outcomes, the focus of most research seems to be on predicting these negative outcomes, as opposed to how workaholics can cope with this trait. There is a clear need for future research to address how workaholics can cope with this tendency and alleviate the known negative outcomes, particularly work-family conflict. Past research tends to make broad recommendations, including that organizations should implement intervention or treatment programs (Aziz & Zickar, 2006); implement information and training workshops educating employees about workaholism (Balducci, Avanzi, & Fraccaroli, in press); and make sure employees are rewarded for balancing performance and detaching from work, rather than simply rewarding employees who may be productive but are displaying workaholic tendencies (Burke, 2001). However, very few studies have examined ways to alleviate the negative outcomes associated with workaholism. One exception is a study by Bakker and colleagues (2013), who found that workaholic employees who exercise during nonwork time (as opposed to working) reported higher well-being. We encourage future research to test potential coping mechanisms, programs, and interventions that may help alleviate the negative outcomes associated with workaholism.

In particular, some type of mindfulness intervention may help reduce the work-family conflict experience by individuals with workaholic tendencies. Mindfulness interventions are becoming increasingly popular, especially in the context of the workplace, as they have been shown to lead to reduced strain (Eby, Allen, Conley, Williamson, Henderson, & Mancini, in press). Utilizing mindfulness techniques (e.g., yoga, body scans, and meditation) may need to be tailored for addressing workaholism and improving work-family conflict (see also Chapter 8). While we may typically think of mindfulness interventions occurring at work to reduce work-related stress, the practice of mindfulness is more useful at home if the goal is to reduce work-family conflict in workaholic employees. For instance, workaholics feel compelled to dive straight into work as soon as they wake up, by checking their email or starting to work from their home computer, which ultimately leads to work-family conflict. However, if workaholic employees practice some type of mindfulness practice upon first waking up, they will be more likely to refrain from these workaholic behaviors and focus on their family life before leaving for and starting work. Similarly, a workaholic would benefit from practicing mindfulness immediately upon returning home from work. This may help remind them to be mindful and aware of what is happening in the moment, potentially helping them to focus more on their family and less on their instinct to continue working.

We also see a need for future research to test the mediating mechanisms regarding crossover theory to understand the complex intersection of workaholism and work-family conflict in the context of home. Although research has demonstrated that workaholism can negatively affect a workaholic's spouse via crossover, few studies have theoretically explained or empirically tested which mediating mechanism is underlying this process. Uncovering mediating mechanisms of workaholism and work-family conflict will also allow researchers to draw from other theoretical perspectives, including resource and role-based theory, and boundary and border theory that could be used in conjunction with crossover theory. Additionally, understanding which mediating mechanism is at play (i.e., direct crossover, indirect crossover, or common stressors) could help suggest practically how spouses of workaholics could cope or avoid some of the negative outcomes they may experience due to the workaholic personality of their partner.

Additionally, there appears to be gaps in the literature regarding certain aspects of study design for workaholism and work-family conflict. Future research should examine the within-level mechanism of workaholism as opposed to the between-level mechanisms, which has largely been the focus of research to date. There also appears to be more research on spillover processes (within individual stress) as opposed to crossover processes (between individual stress) for workaholism and work-family conflict. Finally, much of the research seems to focus on non-American samples, as 13 of the 21 studies reviewed in Table 1 use samples from outside of the United States. Additionally, the majority of the studies reviewed only measured the relationship between workaholism and WIF. Given some of the interesting results from existing studies that have examined the relationship between workaholism and FIW (e.g., gender as a moderator), much more research is needed examining both directions of work-family conflict.

Finally, we see a need for future research to integrate contextual factors into studies, such as the culture of the organization, societal culture, and further examination of gender differences in these relationships. Past research has suggested that organizations fostering a "workaholic culture" can influence workaholic behavior (Griffiths & Karanika-Murray, 2012; Porter, 1996), yet organizational culture is not commonly measured in workaholism studies. Additionally, research suggests that societal values can influence workaholic behavior, in that societies valuing survival (as opposed to self-expression) tend to have higher levels of work investment (Snir & Harpaz, 2009). However, other research suggests cultural origin does not influence workaholism (Aziz et al., 2010a). Future research should seek to address these inconsistent findings. Finally, gender differences are complex for both workaholism (Beiler-May et al., 2017) and work-family conflict (Clark et al., 2015) regarding differences not only in how these constructs operate in men and women but also in potential bias in the measurement of these constructs between men and women. There is a clear need for research to explore the impact gender may have on the workaholism and work-family conflict relationship.

In this chapter, we have reviewed the literature on work-family conflict and workaholism, as well as proposed how these two constructs may be related based on three broad theoretical frameworks. We see a need for future research to examine ways that workaholics (or organizations seeking to help employees with workaholic tendencies) can help to alleviate the known negative outcomes associated with this trait, and specifically work-family conflict. While many suggestions have been made in past articles, very few have tested if potential treatment programs or organizational changes have an impact. Future research should also address the mediating mechanism of workaholism and work-family conflict of a workaholic's spouse, as there is evidence that spouses of workaholics experience negative outcomes but little research examining how this occurs. Uncovering the mediating mechanism of this relationship will allow practical solutions for spouses to alleviate these negative outcomes they may otherwise experience. There also seems to be a need for future research to address within-individual processes of workaholism and work-family conflict, crossover processes between workaholics and their partners, and more studies conducted in the United States. Finally, future research should integrate more contextual factors to extend our understanding of the complex relationship between workaholism and work-family conflict.

REFERENCES

Andreassen, C. S., Griffiths, M. D., Hetland, J., & Pallesen, S. (2012). Development of a work addiction scale. *Personality and Social Psychology, 53*, 265–272. doi:10.1111/j.1467-9450.2012.00947.x.

Andreassen, C. S., Hetland, J., & Pallesen, S. (2013). Workaholism and work-family spillover in a cross-organizational sample. *Journal of Work and Organizational Psychology, 22*, 78–87. doi: 10.1080/1359432X.2011.626201

Andreassen, C. S., Hetland, J., & Pallesen, S. (2014). Psychometric assessment of workaholism measures. *Journal of Managerial Psychology, 29*, 7–24. doi:10.1108/JMP-05-2013-0143.

Ashforth, B. E., Kreiner, G. E., & Fugate, M. (2000). All in a day's work: Boundaries and micro role transitions. *Academy of Management Review, 25*, 472–491. doi:10.2307/259305.

Aziz, S., Adkins, C. T., Walker, A. G., & Wuensch, K. L. (2010a). Workaholism and work-life imbalance: Does cultural origin influence the relationship? *International Journal of Psychology, 45*, 72–79. doi: 10.1080/00207590902913442

Aziz, S., Wuensch, K. L., & Brandon, H. R. (2010b). A comparison among worker types using a composites approach and median splits. *Psychological Record, 60*, 627–642.

Aziz, S., & Zickar, M. J. (2006). A cluster analysis investigation of workaholism as a syndrome. *Journal of Occupational Health Psychology, 11*, 52–62. doi: 10.1037/1076-8998.11.1.52.

Bakker, A. B., Demerouti, E., & Burke, R. (2009). Workaholism and relationship quality: A spillover-crossover perspective. *Journal of Occupational Health Psychology, 14*, 23–33. doi:10.1037/a0013290.

Bakker, A. B., Demerouti, E., & Dollard, M. F. (2008). How job demands affect partners' experience of exhaustion: Integrating work-family conflict and crossover theory. *Journal of Applied Psychology, 93*, 901–911. doi:10.1037/0021-9010.93.4.901.

Bakker, A. B., Demerouti, E., Oerlemans, W., & Sonnentag, S. (2013). Workaholism and daily recovery: A day reconstruction study of leisure activities. *Journal of Organizational Behavior, 34*, 87–107. doi:10.1002/job.1796.

Bakker, A. B., Shimazu, A., Demerouti, E., Shimada, K., & Kawakami, N. (2014). Work engagement versus workaholism: A test of the spillover-crossover model. *Journal of Managerial Psychology, 29*, 63–80. doi:10.1108/JMP-05-2013-0148.

Balducci, C., Avanzi, L., & Fraccaroli, F. (in press). The individual "costs" of workaholism: An analysis based on multisource and prospective data. *Journal of Management*. doi: 10.1177/0149206316658348.

Barber, L. K., & Santuzzi, A. M. (2015). Please respond ASAP: Workplace telepressure and employee recovery. *Journal of Occupational Health Psychology, 20*, 172–189. doi:10.1037/a0038278.

Baruch, Y. (2011). The positive wellbeing aspects of workaholism in cross cultural perspective: The chocoholism metaphor. *Career Development International, 16*, 572–591. doi: 10.1108/13620431111178335.

Beiler-May, A., Williamson, R. L., Clark, M. A., & Carter, N. T. (2017). Gender bias in the measurement of workaholism. *Journal of Personality Assessment*, 1–7. doi: 10.1080/00223891.2016.1198795.

Bolger, N., DeLongis, A., Kessler, R. C., & Wethington, E. (1989). The contagion of stress across multiple roles. *Journal of Marriage and the Family*, 175–183.

Bonebright, C. A., Clay, D. L., & Ankenmann, R. D. (2000). The relationship of workaholism with work-life conflict, life satisfaction, and purpose in life. *Journal of Counseling Psychology, 47*, 469–477. doi: 10.1037/0022-0167.47.4.469.

Brady, B. R., Vodanovich, S. J., & Rotunda, R. (2008). The impact of workaholism on work-family conflict, job satisfaction, and perception of leisure activities. *Psychologist-Manager Journal, 11*, 241–263. doi: 10.1080/10887150802371781.

Burke, R. J. (2001). Workaholism in organizations: The role of organizational values. *Personnel Review, 30*, 637–645. doi:10.1108/EUM0000000005977.

Burke, R. J., Matthiesen, S. B., & Pallesen, S. (2006). Personality correlates of workaholism. *Personality and Individual Differences, 40*, 1223–1233. doi: 10.1016/j.paid.2005.10.017.

Burke, R. J., Richardsen, A. M., & Martinussen, M. (2002). Psychometric properties of Spence and Robbins' measures of workaholism components. *Psychological Reports, 91*, 1098–1104. doi: 10.2466/pr0.2002.91.3f.1098

Carlson, D. S., Kacmar, K. M., Wayne, J. H., & Grzywacz, J. G. (2006). Measuring the positive side of the work-family interface: Development and validation of a work-family enrichment scale. *Journal of Vocational Behavior, 68*, 131–164. doi: 10.1016/j.jvb.2005.02.002

Carlson, D. S., Kacmar, K. M., & Williams, L. J. (2000). Construction and initial validation of a multidimensional measure of work-family conflict. *Journal of Vocational Behavior, 56*, 249–276. doi:10.1006/jvbe.1999.1713.

Cinamon, R. G., Weisel, A., & Tzuk, K. (2007). Work-family conflict within the family: Crossover effects, perceived parent-child interaction quality, parental self-efficacy, and life role attributions. *Journal of Career Development, 34*, 79–100. doi:10.1177/0894845307304066.

Clark, S. C. (2000). Work/family border theory: A new theory of work/family balance. *Human Relations, 53*, 747–770. doi:10.1177/0018726700536001.

Clark, M. A., Beiler, A. A., & Zimmerman, L. M. (2015). Examining the work-family experience of workaholic women. In M. J. Mills (Ed.), *Gender and the Work-Family Experience* (pp. 313–327). Cham, Switzerland: Springer. doi:10.1007/978-3-319-08891-4_16.

Clark, M. A., Michel, J. S., Stevens, G. W., Howell, J. W., & Scruggs, R. S. (2014). Workaholism, work engagement and work-home outcomes: Exploring the mediating role of positive and negative emotions. *Stress and Health, 30*, 287–300. doi: 10.1002/smi.2511

Clark, M. A., Michel, J. S., Zhdanova, L., Pui, S. Y., & Baltes, B. B. (2016). All work and no play? A meta-analytic examination of the correlates and outcomes of workaholism. *Journal of Management, 42*, 1836–1873. doi:10.1177/0149206314522301.

Desrochers, S., & Sargent, L. D. (2004). Boundary/border theory and work-family integration. *Organization Management Journal, 1*, 40–48. doi: 10.1057/omj.2004.11

Dierdorff, E. C., & Ellington, J. K. (2008). It's the nature of work: Examining behavior-based sources of work-family conflict across occupations. *Journal of Applied Psychology, 93*, 883–892. doi:10.1037/0021-9010.93.4.883.

Eby, L. T., Allen, T. D., Conley, K. M., Williamson, R. L., Henderson, T. G., & Mancini, V. S. (in press). Mindfulness-based training interventions for employees: A qualitative review of the literature. *Human Resource Management Review*. doi: 10.1016/j.hrmr.2017.03.004.

Edwards, J. R., & Rothbard, N. P. (2000). Mechanisms linking work and family: Clarifying the relationship between work and family constructs. *Academy of Management Review, 25*, 178–199. doi: 10.5465/AMR.2000.2791609.

Ferguson, M., Carlson, D., Boswell, W., Whitten, D., Butts, M. M., & Kacmar, K. M. (2016). Tethered to work: A family systems approach linking mobile deice use to turnover intentions. *Journal of Applied Psychology, 101*, 520–534. doi:10.1037/apl0000075.

Flaxman, P. E., Menard, J., Bond, F. W., & Kinman, G. (2012). Academics' experiences of a respite from work: Effects of self-critical perfectionism and perseverative cognition on postrespite well-being. *Journal of Applied Psychology, 97*, 854–865. doi:10.1037/a0028055.

Goode, W. J. (1960). A theory of role strain. *American Sociological Review, 25*, 483–496.

Grandey, A. A., & Cropanzano, R. (1999). The conservation of resources model applied to work-family conflict and strain. *Journal of Vocational Behavior, 54*, 350–370. doi: 10.1006/jvbe.1998.1666.

Greenhaus, J. H., & Beutell, N. J. (1985). Sources of conflict between work and family roles. *Academy of Management Review, 10*, 76–88.

Griffiths, M. D., & Karanika-Murray, M. (2012). Contextualising over-engagement in work: Towards a more global understanding of workaholism as an addiction. *Journal of Behavioral Addictions, 1*, 87–95. doi:10.1556/JBA.1.2012.002.

Grzywacz, J. G., Carlson, D. S., Kacmar, K. M., & Wayne, J. H. (2007). A multi-level perspective on the synergies between work and family. *Journal of Occupational and Organizational Psychology, 80*, 559–574. doi: 10.1348/096317906X163081.

Grzywacz, J. G., & Marks, N. F. (2000). Reconceptualizing the work-family interface: An ecological perspective on the correlates of positive and negative spillover between work and family. *Journal of Occupational Health Psychology, 5*, 111–126. doi:0.1037//I076-8998.5.1.111.

Hakanen, J., & Peeters, M. (2015). How do work engagement, workaholism, and the work-to-family interface affect each other? A 7-year follow-up study. *Journal of Environmental Medicine, 57*, 601–609. doi:10.1097/JOM.0000000000000457.

Halbesleben, J. R., Neveu, J. P., Paustian-Underdahl, S. C., & Westman, M. (2014). Getting to the "COR" understanding the role of resources in conservation of resources theory. *Journal of Management, 40*, 1334–1364. doi:10.1177/ 0149206314527130.

Hammer, L. B., Allen, E., & Grigsby, T. D. (1997). Work-family conflict in dual-earner couples: Within individual and crossover effects of work and family. *Journal of Vocational Behavior, 50*, 185–203. doi: 10.1006/jvbe.1996.1557.

Haring, M., Hewitt, P. L., & Flett, G. L. (2003). Perfectionism, coping, and quality of intimate relationships. *Journal of Marriage and Family, 65*, 143–158. doi: 10.1111/j.1741-3737.2003.00143.x.

Harpaz, I., & Snir, R. (2003). Workaholism: Its definition and nature. *Human Relations, 56*, 291–319. doi: 10.1177/0018726703056003613.

Hobfoll, S. E. (1989). Conservation of resource: A new attempt at conceptualizing stress. *American Psychologist, 44*, 513–524.

Hobfoll, S. E. (2001). The influence of culture, community, and the nested-self in the stress process: Advancing conservation of resources theory. *Applied Psychology: An International Review, 50*, 337–421. doi: 10.1111 / 1464-0597.00062.

Huyghebaert, T., Fouquereau, E., Lahiani, F. J., Beltou, N., Gimenes, G., & Gillet, N. (in press). Examining the longitudinal effects of workload on ill-being through each dimension of workaholism. *International Journal of Stress Management*. doi: 10.1037/str0000055.

Kahn, R. L., Wolfe, D. M., Quinn, R. P., Snoek, J. D., & Rosenthal, R. A. (1964). *Organizational stress: Studies in role conflict and ambiguity*. Oxford, UK: Wiley.

Kravina, L., Falco, A., De Carlo, N. A., Andreassen, C. S., & Pallesen, S. (2014). Workaholism and work engagement in the family: The relationship between parents and children as a risk factor. *European Journal of Work and Organizational Psychology, 23*, 875–883. doi: 10.1080/1359432X.2013.832208.

Matthews, R. A., Del Priore, R. E., Acitelli, L. K., & Barnes-Farrell, J. L. (2006). Work-to-relationship conflict: Crossover effects in dual-earner couples. *Journal of Occupational Health Psychology, 3*, 228–240. doi:10.1037/1076-8998.11.3.228.

Mazzetti, G., Schaufeli, W. B., & Guglielmi, D. (2014). Are workaholics born or made? Relations of workaholism with person characteristics and overwork climate. *International Journal of Stress Management, 21*, 227–254. doi:10.1037/a0035700.

McMillan, L. H. W., Brady, E. C., O'Driscoll, M. P., & Marsh, N. V. (2002). A multifaceted validated study of Spence and Robbins' (1992) workaholism battery. *Journal of Occupational and Organizational Psychology, 75*, 357–368. doi: 10.1348/096317902320369758.

Michel, J. S., Kotrba, L. M., Mitchelson, J. K., Clark, M. A., & Baltes, B. B. (2011). Antecedents of work-family conflict: A meta-analytic review. *Journal of Organizational Behavior, 32*, 689–725. doi:10.1002/job.695.

Molino, M., Bakker, A. B., & Ghislieri, C. (2016). The role of workaholism in the job demands-resources model. *Anxiety, Stress, and Coping, 29*, 400–414. doi: 10.1080/10615806.2015.1070833.

Mudrack, P. E. (2006). Understanding workaholism: The case for behavioral tendencies. In R. J. Burke (Ed.), *Research companion to working time and work addiction* (pp. 108–128). Northampton, MA: Edward Elgar.

Mudrack, P. E., & Naughton, T. J. (2001). The assessment of workaholism as behavioral tendencies: Scale development and preliminary empirical testing. *International Journal of Stress Management, 8*, 93–111. doi: 10.1023/A:1009525213213.

Murphy, L. R., & Sauter, S. L. (2003). The USA perspective: Current issues and trends in the management of work stress. *Australian Psychologist, 38*, 151–157. doi:10.1080/00050060310001707157.

Ng, T. W., Sorensen, K. L., & Feldman, D. C. (2007). Dimensions, antecedents, and consequences of workaholism: A conceptual integration and extension. *Journal of Organizational Behavior, 28*, 111–136. doi: 10.1002/job.424.

Nippert-Eng, C. (1996). Calendars and keys: The classification of "home" and "work." *Sociological Forum, 11*, 563–582.

Oates, W. (1971). *Confessions of a workaholic: The facts about work addiction.* New York, NY: World.

Olson-Buchanan, J. B., & Boswell, W. R. (2006). Blurring boundaries: Correlates of integration and segmentation between work and nonwork. *Journal of Vocational Behavior, 68*, 432–445. doi: 10.1016/j.jvb.2005.10.006.

Porter, G. (1996). Organizational impact of workaholism: Suggestions for researching the negative outcomes of excessive work. *Journal of Occupational Health Psychology, 1*, 70–84.

Robinson, B. E. (1999). The work addiction risk test: Development of a tentative measure of workaholism. *Perceptual and Motor Skills, 88*, 199–210. doi: 10.2466/pms.1999.88.1.199.

Robinson, B. E., Carroll, J. J., & Flowers, C. (2001). Marital estrangement, positive affect, and locus of control among spouses of workaholics and spouses of nonworkaholics: A national study. *American Journal of Family Therapy, 29*, 397–410. doi:10.1080/01926180127624.

Russo, J. A., & Waters, L. E. (2006). Workaholic worker type differences in work-family conflict: The moderating role of supervisor support and flexible work scheduling. *Career Development International, 11*, 418–439. doi: 10.1108/13620430610683052.

Schaufeli, W. B., Bakker, A. B., Van der Heyden, F. M. M. A., & Prins, J. T. (2009). Workaholism among medical residents: It is the combination of working excessively and compulsively that counts. *International Journal of Stress Management, 16*, 249–272. doi: 10.1037/a0017537.

Schaufeli, W. B., Shimazu, A., & Taris, T. W. (2009). Being driven to work excessively hard: The evaluation of a two-factor measure of workaholism in the Netherlands and Japan. *Cross-Cultural Research, 43*, 320–348. doi:10.1177/1069397109337239.

Schaufeli, W. B., Taris, T. W., & Bakker, A. B. 2008. It takes two to tango: Workaholism is working excessively and working compulsively. In R. J. Burke & C. L. Cooper (Eds.), *The long work hours culture: Causes, consequences and choices* (pp. 203–225). Bingley, UK: Emerald. doi: 10.1016/B978-1-84855-038-4.00009-9.

Shimazu, A., Demerouti, E., Bakker, A. B., Shimada, K., & Kawakami, N. (2011). Workaholism and well-being among Japanese dual-earner couples: A spillover-crossover perspective. *Social Science and Medicine, 73*, 399–409. doi: 10.1016/j.socscimed.2011.05.049.

Snir, R., & Harpaz, I. (2009). Cross-cultural differences concerning heavy work investment. *Cross-Cultural Research, 43*, 309–319. doi:10.1177/1069397109336988.

Snir, R., & Harpaz, I. (2012). Beyond workaholism: Towards a general model of heavy work investment. *Human Resource Management Review, 22*, 232–243. doi: 10.1016/j.hrmr.2011.11.011.

Spence, J. T., & Robbins, A. S. (1992). Workaholism: Definition, measurement, and preliminary results. *Journal of Personality Assessment, 58*, 160–178.

Taris, T. W., Schaufeli, W. B., & Verhoeven, L. C. (2005). Workaholism in the Netherlands: Measurement and implications for job strain and work-nonwork conflict. *Applied Psychology: An International Review, 54*, 37–60. doi: 10.1111 / j.1464-0597.2005.00195.x.

Taris, T. W., Van Beek, I., & Schaufeli, W. B. (2012). Demographic and occupational correlates of workaholism. *Psychological Reports, 110*, 547–554. doi: 10.2466/03.09.17.PR0.110.2.547-554.

Towers, I., Duxbury, L., Higgins, C., & Thomas, J. (2006). Time thieves and space invaders: Technology, work and the organization. *Journal of Organizational Change Management, 19*, 593–618. doi: 10.1108/09534810610686076.

US Department of Labor, Bureau of Labor Statistics. (2016). American Time Use Survey (ATUS). Retrieved March 2017 from http://www.bls.gov/tus.

Wayne, J. H., Grzywacz, J. G., Carlson, D. S., & Kacmar, K. M. (2007). Work-family facilitation: A theoretical explanation and model of primary antecedents and consequences. *Human Resource Management Review, 17*, 63–76. doi: 10.1016/ j.hrmr.2007.01.002.

Westman, M. (2002). Crossover of stress and strain in the family and workplace. In P. L. Perrewé & D. C. Ganster (Eds.), *Historical and current perspectives on stress and health* (pp. 143–181). Bingley, UK: Emerald Group.

Westman, M., & Etzion, D. 2005. The crossover of work-family conflict from one spouse to the other. *Journal of Applied Social Psychology, 35*, 1936–1957. doi: 10.1111/j.1559-1816.2005.tb02203.x.

In: Work-Life Balance in the 21st Century ISBN: 978-1-53612-526-9
Editor: Jessica M. Nicklin © 2018 Nova Science Publishers, Inc.

Chapter 5

STANDING THE TEST OF TIME:
CHRONOTYPE, SCHEDULING,
AND RECOVERY EXPERIENCES

Lauren O. Gilmer[1],*, Alex P. Lindsey[1], PhD
and Kristen P. Jones[2], PhD

[1]Department of Psychology, Indiana University-Purdue University Indianapolis,
Indianapolis, IN, US
[2]Fogelman College of Business & Economics, University of Memphis,
Memphis, TN, US

ABSTRACT

Work-life balance has much to do with time. Accordingly, this chapter will explore
the biological clocks of individuals (chronotype), the impact of scheduling (including
disparities in schedule access), and the methods that employees use to recover from work.
By integrating the currently disparate literatures on these topics, this chapter will provide
a more complete understanding of how we can maximize work-life balance. One of the
more novel considerations of time in the workplace lies in chronotype research, which
shows that when work schedules do not match employees' chronotype, adverse
consequences can result. As schedules change over time, it is crucial to consider that not
all employees who would benefit from certain schedules are able to utilize them, resulting
in low work-life balance. Research has also demonstrated how difficult it is for
employees to adapt to schedule changes. Therefore, this chapter will review and integrate
a few seminal models of recovery from stress and work-related demands. Overall, this
chapter will emphasize the necessity of considering individual differences when studying
work-life balance. In doing so, we hope to gain a greater understanding of the work-life

---

* Corresponding Author Email: logilmer@iupui.edu.

experience, in addition to what individuals and organizations can do to ensure that workplace well-being is maximized.

STANDING THE TEST OF TIME: CHRONOTYPE, SCHEDULING, AND RECOVERY EXPERIENCES

Most of us wish we had more time—time to sleep, time to spend with loved ones, and time to enjoy our hobbies. Organizations and their employees must also work to achieve their goals under time constraints. These temporal boundaries can add complications to life inside and outside of the workplace. In particular, it can be difficult to maintain an appropriate work-life balance when work schedules and demands are changing, often resulting in a mismatch with individual employee needs.

If all employees started and ended work at the same time, complications would be fewer and further between, but the reality is that schedules vary depending on field of work, organizational culture, and other factors. Employees may work in other countries, work from home, work at night, work rotating shifts, or request flexible working arrangements for caregiving or other reasons. These differences in the use of time result in a lack of consensus among organizations asking, How can we best use our time to achieve our goals? Conversely, employees may wonder, How can I manage the responsibilities of my job and maintain my life outside of work?

In this chapter, we will discuss the history and evolution of work schedules. This discussion will include the impact of individual differences such as chronotype on scheduling, characteristics and implications of flexible work schedules, intersectional disparities in access to preferred scheduling, and job demand recovery processes. Our hope is that this overview will provide a greater understanding of the implications of the widely varied experiences employees face in their work lives. In doing so, we integrate the work-time factors literatures and note gaps that we hope will inspire future research on the aforementioned topics.

Additionally, we provide recommendations to employees and organizations to mitigate work-life and time-specific concerns. These recommendations include creating a flexibility-supportive work environment in addition to implementing formal policies; forming organizational cultures that promote schedule diversity based on chronotype or caregiving responsibilities; and mitigating time-based employee health problems and work-family conflict through organization-sponsored initiatives (e.g., stress management workshops, on-site childcare, and encouragement of work breaks). Overall, it is our hope that these actions will move organizations toward the goal of creating better work-life balance for employees. In turn, work-life balance tends to enhance the organizational bottom-line goals of decreased absenteeism and turnover and increased employee performance.

CHRONOTYPE: NIGHT OWLS AND MORNING LARKS

We begin our discussion of timing in the workplace with an exploration of the impact of chronotype. Have you ever had a friend who loves to stay up late but can never seem to function during the day, even if he tries to change his sleep habits? You might think of your friend as a "night owl," the complete opposite of a "morning lark." However, this person is not simply a party animal. Rather, this is an example of a person with an extreme evening chronotype.

What Is Chronotype?

In the extant literature, chronotype is referred to as a biologically determined individual difference in the preference for sleep and wakeful activity (Nováková, Sládek, & Sumová, 2013) and has a genetic basis (Jones, Huang, Ptáček, & Fu, 2013). People who are considered morning larks are labeled as early chronotypes, whereas those considered night owls are labeled as late chronotypes. While chronotype is a fairly new individual difference variable in workplace-related literature (for a notable exception, see Yam, Fehr, & Barnes, 2014), scientists, called *chronobiologists*, have been studying its existence and impact for decades. German scientist Till Roenneberg brought chronotype into the public eye using the applicable comparison of chronotype to social jet lag, or the difference between midsleep (the midpoint time between going to sleep and waking) on free and work days (Roenneberg, 2012). So, how does the human body know when to go to sleep and wake up, and why does this vary among individuals?

Humans receive cues from outside the body, called *zeitgebers*, or "light-givers," which tell us to wake up or go to sleep. Often, light (natural or artificial) is the main zeitgeber that affects sleep and wake times, but cues can also stem from social obligations, work, or school. Furthermore, cues can vary based on location. For example, in China, political power shifts led to the creation of a single time zone for the whole country, meaning that sunrise and sunset do not match events as they unfold socially (e.g., sunset may occur at midnight), but people are still expected to adhere to schedules set by social and work obligations (Roenneberg et al., 2007). The effects of zeitgebers are also apparent in animal research: Munich-area blackbird populations have different chronotypes depending on whether they live inside or outside of the city (Dominoni, Helm, Lehmann, Dowse, & Partecke, 2013).

In addition to the external cues that affect sleep patterns and preferences, humans also have internal rhythms within the body, called *circadian rhythms*, governed by the suprachiasmatic nucleus (SCN) in the brain's hypothalamus and denoted by changes in hormones, heart rate, and body temperature. This biological clock runs on a schedule close to, but not exactly, 24 hours, without influence from zeitgebers. Under normal circumstances, however, humans are wakeful when light is present and sleep when melatonin is released at night, adhering to the 24-hour schedule dictated by our external world. In this way, the biological clock attempts to synchronize with zeitgebers, but it is a free-running system that may not always match up with external zeitgebers.

Because general life schedules are dynamic in nature, internal and external rhythms oscillate over time in an attempt to adapt to changes, a "catch-up" process referred to as *entrainment*. The goal of entrainment is synchronization of circadian rhythms and external cues, which results in optimal functioning. If changes in sleep/wake schedules are minor, it will likely not take very long for circadian rhythms to synchronize with external rhythms, but this process is much more difficult and time consuming when the body is faced with extreme schedule changes. Individual differences in entrainment result in what we call chronotype differences. When a person has an extreme early (morning lark) or late (night owl) chronotype and a schedule inconsistent with or opposite of that chronotype, entrainment is more difficult, and complications may ensue.

It is difficult to definitively state how many people are classified as morning larks or night owls, or neither, because this depends on the measure used. Various scales have been created to measure chronotype on a continuum, as chronotypes vary a great deal across individuals and populations (Roenneberg et al., 2007). For example, research with European samples shows that 8.2 percent of people fall asleep around 3:00 a.m. or later and would be considered night owls (late chronotype; Roenneberg et al., 2007). Use of different cutoff scores suggests that 20.2 percent of middle-aged nonshift workers are considered night owls (28.1 percent were rated as morning larks, and 51.7 percent were rated as neither morning larks nor night owls; Taillard, Philip, Chastang, & Bioulac, 2004).

Implications of Chronotype

Adages such as "the early bird gets the worm" have influenced the way we think about biologically determined chronotypes, whether these beliefs are accurate or not. Our aforementioned "party-animal" friend (with an extreme late chronotype) appears to face a mismatch between the period during which he is most awake and the period during which he is socially or professionally required to be functioning, productive, and alert. In this case, we would probably call this person a night owl, meaning that life in a morning lark–preferred society can be more difficult.

Research shows that chronotype-zeitgeber mismatch has both short- and long-term implications for individuals. A plethora of evidence documents lower performance for night owls across age groups at both school and work (Scott, 1994). However, the above evidence suggests not that this pattern is attributable to lower levels of general mental ability in night owls but rather that students and employees are asked to perform cognitively demanding tasks in the morning, regardless of their chronotype. The mismatch can also result in health and sleep problems (Martens, Nijhuis, van Boxtel, & Knottnerus, 1999), which are the most widely explored topics in chronotype literature to date. Specifically, data show that night owls are more likely to experience mood disorders, anxiety disorders, substance-use disorders, personality disorders, insomnia, sleep apnea, arterial hypertension, bronchial asthma, type 2 diabetes, and infertility when compared to morning larks (Partonen, 2015). On the extreme end, they also tend to have shorter life spans (Partonen, 2015).

There is also a small but growing body of work on *chronotype bias*, or the belief that people with a morning chronotype are more moral, have more desirable personalities, and are higher performers than night owls, specifically because of their chronotype. Research is establishing this bias and moving toward investigating discrimination based on chronotype bias. Examples include Yam and colleagues' (2014) study, which established that managers use start time as a determinant of performance ratings, even while controlling for objective performance and total work hours, and a study conducted by Bonke (2012), which showed that morning larks have higher earned income than night owls.

Bias in the workplace as a result of perceived personality differences (and assumed performance differences) is another topic that is emerging in the literature. In a study conducted by Yam, Fehr, and Barnes (2014), managers implicitly associated earlier employee start time with high conscientiousness. Follow-up studies with real-life employee-employer dyads and an undergraduate student sample showed managerial bias in performance ratings of employees who start later versus earlier; night owls are not assumed to be conscientious or high-performing individuals. In addition, a study on proactivity and task performance reported a significant correlation between self-reported proactivity and morningness in an undergraduate sample but also noted that morningness moderated the relationship between proactivity and task performance (operationalized as exam scores; Kirby & Kirby, 2006), such that proactivity had a more positive relationship with task performance when training times matched students' chronotype. This suggests that morning people are viewed more positively than night owls in the workplace, but only because their chronotype matches the time constraints and expectations of most organizations. One of the only positive traits that is consistently represented in research on night owls appears to be creativity (Giampietro & Cavallera, 2007).

Chronotype and Work-Life Balance

Having a certain chronotype does not, in and of itself, produce work-life imbalance. However, whether one's chronotype is matched or mismatched with the schedule demands of one's job may have implications for work-life balance. Greenhaus and Beutell (1985) cited the problem of time-based conflict, referring to the reality that when one devotes a certain amount of time to one's job, it takes time away from one's nonwork life. In the case of night owls who work typical day jobs, it is possible they are more able to devote time to nonwork activities or family in the evening, whereas morning larks who work day jobs are more likely to be tired in the evening, thus decreasing their amount of time spent on nonwork activities. Conversely, a chronotype that is mismatched with one's job demands may result in higher levels of exhaustion, such that nonwork activities at the end of the workday/night are limited. Furthermore, awareness of the stigma faced by those with certain chronotypes lead some employees to force themselves into a lifestyle or work schedule that does not match their chronotype, possibly leading to negative physiological and psychological outcomes.

Considering the implausibility of changing one's chronotype, what can be done to mitigate the negative effects of chronotype-zeitgeber mismatch? How can societally accepted chronotype bias against night owls be reduced? Excluding special cases in which one's environment offers little sunlight, and considering the importance of work in our society, we next discuss various work schedules as a main cause of mismatch problems.

WORK SCHEDULES: A BRIEF HISTORY, CURRENT STATUS, AND SCHEDULE ACCESS

People spend the majority of their time either working or sleeping (Mullins, Cortina, Drake, & Dalal, 2014). As we have previously discussed, the timing of working hours is a critical determinant of individual and organizational work outcomes. From medieval times to post-World War II, the work schedule has solidified a sense of order in working life (Snyder, 2016). Employees may punch a time clock at a local office or, in the modern day, report to managers overseas, but the focus on "putting in one's time" remains central to the working world.

Work-Devotion Schema versus Flexibility

Extant literature has examined the continued presence of the *work-devotion schema* (Blair-Loy, 2003), which refers to the cultural assumption that employees should fully pledge their allegiance to work, even if it is at the expense of nonwork or family life. Not only are employees expected to work nine-to-five, but also they may be perceived as uncommitted if they do not work these hours or more (Williams, Blair-Loy, & Berdahl,

2013). As women have joined the workforce, concerns about how to balance life outside of one's work schedule have come to the forefront, as working women are often perceived as responsible for their professional success and maintenance of a home and family (Cheung & Halpern, 2010; Hochschild & Manchung, 1989). Furthermore, men may be, to some extent, still expected to be "breadwinners" while women take care of the home and family (Williams et al., 2013). In the case of chronotype, night owls getting the schedule during which they work best goes directly against the work-devotion schema's nine-to-five mandate.

The work-devotion schema is often observed when managers hesitate to adopt flexible work arrangements (discussed later in this chapter, at length in Silva & Costa, 2017, and in Chapter 6 of this volume) and when employees fear negative outcomes should they request them (Williams et al., 2013). Additionally, a technology-centered culture that allows employees to be potentially available at all times means that the line between work and nonwork may be close to being erased. In the case of the trucking industry, for example, new regulations have given drivers "flexibility" in that they are able to drive at all hours of the day, but in reality, they may have little to no control over their schedules and may be subject to unstable income and fewer protections from the company (Isaac, 2014). Furthermore, because demands may be greater at certain times of day than others, employees are still not working at the times of day congruent with their chronotypically determined wakeful hours. The false notion of flexibility common in the trucking and other industries is concerning for the well-being of employees and maintenance of work-life balance. Not only do organizations face the possibility of employee dissatisfaction, burnout, and turnover, but also they risk facing lawsuits that arise as a result of mistreatment and on-the-job accidents.

What Is Flexibility?

The idea of creating work schedules that meet employees' needs and preferences is not new. Programs ranging from *flextime* (ability to control one's schedule) to *telecommuting* (ability to control where one works, often meaning working from home) have been discussed in the literature and widely implemented in many workplaces (Allen, Johnson, Kiburz, & Shockley, 2013; Hill et al., 2008). Additionally, *reduced work schedules* (working fewer than 40-hour workweeks, or working fewer weeks per year; see Chapter 6 in this volume) are gaining in popularity, although they may be somewhat controversial.

The definition of *flexibility* at work has been described as "the ability of workers to make choices influencing when, where, and for how long they engage in work-related tasks" (Hill et al., 2008, p. 152). Because we know individual differences that affect scheduling needs (e.g., chronotype) are extremely common, it is important for employees to have some control over their own schedules (Kerin & Aguirre, 2005). Furthermore, use of flexible work arrangements can lead to health benefits such as lower stress and burnout (Grzywacz, Carlson, & Shulkin, 2008), resulting in increased productivity (Shepard, Clifton, & Kruse, 1996). The availability of (and acceptability of using) flexible work arrangements is particularly important for "night owls," because they are at a disadvantage within the traditional nine-to-five schedule.

Utilization of Flexible Work Arrangements

Although many organizations are hesitant to adopt flexible policies, or to encourage employees to take advantage of them, some organizations have adopted flexible policies for various reasons. A common framework for articulating the purposes of flexible work arrangements involves a dichotomy of the *worker perspective* and *organizational perspective*, respectively (Hill et al., 2008). This framework notes the difference between granting employees schedules under which they will be successful (worker perspective) and hiring nontraditional schedule employees to save money, and therefore looking out for the well-being of the organization (organizational perspective; Kalleberg, 2001). As seen with just-in-time scheduling (scheduling employees at the last minute, typically on a week-by-week basis), some "flexible" schedules are beneficial to the organization but not to the employee.

Despite the known benefits of flexible work arrangements, research shows that only 28 percent of all full-time wage and salary workers vary their work hours (Beers, 2000). Sometimes, this variation is purely volitional. Other times, employees cannot find other jobs, so they must move to organizations that will match their life or chronotype demands, or they feel pressured to work additional hours in order to be successful. A major reason, cited by 55 percent of surveyed shift workers, that employees (such as night doormen or sanitation workers) work certain schedules is because their type of work requires it (McMenamin, 2007). This calls into question what it means to be a "good worker." Employees may see a vague promise of later job success and security if they prove their commitment by working additional hours (Snyder, 2016), but this can easily lead to what one sociologist refers to as "dangerous, anxious, or morally ambiguous territory" of overinvesting in one's work (Snyder, 2016, p. 165).

Why Flexibility?

Research shows that having the luxury to choose one's schedule may have significant positive influence on work outcomes. For example, a study conducted with night shift nurses showed that those who chose to work a permanent night shift (instead of being asked to work the shift) were better able to tolerate the demands of the night shift (Barton, 1994). Specifically, nurses who chose to work the night shift experienced significantly fewer cardiovascular symptoms and nondomestic disruptions in addition to less neuroticism, job dissatisfaction, and domestic disruption compared to those who did not choose the shift. Overall, research suggests that those who have the least control over their work schedules may be least likely to report adequate work-life balance (Williams, 2008). The next section examines why people are not able to access their preferred schedules and the impact of little to no schedule control on work-life balance.

Intersectional Issues in Access to Flexible Work Arrangements

There are several reasons employees are not granted the work schedules that match their needs, despite the fact that many employees seek flexibility (Richman, Burrus, Buxbaum, Shannon, & Yai, 2009). This lack of flexible or ideal scheduling may be attributable to gender, race, socioeconomic status, chronotype, sector of work, location, lack of unionization, familial obligations, organizational support for schedule changes and flexibility, organizational tenure, or a combination of several of these factors. Intersectionality here refers to the fact that schedule access can be affected by compounded multiple individual differences, such that some employees are more likely than others to experience stigmatization based on these factors. Indeed, there may be significant negative outcomes of flexible schedule inaccessibility for both organizations and employees. As one example, research shows that turnover rates are twice as high for people who cannot access necessary schedule changes compared to those who have access to flexible schedules (Richman et al., 2009). Mills and colleagues also discuss this at length in Chapter 2 of this volume. If managers do not respect employees' time, it is no wonder that some employees want to quit their jobs.

Socioeconomic Status

Literature shows that socioeconomic status can affect schedule outcomes, as upper-class professional employees tend to have more stable schedules and available flexibility, contrasted with lower-class workers, who are less likely to have predictable schedules and flexibility benefits (Williams & Boushey, 2010). Interestingly, professional employees may not actually benefit from higher levels of flexibility because the long hours that their work requires can limit their opportunity for achieving work-life balance (Williams & Boushey, 2010; see Mills, 2017).

On the other hand, low-income employees often face problems such as mandatory overtime, "just-in-time" scheduling, and generally nonflexible schedules that can lead to turnover and negative health, family, and individual/psychological outcomes. Because some employees are not able to work regular full-time jobs (often because of childcare responsibilities), many employees are forced to work nonstandard jobs, which tend to be lower paying and can offer the lowest amount of actual schedule control (Kalleberg, Reskin, & Hudson, 2000). In fact, in one study, 97 percent of low-income employees were not able to adjust their work schedules (Williams & Boushey, 2010). In the face of such challenges, many low-income workers are forced to quit their jobs to meet life demands and may view this as an expected outcome of their employment. Employees whose organizations will not work with their schedules may be unable to hold stable employment and may suffer financial consequences.

Additionally, a lack of flexible options in low-wage jobs can make it difficult for employees to receive promotions and achieve seniority. If employees do advance to a high-ranking position in the workforce, their workload may prevent them from utilizing the time off they have earned (Richman et al., 2009). In the words of Benjamin Snyder, flexible capitalism has given rise to disorienting mantras such as "hurry up and wait" and "relax as quickly as possible so you can recover." Indeed, employees may be left peering out at the "horizon of expectation" (Snyder, 2016, p. 198) while never quite reaching the ultimate goals of career success and work-life balance.

Race

Research exploring the link between race and flexibility outcomes has also emerged in the literature, suggesting people of color are already more likely to be discriminated against in the workplace compared to white employees, especially in subtle ways (Deitch, Barsky, Butz, Chan, Brief, & Bradley, 2003). Furthermore, ethnic minority employees are less likely to receive flexible schedules and more likely to incur discrimination if they do change their schedules as compared to white employees. In fact, Rudman and Mescher (2013) found that black employees who took family leave were more likely than white employees to experience penalties at work such as demotion or even termination. As a result, it is less likely that ethnic minority employees (compared to white employees) request or actually use flexible work arrangements, even if it would lead to better work-life balance, chronotype-work schedule match, or management of nonwork responsibilities such as childcare. For example, a case cited by Williams and Boushey (2010) described a black woman whose necessary flexible schedule reverted to traditional hours in retaliation for filing a race discrimination complaint. Additionally, there is overlap between scheduling issues, race, and work-family conflict. For example, according to the US Census Bureau, one-third of black and Latino children who are left alone while parents are working are forced to stay inside because they live in dangerous neighborhoods (Williams & Boushey, 2010). This lack of exposure to sunlight and stimulation outside the home can be incredibly detrimental to children's development and emotional and physical well-being, although schedule control can easily improve the situation.

Immigrant Employees

There are also many examples demonstrating the increased challenges immigrants face concerning their work schedules. For example, in the United States, research suggests that immigrants work riskier jobs than nonimmigrants (Orrenius & Zavodny, 2009) and commonly work night-shift jobs. One study noted a sizeable gap in sleep duration among African/Caribbean immigrants and whites, but specifically found that a large portion of the gap can be explained by socioeconomic conditions and exposure to night-shift work (Ertel, Berkman, & Buxton, 2011). In a study of Muslim immigrants to the United States and Canada, nonstandard work schedules (shift work and weekend work) were linked to higher job stress and less leisure time spent with family and friends compared to standard work schedules (Jamal & Badawi, 1995).

Furthermore, undocumented immigrants may be subject to unjust working conditions and lack of control over their schedules (Heyman, 1998). Specifically, Heyman's work (1998) outlines evidence of increased likelihood of workplace discrimination, exploitation, and low wages for undocumented Mexican immigrants. Commentaries on the matter indicate that immigrants are less likely to report discrimination, request higher wages, or seek schedule changes than nonimmigrants out of fear of legal backlash (Schulz, 1998). This has especially been the case in US meatpacking plants, an industry comprised of an estimated 50 percent or more immigrant labor (Champlin & Hake, 2006), employing large populations of immigrants since before the dawn of the 20th century (Commons, 1904). Specifically, a report on Midwestern meatpacking plants noted that Hispanic and Asian immigrant workers often work double shifts and overtime for low wages and tend not to unionize (Griffith, Broadway, and Stull, 1995), thereby reducing employee control over work. Furthermore, immigrant workers in these rural Midwestern communities have experienced housing shortages, racial violence, low-quality education for their children, and discrimination, in and outside of the plants (Dalla, Ellis, & Cramer, 2005). Even if immigrant employees are not experiencing overt mistreatment at work, literature implies that there may be unique work-life challenges faced by immigrant employees, especially if they are undocumented.

Gender and Work-Family Culture

Other factors that may impact access to flexible work schedules are familial obligations, employment in an organization that supports flexible work arrangements (Allen, 2001; Thompson, Beauvais, & Lyness, 1999), and organizational tenure. Research has shown that the mere existence of flexible policies is not enough to make employees feel justified and safe in using them; organizations must create a culture that is accepting of flexibility (see Chapter 2 in this volume; Thompson et al., 1999). Indeed, literature notes that lack of manager support for flexibility is a common barrier to availability of flexible work arrangements, along with a lack of information about flexible options (Richman, Johnson, & Noble, 2011). Commonly, organizations support flexible work arrangements as a means of promoting a family-supportive environment. Allen (2001), for example, recognized the importance of family-supportive organizational perception in addition to family-supportive policies and family-supportive supervisors in order to decrease work-family conflict and reduce perceived stigma. Thompson and colleagues (1999) tout the benefits of successfully building a work-family culture, which can include increased utilization of work-family benefits (e.g., job sharing, part-time return-to-work programs, and on-site childcare) and employee affective commitment. Additionally, employees with greater organizational tenure may utilize flexible policies more so than employees with less tenure, presumably because they possess the status that comes with seniority, which can serve to buffer negative consequences (Lambert, Marler, & Gueutal, 2008).

Because managers commonly view time spent at work as a measure of commitment to work, those who require flexible schedules to manage life demands can face stigmatization that in turn can lead to negative consequences. Possible consequences of flexibility stigma are numerous, nuanced, and far reaching. For example, Cech and Blair-Loy (2014) found that in a sample of academic scientists and engineers, employees who perceived flexibility stigma (thought others saw them as uncommitted employees, especially if they were parents) had lower persistence intentions, work-life balance, and job satisfaction than nonstigmatized employees. In the case of professional women, many have accepted flexibility stigma as a norm and do not view actions based on stigmatization as discrimination. As a result, such women may simply leave professional careers because they assume they will not be granted flexible schedules (Stone & Hernandez, 2013). Indeed, research suggests that women and minorities are more likely to be held to stringent time norms compared to men (i.e., more backlash for deviating from schedule norms; Epstein & Kalleberg, 2004) and are less likely to be promoted because of their scheduling needs (Epstein, Seron, Oglensky, & Saute, 2014). Overall, flexibility bias based on gender is complex. For example, both men and women can be victims of flexibility bias but for different reasons: Men may receive a fatherhood bonus for simply having children (Hodges & Budig, 2010) but experience discrimination (perceived as less of a man) and be viewed as less committed to the organization for taking time off for caregiving. On the other hand, women may be viewed as unreliable employees if they have children (although motherhood is a societal expectation of them) and get paid less, especially if they are in a low-wage job (Miller, 2014).

Schedules and Work-Life Balance

Several issues related to flexible schedules and schedule access relate to work-life concerns. We have considered the impact of flexible schedules, socioeconomic status, gender, work-family conflict, race, and immigrant status on employee outcomes. Many of these scheduling topics also intersect to affect overall work-life balance. Employees with lower income may experience unique threats to work-life balance. For example, work-life policies (such as flexible work arrangements) are generally more available to those in higher income brackets (Hammer & Zimmerman, 2011, p. 404). Even if these options are available to low-income workers, they may not be able to take advantage of these policies (e.g., family leave may be available but is likely unpaid leave). As a result, the workplaces of low-wage employees may be less sensitive to, and supportive of, employees' nonwork lives.

Work-family conflict is another concern that plagues those with low work-life balance and has specific connections to work schedules. Employees who are overworked, have rotating schedules, or have a just-in-time schedule, which often requires that employees be available at a moment's notice, tend to experience more work-family conflict. In fact, not only number of hours, but also an inflexible or unpredictable schedule, can result in more work-family conflict (Fox & Dwyer, 1999; Hammer, Cullen, Neal, Sinclair, & Shafiro, 2005). On top of such concerns, low-wage workers may also be more likely to experience work-family conflict than higher earners (Neal, Chapman, Ingersoll-Dayton, & Emlen, 1993). Work-family conflict can also spill over into the workplace, resulting in a feedback loop of possible negative outcomes. In a review of workplace safety, for example, Cullen and Hammer (2007) found that such conflict accounted for 7–10 percent of the variance in workplace safety outcomes, and called work-family conflict a "workplace hazard."

Marital and family relationships are also an aspect of nonwork life that can be affected when employers do not listen to employee schedule concerns. For example, employees whose work schedules do not allow them to see their spouse or children may experience negative emotions, such as feelings of guilt. Furthermore, research has assessed whether men and women experience these types of threats to nonwork life in similar ways. For instance, the relationship between family-to-work and work-to-family conflict and guilt may be moderated by gender role orientation, such that a traditional view of gender roles led to more family-interfering-with-work guilt, while an egalitarian view led to more work-interfering-with-family guilt (Livingston & Judge, 2008). Additionally, employees who are parents serve as role models to their children. Therefore, their experiences with work and affective reactions to work may influence the way children react to work and what they will later expect in the workforce. Literature refers to this as "parent to child crossover effects" and notes that children react more positively to work when they perceive parents have positive affective reactions to work (Porfeli, Wang, & Hartung, 2008), suggesting that whether or not an employer respects an employee's time can have implications not only for that employee but also for family members. Overall, when managers do not consider employee work-life balance when they offer schedules, they ignore outcomes (such as safety concerns and turnover threats) that are organizationally relevant and should be considered. When people do not have the schedules that work best for them, they can experience a myriad of consequences that play out in both their work and nonwork lives.

Considering differences in access to preferred schedules, we see that there are many reasons people do not have the schedules that are most advantageous for them. Lack of control over one's schedule can have many negative consequences. In general, employees need time to recover from work in order to function in the workplace and maintain good health. If people do not have satisfactory recovery experiences, which is more common with unstable or nonpreferred schedules, work and health problems may occur. In the next section, we will review major theories of recovery processes, why they are important, and consequences of insufficient recovery.

RECOVERING FROM WORK

Recovery has been defined as an experience that occurs outside of the workplace in response to everyday workplace stressors, restoring mood and decreasing physiological strain (Sonnentag & Fritz, 2007). Many employees, especially shift workers, do not get sufficient recovery time. In the absence of recovery, employees can experience negative health outcomes. Although work stress is often inevitable, employees and managers could benefit from better understanding how people recover from workplace stressors. By examining this issue, research can shed light on how to mitigate the psychological and physiological issues associated with a lack of sufficient recovery. This is also discussed in Chapter 3 of this volume.

CONSEQUENCES OF A LACK OF RECOVERY

Many employees are not sufficiently recovering from work and, as a result, experience maladaptive fatigue (Winwood, Winefield, & Lushington, 2006), decreased alertness, lower social satisfaction, and increased reaction time (Totterdell, Spelten, Smith, Barton, & Folkard, 1995). Additionally, a lack of recovery over long periods of time, such as a weekend, can lead to burnout and decreased general well-being (Fritz & Sonnentag, 2005). These consequences are a concern for managers because over time they can lead to increased turnover intentions (Kim & Stoner, 2008). Research has also shown that a lack of recovery can have adverse effects on one's health, such as fatigue and psychological overload (Sluiter, de Croon, Meijman, & Frings-Dresen, 2003), acute stress reactions (Geurts & Sonnentag, 2006), and increased risk of cardiovascular morbidity (Härmä, 2006). Fatigue scores are often used as a means of measuring recovery or lack thereof (Bültmann, Kant, Kasl, Schröer, Swaen, & van den Brandt,

2002). Fatigue is not inherently negative, as it is simply a result of exposure to work demands, but a lack of recovery time between two work periods can lead to negative effects, such as chronic fatigue syndrome (Sluiter, Frings-Dresen, van der Beek, & Meijman, 2001). Therefore, varying work demands and subsequent recovery needs should be considered when assessing the most effective recovery experiences.

THEORETICAL FRAMEWORKS

Recovery has been examined within multiple theoretical frameworks, but the dominant theories of stress recovery include conservation of resources theory (Hobfoll, 1989), the demands-resources model (Bakker & Demerouti, 2007), and the recovery model (Sonnentag & Fritz, 2007). We will review each of these theories in turn.

In *conservation of resources theory* (see Chapters 4 and 8 in this volume), Hobfoll explains that people's attempts to build and balance their resources are forms of recovery and that people view a loss of resources as a threat (Hobfoll, 1989). People strive to create an environment in which they will be happy and successful, and utilize resources in this effort. Specifically, *resources* are defined as objects, conditions (e.g., marriage or organizational tenure), personal characteristics (e.g., orientation toward the world and sense of self), and energies (e.g., time, money, and knowledge). Hobfoll also noted that social support is a pervasive and important resource across all categories. When people experience a loss of resources, they may attempt to recover by replacing the resources lost. Hobfoll cited the examples of a divorcee remarrying, a woman who has had a miscarriage attempting to become pregnant again, and an unemployed worker searching for another job. When lost resources are psychological, such as a loss of self-esteem, employees may try to regain these resources by creating conditions that lead to a positive feedback loop. Hobfoll noted that the way people interpret loss of resources (e.g., interpreting threats to resources as challenges) is an important factor that affects how they respond to and recover from stressors.

The *demands-resources model* (Bakker & Demerouti, 2007) extends the conservation of resources model by describing the combinations of job strain and motivation that are evoked by different levels of demands and resources. On the one hand, high-demand conditions, which may be characterized by high cost and potentially low gain, can lead to distress and physiological arousal. On the other hand, high demands are not always harmful. The model stipulates that resources are extremely helpful in responding to high demands. Specifically, Bakker and Demerouti (2007) proposed that when job resources are high, motivation should be high, even if demands are also high. Resources such as social support, performance feedback, and autonomy may be important antecedents to recovery because they motivate employee engagement and learning. Additionally,

Bakker and Demerouti highlighted that employees who have control over how they meet job demands may experience less job strain in multiple job contexts.

RECOVERY EXPERIENCES

Because employees experience recovery in different forms, Sonnentag examined specific recovery experiences outside of the workplace, defined as psychological detachment, relaxation, mastery experiences, and control-based experiences (Sonnentag & Fritz, 2007). *Psychological detachment* is characterized by "disengaging oneself mentally from work" (Sonnentag & Fritz, 2007, p. 205). Employees who work longer hours may have an increased need for detachment, but a higher workload can also make it much more difficult for employees to psychologically detach and, therefore, recover (Sonnentag & Bayer, 2005). Additionally, recovery experiences can only be defined as psychological detachment if they are unrelated to the job. For example, off-job social interaction is a common way to detach from work, but in the case of flight attendants, who constantly interact with others on the job, it can actually decrease well-being (Sonnentag & Natter, 2004).

In general, *relaxation* involves a "state of low activation and increased positive affect" (Stone, Kennedy-Moore, & Neale, 1995, p. 341). Relaxation experiences vary depending on the person and can occur at home or even during work breaks. One common setting in which relaxation occurs is on vacation, which can replenish resources that were depleted during the workweek (Fritz & Sonnentag, 2006). Regardless of the activity, relaxation results in a state of calm and increased positive affect (Sonnentag, Binnewies, & Mojza, 2008).

Mastery experiences involve effortful attempts to better oneself through non-job-related endeavors (Sonnentag & Fritz, 2007). Although mastery experiences require some resources, they can also serve as a form of recovery and reinforce a sense of personal efficacy (Bandura, 1977). For example, Rook and Zijlstra (2006) described the importance of physical activities (i.e., sports) as a means to aid recovery. Other types of mastery experiences can include taking a class or working on a new skill. Mastery experiences were also shown to be especially important for well-being when there is a lack of control (ability to make decisions) in the workplace (Siltaloppi, Kinnunen, & Feldt, 2009). Moreover, research has found that evening mastery experiences had a significant impact on positive activation (positive affect and high arousal) in the morning (Sonnentag et al., 2008).

Finally, *control-based experiences* refer to individuals' freedom to make choices during leisure time that they would otherwise not be able to make in the workplace (Sonnentag & Fritz, 2007). Perceived personal control refers to individuals' sense that they are able to influence their environment (Thompson, 1981) and is crucial to coping with health problems (Berkenstadt, Shiloh, Barkai, Katznelson, & Goldman, 1999). In one study, cancer patients who had higher perceptions of control adjusted better to stressful experiences, even if they were doing worse than other patients physically (Thompson, Sobolew-Shubin, Galbraith, Schwankovsky, & Cruzen, 1993). Indeed, evidence suggests that control is an external resource that aids recovery (Sonnentag & Fritz, 2007). Further, other research has emphasized the necessity of personal control for well-being given that humans naturally want to influence their environment (Greenberger & Strasser, 1986). Job control acts in a similar way to perceived personal control but is related directly to work. Indeed, employee control has been argued to be important for organizations because it can serve as a form of intrinsic motivation (Greenberger & Strasser, 1986). Additionally, personal control was found to have a significant positive influence on job satisfaction and performance in nurses and clerical workers (Greenberger, Strasser, Cummings, & Dunham, 1989).

Organizational Focus on Recovery

Taken together, research has shown that employees need more time to recover than they are currently allowed (Mohren, Jansen, & Kant, 2010). Unsurprisingly, evidence supports the notion that more working hours per day and per week can translate into more recovery time needed by employees (Mohren et al., 2010). Similarly, research supports the hypothesis that working a demanding job can predict higher recovery needs, which are correlated with a decreased sense of well-being (Sonnentag & Zijlstra, 2006). Not only do employees need more time to recover; it may also be more difficult for employees to psychologically detach, and therefore recover, when their workload is higher (Sonnentag & Bayer, 2005).

Recovery and Work-Life Balance

A lack of recovery can have some clear negative impacts on work-life balance. Especially if employees are working too many hours and have too many life demands to recover, they may experience physiological and psychological consequences, as cited earlier. However, the relationships among work, nonwork, and recovery experiences are complex. Generally, when people occupy multiple roles (e.g., mother and employee; caregiver and friend), these roles can provide benefits (resources) and stressors (Hammer & Zimmerman, 2011, p. 406). In other words, more responsibilities in different spheres will not always mean a lack of recovery or decreased work-life balance. Although we have noted that employees are not getting enough recovery time, having both an employee identity and a nonwork identity can lead to different resource gains from work and nonwork/family, resulting in increased recovery.

Social support, often found in nonwork or family life, has also been found to be an important resource for recovery (Hobfoll, 1989). Positive spillover of social support can occur from family to work such that recovery experiences are enhanced. For example, employees who have pride in their family tend to have increased job satisfaction and self-efficacy (Hanson, Hammer, & Colton, 2006). Conversely, a satisfying home life has been found to compensate for an unsatisfactory work environment (especially for blue-collar workers; Piorkowski, 1983). Overall, if employees have the time to foster and grow these supportive relationships outside of the workplace, they may experience enhanced recovery, but this requires employers to allow time for work-life balance.

WHAT CAN EMPLOYEES DO?

Employee control over their time is important for work-life balance and other physical, psychological, and economic outcomes. However, employees' ability to change their schedules can depend on industry, white-collar versus blue-collar status, and privileges often associated with different aspects of identity. It is crucial for employees to be aware of their rights in the workplace and to respond in whatever way they can to attend to issues that affect them and their coworkers. Although the onus of avoiding mistreatment should not be placed on the employee, it is advantageous for employees to look out for their own and others' health and safety. Unionizing is one way to achieve this. For time-related and schedule access issues that have not yet entered into law, such as chronotype bias, employees can make their employers aware of research that has been completed on the topic. Additionally, employees who have the option of flexible work arrangements should take advantage of the opportunity. Over time, as flexibility becomes the norm, flexibility stigma will be reduced.

WHAT CAN ORGANIZATIONS DO?

Organizations have a responsibility to ensure that work-life balance is a value that is upheld both formally and informally. Work-life policies instituted in organizations and at a public policy level have had consistently positive effects, explaining between 3 and 15 percent of variance in absenteeism, turnover, and performance (Hammer & Zimmerman, 2011, p. 403). Specifically, many work-life policies are related to the use of employee time and include scheduling options that are sensitive to individual differences (such as when an employee works best) and nonwork demands.

According to the literature on socioeconomic status and schedule control, adding flexible scheduling options means that low-income employees could be 30 percent less likely to change jobs in a two-year period as compared to employees who lack flexible options (Williams & Boushey, 2010). Furthermore, employers must recognize the culture they create when it comes to flexibility; simply offering flexible schedules and not blatantly discriminating against employees who utilize them is not enough to create a culture that is seen as respecting the work and time of its employees. Employers can ensure they are accepting of diverse applicants during the interview process by telling applicants that they want their employees to work at the times when they will produce the highest-quality results. During the scheduling process, asking about best times to work, based on caregiving responsibilities, chronotype, or other life needs, can also help to create a supportive culture, as would giving employees as much advance notice as possible about their work hours. Taking Google as an example, employers could offer off-site work, a "free day" each week to pursue relevant but noncentral projects, nap rooms, or employee-set schedules. Furthermore, it is apparent that employers have financial incentive to offer preferred schedules to employees, as sleepiness results in more accidents, injuries, lateness, and absenteeism, and decreased performance (Culpepper, 2010). By providing employees with more control over their time, they are likely to minimize time-based stress.

Upon review of the extant literature, it is clear that employers would be prudent to find ways to increase psychological resources for employees without increasing job demands. Introducing wellness programs and stress management workshops, allowing for more breaks during the workday, and providing consistent feedback (especially positive feedback) are all ways that employers can do this. Urban planning research suggests that simply including windows in offices can have positive benefits for employee well-being because they provide access to light and the goings-on of the outside world (recall the impact of natural light on entrainment processes; Kaplan, 1993). Access to vegetation via outdoor picnic benches, courtyards, and walking paths are also valuable possibilities for recovery during work breaks. Additionally, assessing what is blocking employees from recovery may prove helpful in determining ways to enhance recovery experiences. For example, Google recently conducted a study (referred to as gDNA) that essentially measured Sonnentag and Fritz's (2007) psychological detachment via an employee survey. They determined that 31 percent of employees are "segmenters" (are able to psychologically detach), whereas the other 69 percent are "integrators" (unable to psychologically detach; Bock, 2014). Using this information, employers can take action to ensure that those who tend to have trouble psychologically detaching from work are able to do so such that they sufficiently recover.

FUTURE RESEARCH DIRECTIONS

There is still a dearth of research on chronotype that empirically examines bias against night owls, characteristics of owls and larks, distributions of owls and larks across jobs, and ways chronotype can impact work and life outcomes. Studies show that managers tend to champion earlier chronotypes as higher in morality and conscientiousness, but more research could be done on the positive aspects of a late chronotype, such as creativity. Additionally, now that we know chronotype is biologically determined, we can conduct action research, which investigates the most effective ways to utilize chronotype diversity in organizations.

Furthermore, research on issues of intersectionality is crucial when attempting to comprehend the full picture of time in and out of the workplace. Some of this research has already been conducted (e.g., Jamal & Badawi, 1995), but few sources compile this information; rather, researchers have separated their samples of specific demographic groups, and relevant findings have remained isolated and largely forgotten. Additionally, literature reports a complete lack of research on nonstandard work schedules of visible minorities (Jamal & Badawi, 1995), despite the increase of ethnic minorities in the workforce. Research on time issues surrounding immigrant workers is also important. Issues facing immigrants are often overlooked in general, but this troubling lack of attention is compounded by the fact that immigrants tend to work shifts that are overlooked by workforce studies (Orrenius & Zavodny, 2009). As a recent news article (Ellen, 2012) puts it, night shift work can specifically be viewed as the "province of the immigrant, the poorly educated and low-skilled, students, itinerants, also the working elderly," and research should ensure that issues facing multiple demographic groups are represented in the literature.

In general, future research on recovery experiences may have far-reaching implications for employees and managers. If managers are aware of how employees best recover, they can plan to allow sufficient time for these recovery experiences. Additionally, scheduling changes could be implemented to allow for more stable shifts for day and night workers or for more recovery days after working an irregular shift. It is in the best interest of employees and managers for people to receive the recovery time and specific recovery experiences that they require in order to be high functioning during the workday, stay at their jobs, and maintain mental and physical health well-being, as well as maintain their nonwork identities. In addition, future research should more deeply explore the effects of job and academic demands and different measures of recovery. There are several research questions that have yet to be answered in this domain: Who is most likely to have certain recovery experiences, and how can employers encourage these recovery experiences? How are these experiences related to burnout, turnover, and other relevant outcomes? Understanding recovery processes will lead to an understanding of how the concept of time fits into work and life outside of work.

Using research to link the myriad ways in which temporal authority plays a role inside and outside the workplace may provide more comprehensive models of how we conceptualize time and what can be done to improve these conceptualizations for employee well-being and organizational health. For example, investigations of flexible scheduling can be used to determine the most advantageous schedules for different chronotypes. Establishing a greater body of literature on what it means to be at the extreme ends of the chronotype continuum can determine specific recovery experiences that are most beneficial for night owls and morning larks. Finally, examining how extreme chronotypes are treated in the workplace is a simple way to add valuable information to the quickly growing body of literature on workplace diversity and discrimination.

CONCLUSION

Time is power. Time is political, financial, gendered, racial, and geographically bound. Time affects all aspects of workplace experience: start and end times, deadlines, breaks, efficiency and productivity, and employee perceptions. Timing in the workplace also affects employees in ways that manifest outside of the workplace, such as individual health and emotional well-being, social connections, family life/work-family conflict, and recovery processes. The science of chronotype makes clear that we are all on slightly different clocks and should recognize the implications of these individual differences. The importance of time is not likely to go away, especially as the workforce becomes more global, technologically advanced, and unbound by conceptions of a traditional nine-to-five schedule. Keeping this in mind, we remain optimistic that applications of current and forthcoming research will use time considerations as a means of furthering organizational goals and employee work-life balance.

REFERENCES

Åkerstedt, T., Knutsson, A., Westerholm, P., Theorell, T., Alfredsson, L., & Kecklund, G. (2002). Sleep disturbances, work stress and work hours: A cross-sectional study. *Journal of Psychosomatic Research, 53*(3), 741–748.

Allen, T. D. (2001). Family-supportive work environments: The role of organizational perceptions. *Journal of Vocational Behavior, 58*(3), 414–435.

Allen, T. D., Johnson, R. C., Kiburz, K. M., & Shockley, K. M. (2013). Work-family conflict and flexible work arrangements: Deconstructing flexibility. *Personnel Psychology, 66*(2), 345–376.

Bakker, A. B., & Demerouti, E. (2007). The job demands-resources model: State of the art. *Journal of Managerial Psychology, 22*(3), 309–328.

Bandura, A. (1977). Self-efficacy: Toward a unifying theory of behavioral change. *Psychological Review, 84*(2), 191.

Barton, J. (1994). Choosing to work at night: A moderating influence on individual tolerance to shift work. *Journal of Applied Psychology, 79*(3), 449.

Beers, T. M. (2000). Flexible schedules and shift work: Replacing the 9-to-5 workday? *Monthly Labor Review, 123*(6), 33.

Berkenstadt, M., Shiloh, S., Barkai, G., Katznelson, M. B. M., & Goldman, B. (1999). Perceived personal control (PPC): A new concept. *American Journal of Medical Genetics, 82*, 53–59.

Blair-Loy, M. (2003). *Competing devotions: Career and family among women executives*. 1-271. Cambridge, MA: Harvard University Press.

Bock, Laszlo. (2014, March 27). Google's scientific approach to work-life balance (and much more). *Harvard Business Review*. Retrieved from https://hbr.org/2014/03/googles-scientific-approach-to-work-life-balance-and-much-more.

Bonke, J. (2012). Do morning-type people earn more than evening-type people? How chronotypes influence income. *Annals of Economics and Statistics* (pp. 105–106), 55–72.

Bültmann, U., Kant, I., Kasl, S. V., Schröer, K. A., Swaen, G. M., & van den Brandt, P. A. (2002). Lifestyle factors as risk factors for fatigue and psychological distress in the working population: Prospective results from the Maastricht Cohort Study. *Journal of Occupational and Environmental Medicine, 44*(2), 116–124.

Cech, E. A., & Blair-Loy, M. (2014). Consequences of flexibility stigma among academic scientists and engineers. *Work and Occupations, 41*(1), 86-110.

Champlin, D., & Hake, E. (2006). Immigration as industrial strategy in American meatpacking. *Review of Political Economy, 18*(1), 49–70.

Cheung, F. M., & Halpern, D. F. (2010). Women at the top: Powerful leaders define success as work + family in a culture of gender. *American Psychologist, 65*(3), 182.

Commons, J. R. (1904). Labor conditions in meatpacking and the recent strike. *Quarterly Journal of Economics, 19*, 1–32.

Cullen, J. C., & Hammer, L. B. (2007). Developing and testing a theoretical model linking work-family conflict to employee safety. *Journal of Occupational Health Psychology, 12*(3), 266–278.

Culpepper, L. (2010). The social and economic burden of shift-work disorder. *Journal of Family Practice, 59*(1), S3.

Dalla, R. L., Ellis, A., & Cramer, S. C. (2005). Immigration and rural America: Latinos' perceptions of work and residence in three meatpacking communities. *Community, Work and Family, 8*(2), 163–185.

Deitch, E. A., Barsky, A., Butz, R. M., Chan, S., Brief, A. P., & Bradley, J. C. (2003). Subtle yet significant: The existence and impact of everyday racial discrimination in the workplace. *Human Relations, 56*(11), 1299-1324.

Dominoni, D. M., Helm, B., Lehmann, M., Dowse, H. B., & Partecke, J. (2013). Clocks for the city: Circadian differences between forest and city songbirds. *Proceedings of the Royal Society of London B: Biological Sciences, 280*(1763), 2-14.

Ellen, Barbara. (2012, July 28). Unseen and ill-used: The plight of night workers. *Guardian*. Retrieved from https://www.theguardian.com/.

Epstein, C. F., & Kalleberg, A. L. (2004). Time and work: Changes and challenges. In C. F. Epstein & A. L. Kalleberg (Eds.), *Fighting for Time: Shifting Boundaries of Work and Social Life*, 1–21. New York, NY: Russell Sage.

Epstein, C. F., Seron, C., Oglensky, B., & Saute, R. (2014). *The part-time paradox: Time norms, professional life, family and gender*, 14. New York, NY: Routledge.

Ertel, K. A., Berkman, L. F., & Buxton, O. M. (2011). Socioeconomic status, occupational characteristics, and sleep duration in African/Caribbean immigrants and US white health care workers. *Sleep, 34*(4), 509.

Fox, M. L., & Dwyer, D. J. (1999). An investigation of the effects of time and involvement in the relationship between stressors and work-family conflict. *Journal of Occupational Health Psychology, 4*(2), 164.

Fritz, C., & Sonnentag, S. (2005). Recovery, health, and job performance: Effects of weekend experiences. *Journal of Occupational Health Psychology, 10*(3), 187.

Fritz, C., & Sonnentag, S. (2006). Recovery, well-being, and performance-related outcomes: The role of workload and vacation experiences. *Journal of Applied Psychology, 91*(4), 936.

Geurts, S. A., & Sonnentag, S. (2006). Recovery as an explanatory mechanism in the relation between acute stress reactions and chronic health impairment. *Scandinavian Journal of Work, Environment and Health, 32*, 482–492.

Giampietro, M., & Cavallera, G. M. (2007). Morning and evening types and creative thinking. *Personality and Individual Differences, 42*(3), 453-463.

Greenberger, D. B., & Strasser, S. (1986). Development and application of a model of personal control in organizations. *Academy of Management Review, 11*(1), 164–177.

Greenberger, D. B., Strasser, S., Cummings, L. L., & Dunham, R. B. (1989). The impact of personal control on performance and satisfaction. *Organizational Behavior and Human Decision Processes, 43*(1), 29–51.

Greenhaus, J. H., & Beutell, N. J. (1985). Sources of conflict between work and family roles. *Academy of Management Review, 10*(1), 76–88.

Griffith, D., Broadway, M. J., & Stull, D. D. (1995). From city to countryside: Recent changes in the structure and location of the meat- and fish-processing industries. In D. D. Stull, M. J. Broadway, & D. Griffith (Eds.), *Any way you cut it: Meat processing and small-town America*, 17-40. Lawrence: University Press of Kansas.

Grzywacz, J. G., Carlson, D. S., & Shulkin, S. (2008). Schedule flexibility and stress: Linking formal flexible arrangements and perceived flexibility to employee health. *Community, Work and Family, 11*(2), 199–214.

Hammer, L. B., Cullen, J. C., Neal, M. B., Sinclair, R. R., & Shafiro, M. V. (2005). The longitudinal effects of work-family conflict and positive spillover on depressive symptoms among dual-earner couples. *Journal of Occupational Health Psychology, 10*(2), 138.

Hammer, L. B., & Zimmerman, K. L. (2010). Quality of work life. *American Psychological Association Handbook in Psychology, 3,* 399-431. Washington, DC.

Hanson, G. C., Hammer, L. B., & Colton, C. (2006). Development and validation of multidimensional scale of work-family positive spillover. *Journal of Occupational Health Psychology, 11,* 249–265.

Härmä, M. (2006). Workhours in relation to work stress, recovery and health. *Scandinavian Journal of Work, Environment and Health, 32*(6), 502–514.

Heyman, J. M. (1998). State effects on labor exploitation: The INS and undocumented immigrants at the Mexico-United States border. *Critique of Anthropology, 18*(2), 157–180.

Hill, E. J., Grzywacz, J. G., Allen, S., Blanchard, V. L., Matz-Costa, C., Shulkin, S., & Pitt-Catsouphes, M. (2008). Defining and conceptualizing workplace flexibility. *Community, Work and Family, 11*(2), 149–163.

Hobfoll, S. E. (1989). Conservation of resource: A new attempt at conceptualizing stress. *American Psychologist, 44,* 513–524.

Hochschild, A. R., & Manchung, A. (1989). *The second shift: Working women and the revolution at home,* 258-262. New York, NY: Viking.

Hodges, M. J., & Budig, M. J. (2010). Who gets the daddy bonus? Organizational hegemonic masculinity and the impact of fatherhood on earnings. *Gender and Society, 24*(6), 717–745.

Isaac, E. (2014). Disruptive innovation: Risk-shifting and precarity in the age of Uber. *Berkeley Roundtable on the International Economy BRIE Working Paper, 7.*

Jamal, M., & Badawi, J. A. (1995). Nonstandard work schedules and work and nonwork experiences of Muslim immigrants: A study of a minority in the majority. *Journal of Social Behavior and Personality, 10*(2), 395.

Jones, C. R., Huang, A. L., Ptáček, L. J., & Fu, Y. H. (2013). Genetic basis of human circadian rhythm disorders. *Experimental neurology, 243,* 28–33.

Kalleberg, A. L. (2001). Organizing flexibility: The flexible firm in a new century. *British Journal of Industrial Relations, 39*(4), 479–504.

Kalleberg, A. L., Reskin, B. F., & Hudson, K. (2000). Bad jobs in America: Standard and nonstandard employment relations and job quality in the United States. *American Sociological Review, 65*(2), 256–278.

Kaplan, R. (1993). The role of nature in the context of the workplace. *Landscape and urban planning, 26*(1-4), 193-201.

Karasek, R. (1998). Demand/control model: A social, emotional, and physiological approach to stress risk and active behaviour development. *Encyclopedia of Occupational Health and Safety, 2*, 34–36.

Kerin, A., & Aguirre, A. (2005). Improving health, safety, and profits in extended hours operations (shiftwork). *Industrial Health, 43*(1), 201–208.

Kim, H., & Stoner, M. (2008). Burnout and turnover intention among social workers: Effects of role stress, job autonomy and social support. *Administration in Social work, 32*(3), 5–25.

Kirby, E. G., & Kirby, S. L. (2006). Improving task performance: The relationship between morningness and proactive thinking. *Journal of Applied Social Psychology, 36*(11), 2715–2729.

Lambert, A. D., Marler, J. H., & Gueutal, H. G. (2008). Individual differences: Factors affecting employee utilization of flexible work arrangements. *Journal of Vocational Behavior, 73*(1), 107–117.

Livingston, B. A., & Judge, T. A. (2008). Emotional responses to work-family conflict: An examination of gender role orientation among working men and women. *Journal of Applied Psychology, 93*(1), 207–216.

Martens, M. F. J., Nijhuis, F. J. N., van Boxtel, M. P. J., & Knottnerus, J. A. (1999). Flexible work schedules and mental and physical health. A study of a working population with non-traditional working hours. *Journal of Organizational Behavior, 20*(1), 35–46.

McMenamin, T. M. (2007, December). A time to work: Recent trends in shift work and flexible schedules. *Monthly Labor Review*, 3–15.

Means, B., & Seiner, J. A. (2015). Navigating the uber economy. *UCDL Review, 49*, 1511.

Miller, C. C. (2014, September 6). The motherhood penalty vs. the fatherhood bonus. *New York Times,* 1-4.

Mills, M. (2017). We're not there yet: Gender and the work-family interface in the modern workscape. In J. Nicklin (Ed.), *Work-Life Balance in the 21st Century: Perspectives, Practices, and Challenges.* Nova Science Publishers.

Mohren, D. C. L., Jansen, N. W. H., & Kant, I. J. (2010). Need for recovery from work in relation to age: A prospective cohort study. *International Archives of Occupational and Environmental Health, 83*(5), 553–561.

Mullins, H. M., Cortina, J. M., Drake, C. L., & Dalal, R. S. (2014). Sleepiness at work: A review and framework of how the physiology of sleepiness impacts the workplace. *Journal of Applied Psychology, 99*(6), 1096–1112.

Neal, M. B., Chapman, N. J., Ingersoll-Dayton, B., & Emlen, A. C. (1993). *Balancing work and caregiving for children, adults, and elders,* 3-268. Newbury Park, CA: Sage.

Nováková, M., Sládek, M., & Sumová, A. (2013). Human chronotype is determined in bodily cells under real-life conditions. *Chronobiology international, 30*(4), 607–617.

Orrenius, P. M., & Zavodny, M. (2009). Do immigrants work in riskier jobs? *Demography, 46*(3), 535–551.

Partonen, T. (2015). Chronotype and health outcomes. *Current Sleep Medicine Reports, 1*(4), 205-211.

Piorkowski, G. K. (1983). Survivor guilt in the university setting. *Personnel and Guidance Journal, 61*(10), 620–622.

Porfeli, E. J., Wang, C., & Hartung, P. J. (2008). Family transmission of work affectivity and experiences to children. *Journal of Vocational Behavior, 73*(2), 278–286.

Richman, A., Burrus, D., Buxbaum, L., Shannon, L., & Yai, Y. (2009). Innovative workplace flexibility options for hourly workers. *Corporate Voices for Working Families.* Retrieved from http://www.wfd.com/PDFS/Innovative_Workplace_ Flexibility_Options_for_Hourly_Workers.pdf.

Richman, A., Johnson, A., & Noble, K. (2011). Business impacts of flexibility: An imperative for expansion. *Corporate Voices for Working Families.* Retrieved from https://www. wfd.com/PDFS/BusinessImpactsofFlexibility_March2011.pdf.

Roenneberg, T. (2012). *Internal time: Chronotypes, social jet lag, and why you're so tired,* 1-234. Cambridge, MA: Harvard University Press.

Roenneberg, T., Kuehnle, T., Juda, M., Kantermann, T., Allebrandt, K., Gordijn, M., & Merrow, M. (2007). Epidemiology of the human circadian clock. *Sleep medicine reviews, 11*(6), 429–438.

Rook, J. W., & Zijlstra, F. R. (2006). The contribution of various types of activities to recovery. *European Journal of Work and Organizational Psychology, 15*(2), 218–240.

Rudman, L. A., & Mescher, K. (2013). Penalizing men who request a family leave: Is flexibility stigma a femininity stigma? *Journal of Social Issues, 69*(2), 322–340.

Schulz, J. (1998). Grappling with a meaty issue: IIRIRA's effect on immigrants in the meatpacking industry. *Journal of Gender, Race and Justice, 2*(1), 137–162.

Scott, A. J. (1994). Chronobiological considerations in shift worker sleep and performance and shift work scheduling. *Human Performance, 7*(3), 207–233.

Shepard, E., III, Clifton, T. J., & Kruse, D. (1996). Flexible work hours and productivity: Some evidence from the pharmaceutical industry. *Industrial Relations: A Journal of Economy and Society, 35*(1), 123–139.

Siegrist, J. (1996). Adverse health effects of high-effort/low-reward conditions. *Journal of Occupational Health Psychology, 1*(1), 27.

Siltaloppi, M., Kinnunen, U., & Feldt, T. (2009). Recovery experiences as moderators between psychosocial work characteristics and occupational well-being. *Work and Stress, 23*(4), 330–348.

Silva, I.S., & Costa, D. (2017). Non-standard work schedules and work-life balance. In J. Nicklin (Ed.), *Work-Life Balance in the 21ˢᵗ Century: Perspectives, Practices, and Challenges.* Nova Science Publishers.

Sluiter, J. K., de Croon, E. M., Meijman, T. F., & Frings-Dresen, M. H. W. (2003). Need for recovery from work related fatigue and its role in the development and prediction of subjective health complaints. *Occupational and Environmental Medicine, 60*(1), 62–70.

Sluiter, J. K., Frings-Dresen, M. H., van der Beek, A. J., & Meijman, T. F. (2001). The relation between work-induced neuroendocrine reactivity and recovery, subjective need for recovery, and health status. *Journal of Psychosomatic Research, 50*(1), 29–37.

Snyder, B. H. (2016). *The disrupted workplace: Time and the moral order of flexible capitalism,* 1-264. Oxford, UK: Oxford University Press.

Sonnentag, S., & Bayer, U. V. (2005). Switching off mentally: Predictors and consequences of psychological detachment from work during off-job time. *Journal of Occupational Health Psychology, 10*(4), 393.

Sonnentag, S., Binnewies, C., & Mojza, E. J. (2008). "Did you have a nice evening?" A day-level study on recovery experiences, sleep, and affect. *Journal of Applied Psychology, 93*(3), 674.

Sonnentag, S., & Fritz, C. (2007). The Recovery Experience Questionnaire: Development and validation of a measure for assessing recuperation and unwinding from work. *Journal of Occupational Health Psychology, 12*(3), 204–221.

Sonnentag, S., & Natter, E. (2004). Flight attendants' daily recovery from work: Is there no place like home? *International Journal of Stress Management, 11*(4), 366.

Sonnentag, S., & Zijlstra, F. R. (2006). Job characteristics and off-job activities as predictors of need for recovery, well-being, and fatigue. *Journal of Applied Psychology, 91*(2), 330.

Stone, A. A., Kennedy-Moore, E., & Neale, J. M. (1995). Association between daily coping and end-of-day mood. *Health Psychology, 14*(4), 341.

Stone, P., & Hernandez, L. A. (2013). The all-or-nothing workplace: Flexibility stigma and "opting out" among professional-managerial women. *Journal of Social Issues, 69*(2), 235–256.

Taillard, J., Philip, P., Chastang, J. F., & Bioulac, B. (2004). Validation of Horne and Ostberg morningness-eveningness questionnaire in a middle-aged population of French workers. *Journal of biological rhythms, 19*(1), 76-86.

Thompson, C. A., Beauvais, L. L., & Lyness, K. S. (1999). When work-family benefits are not enough: The influence of work-family culture on benefit utilization, organizational attachment, and work-family conflict. *Journal of Vocational Behavior, 54*, 392–415.

Thompson, S. C. (1981). Will it hurt less if I can control it? A complex answer to a simple question. *Psychological Bulletin, 90*(1), 89.

Thompson, S. C., Sobolew-Shubin, A., Galbraith, M. E., Schwankovsky, L., & Cruzen, D. (1993). Maintaining perceptions of control: Finding perceived control in low-control circumstances. *Journal of Personality and Social Psychology, 64*(2), 293.

Totterdell, P., Spelten, E., Smith, L., Barton, J., & Folkard, S. (1995). Recovery from work shifts: How long does it take? *Journal of Applied Psychology, 80*(1), 43–56.

Williams, C. (2008). Work-life balance of shift workers. *Perspectives on Labour and Income, 20*(3), 15.

Williams, J. C., Blair-Loy, M., & Berdahl, J. L. (2013). Cultural schemas, social class, & the flexibility stigma. *Journal of Social Issues, 69*(2), 209–234.

Williams, J. C., & Boushey, H. (2010). The three faces of work-family conflict: *The poor, the professionals, and the missing middle.* Retrieved from https://www. americanprogress.org/issues/economy/reports/2010/01/25/7194/the-three-faces-of-work-family-conflict/.

Winwood, P. C., Winefield, A. H., & Lushington, K. (2006). Work-related fatigue and recovery: The contribution of age, domestic responsibilities and shiftwork. *Journal of Advanced Nursing, 56*(4), 438–449.

Yam, K. C., Fehr, R., & Barnes, C. M. (2014). Morning employees are perceived as better employees: Employees' start times influence supervisor performance ratings. *Journal of Applied Psychology, 99*(6), 1288.

In: Work-Life Balance in the 21st Century   ISBN: 978-1-53612-526-9
Editor: Jessica M. Nicklin   © 2018 Nova Science Publishers, Inc.

Chapter 6

NONSTANDARD WORK SCHEDULES
AND WORK-LIFE BALANCE

Isabel S. Silva[*]*, PhD and Daniela Costa*
School of Psychology, University of Minho, Braga, Portugal

ABSTRACT

Working hours significantly influence the amount of time devoted to other areas of life. In fact, "free time" is often defined as time spent "off work." School schedules, television programming, and programming of cultural activities all tend to be coordinated outside the standard working hours in the majority of the active population. These work hours typically take place during the day from Monday to Friday and are commonly referred to as the "nine to five" schedule. However, due to changes in demographic (e.g., population aging), economic (e.g., increased competitiveness in markets and economic globalization), technological (e.g., greater computerization of jobs), and sociocultural factors (e.g., greater participation of females in the labor market and consumer expectations of extended periods of operation of services), an increasing implementation of different working hours has been observed. In general, such arrangements have been designated as "nonstandard work schedules." This chapter, based on a review of literature, aims to describe and discuss the main positive and negative impacts of nonstandard work schedules on the lives of individuals, especially in terms of family and social life. Specifically, the following work schedules will be examined: shift work, split-shift schedule, compressed workweek, and part-time and flexible working hours. The chapter concludes with recommendations for intervention.

[*] Corresponding Author Email: isilva@psi.uminho.pt.

NONSTANDARD WORK SCHEDULES AND WORK-LIFE BALANCE

Working hours have considerable importance in the temporal organization and operation of any society. According to Fagan (2001), work schedules are structured based on a combination of three factors: the number of working hours, the time of day and week allocated for work, and the degree of autonomy provided to workers. In this regard, working hours influence not only time spent at work but also time allocated to life outside of an organization. In this context, Boulin (1993) pointed out that utilizing time in a particular context depends on the way that time is used in another context, and therefore, the time dedicated to activities of leisure depends upon the time spent at work. The social organization of time is thus defined by the degree of interdependence and synchronization of various activities and is realized by the individual in three levels: (1) microlevel (i.e., individual and family life); (2) mesolevel (i.e., organization and companies); and (3) macrolevel (i.e., society). As further highlighted by Boulin, the three levels have different importance in the temporal organization of societies, as the mesolevel has determinant significance in the temporal structure of other spheres in an individual's life. For example, mass cultural activities or sporting events tend to be planned at the end of the "working day" or on the weekend, and the free time of an individual tends to be defined as the time available "outside of work."

Over the years, as a result of societal evolution, the organization of working hours (working time) has undergone significant changes. The most significant of these changes is the increase in prevalence of working hours designated as nonstandard, that is, working times that differ from conventional or standard hours. Until the middle of the 20th century, the working hours allocated to most workers from industrialized countries were "conventional" or standard working hours (Thierry & Jansen, 1998), that is, work from Monday to Friday, between the morning and evening, with time off on the weekends. However, in the second half of the 20th century, many developments triggered the emergence of workers operating at nonstandard working hours, in order to meet the changing needs of society.

As this chapter highlights, the growth in popularity of nonstandard working hours is predominantly owing to changes in the economic, technological, and sociocultural nature of society. For example, according to Olivetti and Petrongolo (2016), female employment in industrialized countries grew by half a percentage point per year between 1950 and 2005. Extending the research to include the years between 1950 and 2010, and limiting consideration to "economically active" women (i.e., those aged between fifteen and 64 years), the authors observed that in the United States, female employment increased by about 40 percent. While in 1950, only about 30 percent of economically active women were employed, by 2010, the rate was close to 70 percent. Similarly, in Portugal, female employment rates increased by about 50 percent between 1950 and 2010, from around 20 percent in 1950 to about 70 percent in 2010. The growth in the participation of women in the workforce has prompted changes in working hours and schedules, to allow for the joint management of professional life and family and domestic obligations. In this sense, Allan, Brosman, and Walsh (1998) stated that standard working hours were typically suited to men and failed to satisfy female necessities of family-work conciliation. In Table 6.1, a summary of the main changes in this context based on the literature (Boulin, 1993; Hewitt, 1993; Silva, 2012; Smith, Folkard, & Fuller, 2003; Tetrick & Quick, 2003) is presented.

Table 6.1. Economic, technological, and sociocultural changes in society and potential implications for working time management by organizations

Technological and economic changes	Sociocultural changes
• Globalization of the economy • Dissemination of information technology • Consumer demand for the availability of goods and services 24 hours a day • Strong competition within markets • Maximization of productive equipment • Adjustment of production based on market fluctuations • Increase in unemployment rates	• Demographic developments • Changes in lifestyle and career aspirations • Increase in average life expectancy • Increased female participation in the workforce • Increase in average age of workers • Increase in cultural and ethnic diversity of workers • Development of alternate occupational groups (e.g., self-employed) • Modifications in household and professional situations

NONSTANDARD WORK SCHEDULES

As mentioned earlier, the development of nonstandard working hours has been hailed by the professional sphere as the answer to an increasing need for extended operating hours by many companies. Working hours for some companies have been extended up to 24 hours a day, 365 days a year. According to Costa (2003), such arrangements often require alternate schedules such as shift work, part-time work, and compressed workweeks. Presser and Ward (2011) reported in the context of North America that it is problematic to define nonstandard work schedules, owing to the multiplicity of working schedules that are currently practiced. Regardless, it can be said that such a designation can be applied to any working hours that are somehow different from regular daily working hours (regular day shift), as is the case with, for example, a night shift.

In terms of the European context, according to the Sixth European Working Conditions Survey (Eurofound, 2016), a recent growth in atypical working hours has been observed. For example,

- In 2015, about 54 percent of workers from the 28 member states of the European Union were working at least one Saturday per month, which is a similar proportion to 2005 but higher than 2010 (51 percent). Further, 24 percent of workers reported that they work at least three Saturdays per month.
- Additionally, 30 percent work at least one Sunday per month, an increase of 2 percent in comparison to the years of 2005 and 2010. Eleven percent work at least three Sundays per month.
- In 2015, 19 percent of workers performed night shifts, which is an increase of one percentage point as compared to 2010.
- In terms of shift work, 21 percent of workers of the 28 members states of the European Union work in shifts, which is a considerable increase in comparison to the years of 2005 and 2010, where the shift work proportion was only 17 percent.

According to the National Health Interview Survey, the prevalence rate of nonstandard work arrangements in the United States in 2010 was 18.7 percent (Alterman, Luckhaupt, Dahlhamer, Ward, & Calvert, 2013). Men (20.9 percent) more commonly worked nonstandard schedules than women (16.4 percent). Other major demographic groups represented in nonstandard work schedules include workers aged 65 years or older (37.7 percent), workers with lower education (25.3 percent), and workers from the western United States (22.4 percent). In terms of shift work, the prevalence of such arrangements in the United States in 2010 was 28.7 percent.

Although implementing nonstandard work schedules is a solution for increased efficiency and operation capacity for companies, several negative aspects of these arrangements have been noted (Joshi & Bogen, 2007; Li et al., 2014; Strazdins, Clements, Korda, Broom, & D'Souza, 2006) in both the North American and the European contexts. For example, Davis, Goodman, Pirretti, and Almeida (2008), on the basis of two North American studies analyzing how different work schedules interfere with home life, concluded that night work was a particularly strain on a marriage and caused negative mood and fatigue (see also Chapter 5 regarding chronotypes). For these reasons, the creation of positive experiences in both work and family are difficult for those who engage in night work. The authors also observed that work on weekends caused more stress than work from Monday to Friday, regardless of the type of work performed. *White-collar weekday workers* reported less stress with work than white-collar weekend workers ("weekend"), and *blue-collar weekend workers* reported more marital problems than blue-collar weekday workers. Similarly, Albertsen, Rafnsdóttir, Grimsmo, Tómason, and Kauppinen (2008) conducted a review of 66 studies published between 1990 and 2007 that considered the relationship between nonstandard work schedules and work-family balance. All studies showed a relationship between work schedules that fell outside ordinary daytime work hours (8:00 a.m. to 6:00 p.m.) and poor work-life balance. Also, some of these studies found a correlation between nonstandard work schedules and decreased marital satisfaction and well-being of children.

Other studies have examined the impact of such schedule arrangements on conjugal and parental life quality. For example, Craig and Powell (2011) found evidence that parents working nonstandard hours, regardless of gender, spent more time in activities of paid work and less time on housework, on childcare, and in the company of children, in comparison to parents who worked at standard times. Begall, Mills, and Ganzebomm (2015) utilized data from the Netherlands Kinship Panel Study (NKPS) collected during two different temporal moments (moment one was 2002–2004, and moment two was 2005–2007), to investigate the relationship between nonstandard work schedules and the probability of couples having a first or second child. For this, they recruited 742 couples, out of which 432 had no children and 310 had one child at "moment one." The results of the study showed that, for couples that had no children and where the women worked a nonstandard work schedule, the probability of having a first child was smaller. On the other hand, for couples that already had one child and both parents working in a nonstandard work schedule, the probability of having a second child was higher.

More recently, Murtorinne-Lahtinen, Moilanen, Tammelin, Rönkä, and Laakso (2016) sought to study the impact of maternal nonstandard work schedules on family life. Specifically, the authors investigated the impacts of a nonstandard work schedule on single and married mothers and evaluated the importance afforded by these women to time spent with their families while working in such arrangements. In total, 20 Finnish women who worked nonstandard work schedules were interviewed, including 10 single and 10 married mothers. Both groups reported positive and negative aspects of such a schedule. Positive themes included satisfaction with time reserved for family, favorable working conditions, and successful childcare arrangements. Negative aspects raised by the women were the inverse of those issues previously presented: dissatisfaction with time reserved for family (married mothers) and concern for the well-being of children (single mothers), unfavorable working conditions, and childcare-related concerns. The authors concluded that single-parent families face more harm from nonstandard work schedules, and whether mothers experience more positive or negative aspects of such schedules depends on the extent to which regularity and unity between them and their families is created and promoted.

Åkerstedt and Kecklund (2017) analyzed the characteristics of working hours that were perceived by workers as being the most problematic. The most negative characteristics identified (reported by over 20 percent of workers) were short notice (i.e., the workers were informed about schedule changes less than a month in advance); a break between shifts of less than eleven hours; split duty (a break in the middle of working periods for longer than one hour and thirty minutes); working more than five shifts in a row; and working shifts lasting for more than 10 hours. Many of the difficulties associated with such features were of a social nature.

In short, many aspects of nonstandard working hours can create difficulties in managing the relationship between work and outside life. Next, each schedule arrangement—shift work, split shifts, compressed workweeks and long shifts, part-time hours, and flexible working hours—will be reviewed, examining the main difficulties and advantages of each in striking a satisfactory work-life balance. Prior to making such an assessment, a description of each working schedule will be provided, including a definition and consideration of its prevalence in the European and North American contexts.

Shift Work

Shift work has been defined as an organizational model where different teams work in succession in order to extend business working periods, to anywhere up to 24 hours a day (Costa, 1997). In addition to factors such as the number of working days and the start and end times of each shift, this system of work can be further classified based on whether or not working teams switch for different shifts. Shift work can be classified as either fixed (i.e., when working teams are always on the same shift) or rotating (i.e., when working teams switch periodically between shifts).

As discussed, 21 percent of workers from the European Union worked shifts in 2015. Of these, 48 percent worked rotating shifts (a decrease of two percentage points in comparison to the years of 2005 and 2010); 41 percent, fixed shifts (an increase of three percentage points as compared to 2005 and 2010); and 7 percent, daily split shifts (7 percent in 2005 and 8 percent in 2010). Only 4 percent worked under another type of shift work arrangement (5 percent in 2005 and 4 percent in 2010; Eurofound, 2016). In comparison, the percentage of shift workers in the United States in 2010 stood at 28.7 percent (Alterman et al., 2013). Men (29.4 percent) worked shifts more than women (28 percent). Other highly represented groups included workers between 18 and 29 years (43 percent), single workers (41.6 percent), and workers with a high school/GED diploma (28.8 percent).

Like all other working schedules, shift work is associated with both advantages and disadvantages for workers, based on the nature and function of the shifts in question. For example, the study performed by Silva, Prata, Ferreira, and Veloso (2014) based on Portuguese textile workers reported different advantages and disadvantages associated with each considered shift types and systems, including three types of fixed shift (morning, afternoon, and night) and a rotating system. The night shift and rotating system were perceived as having more negative than positive aspects, while afternoon and morning shifts were associated with more advantages than disadvantages.

Noted *advantages* of shift work for workers and their families centered primarily on financial and temporal aspects (e.g., Silva, 2008; Silva et al., 2014; West, Mapedzahama, Ahern, & Rudge, 2012). On a financial level, a shift allowance has the potential to increase the monthly income of workers, while in a temporal regard, shift work offers more free time to workers during the day, which can positively influence social and family relations (see, for example, Agosti, Andersson, Ejlertsson, & Janlöv, 2015). A study performed by Barnett and Gareis (2007) utilized a sample of 55 families with children, in 29 of which mothers worked daytime shifts between 7:00 a.m. and 3:00 p.m., and in 26 of which, mothers worked evening shifts between 3:00 p.m. and 11:00 p.m. Their research verified that the families where mothers worked evening shifts instead of daytime shifts achieved a greater coexistence and increased paternal involvement in the lives and activities of children. More recently, Carneiro and Silva (2015), with the aim of comprehending the advantages of shift work, gathered positive opinions of shift work as perceived by 110 health professionals (nurses and operating assistants), most of whom were married women. The commonly mentioned advantages included time flexibility, the nonexistence of routine, and weekdays off, which facilitate access to services that only operate during the working week.

Regarding the *disadvantages* of shift work, these are more commonly cited for night and weekend shift workers, or shift work during periods that are of high social or familial value. These can be divided into three areas: health, organizational, and family and social life (Caruso, 2014; Silva, 2012). In terms of impact on social and family life, the incompatibility of workers' shift times with the schedules of other family members and members of society can cause problems in marital and parental relations, as well as social lives (Dhande & Sharma, 2011; Handy, 2010; Li et al., 2014; Perrucci et al., 2007).

Tuttle and Garr (2012), using the *2008 National Study of the Changing Workforce*, gathered data from 3,051 participants, out of which 2,242 worked at conventional times, 441 worked shifts (i.e., afternoon, night, split shifts, and rotating shifts), and 268 worked under flexible arrangements. In general, it was observed that when compared with other groups, the shift workers noted greater work-family conflict. Also, Mauno, Ruokolainen, and Kinnunen (2015) studied work-family conflict and enrichment in three groups of workers with different schedules. Their study used a sample of 1,634 Finnish nurses, including 874 daily workers (i.e., those who worked normal working hours from Monday to Friday); 490 rotating two-day shift workers (i.e., those who worked rotating systems that included morning and afternoon shifts, seven days per week); and 270 rotating three-day shift workers (i.e., those who worked rotating systems that included morning, afternoon, and night shifts). The study results indicated that shift workers experience greater work-family conflict than daily workers; however, rotating two-day shift workers reported more work-family conflict than rotating three-day shift workers. Regarding work-family enrichment, no difference was reported between the groups. Still, in the context of work-family conflict, the relationship with marital satisfaction should be noted. For example, Minnotte, Minnotte, and Bonstrom (2015) studied the relationship between work-family conflict and marital satisfaction, based on data provided by 1,822 participants of the *2002 National Study of the Changing Workforce*. Their results indicated a negative association between work-family conflict and marital satisfaction.

Other studies, such as Han and Miller's article (2009), have sought to analyze the impact of working hours on the well-being of children. In this study, the relationship between parents' working hours and depression in teenage children was analyzed, based on data of approximately 4,200 children from the US National Longitudinal Survey of Youth (NLSY). Fifty-four percent were white, 26 percent were African American, and 19 percent were Hispanic. The authors concluded that both families with mothers working night shifts and those with fathers working evening shifts were associated with unfavorable family environments (e.g., fewer meals together) and therefore a higher rate of depression in teens. In addition, Han and Fox (2011) found a positive association between shift work, or parents working night shift, and their children's learning difficulties in mathematics and reading.

Split-Shift Schedules

Another work arrangement that has been studied is the split-shift schedule. Though often included in the category of shift work, this arrangement is characterized by work at preagreed daily hours in split shifts, for example, instead of working eight continuous daily hours, a worker may work for four hours, take a two hour break, and then work for another four hours. According to Centofanti and colleagues (2016), this model is widely used in the transport industry, for marine workers, and in the health field. Split shifts can be fixed (e.g., six hours of work [from 8:00 a.m. to 2:00 p.m.] + six resting hours [from 2:00 p.m. to 8:00 p.m.] + six working hours [from 8:00 p.m. to 2:00 a.m.] + six resting hours [from 2:00 a.m. to 8:00 a.m.], and so on) or rotating (e.g., eight working hours [from 8:00 a.m. to 4:00 p.m.] + eight resting hours [from 4:00 p.m. to 12:00 p.m.] + eight working hours [from 12:00 p.m. to 8 a.m.], and so on). In Spain, this model is more common owing to the cultural practice of *siesta*, with many workers taking an extended lunch break, typically from 2:00 p.m. to 4:00 p.m. (Gracia & Kalmijn, 2016).

Chapela (2015) studied the effects of such working hours on the psychological well-being of workers, in terms of their daily use of time and productivity. To do so, he collected data from the 2002 to 2003 Spanish Time Use Survey (STUS). The author concluded that split-shift workers spent more time sleeping and making meals, and dedicated less time to domestic work, taking care of children, and leisure activities. Interestingly, the study highlighted that women compensated for the reduced amount of time spent on leisure activities on their days off, but men did not. In contrast, men compensated for spending less time with children on their days off, but women did not.

Gracia and Kalmjin (2016) studied the relationship between different working schedules and time dedicated to life outside work, including time for family, time spent with partners, time spent with children, and time spent on leisure activities with family. The work schedules studied included standard work time, between 7:00 a.m. and 6:00 p.m.; evening shifts, encompassing the period from 6:00 p.m. to 12:00 a.m.; and split shifts, defined as work hours between 7:00 a.m. and 2:00 p.m., followed by work hours between 6:00 p.m. and 12:00 a.m. With regard to family time, it was observed that split-shift workers and evening shift workers spent less time on family activities than workers who followed conventional hours. As far as couples were concerned, evening shift workers spent less time with their partners than split-shift workers. In terms of time spent together between parents and children, split-shift schedule workers reported less time spent with their children in comparison to workers of conventional hours. However, no differences were noted between groups in relation to family leisure time.

Compressed Workweek and Long Day Shifts

According to Baltes, Briggs, Huff, Wright, and Neuman (1999), a compressed workweek entails a schedule with a reduced number of days worked per week and, consequently, an increased number of working hours per day. For example, instead of working eight hours a day for five days a week, an employee works ten hours a day for four days a week. Thus, such timetable arrangements are categorized primarily by the number of worked hours and days (e.g., nine daily hours/four days, ten daily hours/four days, or twelve daily hours/three days). In this context, it should also be noted that long hours of daily work, that is, shifts exceeding eight hours per day, are sometimes a requirement, i.e., shifts exceeding eight hours per day.

In the European Union, the prevalence of long days of work (i.e., ten or more hours of work in a day) has progressively declined over the past few years. In 2005, the proportion of workers that worked ten or more hours a day was 36 percent, whereas by 2010 and 2015, this rate had decreased by four percentage points to 32 percent (Eurofound, 2016). In the United States in 2014, 43 percent of organizations allowed some employees to work on a compressed workweek schedule, and only 10 percent of organizations allowed all or nearly all employees to work for a larger number of hours per day on fewer days of the week (Statista, 2016b).

Like any other atypical work schedule, a compressed workweek brings both benefits and costs to workers. For example, in the meta-analysis conducted by Baltes and colleagues (1999), a compressed work schedule was positively associated with increased job satisfaction and satisfaction with working hours and performance. Absenteeism and productivity were not affected by this type of schedule. Considering specifically work-family balance, the meta-analysis by Bambra, Whitehead, Sowden, Akers, and Petticrew (2008) indicated that 19 studies found improvements in family relationships with the introduction of this schedule (e.g., increases in time spent on housework and increases in time spent with partners); five studies found deterioration in work-family balance (e.g., dissatisfaction with time spent with family); and four studies did not find any difference.

It is possible to identify several *positive aspects* of this work schedule. For example, Smith, Wright, Mackey, Milsop, and Yates (1998) investigated the impacts of changing from slowly or rapidly rotating continuous eight-hour shifts to twelve-hour shifts on the health and quality of life of workers from three Australian treatment stations. In total, 72 workers participated, divided into 12 teams of six employees each. The authors concluded that the changes in work schedule brought improvements in the domestic, social, and professional life of workers. Similarly, Mitchell and Williamson (2000) analyzed the transition of power station workers from an eight-hour daily schedule to a twelve-hour day, and results indicated improvements in domestic and social life.

A review of the literature by Knauth (2007), based on 105 English and German studies performed between 1970 and 2005, observed various positive aspects of extending daily working hours. These included (1) less time and expenditure spent on travel; (2) more time for family and social lives; (3) more time for housework; (4) greater satisfaction with work hours; (5) fewer shift changes; and (6) less overtime. More recently, Brown, Bradley, Lingard, Townsend, and Ling (2011) studied the relationship between different work schedules and leisure activities. They concluded that a compressed workweek facilitated an increase in the amount of free time in common with others (i.e., household members and friends), which improved the welfare of workers and their family relationships.

However, not all the available evidence from Bambra and colleagues' meta-analysis (2008) supports the benefits of this working arrangement in terms of life outside the organization. For example, Todd, Robinson, and Reid (1993) examined the transition from an eight-hour daily schedule to a twelve-hour daily schedule for nurses. The study's first moment of evaluation occurred a month before the change; and the second moment, six months after its introduction. Here, it was observed that nurses reported greater dissatisfaction with working schedules in the second phase of the evaluation (i.e., when they were performing twelve-hour shifts per day), reporting an increased sense of having left their nonwork lives in the background, and less time for family activities.

Knauth (2007) also noted some other *negative aspects* associated with such a schedule, namely, (1) higher risk of work accidents; (2) reduction in the quantity and quality of sleep; (3) drowsiness, decreased alertness, and fatigue; (4) adverse effects on performance; (5) prolonged exposure to toxic chemicals; (6) adverse effects on health; (7) increased absenteeism; (8) problems with communication with superiors; and (9) higher risk of accidents when commuting from home to work.

Dall'Ora, Griffths, Ball, Simon, and Aiken (2015) studied how daily work hours (twelve hours or more per day) are related to burnout, job dissatisfaction, dissatisfaction with time flexibility, and intention to leave among hospital nurses. More than 3,100 professionals from twelve European countries participated in the study, and participants were divided into four different work schedules ($\leq$ 8 hours, 8.1–10 hours, 10.1–11.9 hours, and $\geq$ 12 hours). The study results indicated that nurses who worked shifts of twelve or more hours presented higher rates of burnout, greater dissatisfaction with work, less satisfaction with time flexibility, and greater intention to leave their jobs.

Part-Time Work

In Portugal, according to Law n°7/2009 of February 12 (Article 150), "Part-time work . . . corresponds to a normal weekly working period less than the full-time practised in a comparable situation." According to the Sixth European Working Conditions Survey, part-time working arrangements have steadily increased over the past ten years in the European Union. In 2015, the proportion of part-time workers was 20 percent, while this proportion was 18 percent in 2005 and 19 percent in 2010 (Eurofound, 2016). Within this range, the number of women in part-time positions has increased by two percentage points (from 31 percent in 2005 to 33 percent in 2015) and by three percentage points for men (in 2005, the proportion was 7 percent, whereas in 2015, it was 10 percent). Considering only workers aged between 20 and 64 years, 19 percent of EU workers were categorized as part time in 2015, which means there was an increase of 2.5 percent compared to the results from 2005 (Eurostat, 2016). According to the Statistics Portal, the number of part-time workers in the United States has increased by 2.63 million over the past ten years. While in 2005, 24.71 million Americans worked part time, in 2015, this figure had increased to 27.34 million (Statista, 2016a).

Regarding the advantages and disadvantages of this type of work arrangement, the literature has noted more positive than negative aspects in terms of work-life balance. For example, Burke, Dolan, and Fiksenbaum (2013) studied the differences between full-time and part-time workers. The authors collected data from 2,094 nurses who worked in Spain. The main reasons given by part-time workers as to why this time arrangement was preferable were taking care of family members (children and partners), health problems, and to remain active in their profession (i.e., to not get fired). However, the study also pointed out that part-time nurses reported a work environment and attitude less favorable to working and, consequentially, lower levels of involvement in work and less affective commitment.

The literature has identified several *positive aspects* of part-time work, especially where these arrangements are associated with female workers. For example, Higgins, Duxbury, and Johnson (2000) studied the impacts of different work arrangements on the work-home balance, using two different sources of data, a Canadian study related to work-family balance, and data collected in specific interviews about the advantages and disadvantages of part time. The authors concluded that for women, part-time work was associated with lower work-family interference, better time management capacity, and greater satisfaction with life. Accordingly, Hill, Märtinson, Ferris, and Baker (2004) studied 687 women who worked, had at least one child in preschool aged less than five years old, and lived with the child at least half of the time. Their research showed evidence that mothers who worked part time reported greater work-life balance, when compared to mothers who worked full time. Warren (2010) used data from Wave 7 of the Users Database of the European Community Household Panel Survey, a questionnaire aimed at collecting information regarding income, poverty, housing, and other factors in some European countries. The author found evidence that working fewer hours per week contributed to the welfare of women in many countries, by generating greater satisfaction with work schedules and the amount of time available for leisure activities. Other authors (e.g., Beham, Präg, & Drobnič, 2012; Buehler & O'Brien, 2011; Laurijssen & Glorieux, 2013) have also observed similar positive associations between part-time employment and work-family balance.

In comparison to these positive aspects, fewer *negative aspects* of part-time work and work-family balance have been noted. Booth and Van Ours (2008) found contradictory results in relation to part-time work for women. The authors aimed to study the relationship between part-time work and satisfaction with time, work, and life, and thus collected data from Waves 6 to 13 of the British Household Panel Survey (BHPS). Their results showed that women without children reported greater job satisfaction for part-time work schedules than those with full-time schedules but noted no change in satisfaction with life. On the other hand, women with children reported that part-time work schedules resulted in greater satisfaction with the work; however, full-time workers reported greater satisfaction with life. According to Beham and colleagues (2012), in addition to the benefits noted in the evaluation of part-time work, there are differences between professional (i.e., jobs with higher occupational status and authority, good pay, and career prospects) and nonprofessional (i.e., jobs with low status and wage levels, less safe conditions, and less access to family-friendly practices) part-time workers. The workers of nonprofessional part-time positions were the most satisfied, while professional part-time workers revealed levels of satisfaction with work-family balance that were significantly lower than their nonprofessional counterparts.

Flexible Schedules/Flexible Work Arrangements

Flexible hours of work are characterized by the degree of choice that workers have in some aspects of their work schedule, such as hours of starting and ending work, and taking lunch (Thierry & Jansen, 1998). In flexible work arrangements, employers provide workers with the option to choose when and where they intend to work (Lambert, Marler, & Gueutal, 2008). In such work schedules, arrangements such as flexible hours, part time, and telework, among others, are possible.

According to the Sixth European Working Conditions Survey, 26 percent of employees in the European Union in 2015 had the opportunity to take one hour off during business hours to resolve personal or family issues (Eurofound, 2016). On the other hand, 22 percent reported that they were only able to use free time to resolve work-related issues. According to the same survey, the majority of workers (56 percent) do not have the option to choose or influence the working times assigned to them by their organizations. To further highlight this, 43 percent of European workers reported having very regular working hours. In the United States in 2014, 27 percent of organizations reported allowing all or almost all of their employees to change the start and end times of their shifts periodically, and 81 percent of organizations reported allowing some workers to make periodic changes to the start and end times of their shifts (Statista, 2016b).

Russell, O'Connell, and McGinnity (2009) studied the relationship among four different flexible work arrangements, including flexible hours, part time, work from home, and job sharing, and the impacts of such arrangements on pressure at work and work-life conflict. The authors concluded that workers who worked part-time and flexible hours presented lower degrees of work pressure and work-life conflict, whereas workers who worked from home displayed increases in work pressure and work-family conflict.

Additionally, Masuda and colleagues (2012) studied the relationship between flexible work arrangements (flextime, compressed workweek, telecommuting, and part time) and different variables, including job satisfaction, turnover intentions, and work-family conflict. In total, 3,918 managers from fifteen different countries participated in the study and were separated into three groups: Anglo (i.e., 1,492 managers from Australia, Canada, the United States, New Zealand, and the United Kingdom), Asian (i.e., 1,213 managers from Korea, Hong Kong, Japan, the People's Republic of China, and Taiwan), and Latin American (i.e., 1,213 managers from Argentina, Bolivia, Chile, Peru, and Puerto Rico). The results of the study showed that the Anglo group was more likely to have flexible work arrangements available in comparison to the other two groups. The Anglo group also reported greater satisfaction with their work, less turnover intention, and less work-family conflict in comparison to the other groups. In turn, participants from the Latin American group who worked on part-time schedules reported lower turnover intentions and increases in strain-based work-family conflict. For the Asian group, a positive relationship between work-family conflict and teleworking was observed.

Allen, Johnson, Kiburz, and Shockley (2013) explained the relationship between work-family conflict and flexibility, based on four factors: (1) lack of differentiation between flexibility related to the location (i.e., flexplace) and related flexibility with the schedule (i.e., flextime); (2) lack of differentiation between use and availability of flexibility; (3) inconsistencies in the definition of work-family conflict; and (4) sociodemographic characteristics that may interfere with the relationship between flexibility and work-family conflict. To this end, the authors examined 58 studies with 61 independent samples, in the hopes of establishing that flexible work arrangements improved work-family conflict levels. However, it was found that many other organizational strategies focusing on support could have more beneficial effects on work-family conflict than flexible hours. Additionally, situations where flexible work timetables were available but not used were more negatively associated with work-family conflict than the use of flexible hours.

In terms of *positive aspects*, in a sample of approximately 6,500 North American workers, Hill, Hawkins, Ferris, and Weitzman (2001) found evidence that flexibility at work was related to improvements in work-family balance. Costa, Sartori, and Åkerstedt (2006) evaluated how variability (i.e., less fixed working hours subject to company decisions) and flexibility (i.e., less rigid planning of work schedules based on individual discernment and autonomy of choice) of work schedules influenced the health and psychosocial well-being of workers. For this purpose, they used data from the third European Survey of Working Conditions, which included 15 European countries. Evidence showed that greater flexibility and less variability were associated with more favorable effects in the evaluated areas. A justification offered by the authors for these results was the degree of control had by workers in choosing their work schedules, as well as the fact that fixed work schedules allowed for improved planning of additional organizational aspects (e.g., basic physiological functions and planning of daily life with the other members of the household and society).

Further, Hayman (2010) found evidence that flexible working hours reduced the negative impacts of work on family life (i.e., work-family conflict), as well as the negative impacts that family life may have on work performance (i.e., family-work conflict). Hayman also found evidence that flexible work hours contributed to increased well-being of workers, as well as satisfactory work-family balance. Similarly, Rawashded, Almasarweh, and Jader (2016) investigated the relationship between different flexible work arrangements (i.e., flexible hours, compressed workweeks, job sharing, and teleworking) and satisfaction at work and work-family balance. They collected data from 95 employees of a private airline in Jordan. The authors found positive associations between flexible work arrangements and job satisfaction, as well as between these modalities and work-family balance.

Although most studies have found benefits of flexible working hours in terms of work-family balance, there are some *negative aspects* associated with the implementation of flexible work. For example, Thornton (2016) found some problematic implications for a flexible work arrangement (i.e., possibility of working from home) in terms of personal and family life in a sample of Australian workers. While such an arrangement makes it easier for employees to care for other members of the household, such a possibility often reduces productivity and job satisfaction for work completed at home. The author identified the infiltration of the professional sphere on personal and family life, as well as increased working time in comparison to the daily hours worked in an office, as two main negative aspects of such an arrangement.

REFLECTIONS AND RECOMMENDATIONS FOR INTERVENTION

As mentioned earlier, working hours play a vital structural role in the lives of individuals. Indeed, "free time" is commonly defined as areas of individuals' lives that lie outside their work schedule. On the other hand, the chronological position of this "free time" during the day or the week strongly influences the availability of leisure activities with family or other members of the community. Nonstandard working hours, characterized roughly by a divergence in some aspect from what is considered to be conventional working hours, has been associated with both advantages and disadvantages for workers in terms of work-life balance. Therefore, the last section of this chapter provides recommendations for balancing working hours and private life for any managers in charge of time.

A critical aspect of the management of working hours and its impact (not only in work-family relationships but also in other spheres such as health—see, for example, Costa et al., 2006) is the degree of *flexibility* afforded to workers through this management. In fact, various studies have emphasized the importance of flexibility in adaptation to working hours.

Organizations may differ in the way in which they manage the issue of flexibility, that is, in the degree of involvement that they offer workers in the management of working hours. While some organizations encourage the involvement of workers (e.g., in the choice of shifts, the types of shift system used, or the possibility of changes to shifts), others tend to manage such aspects unilaterally. From a conceptual and practical point of view, it can be assumed that promoting the involvement of workers in the management of their own working schedules results in a need for organizational support to assist with managing the difficulties often associated with such.

If we consider the various idiosyncratic and unpredictable demands that often arise in an organizational context (such as a family member becoming sick or celebration of a friend's birthday on a given weekend), the flexibility that organizations offer their employees in the management of working hours (e.g., the ability to change a work shift) can, of course, facilitate the management of work-life interface. On the other hand, if it is recognized that certain nonstandard work schedules create greater difficulties from a family and social point of view (for example, shift systems that involve working evenings, nights, or weekends), flexibility becomes even more crucial in management.

Furthermore, offering flexibility may further facilitate accord between the demands of certain working hours (e.g., working at night or working hours that begin very early) and individual biological differences at a chronotype level (see Chapter 5 of this volume). In short, organizations differ in the manner in which they manage the temporal aspects of work, or to put it another way, in the degree of involvement that they do or do not offer workers in matters such as their assignment to different working schedules available within the organization, their response to requests for shift changes, and even their reorganization of working hours. On the other hand, the possibility of worker involvement has been associated with a better adaptation to working hours, both generally and in terms of work-life interface in particular. As such, *Recommendation 1* is that managers should encourage workers to participate in the management of their own work schedules.

Another key point is the importance of what is termed "family-friendly culture" (Thompson, Beauvais & Lyness, 1999), that is, an environment in which an organization supports those workers who are motivated by a better balance between work life and family life. Various empirical studies (e.g., Allen, 2001; Breaugh & Frye, 2008; Mills, Matthews, Henning, & Woo, 2014; Oliveira, Cavazotte, & Paciello, 2013) support the relevance of this type of organizational culture in attempting to understand the availability of both formal and informal family-friendly practices, and the impact of such on the reduction of conflict between work and family. These studies have drawn worldwide attention to the fact that the mere availability of organizational initiatives (e.g., flexible hours and part-time jobs) may be insufficient in guaranteeing their utilization by workers, since the workers may perceive the use of such as a cause for unfavorable treatment (see Chapter 2 in this volume). For instance, although a worker may prefer working part time to have a better work-life balance, he may not request it. This is because he perceives that the organization will think he is less engaged in her work. As a result, the worker may feel he will be penalized in her performance evaluation and future career promotions. Therefore, he may decide to continue working full time, even though he would rather work part time, for family reasons.

On the whole, and returning to the matter of organizational support in the management of working hours, in order for workers to feel they can express their working hour preferences with the intention of improving work-life balance, it becomes necessary for organizational culture to support such involvement. Otherwise, workers who may potentially be interested in certain working schedules (e.g., part time) will not choose them, due to the perception that management will penalize such a decision based on a view that the worker has less commitment to the organization. In this "management of expectations" between an organization and worker, supervisor support is thus a determining factor in balancing work-family relationships (e.g., Grzywacz & Marks, 2000; Hill, 2005), given their day-to-day role in decision making in aspects of work time management (e.g., whether or not to authorize an occasional change of shifts). As such,

Recommendation 2 is to develop a culture where the organization, and its supervisors, support work-life balance.

In terms of intervention, the role of organizations in promoting adaptation to working hours does not end in flexibility or perceptions of support. As suggested by Åkerstedt and Kecklund (2017), for example, it is important that managers inform workers of changes to working hours well in advance, and respect the recommendation of a minimum interval of 11 hours between shift changes, since such aspects of work schedules have been identified by employees as "big problems." So, *Recommendation 3* is that supervisors should consider the ergonomic recommendations in the design and management of work schedules.

The study of Wong and Ko (2008) on hotel employees enabled them to identify seven factors that would help to improve work-life balance, some of which refer to practices that organizations can adopt. Specifically, the following aspects were discussed: (1) having enough time for life outside work; (2) organizational support in work-life balance; (3) loyalty/fidelity to work (i.e., family support increases fidelity to work, and consequently positively influences work-family relationships); (4) flexibility in working hours; (5) life orientation (i.e., allowing a wider range of options to meet the needs of individuals at different stages of life); (6) voluntary reduction of work hours to satisfy personal needs (e.g., some employees prefer to work less and have more free time for personal life); and (7) interest in job security and career (i.e., the perspective of keeping their job or advancing in their career motivates employees to be more available for overtime work). Thus, our final recommendation is that organizational leaders should maximize the adjustment between the available solutions and employee needs, in terms of work-life balance. This is under the assumption that those needs change throughout life and that different individuals have different needs. In short, work schedules significantly influence the lives of workers, and supervisors can adopt time management practices to facilitate effective work-life interface. Despite the importance of this, as highlighted by Presser and Ward (2011), in contrast to the number of work hours, little academic attention has been given to the impacts of nonstandard work schedules. We hope that this chapter will contribute to the growing interest in developing this issue further, through investigation and intervention, in a way that permits the creation of win-win scenarios, in which organizations and workers can both achieve effective management of work schedules in general, and of work-life balance in particular.

REFERENCES

Agosti, M. T., Andersson, I., Ejlertsson, G., & Janlöv, A. C. (2015). Shift work to balance everyday life: A salutogenic nursing perspective in home help service in Sweden. *BMC Nursing, 14*(2), 1–11. doi:10.1186/s12912-014-0054-6.

Åkerstedt, T., & Kecklund, G. (2017). What work schedule characteristics constitute a problem to the individual? A representative study of Swedish shift workers. *Applied Ergonomics, 59*, 320–325. doi:10.1016/j.apergo.2016.09.007.

Albertsen, K., Rafnsdóttir, G. L., Grimsmo, A., Tómason, K., & Kauppinen, K. (2008). Workhours and worklife balance. *Scandinavian Journal of Work, Environment and Health, 5*, 14–21.

Allan, C., Brosnan, P., & Walsh, P. (1998). Non-standard working-time arrangements in Australia and New Zealand. *International Journal of Manpower, 19*(4), 234–249. doi:10.1108/01437729810220419.

Allen, T. D. (2001). Family-supportive work environments: The role of organizational perceptions. *Journal of Vocational Behavior, 58*(3), 414–435. doi:10.1006/jvbe.2000.1774.

Allen, T. D., Johnson, R. C., Kiburz, K. M., & Shockley, K. M. (2013). Work-family conflict and flexible work arrangements: Deconstructing flexibility. *Personnel Psychology, 66*(2), 345–376. doi:10.1111/peps.12012.

Alterman, T., Luckhaupt, S. E., Dahlhamer, J. M., Ward, B. W., & Calvert, G. M. (2013). Prevalence rates of work organization characteristics among workers in the U.S.: Data from the 2010 national health interview survey. *American Journal of Industrial Medicine, 56*(6), 647–659. doi:10.1002/ajim.22108.

Baltes, B. B., Briggs, T. E., Huff, J. W., Wright, J. A., & Neuman, G. A. (1999). Flexible and compressed workweek schedules: A meta-analysis of their effects on work-related criteria. *Journal of Applied Psychology, 84*(4), 496–513. doi:10.1037/0021-9010.84.4.496.

Bambra, C., Whitehead, M., Sowden, A., Akers, J., & Petticrew, M. (2008). "A hard day's night?" The effects of compressed working week interventions on the health and work-life balance of shift workers: A systematic review. *Journal of Epidemiology and Community Health, 62*, 764–777. doi:10.1136/jech.2007.067249.

Barnett, R. C., & Gareis, K. C. (2007). Shift work, parenting behaviors, and children's socioemotional well-being: A within-family study. *Journal of Family Issues, 28*(6), 727–748. doi:10.1177/0192513X06298737.

Begall, K., Mills, M., & Ganzeboom, H. B. G. (2015). Non-standard work schedules and childbearing in the Netherlands: A mixed-method couple analysis. *Social Forces, 93*(3), 957–988. doi:10.1093/sf/sou110.

Beham, B., Präg, P., & Drobnič, S. (2012). Who's got the balance? A study of satisfaction with the work-family balance among part-time service sector employees in five western European countries. *International Journal of Human Resource Management, 23*(18), 3725–3741. doi:10.1080/09585192.2012.654808.

Booth, A. L., & Van Ours, J. C. (2008). Job satisfaction and family happiness: The part-time work puzzle. *Economic Journal, 118*(526), F77-F99. doi:10.1111/j.1468-0297.2007.02117.x.

Boulin, J. (1993). The social organization of time. *Futures, 25*(5), 511–520. doi:10.1016/0016-3287(93)90093-9.

Breaugh, J., & Frye, K. (2008). Work-family conflict: The importance of family-friendly employment practices and family-supportive supervisors. *Journal of Business and Psychology, 22*(4), 345–353. doi:10.1007/s10869-008-9081-1.

Brown, K., Bradley, L., Lingard, H., Townsend, K., & Ling, S. (2011). Labouring for leisure? Achieving work-life balance through compressed working weeks. *Annals of Leisure Research, 14*(1), 43–59. doi:10.1080/11745398.2011.575046.

Buehler, C., & O'Brien, M. (2011). Mothers' part-time employment: Associations with mother and family well-being. *Journal of Family Psychology, 25*(6), 895–906. doi:10.1037/a0025993.

Burke, R. J., Dolan, S. L., & Fiksenbaum, L. (2013). Part-time versus full-time work: An empirical evidence-based case of nurses in Spain. *Evidence-Based HRM: A Global Forum for Empirical Scholarship, 2*(2), 176–191. doi:10.1108/EBHRM-02-2013-0001.

Carneiro, L., & Silva, I. S. (2015). Trabalho por turnos e suporte do contexto organizacional: Um estudo num centro hospitalar [Shift work and organizational support: A study in a hospital]. *International Journal on Working Conditions, 9*, 142–160.

Caruso, C. C. (2014). Negative impacts of shiftwork and long work hours. *Rehabilitation Nursing, 39*, 16–25. doi:10.1002/rnj.107.

Centofanti, S., Short, M., Hilditch, C. J., Dorrian, J., Kohler, M., & Banks, S. (2016). The impact of returning to a daytime schedule on sleep, performance and mood after simulated fixed and rotating split shift schedules. *Eat, Sleep, Work, 1*, 35–48.

Chapela, J. G. (2015). Split or straight? Evidence of the effects of work schedules on workers' well-being, time use, and productivity. *SERIEs, 6*(2), 153–177. doi:10.1007/s13209-015-0125-2.

Costa, G. (1997). The problem: Shiftwork. *Chronobiology International, 14*(2), 89–98. doi:10.3109/07420529709001147.

Costa, G. (2003). Shift work and occupational medicine: An overview. *Occupational Medicine, 53*, 83–88. doi:10.1093/occmed/kqg045.

Costa, G., Sartori, S., & Åkerstedt, T. (2006). Influence of flexibility and variability of working hours on health and well-being. *Chronobiology International, 23*(6), 1125–1137. doi:10.1080/07420520601087491.

Craig, L., & Powell, A. (2011). Non-standard work schedules, work-family balance and the gendered division of childcare. *Work, Employment and Society, 25*(2), 274–291. doi:10.1177/0950017011398894.

Dall'Ora, C., Griffiths, P., Ball, J., Simon, M., & Aiken, L. H. (2015). Association of 12 h shifts and nurses' job satisfaction, burnout and intention to leave: Findings from a cross-sectional study of 12 European countries. *BMJ Open, 5*(9), 1–7. doi:10.1136/bmjopen-2015-008331.

Davis, K. D., Goodman, W. B., Pirretti, A. E., & Almeida, D. M. (2008). Nonstandard work schedules, perceived family well-being, and daily stressors. *Journal of Marriage and Family, 70*(4), 991–1003. doi:10.1111/j.1741-3737.2008.00541.x.

Dhande, K. K., & Sharma, S. (2011). Influence of shift work in process industry on workers' occupational health, productivity, and family and social life: An ergonomic approach. *Human Factors and Ergonomics in Manufacturing and Service Industries, 21*(3), 260–268. doi:10.1002/hfm.20231.

European Foundation for the Improvement of Living and Working Conditions (Eurofound). (2016). Sixth European working conditions survey: Overview report. Luxembourg: Publications Office of the European Union. doi:10.2806/518312.

Eurostat. (2016). Part-time employment rate. Retrieved on November 10, 2016, from http://ec.europa.eu/.

Fagan, C. (2001). Time, money and the gender order: Work orientations and working time preferences in Britain. *Gender, Work and Organization, 8*(3), 239–266. doi:10.1111/1468-0432.00131.

Gracia, P., & Kalmijn, M. (2016). Parents' family time and work schedules: The split-shift schedule in Spain. *Journal of Marriage and Family, 78*(2), 401–415. doi:10.1111/jomf.12270.

Grzywacz, J. G., & Marks, N. F. (2000). Reconceptualizing the work-family interface: An ecological perspective on the correlates of positive and negative spillover between work and family. *Journal of Occupational Health Psychology, 5*, 111–126. doi:0.1037//I076-8998.5.1.111. ˙

Han, W. J., & Fox, L. E. (2011). Parental work schedules and children's cognitive trajectories. *Journal of Marriage and Family, 73*, 962–980. doi:10.1111/j.1741-3737.2011.00862.x.

Han, W. J., & Miller, D. P. (2009). Parental work schedules and adolescent depression. *Health Sociology Review, 18*(1), 36–49. doi:10.5172/hesr.18.1.36.

Handy, J. (2010). Maintaining family life under shiftwork schedules: A case study of a New Zealand petrochemical plant. *New Zealand Journal of Psychology, 39*(1), 29–37.

Hayman, J. (2010). Flexible work schedules and employee well-being. *New Zealand Journal of Employment Relations, 35*(2), 76–87.

Hewitt, P. (1993). *About time: The revolution in work and family life.* London, UK: Rivers Oram Press.

Higgins, C., Duxbury, L., & Johnson, K. L. (2000). Part-time work for women: Does it really help balance work and family? *Human Resource Management, 39*(1), 17–32. doi:10.1002/(SICI)1099-050X(200021)39:1<17::AID-HRM3>3.0.CO;2-Y.

Hill, E. J. (2005). Work-family facilitation and conflict, working fathers and mothers, work-family stressors and support. *Journal of Family Issues, 26*(6), 793–819. doi:10.1177/0192513X05277542.

Hill, E. J., Hawkins, A. J., Ferris, M., & Weitzman, M. (2001). Finding an extra day a week: The positive influence of perceived job flexibility on work and family life balance. *Family Relations, 50*(1), 49–58. doi:10.1111/j.1741-3729.2001.00049.x.

Hill, E. J., Märtinson, V. K., Ferris, M., & Baker, R. Z. (2004). Beyond the mommy track: The influence of new-concept part-time work for professional women on work and family. *Journal of Family and Economic Issues, 25*(1), 121–136. doi:10.1023/B:JEEI.0000016726.06264.91.

Joshi, P., & Bogen, K. (2007). Nonstandard schedules and young children's behavioral outcomes among working low-income families. *Journal of Marriage and Family, 69*(1), 139–156. doi:10.1111/j.1741-3737.2006.00350.x.

Knauth, P. (2007). Extended work periods. *Industrial Health, 45*, 125–136. doi:10.2486/indhealth.45.125.

Lambert, A. D., Marler, J. H., & Gueutal, H. G. (2008). Individual differences: Factors affecting employee utilization of flexible work arrangements. *Journal of Vocational Behavior, 73*(1), 107–117. doi:10.1016/j.jvb.2008.02.004.

Laurijssen, I., & Glorieux, I. (2013). Balancing work and family: A panel analysis of the impact of part-time work on the experience of time pressure. *Social Indicators Research, 112*(1), 1–17. doi:10.1007/s11205-012-0046-4.

Li, J., Johnson, S. E., Han, W., Andrews, S., Kendall, G., Stradzins, L., et al. (2014). Parents' nonstandard work schedules and child well-being: A critical review of the literature. *Journal of Primary Prevention, 35*, 53–73. doi:10.1007/s10935-013-0318-z.

Masuda, A. D., Poelmans, S. A. Y., Allen, T. D., Spector, P. E., Lapierre, L. M., Cooper, C. L., et al. (2012). Flexible work arrangements availability and their relationship with work-to-family conflict, job satisfaction, and turnover intentions: A comparison of three country clusters. *Applied Psychology: An International Review, 61*(1), 1–29. doi:10.1111/j.1464-0597.2011.00453.x.

Mauno, S., Ruokolainen, M., & Kinnunen, U. (2015). Work-family conflict and enrichment from the perspective of psychosocial resources: Comparing Finnish health care workers by working schedules. *Applied Ergonomics, 48*, 86–94. doi:10.1016/j.apergo.2014.11.009.

Mills, M. J., Matthews, R. A., Henning, J. B., & Woo, V. A. (2014). Family-supportive organizations and supervisors: How do they influence employee outcomes and for whom? *International Journal of Human Resource Management, 25*(12), 1763–1785. doi:10.1080/09585192.2013.860387.

Minnotte, K. L., Minnotte, M. C., & Bonstrom, J. (2015). Work-family conflicts and marital satisfaction among US workers: Does stress amplification matter? *Journal of Family and Economic Issues, 36*(1), 21–33. doi:10.1007/s10834-014-9420-5.

Mitchell, R. J., & Williamson, A. M. (2000). Evaluation of an 8-hour versus a 12-hour shift roster on employees at a power station. *Applied Ergonomics, 31*(1), 83–93. doi:10.1016/S0003-6870(99)00025-3.

Murtorinne-Lahtinen, M., Moilanen, S., Tammelin, M., Rönkä, A., & Laakso, M.-L. (2016). Mothers' non-standard working schedules and family time: Enhancing regularity and togetherness. *International Journal of Sociology and Social Policy, 36*(1/2), 119–135. doi:10.1108/IJSSP-02-2015-0022.

Oliveira, L. B., Cavazotte, F. S. C. N., & Paciello, R. R. (2013). Antecedentes e consequências dos conflitos entre trabalho e família. *Revista de Administração Contemporânea* [Antecedents and consequences of conflicts between work and family. *Journal of Contemporary Management*], *17*(4), 418–437.

Olivetti, C., & Petrongolo, B. (2016). The evolution of gender gaps in industrialized countries. *Annual Review of Economics, 8,* 405–434. doi:10.1146/annurev-economics-080614-115329.

Perrucci, R., MacDermid, S., King, E., Tang, C., Brimeyer, T., Ramadoss, K., et al. (2007). The significance of shift work: Current status and future directions. *Journal of Family and Economic Issues, 28,* 600–617. doi:10.1007/s10834-007-9078-3.

Presser, H. B., & Ward, B. W. (2011). Nonstandard work schedules over the life course: A first look. *Monthly Labor Review, 134*(7), 3–16.

Rawashdeh, A. M., Almasarweh, M. S., & Jaber, J. (2016). Do flexible work arrangements affect job satisfaction and work-life balance in Jordanian private airlines? *Business and Management, 8*(3), 172–184.

Russell, H., O'Connell, P. J., & McGinnity, F. (2009). The impact of flexible working arrangements on work-life conflict and work pressure in Ireland. *Gender, Work and Organization, 16*(1), 73–97. doi:10.1111/j.1468-0432.2008.00431.x.

Silva, I. S. (2008). *Adaptação ao trabalho por turnos* [Adaptation to shift work] (Unpublished doctoral dissertation in work and organizational psychology). University of Minho, Braga, Portugal.

Silva, I. S. (2012). *As condições de trabalho no trabalho por turnos. Conceitos, efeitos e intervenções* [*The working conditions in shift work. Concepts, effects and interventions*]. Lisbon, Portugal: Climepsi Editores.

Silva, I. S., Prata, J., Ferreira, A. I., & Veloso, A. (2014). Shiftwork experience: Worker's vision of its impacts. In P. Arezes et al. (Eds.), *Occupational Safety and Hygiene II* (pp. 651–656). London, UK: Taylor & Francis. doi:10.1201/b16490-115.

Smith, C. S., Folkard, S., & Fuller, J. A. (2003). Shiftwork and working hours. In J. C. Quick & L. E. Tetrick (Eds.), *Handbook of occupational health psychology* (2nd ed.;

pp. 163–183). Washington, DC: American Psychological Association. doi:10.1037/10474–008.

Smith, P. A., Wright, B. M., Mackey, R. W., Milsop, H. W., & Yates, S. C. (1998). Change from slowly rotating 8-hour shifts to rapidly rotating 8-hour and 12-hour shifts using participative shift roster design. *Scandinavian Journal of Work, Environment and Health, 24*(suppl. 3), 55–61.

Statista: The Statistics Portal. (2016a). *Number of part-time employees in the United States from 1990 to 2015* (in millions). Retrieved on November 10, 2016, from https://www.statista.com/.

Statista: The Statistics Portal. (2016b). *Percentage of U.S. employers allowing flex time to their employees in 2014*. Retrieved on November 13, 2016, from https://www.statista.com/.

Strazdins, L., Clements, M. S., Korda, R. J., Broom, D. H., & D'Souza, R. M. (2006). Unsociable work? Nonstandard work schedules, family relationships, and children's well-being. *Journal of Marriage and Family, 68*, 394–410. doi:10.1111/j.1741-3737.2006.00260.x.

Tetrick, L. E., & Quick, J. C. (2003). Prevention at work: Public health in occupational settings. In J. C. Quick & L. E. Tetrick (Eds.), *Handbook of occupational health psychology* (2nd ed.; pp. 3–17). Washington, DC: American Psychological Association. doi:10.1037/10474-001.

Thierry, H., & Jansen, B. (1998). Work time and behaviour at work. In P. J. D. Drenth, H. Thierry, & C. J. de Wolff (Eds.), *Handbook of work and organizational psychology* (Vol. 2: *Work psychology*; 2nd ed., pp. 89–119). East Sussex, UK: Psychology Press.

Thompson, C. A., Beauvais, L. L., & Lyness, K. S. (1999). When work-family benefits are not enough: The influence of work-family culture on benefit utilization, organizational attachment, and work-family conflict. *Journal of Vocational Behavior, 54*, 392–415. doi:10.1006/jvbe.1998.1681.

Thornton, M. (2016). The flexible cyborg: Work-life balance in legal practice. *Sydney Law Review, 38*(1), 1–21.

Tood, C., Robinson, G., & Reid, N. (1993). 12 hour shifts: Job satisfaction of nurses. *Journal of Nursing Management, 1*(5), 215–220. doi:10.1111/j.1365-2834.1993.tb00216.x.

Tuttle, R., & Garr, M. (2012). Shift work and work to family fit: Does schedule control matter? *Journal of Family Economic Issues, 33*, 261–271. doi:10.1007/s10834-012-9283-6.

Warren, T. (2010). Work time. Leisure time. On women's temporal and economic wellbeing in Europe. *Community, Work and Family, 13*(4), 365–392. doi:10.1080/13668801003765713.

West, S., Mapedzahama, V., Ahern, M., & Rudge, T. (2012). Rethinking shiftwork: Mid-life nurses making it work. *Nursing Inquiry, 19*(2), 177–187. doi:10.1111/j.1440-1800.2011.00552.x.

Wong, S. C. K., & Ko, A. (2008). Exploratory study of understanding hotel employees' perceptions on work-life balance issues. *International Journal of Hospitality Management, 28*, 195–203. doi:10.1016/j.ijhm.2008.07.001.

In: Work-Life Balance in the 21st Century
Editor: Jessica M. Nicklin

ISBN: 978-1-53612-526-9
© 2018 Nova Science Publishers, Inc.

Chapter 7

EXPATRIATE WORK-LIFE BALANCE: RESOURCES, WORK-TO-LIFE ENRICHMENT, AND WORK OUTCOMES

Kevin A. Byle[1,*], PhD, Jeffrey M. Cucina[1], PhD,
Laurel A. McNall[2], PhD
and Jessica M. Nicklin[3], PhD
[1]US Customs and Border Protection, Washington, DC, US
[2]The College at Brockport, State University of New York, Brockport, NY, US
[3]University of Hartford, West Hartford, CT, US

ABSTRACT

Increasingly, organizations send employees to work internationally, and these assignments are costly for organizations. As organizations become more global, the demand for highly skilled and specialized professionals to be sent to foreign locations is increasing, with organizations employing over 1.3 million expatriates from the United States (Van Vianien, De Pater, & Kristof-Brown, 2004). Because of the costs associated with placing expatriates abroad and importance of choosing the right employees for these assignments, there is a need to examine factors that are linked to the success of expatriate placements. This chapter explores the links among resources (i.e., coworker support and personality), work-to-life enrichment, and critical expatriate work outcomes (i.e., job satisfaction, burnout, and intentions to leave an international assignment early).

* Author Notes: The views expressed in this chapter are those of the authors and do not necessarily reflect the views of US Customs and Border Protection or the US federal government. A portion of this article was presented at the 125th meeting of the American Psychological Association in Washington, DC.
Address correspondence to: Kevin.Byle@dhs.gov.

Work in the 21st century is becoming more global as organizations seek to expand their international footprints. Consequently, expatriates are increasingly being deployed from an organization's home country to overseas settings for various periods of time. A 2012 survey of organizations reported significant growth in expatriate assignments (Brookfield Global Relocation Services, 2012). Having expatriate employees potentially benefits organizations by increasing liaisons and communication between headquarters and overseas employees. At the same time, being an expatriate can benefit an employee as it provides an opportunity to experience a new culture and gain perspective on the global role of an organization. However, the process of moving to a new country and adjusting to life overseas can be a strain to employees and their families and requires a period of adjustment. A longitudinal study of expatriates revealed that it takes about six months for them to adjust to their work assignments in the host country (Zhu, Wanberg, Harrison, & Diehn, 2015).

Unfortunately, many expatriate employees fail to adjust to their new environment. Failure rates of expatriates (i.e., the rate of expatriates prematurely terminating their overseas assignments) are high (20–40 percent overall and as high as 70 percent for assignments in developing countries) and costly to organizations (Dowling, Schuler, & Welch, 1999; Shay & Tracey, 1997). Harvey and Moeller (2009) estimated the cost of repatriating failed expatriates at between $200,000 and $500,000, resulting in approximately $6 billion in annual costs across all US companies. Even when expatriate employees are successful, expatriation is a costly endeavor for an organization and the employee. Figar (2016) suggested that the costs associated with expatriate workers is second only to the president of a company and can exceed $1 million per person, especially when housing, children's schooling, and other costs are included. O'Neill (2009) reported that a three- to five-year expatriate assignment can cost two to three times the expatriate's base salary.

Regarding employee costs, expatriates may face increased demands that reduce their work-life balance. For example, many expatriates report working extended hours compared to their home country positions. A 2007 survey reported that 66 percent of expatriates stated they worked longer hours in their host country compared to their previous home country positions; expatriates' workweeks increased by a mean of 13.4 hours (Shortland & Cummins, 2007). Shortland (2015) also reported that expatriates work longer hours and termed this the "expat factor" (p. 1452). Indeed, it is not uncommon for expatriate employees to be asked to attend meetings and phone calls with their home country colleagues during off hours. Many are also expected to attend networking and other events outside of their normal working hours.

Although many expatriates move to a host country with their family, others must maintain long-distance relationships with their spouses, significant others, and children. For those who expatriate with their families, the need for family members to adjust to overseas living adds an extra strain. Failure to adjust for even one family member can lead to an early termination of assignment. In addition, expatriates often leave their extended social contacts (e.g., extended family, friends, and acquaintances) behind and must forge new relationships and build a new social life within their host country. Developing new relationships requires an investment of time and psychological resources, which could set up further demands on the expatriate. Taken together, each of these factors may contribute to greater work-family conflict for expatriates, defined as "a form of inter-role conflict in which role pressures from the work and family domains are mutually incompatible in some respect" (Greenhaus & Beutell, 1985, p. 77). Indeed, van der Zee and colleagues (2005) found that negative spillover of an expatriate's demands influenced well-being for both the expatriate and his or her spouse. Moreover, Shaffer, Harrison, Gilley, and Luk (2001) found that work-family conflict positively predicted expatriate withdrawal cognitions.

However, the positive psychology movement has helped usher in a new era of research in the work-family interface, which emphasizes the potential for positive interactions between multiple life domains (see also Chapter 8 in this volume). In other words, balancing the demands of expatriate assignments with family and personal demands need not always result in conflict. Accordingly, Greenhaus and Powell (2006) defined work-family enrichment as "the extent to which experiences in one role improves the quality of life in the other role" (p. 73). For example, expatriates may develop new, high-quality relationships with their fellow expatriates or host country nationals at work, which help their family acclimate to their new surroundings, thereby experiencing greater enrichment. In other words, various forms of social support for expatriates may be critical variables for adjustment (Bhatti, Kaur, & Battour, 2013b; Shaffer et al., 2001). In addition, individual differences have been linked to expatriate effectiveness (Shaffer, Harrison, Gregersen, Black, & Ferzandi, 2006), which could mean that certain individuals are more likely to see the benefits of expatriation. Given the high-stakes nature of expatriate positions, there is a need for both researchers and practitioners to better understand the antecedents and consequences of expatriate work-life enrichment (WLE). Although it has been understudied relative to work-life conflict, WLE may be of great importance for expatriates trying to balance multiple life domains. Specifically, coworker support and individual differences may be two important resources related to enrichment, which could in turn drive important expatriate outcomes.

GOALS OF THIS CHAPTER

In this chapter, we review theoretical and empirical research on work-life enrichment as it pertains to the expatriate experience. Drawing on a model by Lazarova, Westman, and Shaffer (2010), we argue that resources can contribute to perceptions of WLE, which in turn can lead to important expatriate work outcomes. In addition, personal resources (coworker support and personality) may have a direct impact on these outcomes. Mediation analyses can shed light on whether personal resources directly impact outcomes or if the relationship is mediated by WLE. Next, we present the results of work we did with a group of law enforcement expatriates. Many law enforcement agencies, especially at the federal and national levels, deploy expatriates to host countries to facilitate cooperation with host country counterparts. We describe the quantitative and qualitative research we conducted with a sample of these individuals. Our quantitative findings examined the relationships among resources (coworker support and personality), work-life enrichment, and important expatriate work outcomes (i.e., job satisfaction, burnout, and intentions to leave an international assignment early). This work is important because it incorporates newer developments in the work-family literature. In particular, we expand our focus to study work-*life* enrichment, recognizing that nonwork domains go beyond the family and focus on one direction relevant to this sample: work-*to*-life enrichment, which occurs when work experiences improve the quality of one's private life. In addition, we focus on the positive side of the work-life interface to acknowledge the potential benefits associated with expatriate workers, an understudied area of research. Our qualitative findings include a realistic preview of expatriation and considerations that expatriates may not typically think about before taking an assignment.

EXPATRIATE WORK-LIFE ENRICHMENT

Lazarova and colleagues (2010) proposed a four-stage model integrating work-family enrichment with the expatriate literature. The model incorporates both the job demands-resources (JD-R) model (Bakker & Demerouti, 2007) and the conservation of resources theory (COR; Hobfoll, 1989; 2002). According to the JD-R model, environments with greater resources and fewer demands foster readiness to put forth effort to perform well. That is, resources can trigger a process that motivates employees to reach their goals and, at the same time, can also buffer the effect of demanding situations. This suggests that if expatriates can draw upon resources to help them more effectively navigate their new environments, they could in turn experience greater success and engagement in their roles. Similarly, COR is also used to help explain the enrichment process. Simply put, individuals strive to collect and maintain resources, and to ultimately accumulate "resource banks" to help them deal with stressful situations. Those with a greater number or higher quality of resources feel less threatened by stressful situations since they have a surplus of resources in their bank (see also Chapters 4 and 8). Thus, an expatriate with an abundance of resources may experience less negative reactions to an international assignment compared to someone with fewer or lower quality resources.

EXPATRIATE RESOURCES: COWORKER SUPPORT AND PERSONALITY

Lazarova and colleagues (2010) proposed a large number of expatriate resources and demands that could be categorized as general, personal, work, and family attributes. Given our focus on broadening the understanding of positive interactions between work and nonwork domains, we focused on expatriate resources and, more specifically, a work resource (coworker support) and personal resources (individual differences) that may be drivers of work-to-life enrichment.

Social Support

Greenhaus and Powell (2006) argued that social support is one type of social-capital resource that can be transferred from one domain to another. Social support is an individual's perception that they are "cared for and loved, esteemed, and valued, and a member of a network of mutual obligations" (Cobb, 1976, p. 300) and can be experienced from many different sources. The role of support has been examined extensively in the work-family literature among domestic workers (e.g., Thomas & Ganster, 1995). For example, higher levels of perceived support from various sources have been related to lower levels of work-family conflict (e.g., Ayman & Antani, 2008; O'Driscoll et al., 2003; Seiger & Wiese, 2009; Thomas & Ganster, 1995) and higher levels of work-family enrichment (e.g., Baral & Bhargava, 2010; Cinamon & Rich, 2010; Grzywacz & Marks, 2000). In a sample of expatriates, Shaffer and colleagues (2001) found that a lack of perceived organizational support prompted expatriates to think of leaving their assignments early, and noted that very little attention has been paid to expatriates' perceptions of organizational support. Along similar lines, Bhatti and colleagues (2013b) suggested that having a large host country social support network assists expatriates in adapting to a new culture by way of providing information about the culture and expanding expatriates' social reputation. One specific form of social support that may be particularly relevant is coworker support, which is critical to the current sample because they often work in teams of law enforcement expatriates, alongside large numbers of other expatriates at US embassies and consulates. This indicates that support, and specifically coworker support, may help individuals build upon and generate even more resources, making the enrichment process more likely. Thus, coworker support can be expected to have a positive association with WLE.

Personality

A considerable amount of research demonstrates that the big five personality traits are related to managing multiple role memberships in a variety of domestic work environments (e.g., Allen, Johnson, Saboe, Choe, & Soner, 2012; Michel, Clark, & Jaramillo, 2011). For example, Allen and colleagues (2012) found that negative trait-based variables (e.g., negative affect and neuroticism) are related to work-family conflict whereas positive trait-based variables (e.g., positive affect and self-efficacy) are related to less work-family conflict. Michel and colleagues' (2011) meta-analysis found that extraversion, agreeableness, conscientiousness, and neuroticism are related to negative work-nonwork spillover, while extraversion, agreeableness, conscientiousness, and openness to experience are related to positive work-nonwork spillover. Less research has been conducted on the relationship between personality traits and work-life balance in the international environment, but there is evidence to suggest that individual differences can have implications for expatriate work outcomes. We will review the personality dimensions (i.e., the big five, tolerance of ambiguity, and coping with change) in the following subsections, offering insight into how these personality traits may influence the expatriate experience, followed by the empirical research on personality, work-life enrichment, and expatriate success. The Big Five personality traits are the most established and commonly used taxonomy of personality (Digman, 1990). Tolerance of ambiguity (McLain, 1993) and coping with change (Judge, Thoresen, Pucik, & Welbourne, 1999) are more specific change-related personality characteristics that may be important when individuals expatriate overseas and could be helpful in understanding expatriate work outcomes.

Extroversion

Extroversion appears important for expatriate outcomes as extroverts are more likely to interact with strangers and take the initiative to build relationships with host country colleagues (Bhatti et al., 2013b). Indeed, many expatriates are sent overseas to build relationships with host country colleagues and represent the employing organization overseas. Additionally, expatriates must develop new friendships overseas to build social lives, and extroversion plays a role in developing new relationships. Thus, extroverted expatriates may more naturally cultivate coworker and other support networks overseas than more introverted expatriates.

Neuroticism

Neuroticism (which is emotional stability reversed) also plays a conceptual role in expatriates' outcomes as individuals low in neuroticism are less likely to experience stress and negative emotions and thus are more likely to be well adjusted. Bhatti and colleagues (2013b) suggested that emotional stability (i.e., low neuroticism) is associated with the ability to handle problems and unpleasant situations overseas. Taking a new position in a foreign country can be a stressful event for expatriates. A study by Valantin (2015) provided evidence of sleep problems, depression, anxiety, and alcohol use in expatriates in Hong Kong, which suggests that expatriates experience greater levels of stress. Thus, emotional stability may help expatriates better cope with stressful situations resulting in better adjustment and other work outcomes.

Conscientiousness

Conscientiousness has been shown to predict performance in nearly all jobs (Barrick & Mount, 1991), and this is likely no exception for expatriates. Individuals who are high in conscientiousness are more motivated to achieve and are dependable, which could relate to the quality and quantity of work overseas. Indeed, host country colleagues may prefer to interact with expatriates who are high in conscientiousness as they know these individuals are reliable and productive. Conscientious expatriates may also be more motivated to take steps to learn about and adapt to the host country.

Openness to Experience

Openness is also conceptually related to expatriate outcomes. Expatriates need to learn about a new culture and possibly a new language, and openness has been shown to predict training performance (Barrick & Mount, 1991). Openness also reflects interest in learning new things, mental flexibility, and imagination. These are traits that help an individual learn, comprehend, and understand a new culture.

Agreeableness

Although extroversion concerns the likelihood of meeting new people and interacting with others, agreeableness is related to the quality of those interactions. By quality, we refer to traits such as politeness, kindness, and tactfulness. These traits seem linked to interpersonal skills, which were related to expatriate adjustment ($\rho = .24$) in a meta-analysis (albeit with only two studies; Hechanova, Beehr, & Christiansen, 2003). Thus, it seems likely that agreeable individuals will be more likely to build quality relationships in their host countries than disagreeable expatriates. Agreeableness is also associated with a decreased likelihood for building negative relationships, antagonism, and being argumentative. Thus, agreeable expatriates are likely better able to adapt to their host countries.

Tolerance of Ambiguity

Tolerance of ambiguity is a personality trait or cognitive style that tends to influence decision making and the perception of new and unfamiliar situations (McLain, 1993). Individuals high in tolerance of ambiguity have a tendency to view novel experiences as desirable (Budner, 1962) and are comfortable with situations that are uncertain, incomplete, and vague. In contrast, individuals low in tolerance of ambiguity tend to avoid situations that are new and unique, are risk aversive, and prefer familiarity. Individuals scoring high in tolerance of ambiguity seem likely to better adapt to their new environments than their low-scoring counterparts. In fact, researchers have suggested that tolerance for ambiguity influences performance of expatriates (Arthur & Bennett, 1995; Mol, Born, Willemsen, & Van Der Molen, 2005), and the two studies to date that have examined the influence of tolerance of ambiguity on expatriate success have a meta-analytic correlation of .35.

Coping with Change

Coping with change is the response an individual in the workplace has to organizational change (Judge et al., 1999), and it consists of positive self-concept and risk tolerance. Individuals high in coping with change tend to embrace change, view change as positive, and feel comfortable with adapting to change. Individuals low in coping with change tend to react negatively to and experience stress during periods of change. While the construct was originally conceptualized as a response to organizational change, it may influence expatriate success while moving within the organization from one country to another, and managing the changes associated with that move.

Empirical Research

Personality may influence not only WLE but also expatriate outcomes. To understand these relationships, we can draw upon Friede and Ryan's (2005) framework that describes how personality may impact the work-family interface through several mechanisms, which can generalize to work-life issues among expatriates. For example, Friede and Ryan argue that an individual's personality will likely affect the manner in which a person perceives and responds to a situation. That is, expatriates may perceive their work-life situation as conflicting, but to others, it could be enriching. In addition, personality is likely to have an influence on the types of psychological resources and coping strategies that individuals draw upon during the stress of their new international assignment. Individuals with certain personalities may select more effective coping strategies, which may assist them in managing work and nonwork domains. Unfortunately, to our knowledge, no empirical research has investigated the link between expatriate personality and WLE.

Regarding empirical research on the link between personality and expatriate outcomes, Ones and Viswesvaran (1999) found that conscientiousness was perceived by expatriate staffing managers to be the most important personality factor for adjustment and completion of an international assignment, and openness was perceived to be important for completion of overseas assignment. Caligiuri (2000) found that extroversion, agreeableness, and emotional stability were negatively related to whether expatriates desire to terminate their assignment, and conscientiousness was positively related to performance. In a meta-analysis, Mol and colleagues (2005) found that all of the big five personality traits except openness were related to expatriate performance. Combining data from a handful of studies, regression analyses by Shaffer and colleagues (2006) reported that all of the big five personality traits predicted at least one important expatriate outcome (i.e., task performance, contextual performance, withdrawal cognitions, cultural adjustment, interaction adjustment, and work adjustment). They also found that other individual differences (i.e., cultural flexibility, task orientation, people orientation, and ethnocentrism) predicted at least one important outcome. Huang, Chi, and Lawler (2005) found that extraversion and openness were positively related to expatriate adjustment. Freeman and Olson-Buchanan (2013) reported that agreeableness, openness, and conscientiousness were related to adjustment variables. Bhatti, Battour, Ismail, and Sundram (2013a) studied the relationship between the big five personality traits, adjustment, and performance using structural equation modeling. They found that adjustment mediated the relationship between all of the big five traits on performance.

However, surprisingly, Stockert (2015) found that none of the big five traits were related to adjustment. Furthermore, historical Peace Corps research reviewed by Sinangil and Ones (2001) indicated that personality tests (and structured interviews) were not very successful predictors of expatriate success. The conflicting results of these studies suggest that further research is needed on the relationships between personality and expatriate outcomes as Bhatti, Kaur, and Battour (2013b) noted the lack of clarity in the research literature on this topic. Previous studies have also been limited by the scope of personality variables studied (only the big five) and have used samples that are limited to only a few countries in which expatriates might work.

OUR STUDIES

We conducted both a quantitative and a qualitative research study on a sample of law enforcement expatriates, an underresearched group. Many crimes and criminal organizations cross international borders. Suspects flee the United States for other countries; drugs and contraband are smuggled into the United States and money is smuggled out of the United States; criminal organizations have presences in multiple countries; and fugitives seek safe harbor in foreign countries. In order to combat transnational crime, many law enforcement agencies send expatriates overseas to serve as liaisons with their host country counterparts, to conduct training in host countries, to share information, and to build relationships. The purpose of the quantitative study was to examine the empirical links among support, personality, WLE, and expatriate outcomes. This work was conducted using an online survey administered to a sample of federal law enforcement expatriates. The qualitative study was conducted to collect narrative information on the work-life experiences of expatriates, which can affect expatriate outcomes.

Predictions

Based on our review of the work-family and expatriate literature, along with Lazarova and colleagues' (2010) model of the positive side of the work-family interface on international assignments, we hypothesized that a work resource (coworker support) and personal resources including extraversion and adaptability variables (i.e., openness, tolerance for ambiguity, and coping with change) would be positively related to WLE. In turn, WLE would be positively related to job satisfaction and negatively related to burnout and intentions to leave an international assignment early. Lazarova and colleagues' (2010) model also implied that WLE mediates the relationship between resources and expatriate work outcomes, and we tested this hypothesis with our data. Finally, we hypothesized that emotional stability (neuroticism reversed), conscientiousness, agreeableness, extroversion, openness to experience, coping with change, and tolerance for ambiguity would be positively related to job satisfaction and negatively related to burnout and turnover intentions.

QUANTITATIVE STUDY

Method

Participants

An online survey was administered to federal agents working internationally at US embassies and consulates around the world. The participants worked for a large federal law enforcement agency and served as liaisons between their agency and foreign counterparts. A census survey of expatriates was conducted, and 86 voluntary responses were obtained. Table 7.1 provides demographic information for the respondents.

Measures

Participants were asked to rate each item on a five-point scale labeled 1 (strongly disagree) to 5 (strongly agree) unless otherwise noted. The internal consistencies for the measures were all acceptable, as they ranged from .78 to .89.

Table 7.1. Demographic information on study participants

Variable	Frequency	Percent
Gender:		
Male	82	95.3
Female	4	4.7
Race/ethnicity:		
Caucasian	53	61.6
Hispanic	18	20.9
Asian	8	9.3
Other	7	8.2
Host country location:		
Central and South America	23	26.7
Europe	15	17.4
Asia	20	23.3
Greater Middle East	23	26.7
North American (e.g., Canada)	4	5.9
	N	
Total number of countries represented[a]	38	
	Mean	*SD*
Age	41.6	6.48

Note: Total $N = 86$; [a] Many countries had more than one participant.

- *Coworker support.* A modified, three-item version of the Survey of Perceived Organizational Support (Eisenberger, Huntington, Hutchinson, & Sowa, 1986) was used to assess coworker support. A sample item is "My coworkers really care about my well-being."
- *Big five personality.* To assess the five factors of personality, a brief version of Goldberg's (1992) mini-marker set was used. This version (Gosling, Rentfrow, & Swann, 2003) consists of two items for each factor. Participants were asked to respond to the items using a nine-point Likert-type scale ranging from 1 (disagree strongly) to 9 (agree strongly). The total scores were calculated by summing the two positive or negative items for each personality construct.
- *Tolerance of ambiguity.* Four items from the McLain study (1993) were used to measure tolerance of ambiguity. A sample item is, "I am good at managing unpredictable situations."
- *Coping with change.* A five-item measure from Judge and colleagues' work (1999) was used to assess how participants cope with change. A sample item is, "When dramatic changes happen, I feel I can handle them with ease."

- *Work-life enrichment.* Work-life enrichment was assessed using a modified version of Carlson and colleagues' (2006) enrichment scales. Given our focus on "work-life" rather than "work-family," we replaced the word "family" with "private life." A sample item is, "My involvement in my work helps me to understand different viewpoints, and this helps me be better in my private life."
- *Job satisfaction.* A two-item measure of job satisfaction from Spector et al. (2007; e.g., "Overall, I am satisfied with my work") was assessed.
- *Burnout.* An abbreviated version of the Maslach Burnout Inventory (Maslach & Jackson, 1981) was used to assess the emotional exhaustion component of burnout. A sample item is, "I feel emotionally drained from my work."
- *Turnover intentions.* Intentions to leave the host country before one's assignment was complete were assessed using three items created by authors. A sample item is, "I am planning to voluntarily leave my position in this host country before my tour is complete."

Results

The intercorrelations for the variables are presented in Table 7.2. Our hypothesis indicating that coworker support was significantly related to WLE was not supported ($r = .20$, ns). In addition, only agreeableness was significantly positively correlated with WLE ($r = .33$, $p < .01$), but no other individual difference variables were significantly correlated with WLE, so our hypothesis was only partially supported. On the other hand, WLE was significantly related to burnout ($r = -.22$, $p < .05$), turnover intentions ($r = -.32$, $p < .01$), and job satisfaction ($r = .50$, $p < .01$). In addition, personality had direct relationships with expatriate outcomes (i.e., burnout, turnover intentions, and job satisfaction). For example, extraversion was significantly related to burnout ($r = -.297$, $p < .01$) but not to turnover intentions ($r = -.07$, ns). Emotional stability was significantly related to burnout ($r = -.29$, $p < .01$), and agreeableness was significantly related to job satisfaction ($r = .25$, $p < .05$). Of the other big five personality traits, openness was not significantly related to either burnout ($r = -.20$, ns) or turnover intentions ($r = -.18$, ns). Interestingly, conscientiousness was not related to any of the work outcomes. Tolerance of ambiguity was significantly related to burnout ($r = -.21$, $p < .05$) and turnover intentions ($r = -.29$, $p < .01$). Coping with change was also significantly related to burnout ($r = -.27$, $p < .05$) and turnover intentions ($r = -.29$, $p < .01$). Although not hypothesized, coworker support was significantly related to burnout ($r = -.21$, $p < .05$), turnover intentions ($r = -.29$, $p < .01$), and job satisfaction ($r = .29$, $p < .01$).

Table 7.2. Intercorrelations among predictor and job outcome variables

Variable	1	2	3	4	5	6	7	8	9	10	11	12
1. Turnover intentions	---											
2. Burnout	.210	---										
3. Job satisfaction	-.369**	-.254*	---									
4. Coworker support	-.287**	-.214*	.286**	---								
5. Work-life enrichment	-.320***	-.217*	.498***	.200	---							
6. Coping with change	-.292***	-.265*	.142	.123	.143	---						
7. Tolerance of ambiguity	.027	-.215*	.080	-.017	.007	.397**	---					
8. Extraversion	-.066	-.297**	.139	.174	.112	.066	.283**	---				
9. Agreeableness	-.090	-.135	.252*	.321**	.333**	.233*	-.112	.124	---			
10. Conscientiousness	-.098	-.204	.130	.062	.190	.427**	.148	-.005	.241*	---		
11. Emotional stability	-.151	-.289**	.053	.167	.119	.358**	.334**	.170	.424**	.496**	---	
12. Openness	-.176	-.201	.184	.281**	.191	.417**	.358**	.333**	.314**	.335**	.537**	---

Table 7.3. Analyses conducted to determine if WLE mediates the relationship between resources and outcomes

Resource (X)	Outcome (Y)	Step 1 (X predicts Y)	Step 2 (X predicts M)	Step 3 (M predicts Y, controlling for X)	Step 4 (X does not predict Y, controlling for M)	Conclusion
Coping with change	Turnover intentions	Yes; $r = -.292^{**}$	No; $r = .143$	---	---	No Mediation
	Burnout	Yes; $r = -.265^{*}$	No; $r = .143$	---	---	No Mediation
	Job satisfaction	No; $r = .142$	---	---	---	No Mediation
Tolerance of ambiguity	Turnover intentions	No; $r = .027$	No; $r = .007$	---	---	No Mediation
	Burnout	Yes; $r = -.215^{*}$	No; $r = .007$	---	---	No Mediation
	Job satisfaction	No; $r = .080$	---	---	---	No Mediation
Extraversion	Turnover intentions	No; $r = -.066$	---	---	---	No Mediation
	Burnout	Yes; $r = -.297^{**}$	No; $r = .112$	---	---	No Mediation
	Job satisfaction	No; $r = .139$	---	---	---	No Mediation
Agreeableness	Turnover intentions	No; $r = -.090$	---	---	---	No Mediation
	Burnout	No; $r = -.135$	---	---	---	No Mediation
	Job satisfaction	Yes; $r = .252^{*}$	Yes; $r = .333^{**}$	Yes, $\beta = .466^{**}$	Yes, $\beta = .096$	Mediation
Conscientiousness	Turnover intentions	No; $r = -.098$	---	---	---	No Mediation
	Burnout	No; $r = -.204$	---	---	---	No Mediation
	Job satisfaction	No; $r = .130$	---	---	---	No Mediation
Emotional stability	Turnover intentions	No; $r = -.151$	---	---	---	No Mediation
	Burnout	Yes; $r = -.289^{**}$	No; $r = .119$	---	---	No Mediation
	Job satisfaction	No; $r = .053$	---	---	---	No Mediation
Openness	Turnover intentions	No; $r = -.176$	---	---	---	No Mediation
	Burnout	No; $r = -.201$	---	---	---	No Mediation
	Job satisfaction	No; $r = .184$	---	---	---	No Mediation

Resource (X)	Outcome (Y)	Step 1 (X predicts Y)	Step 2 (X predicts M)	Step 3 (M predicts Y, controlling for X)	Step 4 (X does not predict Y, controlling for M)	Conclusion
Coworker support	Turnover intentions	Yes; r = −.287**	No; r = .200	---	---	No Mediation
	Burnout	Yes; r = −.214*	No; r = .200	---	---	No Mediation
	Job satisfaction	Yes; r = .286**	No; r = .200	---	---	No Mediation

Note: $N = 86$. **Correlation is significant at the 0.01 level (2-tailed). *Correlation is significant at the 0.05 level (2-tailed). M represents the mediator, WLE, X represents resource variables, and Y represents outcome variables.

Mediated versus Direct Effects

We were also interested in whether WLE served as a mediating mechanism between resources and work outcomes. We used the classic four-step procedure for establishing mediation, whereby a variable M mediates the relationship X and Y (Baron & Kenny, 1986; James & Brett, 1984; Judd & Kenny, 1981; Kenny, 2016). In the first step, a researcher determines whether or not X predicts Y (via regression or, equivalently, correlation in the bivariate case). In the second step, a researcher determines whether or not X predicts M. In the third step, a regression analysis is conducted using X and M to predict Y and it is determined whether the relationship between M and Y is significant (controlling for X). The regression analysis results are used again in the fourth step, during which the researcher determines whether the relationship between X and Y is significant, controlling for M. A nonsignificant relationship between X and Y (controlling for M) is evidence of full mediation. We applied this four-step procedure to each of the mediation analyses, stopping whenever one of the steps did not yield a result supporting mediation. The results of this analysis are detailed in Table 7.3.

In total we tested 24 models for which WLE mediated the relationship between various resources and the three outcome variables. As shown in Table 7.3, we only found evidence of mediation in 1 of the 24 models. WLE mediated the relationship between agreeableness and job satisfaction. There was a significant relationship between agreeableness and job satisfaction ($r = .25$, $p < .01$) and between agreeableness and WLE ($r = .33$, $p < .01$), providing support in Steps 1 and 2. WLE predicted job satisfaction when controlling for agreeableness ($\beta = .47$, $p < .01$), and agreeableness did not predict job satisfaction when controlling for WLE ($\beta = .10$, $p > .05$), providing support in Steps 3 and 4.

Post Hoc Analyses

Given our results found that resources were more strongly connected to expatriate outcomes rather than WLE, we conducted post hoc multiple regression analyses to determine which personality traits and support variables were explaining the most variance in predicting expatriate burnout, job satisfaction, and turnover intentions. Tables 7.3–7.5 present the independent variables, standardized β-weights, and $R2$ statistics for each of the models predicting work outcomes. Table 7.4 presents the multiple regression results for expatriate burnout. Model 1 is the baseline model, and in this model extraversion accounted for the most variance in predicting burnout, while coping with change, emotional stability, and tolerance of ambiguity (despite being correlated with burnout) added little to the model. Model 2 dropped tolerance of ambiguity; in this model each of the remaining predictor variables changed very little with respect to prediction of burnout. Model 3 dropped emotional stability, and doing this resulted in extraversion ($\beta = -.22$, $p < .01$) and coping with change ($\beta = -.22$, $p < .05$), each predicting burnout significantly. Models 4 and 5 test whether coworker support and WLE added significantly to Model 3. Neither coworker support ($\beta = -.14$, ns) nor WLE ($\beta = -.16$, ns) were statistically significant when added to Model 3. The best predictors of expatriate burnout are extraversion and coping with change, and together they account for 14.9 percent of the variance in burnout (representing an R of .368).

Table 7.4. Multiple regression results for job burnout

Predictor	Model 1	Model 2	Model 3	Model 4	Model 5
Extraversion	−.251*	−.254*	−.281**	−.257*	−.265*
	(.136)	(.131)	(.131)	(.132)	(.131)
Coping with change	−.179	−.183+	−.246*	−.230*	−.225*
	(.194)	(.183)	(.173)	(.173)	(.173)
Emotional stability	−.178	−.180			
	(.190)	(.185)			
Tolerance of ambiguity	−.014				
	(.208)				
Coworker support				−.141	
				(.160)	
Work-life enrichment					−.155
					(.558)
Model fit statistics					
Model R^2	.176***	.149***	.149***	.168***	.172***
Model R	.420***	.386***	.368***	.410***	.415***

Note: $N = 86$. Standard errors appear below the coefficient in parentheses.
Significance is denoted by the following markers: $+p < .10$; $*p < .05$; $**p < .01$; $***p < .001$.

Table 7.5 presents the multiple regression results for expatriate turnover intentions. Model 1 (the only model) included the variables significantly correlated with turnover intentions. Here, coworker support ($\beta = -.21$, $p <.05$), coping with change ($\beta = -.23$, $p <.01$), and WLE ($\beta = -.25$, $p <.05$) each contributed uniquely to explaining expatriate turnover intentions. Together, these variables accounted for 20.6 percent of the variance in explaining turnover intentions (representing an R of .454).

Table 7.5. Multiple regression results for turnover intentions

Predictor	Model 1
Coworker support	−.209*
	(.132)
Coping with change	−.231*
	(.143)
Work-life enrichment	−.245*
	(.465)
Model fit statistics	
Model R^2	.206***
Model R	.454***

Note: $N = 86$. Standard errors appear below the coefficient in parentheses.
Significance is denoted by the following markers: $+p < .10$; $*p < .05$; $**p < .01$; $***p < .001$.

Table 7.6 presents the multiple regression results for expatriate job satisfaction. Model 1 included WLE and coworker support; both variables contributed to the explanation of job satisfaction, with WLE ($\beta = .46$, $p <.001$) carrying more weight than coworker support ($\beta = .19$, $p <.05$). Model 2 added agreeableness, but it did not add significantly ($\beta = .04$, ns) to Model 1. Model 1 is retained, and together WLE and coworker support account for 28.4 percent of the variance in expatriate job satisfaction (representing an R of .53).

Table 7.6. Multiple regression results for job satisfaction

Predictor	Model 1	Model 2
Work-life enrichment	.459***	.447***
	(.231)	(.243)
Coworker support	.194*	.183+
	(.066)	(.069)
Agreeableness		.044
		(.062)
Model fit statistics		
Model R^2	.284***	.286**
Model R	.533***	.535**

Note: $N =86$. Standard errors appear below the coefficient in parentheses.
Significance is denoted by the following markers: $+p < .10$; $*p < .05$; $**p < .01$; $***p < .001$.

Discussion

The quantitative study did not find support for the hypothesized relationships between work and personal resources with WLE, with the exception of a positive bivariate relationship between agreeableness and WLE, such that more agreeable individuals experience greater work-to-life enrichment. By extension, WLE is only a mediating mechanism between agreeableness and job satisfaction. Instead, we found evidence that coworker support, individual differences, and WLE contribute directly to expatriate outcomes. The finding that individual differences such as agreeableness are directly related to expatriate outcomes lends support to Greenhaus and Powell's (2006) work-family enrichment theory that developing high-quality relationships with others (e.g., fellow expatriates and host country nationals) may facilitate an individual acclimating to new surroundings and experiencing greater enrichment.

The fact that coworker support, individual differences, and WLE were related to expatriate work outcomes fits with past research. For example, both WLE and coworker support have been linked to work outcomes for domestic positions (Innstrand, Langballe, Espnes, Falkum, & Aasland, 2008; McNall, Masuda, & Nicklin, 2010; McNall, Nicklin, & Masuda, 2010), but little research has been done in an expatriate context. These findings suggest that both coworker support and WLE play a role for expatriates in adjusting to and succeeding in an international assignment. While the roles of coworker support and WLE in predicting burnout overlaps with the roles of extroversion and coping with change in predicting burnout, neither was a significant predictor after controlling for extraversion and coping with change. Thus, organizations might be able to prevent burnout by selecting employees who are extroverted and who can cope with change or by enhancing WLE. This furthers a call for a more whole-person assessment of candidates for international assignments while also having implications for training and programs designed to prepare employees for international assignments. Regardless, having sufficient resources available (e.g., close networking of coworkers abroad) may help expatriates adjust and prevent negative work outcomes such as intention to leave an international assignment early as WLE uniquely predicted turnover intentions (and job satisfaction).

The results of this study have theoretical implications for the Lazarova and colleagues (2010) model of expatriate work and family performance, which suggests that resources and demands play a role on expatriate and partner adjustment, which in turn influence engagement and performance in work and family domains. The findings of this study suggest that resources and WLE are directly related to important expatriate work outcomes. Future research should expand on our research by including more work resources (beyond coworker support) and personal resources (beyond individual differences) to include other forms of resources, such as family resources, while also factoring in personal, work, and family demands. In addition, to provide a true test of this model, expatriate and partner role engagement and performance should be examined.

As expected, many of the adaptability-related variables (coping with change and tolerance of ambiguity) were significantly related to expatriate burnout and intentions to leave an international assignment early. This makes sense, as expatriates are asked to move to a different country where norms, practices, and living standards are different than those in the United States. In addition to some of the big five personality traits that research has indicated or suggested are related to expatriate work outcomes (Caligiuri, 2000; Huang, Chi, & Lawler, 2005; Ones & Viswesvaran, 1999), flexibility variables, such as those in this study, may help an expatriate better adapt to new environments and serve as a buffer to undesirable and costly (from both the organizational and the personal perspective) outcomes such as burnout and leaving an international assignment earlier than expected. Practitioners would do well to use these personality variables to assist them in assessing employees who are under consideration for international assignments.

Limitations

Several limitations of this study should be noted. First, the sample used was small, which limits the inferences from the statistical analyses. Second, the expatriates who participated were largely Caucasian male law enforcement agents, and this limits the generalizability of the results. However, this was a worldwide field study with an applied population of expatriates. Third, the data were collected using a single instrument, which suggests the possibility of common method bias; however, Spector's (1987, 2006) work suggests that concerns about common method bias may be overstated, and Doty and Glick (1998) noted that it "does not invalidate many research findings" (p. 374). Fourth, due to time restrictions, only two items were used to measure the big five personality dimensions; however, past research suggests that shorter personality scales are reliable and valid and are a good alternative when it is not feasible to administer a full personality inventory (Donnellan, Oswald, Baird, & Lucas, 2006; Ehrhart, Ehrhart, Roesch, Chung-Herrera, Nadler, & Bradshaw, 2009; Gosling et al., 2003; Muck, Hell, & Gosling, 2007; Rammstedt & John, 2006; cf. Credé, Harms, Niehorster, & Gaye-Valentine, 2012).

QUALITATIVE STUDY

In addition to collecting quantitative information, we also collected qualitative information during our work with this expatriate population. This information sheds light on the unique work and life experience of expatriates and provides context for the work-life situation of expatriates. Two sources of qualitative information were used: job analysis interviews and subject matter expert (SME) panels. Job analysis is the process of documenting the tasks, duties, knowledge, skills, abilities, and other characteristics of a position. It often entails the use of qualitative methodology (Brawley & Pury, 2016), especially when job observations and incumbent interviews are conducted. As part of this work, two of the authors visited expatriates working overseas and conducted job observations and interviews. In addition to collecting information on the tasks, duties, and technical knowledge, skills, and abilities, the interviews also covered the other nontechnical characteristics, skills, and abilities that are associated with expatriate adjustment. These topics were also discussed during a series of SME panels held with expatriates. The interviews and SME panels provided rich information on expatriate experiences.

Many of the expatriates we spoke with provided qualitative information that is consistent with previous quantitative research on expatriation. For example, many reported working longer hours, which is consistent with the findings reported by Shortland and Cummins (2007). Time zone issues played a role in the extra hours as many expatriates had to interact with home country staff members during home country working hours. Travel was another significant factor. Depending on the size of the organization's expatriate footprint, expatriates may be responsible for covering large geographic regions and multiple countries, necessitating extensive travel commitments. For instance, an expatriate who is assigned to work in a specific host country might be responsible for conducting business in neighboring countries or in the host country's outlying possessions and territories. Many expatriates were also aware of the costs associated with their assignments. The sponsoring agency must provide for travel, office space rent, housing, schooling (for the expatriate's children), and other expenses. Thus, many of the expatriates we met indicated that they felt an obligation to increase their work output to make up for these benefits. This is consistent with equity theory in that expatriates increase their work inputs due to an underpayment inequity that occurs when comparing their ratio of inputs to outputs to those for their previous home country position (Adams, 1965).

In order to collect information that could be used to create noncognitive predictive measures and a realistic job preview, we also asked the expatriates what things they wish they knew about expatriation before becoming an expatriate. This information was collected during job interviews and SME panels and was presented to a group of SMEs who reviewed and edited the information and came to a consensus on the topics. The SMEs organized the information into 11 topical categories, covering financial, housing, family, convenience, moving, quality of life, transportation, health care, work schedule, cultural, and transition issues and recommendations. In Table 7.7, we provide a summary of the information we collected. In general, expatriation requires many personal sacrifices and considerations as an expatriate's personal life is often changed dramatically when moving overseas.

Table 7.7. Qualitative information on becoming an expatriate

Topical category	Theme
Financial	Although the organization may provide reimbursements for certain expenses, there are often additional expenses that an expatriate must pay for out of pocket (e.g., moving pets, tips, medical expenses, and school field trips)
	Oftentimes, host country banking systems are not well integrated with US banking systems. Some countries are primarily cash-based societies. It can be difficult to deposit checks into home country bank accounts when overseas and credit card companies and banks often charge higher rates for overseas transactions.
	Paying bills in your host country (e.g., utilities) often requires the creation of a foreign bank account. However, in some financially unstable countries, there is a risk of the host country government nationalizing bank accounts.
	Moving overseas requires preparation regarding your home country expenses and assets. There is a need to notify insurance companies of your move; home country bank accounts and investments must be maintained; and so forth.
	The strength of the US dollar impacts your quality of life overseas.
	Oftentimes local products (e.g., paper products, paper towels, napkins, and toilet paper) can be of lower quality or more expensive than in the United States, and it might be best to bring these with you when moving overseas.
	It can be difficult and expensive to obtain American toys overseas, therefore, if an expatriate has children, it is often a good idea to purchase toys for birthdays and holidays in advance and to bring them when moving overseas.
	Some products (e.g., liquor and cigarettes) can be very expensive overseas, making it wise to bring these items when moving.
	Filing federal and state taxes can be more complicated when moving overseas, and there is often ambiguity and differing opinions about what can be officially considered as income (e.g., moving expenses and school tuition).
Housing	In some countries, the quality of local construction might be lower than in the United States. Many expatriates we spoke to indicated constant maintenance issues in their local housing (leaks and power outages).
	Many American appliances and electronics are not suitable for use with a foreign country's electrical system or require converters.
	Depending on the host country, additional security might be needed for an expatriate's housing (e.g., alarms, barred windows, and barbed wires).
	Depending on the origin and host country, living accommodations may be very different, particularly in size of living space.
	Some housing includes used furniture, which may be of lower quality than what an expatriate is used to.
	Response to home maintenance requests can be slow.
Family	The host country school year may be quite different from the United States (e.g., longer winter break and shorter summer break).
	An expatriate's spouse may not be able to find meaningful work overseas and have to transition into either domestic life or a new field.
	Expatriation can be a benefit for children as it provides more bonding time and an opportunity to learn about other cultures.

Table 7.7. (Continued)

Topical category	Theme
	Family issues can spill over into the work environment quite easily. Sometimes children wish to return home and may act inappropriately on purpose to make the sponsoring organization send the expatriate back to the home country.
	Moving to and from the home and host countries can be a traumatic experience for children.
Conveniences	In many urbanized areas of the United States, it is very convenient to purchase items and obtain food at nearly all hours of the day. This is not the case in many foreign countries. The one-stop shopping stores that Americans are used to (e.g., Target, Walmart, Costco, and CVS) may not have any equivalents overseas, necessitating multiple shopping trips to different stores.
	Children (and some adults) are often used to food chains and brands (e.g., McDonalds, Taco Bell, Burger King, and certain cereals and snacks) that may either not exist overseas or be very expensive to obtain.
	Television stations overseas are often in another language, and typical American stations and programming are not available overseas. Some host country Internet providers and home country service providers block overseas access to websites containing television programming.
Moving	When moving overseas, household and personal items are usually transported using three modes: extra luggage, air freight (which is often limited to a small amount due to cost), and surface freight (which can take two to three months for transport). As a result, an expatriate and his or her family may arrive overseas several weeks or months before all of their household goods. Privately owned vehicles often take an extensive amount of time to arrive.
	Sometimes expatriates are placed into temporary housing when arriving overseas, resulting in a total of three moves (i.e., moving to the host country temporary quarters, moving to the host country permanent quarters, and moving back to the home country).
	Moving with pets can be expensive and may require extensive quarantine periods (e.g., 6 months).
Quality of life	The farther your host country is from the United States, the more difficult it can be to obtain products that are not available in certain overseas countries (e.g., cereals, maple syrup, waffles, peanut butter, turkey for Thanksgiving, and a gallon of milk). It can be difficult to obtain high-quality seafood in landlocked countries. Consequently, expatriates must be open to changing their eating and shopping habits.
	The host country daily schedule (e.g., hours of operation of businesses) may be very different from that in the United States.
	Clothing can be of poorer quality when purchased overseas.
	In some countries, electronics (e.g., computers, tablets, and stereo equipment) can be difficult to obtain.
Transportation	Adjusting to driving overseas can be difficult. Some countries drive on the opposite side of the road, use roundabouts, or have no stop signs or traffic lights. Traffic can very busy and chaotic, safety may not be up to American standards, and carjackings and break-ins may be common.
	It may be easier to purchase a new car overseas rather than bringing a privately owned vehicle; however, selling that car when returning to the United States can be difficult.

Topical category	Theme
	Car maintenance (e.g., oil changes and repairs) can be very expensive overseas.
Health care	Health insurance overseas can be more complicated as oftentimes all health care is considered out of network using a domestic insurance policy. Some countries have free public health care that cannot be used by noncitizens.
	Orthodontics can be very expensive overseas and of poor quality.
	Special vaccinations (e.g., malaria and yellow fever) may be required.
Work schedule	The daily and weekly work schedule may be very different overseas (e.g., Sunday may be considered a workday, work may halt between 2:00 p.m. and 5:00 p.m. for a siesta and then resume later at night).
	In Arab countries nearly everything is closed during Ramadan.
	In European countries August is a vacation month, which can slow down work.
	In Asian countries, a six-day workweek is common.
	Domestic colleagues may not be aware of or sensitive to time zone differences and can contact expatriates at odd hours.
Cultural adjustments	In some countries, the common way of thinking is quite different. Customer service may be of lower quality, priorities may differ, and law enforcement responses to crimes (e.g., robberies) may be weak or nonexistent, and some foreign countries have anti-American sentiments.
Transition	Oftentimes an incoming expatriate is replacing an outgoing one. It is often a good idea for the two to connect and share information.

CONCLUSION AND RECOMMENDATIONS

Expatriation can be both a rewarding and a stressful experience for employees and their families. Consequently, there is a need to fully understand the work-life experiences of expatriate employees. We have made a contribution to the literature through the use of quantitative study of law enforcement expatriates. First, we found that coworker support and WLE were related to burnout, turnover intention, and job satisfaction. Thus, organizations with expatriates should focus on fostering greater coworker support and facilitating WLE. This could be done by facilitating coworker support through the creation of mentoring relationships (with current and previous expatriates in the host country) and support groups (for coworkers and their families). WLE can be facilitated through training on how to extend knowledge gained through working in the host country to one's personal life. Organizations would do well to provide information on the cultural differences of the host country and any necessary training to prepare expatriates for their assignments. Although previous research has examined these relationships using domestic samples, our study is among the first (to our knowledge) to examine these variables in an expatriate context. The only other study we located was by Kempen and colleagues (2015), who found that WLE predicted job satisfaction ($r = .46$) and turnover intentions ($r = -.31$), with very similar magnitudes to the results in our study ($r = .50$ and $r = -.32$, respectively).

At the same time, we also examined the relationship among several individual differences with expatriate outcomes. We found that extroversion, emotional stability, coping with change, and tolerance of ambiguity were all negatively related to burnout. Additionally, coping with change was negatively related to turnover intentions. Therefore, burnout and turnover intentions can be minimized when expatriates are extroverted and emotionally stable and when they can cope well with change and tolerate ambiguity. We recommend that organizations consider measuring these variables in selection systems for expatriation or that they use this information to help expatriate candidates to self-select into expatriate positions. We only found limited support for the mediated model (whereby WLE mediated the relationship between resources and outcomes) that Lazarova and colleagues (2010) proposed.

Additionally, our qualitative study results provide rich information that can be used for creating realistic job previews of expatriate positions and informing potential expatriate employees of the realities of living overseas. Indeed, Kraimer, Bolino, and Mead (2016) recommended that practitioners develop realistic job previews for expatriate positions. Overall, we found that expatriation is a complex process that requires thought and consideration on behalf of the organization and the employee in order for it to be successful. Organizations and potential expatriates should be mindful of the correlates of expatriate outcomes, and researchers and practitioners should use this information to develop successful expatriation programs.

REFERENCES

Adams, J. G. (1965). Inequity in social exchange. In L. Berkowitz (Ed.), *Advances in experimental social psychology* (Vol. 2; pp. 267–299). New York, NY: Academic Press.

Allen, T. D., Johnson, R. C., Saboe, K. N., Cho, E., Dumani, S., & Evans, S. (2012). Dispositional variables and work-family conflict: A meta-analysis. *Journal of Vocational Behavior, 80*(1), 17–26.

Arthur, W., & Bennett, W. (1995). The international assignee: The relative importance of factors perceived to contribute to success. *Personnel Psychology, 48*, 99–114.

Ayman, R., & Antani, A. (2008). Social support and work-family conflict. In K. Korabik, D. S. LEro, & D. L. Whitehead (Eds.), *Handbook of work-family integration: Research, theory, and best practices* (pp. 287–304). New York, NY: Elsevier.

Bakker, A. B., & Demerouti, E. (2007). The job demands-resources model: State of the art. *Journal of Managerial Psychology, 22*(3), 309–328.

Baral, R., & Bhargava, S. (2010). Work-family enrichment as a mediator between organizational interventions for work-life balance and job outcomes. *Journal of Managerial Psychology, 25*(3), 274–300.

Baron, R. M., & Kenny, D. A. (1986). The moderator-mediator variable distinction in social psychological research: Conceptual, strategic and statistical considerations. *Journal of Personality and Social Psychology, 51*, 1173–1182.

Barrick, M. R., & Mount, M. K. (1991). The big five personality dimensions and job performance. *Personnel Psychology, 41*, 1–26.

Bhatti, M. A., Battour, M. M., Ismail, A. R., & Sundram, V. P. (2013a). Effects of personality traits (big five) on expatriates adjustment and job performance. *Equality, Diversity, and Inclusion: An International Journal, 33*(1), 73–96.

Bhatti, M. A., Kaur, S., & Battour, M. M. (2013b). Effects of individual characteristics on expatriates' adjustment and job performance. *European Journal of Training and Development, 37*(6), 544–563.

Brawley, A. M., & Pury, C. L. S. (2016). It's like doing a job analysis: You know more about qualitative methods than you might think. *Industrial and Organizational Psychology, 9*(4), 753–760.

Brookfield Global Relocation Services. (2012). *2012 Global relocation trends survey.* Woodridge, IL: Brookfield Global Relocation Services.

Budner, S. (1962). Intolerance of ambiguity as a personality variable. *Journal of Personality, 30*, 29–50.

Caligiuri P. M. (2000). The big five characteristics as predictors of expatriate's desire to terminate the assignment and supervisor-rated performance. *Personnel Psychology, 53*, 67–88.

Carlson, D. S., Kacmar, K. M., Wayne, J. H., Grzywacz, J. G. (2006). Measuring the positive side of the work-family interface: Development and validation of a work-family enrichment scale. *Journal of Vocational Behavior, 68*, 131–164.

Cinamon, G. R., & Rich, Y. (2010). Work family relations: Antecedents and outcomes. *Journal of Career Assessment, 18*(1), 59–70.

Cobb, S. (1976). Social support as a moderator of life stress. *Psychosomatic Medicine, 38*(5), 300–314.

Credé, M., Harms, P., Niehorster, S., & Gaye-Valentine, A. (2012). An evaluation of the consequences of using short measures of the big five personality traits. *Journal of Personality and Social Psychology, 102*(4), 874.

Digman, J. M. (1990). Personality structure: Emergence of the five-factor model. *Annual Review of Psychology, 41*(1), 417–440.

Donnellan, M. B., Oswald, F. L., Baird, B. M., & Lucas, R. E. (2006). The mini-IPIP scales: Tiny-yet-effective measures of the big five factors of personality. *Psychological Assessment, 18*(2), 192.

Doty, D. H., & Glick, W. H. (1998). Common methods bias: Does common methods variance really bias results? *Organizational Research Methods, 1*, 374–406.

Dowling, P. J., Schuler, R. S., & Welch, D. E. (1999). *International human resource management.* Cincinnati, OH: South-Western College Publishing.

Ehrhart, M. G., Ehrhart, K. H., Roesch, S. C., Chung-Herrera, B. G., Nadler, K., & Bradshaw, K. (2009). Testing the latent factor structure and construct validity of the Ten-Item Personality Inventory. *Personality and Individual Differences, 47*(8), 900–905.

Eisenberger, R., Huntington, R., Hutchinson, S., & Sowa, D. (1986). Perceived organizational support. *Journal of Applied Psychology, 71*, 500–507.

Figar, N. (2016). Managing the expatriation process. *Facta Universitatis: Economics and Organization, 13*(3), 233–246.

Freeman, M. M., & Olson-Buchanan, J. B. (2013). The relations between expatriate personality and language fluency and its effect on host country adjustment: An empirical study. *International Journal of Management, 30*(2, pt. 1), 393–401.

Friede, A., & Ryan, A. M. (2005). The importance of the individual: How self-evaluations influence the work-family interface. In E. E. Kossek & S. J. Lambert (Eds.), *Work and life integration: Organizational, cultural, and individual perspectives* (pp. 193–209). Mahwah, NJ: Erlbaum.

Goldberg, L. R. (1992). The development of markers for the big-five factor structure. *Psychological Assessment, 4*, 26–42.

Gosling, S. D., Rentfrow, P. J., & Swann, W. B. (2003). A very brief measure of the big five personality domains. *Journal of Research in Personality, 37*, 504–528.

Greenhaus, J. H., & Beutell, N. J. (1985). Sources of conflict between work and family roles. *Academy of Management Review, 10*(1), 76–88.

Greenhaus, J. H., & Powell, G. N. (2006). When work and family are allies: A theory of work-family enrichment. *Academy of Management Review, 31*(1), 72–92.

Grzywacz, J. G., & Marks, N. F. (2000). Reconceptualizing the work-family interface: An ecological perspective on the correlates of positive and negative spillover between work and family. *Journal of Occupational Health Psychology, 5*, 111–126.

Harvey, M., & Moeller, M. (2009). Expatriate managers: A historical review. *International Journal of Management Reviews, 11*, 275–296.

Hechanova, R., Beehr, T. A., & Christiansen, N. D. (2003). Antecedents and consequences of employees' adjustment to overseas assignment: A meta-analytic review. *Applied Psychology: An International Review, 52*(2), 213–236.

Hobfoll, S. E. (1989). Conservation of resources: A new attempt at conceptualizing stress. *American Psychologist, 44*, 513–524.

Hobfoll, S. E. (2002). Social and psychological resources and adaptation. *Review of General Psychology, 6*(4), 307–324.

Huang, T. J., Chi, S. C., & Lawler, J. J. (2005). The relationship between expatriate's personality traits and their adjustment to international assignments. *International Journal of Human Resource Management, 16*(9), 1656–1670.

Innstrand, S. T., Langballe, E. M., Espnes, G. A., Falkum, E., & Aasland, O. G. (2008). Positive and negative work-family interaction and burnout: A longitudinal study of reciprocal relations. *Work Stress, 22*(1), 1–15.

James, L. R., & Brett, J. M. (1984). Mediators, moderators and tests for mediation. *Journal of Applied Psychology, 69*, 307–321.

Judd, C. M., & Kenny, D. A. (1981). Process analysis: Estimating mediation in treatment evaluations. *Evaluation Review, 5*, 602–619.

Judge, T. A., Thoresen, C. J., Pucik, V., & Welbourne, T. M. (1999). Managerial coping with organizational change: A dispositional perspective. *Journal of Applied Psychology, 84*, 107–122.

Kempen, R., Pangert, B., Hattrup, K., Mueller, K., & Joens, I. (2015). Beyond conflict: The role of life-domain enrichment for expatriates. *International Journal of Human Resource Management, 26*, 1–22.

Kenny, D. A. (2006). Mediation. Retrieved May 2, 2017, from http://davidakenny.net/.

Kraimer, M., Bolino, M., & Mead, B. (2016). Themes in expatriate and repatriate research over four decades: What do we know and what do we still need to learn? *Annual Review of Organizational Psychology and Organizational Behavior, 3*, 83–109.

Lazarova, M., Westman, M., & Shaffer, M. A. 2010. Elucidating the positive side of the work-family interface on international assignments: A model of expatriate work and family performance. *Academy of Management Review, 35*(1), 93–117.

Maslach, C., & Jackson, S. E. (1981). The measurement of experienced burnout. *Journal of Organizational Behavior, 2*, 99–113.

McLain, D. L. (1993). The MSTAT-I: A new measure of an individual's tolerance of ambiguity. *Educational and Psychological Measurement, 53*, 183–189.

McNall, L. A., Masuda, A. D., & Nicklin, J. M. (2010). Flexible work arrangements, job satisfaction, and turnover intentions: The mediating role of work-to-family enrichment. *Journal of Psychology: Interdisciplinary and Applied, 144*(1), 61–81.

McNall, L. A., Nicklin, J. M., & Masuda, A. D. (2010). A meta-analytic review of the consequences associated with work–family enrichment. *Journal of Business and Psychology, 25*(3), 381–396.

Michel, J. S., Clark, M. A., & Jaramillo, D. (2011). The role of the five factor model of personality in the perceptions of negative and positive forms of work-nonwork spillover: A meta-analytic review. *Journal of Vocational Behavior, 79*(1), 191–203.

Mol, S. T., Born, M. P., Willemsen, M. E., & Van Der Molen, H. T. (2005). Predicting expatriate job performance for selection purposes: A quantitative review. *Journal of Cross-Cultural Psychology, 36*(5), 590–620.

Muck, P. M., Hell, B., & Gosling, S. D. (2007). Construct validation of a short five-factor model instrument: A self-peer study on the German adaptation of the Ten-Item

Personality Inventory (TIPI-G). *European Journal of Psychological Assessment, 23*(3), 166.

O'Driscoll, M. P., Poelmans, S., Spector, P. E., Kalliath, T., Allen, T. D., Cooper, C. L., & Sanchez, J. I. (2003). Family-responsive interventions, perceived organizational and supervisor support, work-family conflict, and psychological strain. *International Journal of Stress Management, 10*(4), 326.

O'Neill, J. (2009). Relocating employees overseas: Beyond cost projections and into the world of cost modeling. *Compensation Benefits Review, 41,* 55–60.

Ones, D. S., & Viswesvaran, C. (1999). Relative importance of personality dimensions for expatriate selection: A policy capturing study. *Human Performance, 12,* 275–294.

Peltokorpi, V., & Froese, F. (2014). Expatriate personality and cultural fit: The moderating role of host country context on job satisfaction. *International Business Review, 23,* 293–302.

Rammstedt, B., & John, O. P. (2007). Measuring personality in one minute or less: A 10-item short version of the big five inventory in English and German. *Journal of Research in Personality, 41*(1), 203–212.

Seiger, C. P., & Wiese, B. S. (2009). Social support from work and family domains as an antecedent or moderator of work-family conflicts? *Journal of Vocational Behavior, 75*(1), 26–37.

Shaffer, M. A., Harrison, D. A., Gilley, K. M., & Luk, D. M. (2001). Struggling for balance amid turbulence on international assignments: Work-family conflict, support and commitment. *Journal of Management, 27*(1), 99–121.

Shaffer, M. A., Harrison, D. A., Gregersen, H., Black, J. S., & Ferzandi, L. A. (2006). You can take it with you: Individual differences and expatriate effectiveness. *Journal of Applied Psychology,* 91(1), 109–125.

Shay, J., & Tracey, J. B. (1997). Expatriate managers: Reasons for failure and implications for training. *Cornell Hotel and Restaurant Administration Quarterly, 38*(1), 30–35.

Shortland, S. (2015). The "expat factor": The influence of working time on women's decisions to undertake international assignments in the oil and gas industry. *International Journal of Human Resources Management, 26*(11), 1452–1473.

Shortland, S., & Cummins, S. (2007). Work-life balance: Expatriates reflect the international dimension. *Global Business and Organizational Excellence, 26*(6), 28–42.

Sinangil, H. K., & Ones, D. S. (2001). Expatriate management. In N. Anderson, D. S. Ones, H. K. Sinangil, & C. Viswesvaran (Eds.), *Handbook of industrial, work and organizational psychology* (Vol. 1; pp. 425–443). Thousand Oaks, CA: SAGE.

Spector, P. E. (1987). Method variance as an artifact in self-reported affect and perceptions at work: Myth or significant problem? *Journal of Applied Psychology, 72*(3), 438.

Spector, P. E. (2006). Method variance in organizational research: Truth or urban legend? *Organizational Research Methods, 9*(2), 221–232.

Spector, P. E., et al. (2007). Cross-national differences in relationships in relationships of work demands, job satisfaction, and turnover intentions with work-family conflict. *Personnel Psychology, 60*, 805–835.

Stockert, J. P. (2015). *Expatriate adjustment of U.S. military on foreign assignment: The role of personality and cultural intelligence in adjustment* (Unpublished master's thesis). Minnesota State University, Mankato, MN.

Thomas, L. T., & Ganster, D. C. (1995). Impact of family-supportive work variables on work-family conflict and strain: A control perspective. *Journal of Applied Psychology, 80*(1), 6.

Valantin, C. (2015). *Lifestyle, sleep quality and mental health of Hong Kong expatriates* (Unpublished doctoral dissertation). California School of Professional Psychology, Alliant International University, Hong Kong, China.

van der Zee, K. I., Ali, A. J., & Salomé, E. (2005). Role interference and subjective well-being among expatriate families. *European Journal of Work and Organizational Psychology, 14*(3), 239–262.

Van Vianien, A. E. M., De Pater, I. E., & Kristof-Brown, A. L. (2004). Fitting in: Surface and deep level cultural differences and expatriates' adjustment. *Academy of Management Journal, 47*, 697–709.

Zhu, J., Wanberg, C. R., Harrison, D. A., & Diehn, E. W. (2015). Ups and downs of the expatriate experience? Understanding work adjustment trajectories and career outcomes. *Journal of Applied Psychology, 101*(4), 549–568.

PART 2. BEYOND WORK-FAMILY CONFLICT

In: Work-Life Balance in the 21st Century   ISBN: 978-1-53612-526-9
Editor: Jessica M. Nicklin   © 2018 Nova Science Publishers, Inc.

Chapter 8

AN EXAMINATION OF POSITIVE PSYCHOLOGICAL RESOURCES FOR PROMOTING WORK-LIFE BALANCE

Jessica M. Nicklin[1,], Laurel A. McNall[2] and Anneliese Janssen[1]*
[1]University of Hartford, West Hartford, CT, US
[2]The College at Brockport, State University of New York
Brockport, NY, US

ABSTRACT

Over the past few decades, researchers and practitioners have called attention to the consequences associated with balancing work and family demands. This led to an increased interest in finding ways to minimize the negative impact of *work-family conflict* (when role demands stemming from one domain are incompatible with the role demands stemming from another domain; Greenhaus & Beutell, 1985). In recent years, however, the field has evolved in a number of ways. First, with the introduction of *work-family enrichment* (the extent to which experiences in one role *improve* the quality of life in another role; Carlson, Kacmar, Wayne, & Grzywacz, 2006; Greenhaus & Powell, 2006), scholars now recognize that there are also *positive outcomes* resulting from balancing dual roles (McNall, Nicklin, & Masuda, 2010). Second, the push to examine the positive aspects of multirole memberships corresponds with the recent attention devoted to *positive psychology* in organizations (e.g., Allen & Kiburz, 2012; Seligman & Csikszentmihalyi, 2000). This research reveals the importance of psychological resources such as mindfulness and resilience for enhanced well-being at work and home. Third, with the changing nature of work and home life, researchers have shifted focus in recent years from work-family balance to work-*life* balance. This approach recognizes domains outside of work and family; thus, a more comprehensive understanding of *work-life*

---

* Corresponding Author Email: nicklin@hartford.edu.

balance is needed. To meet the needs of our evolving field, we use conservation of resources theory (Hobfoll, 2002) to focus on the impact of three psychological resources (resilience, mindfulness, and self-compassion) for minimizing work-life conflict and maximizing work-life enrichment. To that end, we (1) review the state of the current research literature; (2) make recommendations for future research needs; and (3) provide actionable recommendations for practitioners seeking to approach work-life balance issues through the lens of positive psychology.

"*Balance is not something you find, it's something you create.*
—Jana Kingsford, *UNJUGGLED: Lessons from a Decade of Blending Business, Babies, Balance, and Big Dreams*

It is no surprise that many workers struggle with balancing work and life issues (Gurchiek, 2010); being out of balance can have long-term negative consequences for individuals, organizations, and society as a whole in the form of increased stress, depression, psychological strain, and physical symptoms. With the ever-changing nature of work, this may only get worse unless countermeasures are taken to help employees move toward a greater state of balance. For instance, work roles are being redefined to reflect growth in technology and globalization (e.g., SHRM Foundation, 2014); employees' values and needs are evolving, with greater emphasis on autonomy and meaningful work (e.g., Katzenbach & Khan, 2010); and the demographic makeup of the workforce is changing. People are living and working longer, women now make up nearly 40 percent of managers in the United States (Bureau of Labor Statistics, 2016b), and in about half of married-couple families, both partners work (Bureau of Labor Statistics, 2016a). What is considered "family" has also evolved, with an increase in nonfamily-, single parent-, and same-sex couple-households (e.g., Vespa, Lewis, & Krieder, 2013).

Fortunately, as the world of work evolves, so too has our approach for understanding human behavior. We now have a better understanding that managing multiple roles not only creates conflict but also can lead to benefits in the form of work-family enrichment (e.g., Carlson et al., 2006; Greenhaus & Powell, 2006). This fits nicely with Dr. Martin Seligman's call for scholars to examine what makes people *flourish*, which effectively started the positive psychology movement in the late 1990s. Since this call, many studies have explored *what goes right* in individuals—how to make people go from good to great. The workplace literature is no exception. Over the past 20 years we have seen tremendous growth in applying positive psychology principles in the workplace. More recently, there has been increased attention devoted to factors that promote these positive work-family balance experiences. In addition, given the complexity and diversity of today's "family," the field is moving beyond "work-*family*" as was historically conceptualized, to "work-*life*" issues, which address how many employees may not fit the "traditional" family model yet are still seeking balance across multiple life domains (e.g., school, religion, hobbies, and health).

Taken together, the purpose of this chapter is to provide a review of the literature on positive psychological resources, namely, resilience, mindfulness, and self-compassion, that contribute to work-life balance through the lens of conservation of resources theory (Hobfoll, 2002). This is an important area of exploration in that organizations are increasingly interested in finding ways to minimize stress and burnout for employees. With health-care costs at an all-time high for both employers and employees, there needs to be a better understanding of resources and skills that employees can easily develop. We believe that resilience, mindfulness, and self-compassion are all psychological resources that can be trained and incorporated into daily life. At the same time, these resources have all been linked to lower levels of stress and greater physical and psychological well-being, and can apply to work-life issues. After reviewing the research literature, we provide areas of opportunity for both researchers and practitioners seeking to approach work-life balance problems through the lens of positive psychology.

OVERVIEW OF CONFLICT AND ENRICHMENT

Balancing work and life concerns prioritizing and allocating time and resources between work and other life domains (family, school, hobbies, spiritual, etc.). Only recently have scholars focused on the idea of *balance* as a holistic and bi-directional construct (see also Chapters10 and 11 in this volume). Instead, work-life balance has historically been conceptualized and understood in terms of the negative (conflict) and positive (enrichment) sides of the work-family interface. We review the literature on work-family conflict and enrichment in order to provide a theoretical framework for how positive psychological resources enhance work-life balance and overall well-being.

Conflict

Work-family conflict has been defined as "a form of inter-role conflict in which the role pressures from the work and family domains are mutually incompatible in some respect" (Greenhaus & Beutell, 1985, p. 77). Work can interfere with family (work-family conflict [WFC]) if an employee cannot attend her son's soccer game because she has a late meeting; and family can interfere with work (family-to-work conflict [FWC]) if an employee misses an important client meeting because of a sick child who must be picked up from school.

Conflict is not a homogenous or a generic concept. It can be complex, dynamic, and multiply determined. Conflict is posited to originate from three sources: time, strain, and behavior (Greenhaus & Beutell, 1985).

- *Time-based conflict* occurs when the time devoted to one role (i.e., work) makes it difficult to fulfill the requirements of another role (i.e., home). An example of this might be if a parent is working late so does not have the *time* to make a child's Halloween costume.
- *(Role) strain-based conflict* occurs when one role makes it difficult to fulfill the obligations of another role. For instance, if a person is having marital difficulties, this stress and anxiety may interfere with work due to the strain associated with the personal problems.
- *Behavioral-based conflict* occurs when the behaviors required in one role make it difficult to fulfill the requirements of another role. For example, a mother may be warm, nurturing, and caring in her family role, but that behavior is less effective in her managerial role where authority, direction, and decisiveness are needed.

These three sources can act alone, or they can interact with and exacerbate the others. For example, a recently promoted manager may find conflicts not only between current and previous roles but also with additional time demands and changes in responsibility that overlap with (and impinge upon) his nonwork relationships.

Research and theory helps us understand how the three types of conflict impact individuals. Based on the *scarcity perspective*, people only have a fixed amount of resources (e.g., time and energy), and given the culmination of role expectations from various life domains (i.e., work and family), they will ultimately become overwhelmed. Because it is difficult, if not impossible, to fully commit to the expectations of each life role, this felt difficulty results in role strain (Goode, 1960; Marks, 1977), that is, "the difficulty of fulfilling role demands" (Goode, 1960, p. 493). Thus, work and family roles can drain resources, and when the expectations of these roles clash, it leads to a number of negative consequences for individuals and for organizations.

There is an emerging consensus in the empirical literature that conflict has demonstrable negative effects. Recent meta-analyses (summarized in Table 1[1]) have examined the adverse outcomes that can arise from perceptions of work-family conflict. As can be seen, a variety of work, family, and non-domain-specific factors are adversely associated with work-family conflict. Work-family conflict is consistently negatively related to job, life, and family satisfaction, and positively associated with stress, depression, psychological strain, and physical symptoms. What is especially interesting is that both WFC and FWC are associated with variables that stem from the competing domain. In other words, FWC is negatively associated with job satisfaction, even though the source of conflict originates from the family domain. In many cases, but not in all, the

---

[1] It should be noted that this table is not inclusive of all of the findings of these meta-analyses. For instance, the Ford, Heinen, & Langkamer (2007) meta-analysis examined several cross-domain relationships not included in this table. The purpose was to provide illustrative samples of the consequences of work-family conflict, not to provide a thorough overview of each meta-analysis.

relationships between conflict and the outcomes are stronger when the source of conflict and the outcome come from the same domain. Thus, job satisfaction is typically more strongly related to WFC conflict than is FWC. Nevertheless, both WFC and FWC are negatively associated with a host of important work and nonwork outcomes.

Table 8.1. Meta-analyses examining outcomes of work-family conflict

Authors	Work-to-family	Family-to-work
Kossek & Ozeki (1998)	*(−) job satisfaction* *(−) life satisfaction*	(−) job satisfaction (−) life satisfaction
Allen, Herst, Bruck, & Sutton (2000)	*Work outcomes:* (−) job satisfaction (−) career satisfaction (−) organizational commitment (+) turnover intentions (−) job performance *Nonwork outcomes:* (−) life satisfaction (−) marital satisfaction (−) family satisfaction *Stress outcomes:* (+) general psychological strain (+) somatic/physical symptoms (+) depression (+) alcohol abuse (+) burnout (+) work-related stress (+) family-related stress	
Ford, Heinen, & Langkamer (2007)	(+) overall job stress (+) anxiety (+) role overload (+) role conflict (+) role ambiguity (+) tension (−) family satisfaction	(+) family stress (−) job satisfaction
Amstad, Meier, Fasel, Elfering, & Semmer (2011)	*Work outcomes:* *(−) work satisfaction* *(−) organizational commitment* *(+) turnover intentions* *(+) burnout/exhaustion* (+) absenteeism (−) work-related performance (+) work-related stress (−) career satisfaction *(−) organizational citizenship behaviors*	*Work outcomes:* (−) work satisfaction (−) organizational commitment (+) turnover intentions (+) burnout/exhaustion *(+) absenteeism* *(−) work-related performance* (+) work-related stress (−) organizational citizenship behaviors

Table 8.1. (Continued)

Authors	Work-to-family	Family-to-work
	Family-related outcomes: (−) marital satisfaction (−) family satisfaction *(−) family-related performance* *(+) family-related stress*	*Family-related outcomes:* *(−) marital satisfaction* *(−) family satisfaction* (+) family-related stress
	Domain-unspecific outcomes: *(−) life satisfaction* *(+) health problems* *(+) psychological strain* *(+) somatic/physical symptoms* *(+) depression* (+) substance abuse *(+) stress* (+) anxiety	*Domain-unspecific outcomes:* (−) life satisfaction (+) health problems (+) psychological strain (+) somatic/physical symptoms (+) depression (+) substance abuse (+) stress *(+) anxiety*

Note: Only "significant" effects are included; this typically meant that the confidence intervals did not include zero. When the same variable was examined for both work-family and family-work directions, the stronger effect is indicated in bold italics. (+) implies a positive relationship and (−) implies a negative relationship.

As discussed earlier, recent research has also explored sources of conflict from other life domains outside of the traditional family. For instance, given the increase in undergraduate students working full time (e.g., Davis, 2012; King, 2006) and many working adults returning to school for graduate education (Council of Graduate Students, 2015), attention has been devoted toward understanding *work-school conflict*, that is, the extent to which work interferences with a student's ability to meet school-related demands and responsibilities (Markel & Frone, 1998; Park & Sprung, 2013, 2015). Likewise, medical professionals have revealed negative consequences associated with *work-health conflict* for those living with a chronic illness (e.g., Gignac, Lacaille, Beaton, Backman, Cao, & Badley, 2014; Jetha, Cao, & Gignac, 2012). Scholars have even examined the complexities of *work-friends conflict* (Pedersen & Lewis, 2012). As such, we believe it is important to broaden our understanding of multirole memberships to *work-life conflict*—which includes, but is not limited to, role demands stemming from the family.

Enrichment

Recall, however, that a more balanced understanding of the work-personal life interface requires recognition of both the negative and positive consequences of balancing multiple role memberships. We now recognize that participation in multiple roles provides individuals with opportunities to *positively* impact their various life domains. While in its relative infancy compared to conflict research, scholars have indeed recognized and considered the positive relationship between work and family domains. As illustrated in Table 8.2, several construct conceptualizations have been offered to identify and describe the positive side of the work-family interface, although distinctions among these labels are not always clear, and some authors use them interchangeably (e.g., Frone, 2003). Masuda, McNall, Allen and Nicklin (2012) found that enrichment and positive spillover were unique but related constructs. We favor Greenhaus and Powell's (2006) construct of work-family enrichment because it is the most inclusive and captures not only the transfer of resources but also the improvement in well-being and quality of life due to transfer (see Wayne, 2009).

As mentioned earlier, work-family enrichment is defined as "the extent to which experiences in one role improves the quality of life in the other role" (Greenhaus & Powell, 2006, p. 73). Like conflict, enrichment is bi-directional. *Work-to-family enrichment* (WFE) occurs when work experiences improve the quality of family life, and *family-to-work enrichment* (FWE) occurs when family experience improves the quality of work life. For instance, if an employee receives a bonus at work this may create enrichment due to the fiscal improvements in the family life. Alternatively, if an employee has a great weekend with his family and goes back to work happy and enthusiastic on Monday, this can create improvements in his work life. Given the variety of possible benefits, Greenhaus and Powell (2006) proposed five categories of resources that may be acquired through various role experiences via an instrumental (direct) or affective path (indirect). They are as follows:

- Skills and perspectives (interpersonal skills, coping skills, and organization skills)
- Psychological and physical resources (self-efficacy, optimism, and self-compassion)
- Social-capital resources (networking, information gathering, and socializing)
- Flexibility (flexible work arrangements, scheduling, and planning)
- Material resources (money, gifts, and benefits)

Similar to the sources of conflict discussed, these experiences are not mutually exclusive and can interact with one another. This has been explained by the *role accumulation* perspective, such as Sieber (1974) and Marks (1977) discuss. Sieber proposed that resources acquired in one role can be invested in other roles. Marks argued that participation in one role can create energy that is used to improve experiences in other roles. This suggests that by participating in multiple roles, resources are generated (e.g., skills, social capital, and material) that can spillover and benefit the other roles in one's life.

Table 8.2. Terms and definitions describing positive work-family synergies

Label	Description
Work-family positive spillover	Transfer of positively valenced affect, skills, behaviors, and values from the originating domain to the receiving domain, thus having a beneficial effect on the receiving domain (Edwards & Rothbard, 2000).
Work-family facilitation	Extent to which participation at work (or home) is made easier by virtue of the experiences, skills, and opportunities gained or developed at home (or work; Frone, 2003).
Work-family enrichment	The extent to which experiences in one role improve the quality of life in the other role (Greenhaus & Powell, 2006).

In support of enrichment theory, empirical research demonstrates that it is beneficial for individuals and organizations for employees to be involved in multiple roles. The results of two meta-analyses summarizing the literature are presented in Table 8.3. Both studies demonstrate that like conflict, enrichment is related to work, nonwork, and health-related outcomes, and the relationships are typically stronger when the source of the enrichment is consistent with the outcome. WFE is more strongly associated with job satisfaction than is FWE, and FWE is more strongly associated with family satisfaction than is WFE. Interestingly, McNall and colleagues (2010) found that enrichment stemming from work and family were equally important for health-related outcomes. Other empirical studies have also revealed that work-family enrichment is positively associated with job performance (Carlson, Kacmar, Zivnuska, Ferguson, & Whitten, 2011), work engagement (Siu et al., 2010), and relationship satisfaction (Gareis, Barnett, Ertel, & Berkman, 2009), and negatively associated with turnover intentions (Wayne, Randel, & Stevens, 2006).

Table 8.3. Meta-analyses examining potential outcomes of work-family enrichment

Authors	Work-to-family . . .	Family-to-work . . .
McNall, Nicklin, & Masuda (2010)	*Work outcomes:* *(+) job satisfaction* *(+) affective commitment* *Nonwork outcomes:* (+) family satisfaction (+) life satisfaction *Health outcomes:* (+) physical/mental health	*Work outcomes:* (+) job satisfaction (+) affective commitment *Nonwork outcomes:* *(+) family satisfaction* *Health outcomes:* (+) physical/mental health
Shockley & Singla (2011)	*(+) job satisfaction* (+) family satisfaction	(+) job satisfaction *(+) family satisfaction*

Note: Only "significant" effects are included; this typically meant that the confidence intervals did not include zero. When the same variable was examined for both work-family and family-work directions, the stronger effect is indicated in bold italics. (+) implies a positive relationship and (−) implies a negative relationship.

Similar to the conflict literature, enrichment theory and research includes areas of life beyond the traditional family. *Work-school enrichment*, for instance, occurs when the quality of the school role improves as a function of the work role (and vice versa). Creed, French, and Hood (2015) demonstrated that work-university facilitation was associated with more engagement and general well-being; and McNall and Michel (2011) found that work-school enrichment was positively associated with job satisfaction and school satisfaction and performance. As such, enrichment can come from many life roles, including but not limited to school, work, family, friends, community involvement, volunteer work, extracurricular activities, travel, and even pets. The resources acquired through one's book club (support, commitment, and relatedness), for instance, can benefit other life domains such as school, home, and work.

CONSERVATION OF RESOURCES THEORY

Given the breadth and depth of research reviewed thus far, we adopt an all-inclusive model, by which we explore *work-life balance* through the lens of conservation of resources theory (COR). In this section, we propose that COR helps explain how resources, such as resilience, mindfulness, and self-compassion, strengthen enrichment and reduce conflict for today's working professionals.

Recall that conflict models assume that multiple roles deplete resources (e.g., energy), whereas enrichment approaches propose that multiple roles produce and protect resources (e.g., time management skills) that can be shared among life domains. Hobfoll (2002) defined *resources* as "those entities that either are centrally valued in their own right (e.g., self-esteem, close attachments, health, and inner peace) or act as a means to obtain centrally valued ends (e.g., money, social support, and credit)" (p. 307). Conservation of resources theory (Hobfoll, 1998) suggests that people seek to "obtain, retain, and protect resources and that stress occurs when resources are threatened with loss or lost when individuals fail to gain resources after substantive resource investment" (Hobfoll, 2002, p. 312). When individuals are faced with resource loss, they will be motivated to acquire and protect additional resources; if they are unsuccessful, stress and strain will ultimately occur. When individuals encounter stressful circumstances, those with a solid resource reservoir will be more successful at navigating problems and avoiding strain. Take, for instance, the employee who works 60 hours per week, has three children, and attends graduate school online. Naturally, this busy lifestyle will deplete her resources (e.g., less sleep and free time) and will potentially result in increased stress and burnout, and decreased job and life satisfaction. Yet, if she has an arsenal of stored resources, she is less likely to be impacted by stressful work and life events. Being a student may give her an opportunity to socialize and network with her fellow graduate students and professors (social capital resources); as a parent she has perspective-taking and coping skills (skills and perspective resources); and as an employee she is flexible, autonomous, and goal directed (flexibility and psychological resources). Because of the resources generated in her various life roles, she is more effective at solving problems, less affected by stress, and resistant to the resource drain that may occur. Hobfoll purports that resource gain in general is important but is especially valuable following stressful circumstances—in the face of resource loss.

Many empirical studies demonstrate the importance of resources for reducing conflict and enhancing enrichment. In a meta-analysis, organizational and supervisor support were related to reductions in work-family conflict (Kossek, Pichler, Bodner, & Hammer, 2011), and Nicklin and McNall (2013) showed that family support and supervisor support were positively correlated with work-family enrichment. Similarly, McNall and Michel (2016) found that perceived organizational support for school was linked to less work-school conflict and greater work-school enrichment. In a meta-analytic review of over 60 studies, Byron (2005) showed that coping skills and scheduling flexibility were negatively related to work-family conflict; and McNall, Masuda, and Nicklin (2010) showed that flexible work arrangements were positively associated with enrichment. Several psychological resources such as self-esteem (Grandey & Cropanzano, 1999), conscientiousness (Wayne, Musisca, & Fleeson, 2004), proactive personality, optimism (Aryee, Srinivas, & Tan, 2005), and core self-evaluations (Haines, Harvey, Durand, & Marchand, 2013) have been linked to reductions in conflict, while openness to experience, extraversion, agreeableness, consciousness (Wayne et al., 2004), proactive personality (McNall & Michel, 2011), optimism (Aryee et al., 2005), and core-self evaluations (McNall, Masuda, Shanock, & Nicklin, 2011) are positively associated with enrichment.

Thus, consistent with COR theory and Greenhaus and Powell's (2006) categories of resources (skills/perspectives, psychological/physical, social capital, flexibility, and material), it is evident that people benefit from and rely on a variety of resources made available to them in their daily lives. We believe that the resources generated in various life domains are essential for reducing conflict and promoting enrichment, ultimately leading to enhanced well-being. Because the positive psychology movement encourages us to move beyond "fixing" to a focus on "flourishing" (helping people reach their maximal human potential and quality of life), we expand upon three psychological resources we believe have the potential to help employees manage work and life roles, and ultimately flourish: (1) resilience, (2) mindfulness, and (3) self-compassion. Our goal is to help working adults not only reduce perceptions of conflict but also move the needle from good to great through their multiple role memberships.

Resilience

Quotes such as, "It's not whether you get knocked down; it's whether you get back up" (Vince Lombardi) and, "The harder you fall, the higher you bounce" (Douglas Horton) are all too common on motivational posters and cards of encouragement. Popular media consistently credits resilience as an important factor enabling people to cope with daily life stressors and massive life tragedies. Over the years, however, many different definitions of resilience have been offered across a variety of disciplines, which has led to conceptual confusion (Leon & Halbesleben, 2014). For our purposes, we define resilience as an individual, personality-based resource that allows individuals to "bounce back" after adversity (Britt, Shen, Sinclair, Grossman, & Klieger, 2016).

In general, resilience is positively associated with a number of other positive psychology constructs such as purpose in life, social support, positive reframing, active coping, and optimism, and is negatively related to substance use, perceived stress, fatigue, depression, anxiety, and physical symptoms (e.g., Smith, Dalen, Wiggins, Tooley, Christopher, & Bernard, 2008). In a meta-analysis of over 100 effect sizes, Hu, Zhang, and Wang (2014) found that trait resilience was positively correlated with positive indicators of mental health and negatively correlated with negative indicators of mental health. They argued that "resilience plays a major role in helping individuals achieve a state of positive mental health and reduce negative indicators" (p. 24).

Resilience has been studied in the context of work-life issues as a personality profile that reflects various configurations of the five-factor model of personality. For example, Braunstein-Bercovitz, Frish-Burstein, and Benjamin (2012) found that resilient people experienced lower levels of work-family conflict compared with other personality types. Krisor, Diebig, and Rowold (2015) examined the relationship of cortisol, an objective biomarker to stress, with resilience, and work-family issues. In a study of 35 employed parents, they found that cortisol was negatively related to resilience. In addition, they found that resilience was positively related to work-family balance (but not work-family conflict).

Additionally, resilience has been studied as a subcomponent of psychological capital (PsyCap; Luthans, Avolio, Avey, & Norman, 2007). Karatepe and Karadas (2014) found that PsyCap can mitigate work-family conflict, but PsyCap is a single, overall measure that does not examine the direct effects of resilience on the work-life interface. Resilience has also been studied as a cluster of multiple traits, with hardiness being the most common example. Hardiness refers to how individuals view events in their lives, and includes commitment (i.e., ability to find purpose and meaning in life along with the belief that one's efforts are meaningful and valuable), challenge (i.e., tendency to interpret demanding events as opportunities for personal growth), and control (i.e., belief that the individual can affect the world in positive ways). Bernas and Major (2000) found that hardiness did affect work interference with family through job stress but did not impact family interference with work through family stress.

In addition to examining resilience as a trait, research shows that training programs can be effective at strengthening resilience. For instance, Rose and colleagues (2013) found that a six-session resilience training program called SMART-OP was effective at reducing self-reported stress among graduate students. Reivich, Seligman, and McBride (2011) describe the Army Master Resilience Trainer (MRT) course, a 10-day program of study that teaches resilience skills to officers based on the Penn Resilience Program (PRP) curriculum. Therefore, it is evident that while resilience is a personality-based resource, it is possible (and encouraged) to develop resilience among working adults in a variety of domains.

In line with COR theory, we argue that resilience is an important resource that helps individuals recover from the stresses associated with balancing multiple life roles (conflict). Consistent with enrichment theory, those who are more resilient should also benefit more from the resources gained and transferred through multirole memberships. In other words, someone who is resilient should be better able to handle the demands of work, school, family, and friends, thus benefiting more from the resources gained from each domain.

Mindfulness

Anyone who is faced with balancing the demands of everyday life has been guilty of checking emails while spending time with loved ones, eating an entire bag of potato chips without thinking (or being hungry), or arriving at a destination but not remembering most of the drive. We live in a time where we are perpetually connected to the world through social media and would rather post a photo of our food (#delicious) than live in the moment, distracting us from enjoying and appreciating our full experiences (Brown, 2013). Recently however, there has been a movement toward educating people (from children in the classroom to adults in the boardroom and athletes on the playing field) to live in the moment. According to Jon Kabat-Zinn, *mindfulness* is awareness that arises through paying attention, on purpose, in the present moment, nonjudgmentally. While mindfulness has existed for centuries through Buddhist tradition, it has recently made its debut in Western culture (Kabat-Zinn, 1990). As evidence of its popularity, dozens of meta-analyses over the past decade have demonstrated the benefits of mindfulness-based interventions, including but not limited to interventions in schools (e.g., Zenner, Herrnleben-Kurz, & Walach, 2014) and interventions for breast cancer patients (e.g., Cramer, Lauche, Paul, Langhorst, Michalsen, & Dobos, 2015). Meta-analytic evidence also supports that one not need be ill or suffering to benefit from practicing mindfulness. Chiesa and Serretti (2009) showed that mindfulness-based stress reduction was effective at reducing stress, even in healthy individuals. Thus, we believe that mindfulness is an important well-being resource (Roche, Haar, & Luthans, 2014) and cognitive emotional segmentation strategy (Michel, Bosch, & Rexroth, 2014) that enables people to successfully balance work and life. For instance, Singh and colleagues (2010) found that mothers were able to use the resource of mindful behavior learned at work with their children at home, obtaining benefit from this resource at home.

Similar to resilience, people have a baseline level of trait mindfulness (e.g., Brown & Ryan, 2003), but this resource can also be fostered through training and intervention (e.g., Brown, Ryan, & Creswell, 2007). Roeser and colleagues (2013) found that teachers who completed mindfulness training reported feeling less stressed, anxious, depressed, exhausted, and burned out due to their jobs than those who did not complete the training. Forteny, Luchterband, Zaklestkaia, Zgicrska, and Rakel (2013) found in a sample of primary-care clinicians that a mindfulness intervention significantly reduced burnout, depression, anxiety, and stress. Interestingly, Roche and colleagues (2014) found that mindfulness was not only negatively related to anxiety, depression, and emotional exhaustion among several samples of managers but also positively related to psychological capital. This suggests that positive resources can breed other positive resources to foster well-being.

Allen and Paddock (2015) note that only a few studies have examined the link between mindfulness and work-family variables. Allen and Kiburz (2012) found among a sample of working adults that trait mindfulness was positively associated with work-family balance, sleep quality, and vitality, and that sleep quality and vitality mediated the relationship between mindfulness and work-family balance. Michel, Bosch, and Rexroth (2014) also found that those in a mindful intervention group were better able to psychologically detach from work, experienced less strain-based work-family conflict, and were more satisfied with their work-life balance. Interestingly, Allen and Kiburz (2012) found that trait mindfulness explained significant unique variance in work interference with family and family interference beyond demographic, work, and personality factors (as cited in Allen & Paddock, 2015).

Although most of the research to date on work-life balance and mindfulness has focused on family, there is an abundance of research support for mindfulness as a valuable resource for reducing stress and promoting well-being across many life domains. Being present, paying attention on purpose, and being nonjudgmental is a way for people to avoid the stresses associated with work-life conflict and enjoy the benefits of work-life enrichment. For instance, if individuals are truly mindful, they will be present with their family when they are at the dinner table, rather than rushing through the meal to answer emails. This will ultimately lead to less chaos, stress, and conflict. Similarly, if individuals are truly present and in the moment with their friends, they can genuinely enjoy and appreciate the moments, which can later benefit other life domains through increased affect.

Self-Compassion

We tend to be very sympathetic and supportive of others in the face of adversity and failure. For instance, when a friend loses a job, a child fails an exam, or a partner gets in a squabble, we are often listen and provide encouragement. We typically do not judge and criticize; we are accepting and merciful. How many times have you heard "don't worry, it happens to everyone" or "chin up—it will get better"? Compassion for others is a beneficial resource not only for the receiving party but also for the self (Sheldon & Cooper, 2008). Yet, we do not always seem to offer ourselves the same kindness and leniency. We are much more likely to say "how could you do that" or "I can't believe I could be so dumb!" In fact, research shows that people are typically much harder on themselves than they are on others, and this sort of negativity can be emotionally and physically damaging (Neff & Germer, 2013), resulting in low self-esteem and decreased mental health (Neff, Rude, & Kirkpatrick, 2007). As such, researchers have begun examining *self-compassion*, defined as "being open to and moved by one's own suffering, experiencing feelings of caring and kindness towards oneself, taking an understanding, non-judgmental attitude toward one's inadequacies and failures, and recognizing that one's experience is part of the common human experience" (Neff, 2003, p. 224). The three elements of self-compassion, as identified by Dr. Kristin Neff, include the following:

1. *Self-kindness versus self-judgment* involves extending kindness and understanding to oneself rather than harsh self-criticism and judgment. Simply stated, self-compassion means to *treat oneself* with the same kindness, understanding, and compassion that one would show a friend and not judging one's shortcomings.
2. *Common humanity versus isolation* concerns seeing one's experiences as part of the larger human experience rather than as separating and isolating. This reflects an understanding that hardships are part of the human experience and it is possible to learn from them (rather than isolating ourselves due to those sufferings).
3. *Mindfulness versus overidentification* describes holding one's painful thoughts and feelings in balanced awareness rather than overidentifying with them. This represents recognizing that hardships are part of everyday life, but feelings of imbalance can be managed. In other words, this is a willingness to observe our negative thoughts and emotions with openness and clarity, which allows for mindful awareness.

Self-compassion has been viewed as an emotionally based resource that assists with coping and performance-based pressures (Mosewich, Kowalski, Sabiston, Sedgwick, &

Tracy, 2011); individuals have a baseline level of self-compassion, but it is also viewed as a teachable skill that can be strengthened in order to promote optimal functioning (similar to resilience and mindfulness). For instance, trait self-compassion has been associated with higher positive emotions and lower negative emotions (Zhang & Chen, 2016), as well as higher levels happiness, optimism, personal initiative, and curiosity (Neff et al., 2007). Self-compassion has also been shown to influence how individuals react to negative daily life events (Leary, Tate, Adams, Batts Allen, & Hancock, 2007). However, for those who have lower levels of self-compassion, research shows that it can be strengthened through formal interventions or daily self-initiated exercises. For instance, Neff and Germer (2013) found that participation in an eight-week mindfulness self-compassion program led to a decrease in depression, anxiety, and stress compared to a control group two weeks after the program was completed (Study 2). Shapira and Mongrain (2010) showed that an online self-compassion exercise led to increases in happiness six months later and decreases in depression three months later. Therefore, it seems that practicing self-compassion leads to other benefits of positive psychology, and this resource can be cultivated and strengthened.

While research is in its early stages in regard to how self-compassion influences work-life issues, the initial research is promising. Research shows that self-compassion helps promote healthy relationships, intimacy, and conflict-resolution strategies (e.g., La Guardia et al., 2007; Yarnell & Neff, 2013; Zacchilli, Hendrick, & Hendrick, 2009). Similarly, self-compassion reduces shame proneness, fear of failure, negative evaluation (Mosewich et al., 2011), and the negative emotional reactions from failure on learning and motivation to try again (e.g., Shepherd & Cardon, 2009). In line with COR theory, we see self-compassion as an important resource for balancing multirole memberships, because those higher in self-compassion understand their strengths and limitations, value their needs and desires, and can better adapt to life's daily hardships than those lower in self-compassion. Flavin and Swody (2016) found in a sample of working mothers in leadership roles that self-compassion was negatively related to unproductive guilt and positively related to work-family enrichment. In a sample of undergraduate students, Nicklin, Varga, Meachon, Healy, Ewashkow, and Gentiles (2015) found that self-compassion was related to a reduction in stress and school-to-life conflict, and increased levels of life-to-school enrichment, self-efficacy, and resilience. In a sample of graduate students, Meachon, Nicklin, Varga, Ewashkow, and Healy (2016) found that self-compassion was negatively related to stress and overall conflict, and positively related to overall enrichment, self-efficacy, and resilience.

Taken together, it is evident that self-compassion not only leads to higher levels of well-being but also is an important resource for flourishing in many life domains. Similar to mindfulness, research also highlights that self-compassion is related to other positive resources, such as resilience. Thus, those who are self-compassionate will likely be more forgiving when they forget to pack their child's lunch or arrive late to a meeting than those who exhibit less compassion toward themselves. These people are also likely to be more resilient in the face of adversity and able to thrive in the face of completing life domains—ultimately leading to lower levels of conflict and higher levels of enrichment with work and life balance.

Summary

Taken together, both research and theory offer the idea of resource generation as a means for achieving a more balanced life. Fortunately, teaching individuals the skills of resilience, mindfulness, and self-compassion is possible and can be an important step in helping employees flourish in all aspects of life.

AN AGENDA FOR THE RESEARCH AND PRACTICE OF POSITIVE PSYCHOLOGY AND WORK-LIFE ISSUES

The studies reviewed in this chapter provide an excellent starting point for understanding how positive resources, including resilience, mindfulness, and self-compassion, influence work-life conflict and enrichment. Yet, there is still a lot of work to be done to promote the well-being of the future workforce. As illustrated in Figure 8.1, we suggest that the nurturing of positive resources promotes the successful navigation of multirole memberships through reduced conflict and enhanced enrichment. This leads us to several opportunities for future research and practice, which we discuss in the pages to follow. These agenda items can help realize the potential in capitalizing on these trainable resources to help people balance their work and life demands.

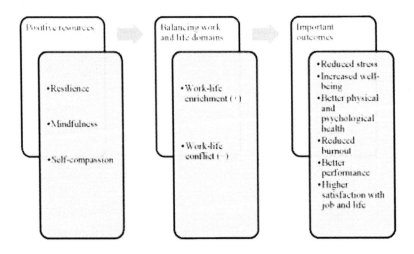

Figure 8.1. How positive resources impact balancing work and life.

Agenda Item 1: Use More Rigorous Research Designs

Much of the work-family research to date is based on cross-sectional and correlational designs, not allowing for causality to be determined (Eby, Casper, Lockwood, Bordeaux, & Brinley, 2005). In most cases, we cannot confidently conclude that mindfulness *causes* work-life enrichment to occur; it is possible that work-life enrichment causes people to be more mindful or that the relationship is due to the effects of another variable, such as resilience. As mentioned earlier, positive resources likely breed the presence of other positive resources, making it difficult to isolate the specific resources that are responsible for the changes in conflict and enrichment. This represents a challenge for researchers to untangle the combination of multiple resources that may boost well-being, and as such, more advanced research designs are needed.

This is further complicated by the fact that much of the research to date has been collected from a single source during a single point in time; it is possible that our conclusions are somewhat inflated due to single-source bias (Campbell & Fiske, 1959). There can be overlapping variability due to the data being collected from self-reports— not necessarily due to a genuine relationship between the variables of interest. While we believe there is a meaningful relationship between the positive resources discussed in this chapter and conflict and enrichment, we also have concerns about an overreliance on self-report measures in the work-family literature. We already know that resilience, mindfulness, and self-compassion are related and may be somewhat overlapping constructs. What is unclear is whether their influence on conflict and enrichment is in fact unique and significant or due to shared within-person variability associated with survey designs.

The laboratory research discussed in this chapter can aid in isolating the effects of positive resources on individual and organizational outcomes in order to determine causality (e.g., Rose et al., 2013). Yet, much of the experimental evidence discussed has emerged from laboratories with nonworkplace samples, raising the question of generalizability. Furthermore, many experimental and quasi-experimental studies utilize abbreviated versions of well-validated programs such as mindfulness-based stress reduction, which can limit their effects (e.g., Bowen & Marlatt, 2009). Improving research design will not only advance theory and research but also strengthen the applicability of positive interventions in the workplace. Managers will be more likely to implement such strategies if they are shown to be effective in the workplace and we encourage organizational leaders to be open to this type of research to move the field forward. Taking these concerns into account, we recommend that future research consider the following:

1. *Collect data from multiple sources.* Avoid designs that rely exclusively on self-reports measures; instead, consider multiple sources such as coworkers, supervisors, spouses, children, friends, or roommates. For instance, it would be beneficial to measure perceptions of self-compassion from an employee but assess a coworker's perception of life-to-work conflict. Another suggestion is to measure employee resilience and perceptions of work-life enrichment from a spouse. This would help to determine the effect of resources on work-life conflict and enrichment without the concern for single-source bias.

2. *Use longitudinal designs.* Another way to avoid common method bias is by assessing changes over multiple points in time. Instead of examining self-reported resilience, mindfulness, and self-compassion from a trait approach, these resources could be assessed as trajectories that examine the demonstration of the resources (e.g., Britt et al., 2016). In other words, researchers should first establish a baseline measure and then assess these positive resources at multiple points in time in various domains. This would allow us to explore how individuals adapt to conflict and benefit from enrichment over time. Given Frederickson's (1995) broaden-and-build model, we expect that gaining and protecting these positive resources allows individuals, *over time*, to gain other positive resources, supporting better problem solving, creativity, and decision making. This also fits with Hobfoll's (2002) idea of gain spirals in conservation of resources theory, where individuals with more resources to invest generate additional resources that could help reduce conflict and promote enrichment, leading to positive outcomes for work and the self. Without longitudinal designs, it is difficult to determine the trajectory of resilience, mindfulness, and self-compassion. Longitudinal designs may also help with the temporal ordering of positive resources—for example, mindfulness and self-compassion may come first, whereas resilience is after the adversity (i.e., conflict).

3. *Conduct research in organizational settings.* Even though experimental research has its benefits (e.g., greater control), we need to partner with organizations to conduct more field research. Although there has been an increase in resilience and mindfulness training in corporations (e.g., HardiTraining; Maddie et al., 1998), we need more rigorous designs including quasi-experimental and longitudinal designs. For instance, Good and colleagues (2016) recommended that more rigorous research is needed to assess whether employees randomly assigned to mindfulness leader training are significantly different than those in other corporate training programs. We recommend that researchers start by developing partnerships with local organizations that have an interest in worker well-being. For example, nonprofit organizations that employ human service workers may be especially prone to negative work outcomes (Hastings, Horne, & Mitchell, 2004), such as high turnover and burnout. This may be an opportunity

for researchers to collaborate with organizational leaders to conduct quasi-experimental designs.

Agenda Item 2: Clarify and Expand Positive Psychology Constructs

One point we have emphasized throughout this chapter is that while positive resources have a unique impact on conflict and enrichment (and ultimately well-being), they are indeed overlapping. For instance, mindfulness, by definition, is embedded in the construct of self-compassion, and mindfulness has been linked to the development of self-compassion (Roeser et al., 2013) and resilience in both managers and entrepreneurs (Roche et al., 2014). We selected these three personal resources because they likely serve an affective and instrumental function for work-life conflict and enrichment, and can be harnessed through training and development. However, what is not clear is *how* these three resources tie together: is there an overarching positive resource driving these subresources, or is one of these resources the causal mechanism linking positive resources to work-life enrichment and conflict (see Figure 8.2)?

Figure 8.2 provides only two examples of the possible ways in which these resources could be linked. For instance, Good and colleagues (2016) argue that mindfulness fosters resilience through recovery from toxic and stressful work experiences. Mindful employees may experience more positive emotions, and in turn, this helps them recover from the demands of balancing work and life. Yet, how self-compassion fits into this scheme is unclear; is self-compassion fostered through mindfulness, or vice versa? More work is needed to understand how these underlying mechanisms link mindfulness and self-compassion with well-being and other outcome variables, specifically related to the work-life interface.

Additionally, there are a number of other positive psychology constructs not discussed in this chapter, including but not limited to optimism, gratitude, signature strengths, hope, hardiness, spirituality, and positive affect. Researchers need to develop a parsimonious nomological network of positive psychology resources for managing work and life roles, and a construct validation study may be a useful starting point. The point is that we are confident these resources are related, but specifically *how* they operate is less understood. The suggestions for future research discussed in agenda Item 1 will help untangle the relationships among the positive psychology resources. Specifically, longitudinal data collection and multilevel modeling will provide valuable insights into *how* resources such as resilience, self-compassion, and mindfulness influence the work-life interface, and in turn, worker well-being.

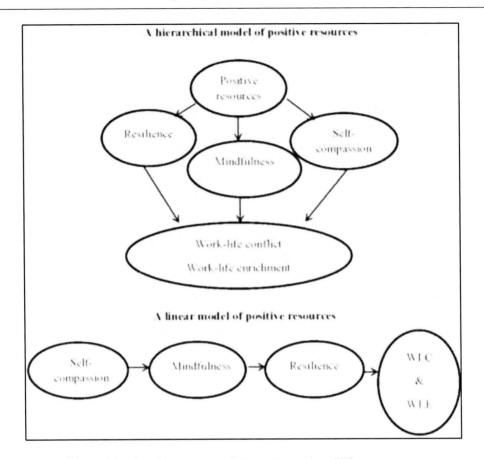

Figure 8.2. Possible models of positive resources influencing work and life.

From a practitioner standpoint, this is important because managers and consultants can better understand the foundations of training programs and then determine what specific interventions are most effective for thriving. While we know that resilience training, mindfulness-based stress reduction, and self-compassion exercises are at least somewhat effective in insolation, should we develop one overarching training program to improve return on investment? Or, if we know that mindfulness fosters resilience and self-compassion through one of the aforementioned channels, then should we really be focused on resilience-based mindfulness training—or self-compassion training with a focus on building resilience? Can both resources be enhanced through the same learning opportunity?

Agenda Item 3: Develop/Deploy Training to Increase Psychological Resources

One of the primary reasons we focused on resilience, mindfulness, and self-compassion in this chapter is that with increased awareness these resources can be strengthened and leveraged in any employee. Hefferon and Boniwell (2011) stated that "anyone can be trained to be resilient" (p. 117), and Neff and Yarnell (2013) argued that with proper tools, self-compassion could be easily adopted in one's everyday life. A useful first step for businesses is to provide employees with educational opportunities to increase their awareness about the benefits of developing positive psychological resources. For example, human resource professionals can provide employees with easy-to-implement strategies for balancing work and life—specifically surrounding building resilience, self-compassion, and mindfulness. Monthly "lunch and learns" that explain self-compassion guided meditations or exercises, inspirational tips of week, or monthly company newsletters would be a great place to start conveying the benefits of these positive resources for working adults. Interventions do not always have to be expensive or elaborate, but making employees aware of the power of these resources in their personal and professional lives is the first step to a more positive and balanced workforce. It could also help create a culture of mindfulness.

In the future, higher-quality research designs coupled with a better understanding of the relationships among positive psychology resources should guide the decisions we make about what types of training to put into practice in organizations. This is why it is critical that there is transparency and flexibility in the research-practice process. Facilitating these interventions in the workplace will not only enhance employee well-being but also help to answer the calls discussed in agenda Items #1 and #2.

Agenda Item #4: Drive Partnerships among Stakeholders

It can be easy to get siloed in our areas of expertise, neglecting potential fruitful partnerships for advancing research and practice. We believe in order to continue to integrate positive psychology into the workplace literature, clinical psychologists, neuroscientists, organizational psychologists, consultants, and human resource and other business professionals must work together to leverage each other's knowledge and strengths. For instance, academics are experts at designing and conducting laboratory research (agenda items #1 and #2), but partnering with a consultant or local organization results in more field work that helps us answer some of the questions we have raised in this chapter (agenda item #3). Or a human resources professional may want to start a mindfulness training program but not know where to start, and could benefit from working with a clinical psychologist who could implement an empirical-based program. These partnerships can cultivate a better understanding of the mind, body, and workplace connection. We urge professionals, both academic and applied, to partner with folks outside of their primary area of experience to discover ways to leverage positive psychology practices in organizations.

CONCLUSION

Through awareness and training, positive psychology resources such as resilience, mindfulness, and self-compassion can aid working professionals from all backgrounds and industries to transform their lives from *good* to *great*. Many people already embody some elements of these positive resources, but perhaps even more importantly, they can learn the skills needed to leverage the benefits of the resources in order to successfully manage work and life roles. This in turn can help individuals lead more enriching and satisfied lives. Dr. Seligman states that by 2051, 51 percent of people could be flourishing (Chamberlin, 2011). We believe that resilience, mindfulness, and self-compassion are essential ingredients for meeting this charge.

REFERENCES

Allen, T. D., Herst, D. E., Bruck, C. S. & Sutton, M. (2000). Consequences associated with work-to-family conflict: A review and agenda for future research. *Journal of Occupational Health Psychology, 5*(2), 278–308. doi:10.1037/1076-8998.5.2.278.

Allen, T. D. & Kiburz, K. M. (2012). Trait mindfulness and work-family balance among working parents: The mediating effects of vitality and sleep quality. *Journal of Vocational Behavior, 80*, 372–379. doi:10.1016/j.jvb.2011.09.002.

Allen, T. D. & Paddock, E. L. (2015). How being mindful impacts individuals' work-family balance, conflict, and enrichment: A review of existing evidence, mechanisms and future directions. In J. Reb, P. B. Atkins, J. Reb, P. B. Atkins (Eds.), Mindfulness in organizations: *Foundations, research, and applications*, (pp. 213–238). New York, NY: Cambridge University Press.

Amstad, F. T., Meier, L. L., Fasel, U., Elfering, A. & Semmer, N. K. (2011). A meta-analysis of work-family conflict and various outcomes with a special emphasis on cross-domain versus matching-domain relations. *Journal of Occupational Health Psychology, 16*(2), 151. doi:http://psycnet.apa.org/doi/10.1037/a0022170.

Aryee, S., Srinivas, E. S. & Tan, H. H. (2005). Rhythms of life: Antecedents and outcomes of work-family balance in employed parents. *Journal of Applied Psychology, 9*, 132–146. doi:10.1037/0021-9010.90.1.132.

Bernas, K. H. & Major, D. A. (2000). Contributors to stress resistance: Testing a model of women's work-family conflict. *Psychology of Women Quarterly, 24*(2), 170–178. doi:10.1111/j.1471-6402.2000.tb00198.x.

Bowen, S. & Marlatt, A. (2009). Surfing the urge: Brief mindfulness-based intervention for college student smokers. *Psychology of Addictive Behaviors, 23*(4), 666.

Braunstein-Bercovitz, H., Frish-Burstein, S. & Benjamin, B. A. (2012). The role of personal resources in work-family conflict: Implications for young mothers' well-being. *Journal of Vocational Behavior*, *80*(2), 317–325. doi:10.1016/ j.jvb. 2011.10.003.

Britt, T. W., Shen, W., Sinclair, R. R., Grossman, M. R. & Klieger, D. M. (2016). How much do we really know about employee resilience? *Industrial and Organizational Psychology: Perspectives on Science and Practice*, *9*(2), 378–404. doi:10.1017/ iop.2015.107.

Brown, D. (2013). Our virtual shadow: Why we are obsessed with documenting our lives online. New York: Ted Conferences.

Brown, K. W. & Ryan, R. M. (2003). The benefits of being present: Mindfulness and its role in psychological well-being. *Journal of Personality and Social Psychology*, *84*, 822–848. doi:10.1037/0022–3514.84.4.822.

Brown, K. W., Ryan, R. M. & Creswell, D. (2007). Mindfulness: Theoretical foundations and evidence for its salutary effects. *Psychological Inquiry*, *18* (4), 211-237. doi: 10.1080/10478400701598298.

Bureau of Labor Statistics. (2016b). Husband and wife employed in 48 percent of married-couple families in 2015. *Economics Daily*. Retrieved from http:// www.bls.gov/.

Bureau of Labor Statistics. (2016b). 39 percent of managers in 2015 were women. *Economics Daily*. Retrieved from http://www.bls.gov/.

Byron, K. (2005). A meta-analytic review of work-family conflict and its antecedents. *Journal of Vocational Behavior*, *67*(2), 169–198. http://doi.org/10.1016/j.jvb. 2004.08.009.

Campbell, D. T. & Fiske, D. (1959). Convergent and discriminant validation by the multitrait-multimethod matrix. *Psychological Bulletin*, *56*(2), 81–105.

Carlson, D. S., Kacmar, K. M., Wayne, J. H. & Grzywacz, J. G. (2006). Measuring the positive side of the work-family interface: Development and validation of a work-family enrichment scale. *Journal of Vocational Behavior*, *68*, 131–164. doi:10.1016/ j.jvb.2005.02.002.

Carlson, D. S., Kacmar, K. M., Zivnuska, S., Ferguson, M. & Whitten, D. (2011). Work-family enrichment and job performance: A constructive replication of affective events theory. *Journal of Occupational Health Psychology*, *16*(3), 297. http://psycnet.apa.org/doi/10.1037/a0022880.

Chamberlin, J. (2011). Martin E. P. Seligman's new initiative calls for a global boost in well-being by 2051. *APA Monitor*, *42*. Retrieved from http://www.apa.org/.

Chiesa, A. & Serretti, A. (2009). Mindfulness-based stress reduction for stress management in healthy people: A review and meta-analysis. *Journal of Alternative and Complementary Medicine*, *15*(5), 593–600.

Council of Graduate Students. (2015). *Graduate schools report 3.5% increase in first-time enrollment*. Retrieved from http://cgsnet.org/.

Cramer, H., Lauche, R., Paul, A., Langhorst, J., Michalsen, A. & Dobos, G. (2015). Mind-body medicine in the secondary prevention of coronary heart disease: A systematic review and meta-analysis. *Deutsches Ärzteblatt International, 112*(45), 759–767.

Creed, P. A., French, J. & Hood, M. (2015). Working while studying at university: The relationship between work benefits and demands and engagement and well-being. *Journal of Vocational Behavior, 86*, 48–57. http://dx.doi.org/10.1016/ j.jvb.2014.11. 002.

Davis, J. (2012). *School enrollment and work status: 2011*. United States Census Bureau. Retrieved from https://www.census.gov/.

Diener, E. (1996). Subjective well-being in cross-cultural perspective. In H. Grad, A. Blanco, & J. Georgas (Eds.), *Key issues in cross-cultural psychology*, (pp. 319–330). Lisse, Netherlands: Swets & Zeitlinger.

Eby, L. Casper, W., Lockwood, A., Bordeaux, C. & Brinley, A. (2005). Work and family research in IO/ OB: Content analysis and review of the literature (1980-2002). *Journal of Vocational Behavior, 66*, 124-197.

Edwards, J. R. & Rothbard, N. P. (2000). Mechanisms linking work and family: Clarifying the relationship between work and family constructs. *Academy of Management Review, 25*, 178–199. doi:10.5465/AMR.2000.2791609.

Flavin, C. & Swody, C. (2016). LeaderMoms Use Self-Compassion as Antidote to Unproductive Guilt. *Tech report*. Thrive Leadership.

Ford, M. T., Heinen, B. A. & Langkamer, K. L. (2007). Work and family satisfaction and conflict: A meta-analysis of cross-domain relations. *Journal of Applied Psychology, 92*(1), 57–80. doi:10.1037/0021-9010.92.1.57.

Fortney, L., Luchterhand, C., Zakletskaia, L., Zgierska, A. & Rakel, D. (2013). Abbreviated mindfulness intervention for job satisfaction, quality of life, and compassion in primary care clinicians: A pilot study. *Annals of Family Medicine, 11*(5), 412–420.

Fredrickson, B. L. (1998). What good are positive emotions? *Review of General Psychology: Journal of Division 1, of the American Psychological Association, 2*(3), 300–319. http://doi.org/10.1037/1089-2680.2.3.300.

Frone, M. R. (2003). Work-family balance. In J. C. Quick & L. E. Tetrick (Eds.), *Handbook of occupational health psychology*, (pp. 143–162). Washington, DC: American Psychological Association.

Gareis, K. C., Barnett, R. C., Ertel, K. A. & Berkman, L. F. (2009). Work-family enrichment and conflict: Additive effects, buffering, or balance? *Journal of Marriage and Family, 71*(3), 696–707. doi:10.1111/j.1741–3737.2009.00627.x.

Gignac, M. A., Lacaille, D., Beaton, D. E., Backman, C. L., Cao, X. & Badley, E. M. (2014). Striking a balance: Work-health-personal life conflict in women and men with arthritis and its association with work outcomes. *Journal of Occupational Rehabilitation*, *24*(3), 573–584. doi:10.1007/s10926-013-9490-5.

Good, D. J., et al. (2016). Contemplating mindfulness at work: An integrative review. *Journal of Management*, *42*, 114–142. doi:10.1177/0149206315617003.

Goode, W. J. (1960). A theory of role strain. *American Sociological Review*, *25*, 483–496. doi:10.2307/2092933.

Gottman, J. M. (1994). *What predicts divorce? The relationship between marital processes and marital outcomes*. Hillsdale, NJ: Erlbaum.

Grandey, A. A. & Cropanzano, R. (1999). The conservation of resources model applied to work-family conflict and strain. *Journal of Vocational Behavior*, *54*(2), 350–370. doi:10.1006/jvbe.1998.1666.

Greenhaus, J. H. & Beutell, N. J. (1985). Sources of conflict between work and family roles. *Academy of Management Review*, *10*(1), 76–88. doi:10.2307/258214.

Greenhaus, J. H. & Powell, G. N. (2006).When work and family are allies: A theory of work-family enrichment. *Academy of Management Review*, *31*, 72–92. doi:10.1016/j.jvb.2005. 02.002.

Gurchiek, K. (2010, September 15). Nine-year study documents benefits of wellness program. *SHRM*. https://www.shrm.org/.

Haines, V. Y., Harvey, S., Durand, P. & Marchand, A. (2013). Core self-evaluations, work-family conflict, and burnout. *Journal of Marriage and Family*, *75*(3), 778–793. doi:10.1111/jomf.12026.

Hardy, M. E. & Conway, M. E. (1988). *Role theory: Perspectives for health professionals* (2nd ed.). Norwalk, CT: Appelton & Lange.

Hastings, R. P., Horne, S. & Mitchell, G. (2004). Burnout in direct care staff in intellectual disability services: a factor analytic study of the Maslach Burnout Inventory. *Journal of Intellectual Disability Research*, *48*(3), 268-273.

Hefferon, K. & Boniwell, I. (2011). Positive psychology: *Theory, research and applications*. Maidenhead, UK: McGraw-Hill Education.

Hobfoll, S. E. (1988). *The ecology of stress*. New York, NY: Hemisphere.

Hobfoll, S. E. (2002). Social and psychological resources and adaptation. *Review of General Psychology*, *6*(4), 307–324. doi:10.1037/1089-2680.6.4.307.

Hu, T., Zhang, D. & Wang, J. (2014). A meta-analysis of the trait resilience and mental health. *Personality and Individual Differences*, *76*, 18–27.

Jetha, A., Cao, X. & Gignac, M. A. (2012). Balancing work and health: Do younger workers experience more work-health conflict than middle- and older-aged workers with rheumatic diseases? *Arthritis and Rheumatism*, *64*, S1023–S1023.

Kabat-Zinn, J. (1990). Full catastrophe living. Program of the stress-reduction clinic at the University of Massachusetts Medical Center, Shrewsbury, MA.

Karatepe, O. M. & Karadas, G. (2014). The effect of psychological capital on conflicts in the work-family interface, turnover and absence intentions. *International Journal of Hospitality Management*, *43*, 132–143. doi:10.1016/j.ijhm.2014.09.005.

Katzenbach, J. R. & Khan, Z. (2010). Money is not the best motivator. *Forbes*. Retrieved November 5, 2012, from http://www.forbes.com/.

King, J. (2006). Working their way through college: Student employment and its impact on the college experience. *ACE* Issue Brief. Retrieved from http://www.acenet.edu/.

Kossek, E. E. & Ozeki, C. (1998). Work-family conflict, policies, and the job–life satisfaction relationship: A review and directions for organizational behavior–human resources research. *Journal of Applied Psychology*, *83*(2), 139. doi:10.1037/0021-9010.83.2.139.

Kossek, E. E., Pichler, S., Bodner, T. & Hammer, L. B. (2011). Workplace social support and work-family conflict: A meta-analysis clarifying the influence of general and work-family-specific supervisor and organizational support. *Personnel Psychology*, *64*(2), 289–313. doi:10.1111/j.1744–6570.2011.01211.x.

Krisor, S. M., Diebig, M. & Rowold, J. (2015). Is cortisol as a biomarker of stress influenced by the interplay of work-family conflict, work-family balance and resilience? *Personnel Review*, *44*(4), 648–661. doi:10.1108/PR-09-2013-0168.

La Guardia, J. G. (2007). Need fulfillment in couples: Emotional engagement and consequences for personal and relational functioning. Paper presented at the Third International Conference on Self-Determination Theory, Toronto, Ontario, Canada.

Leary, M. R., Tate, E. B., Adams, C. E., Batts Allen, A. & Hancock, J. (2007). Self-compassion and reactions to unpleasant self-relevant events: The implications of treating oneself kindly. *Journal of Personality and Social Psychology*, *92*(5), 887–904. doi:10.1037/0022-3514.92.5.887.

Leon, M. R. & Halbesleben, J. B. (2014). Building resilience to improve employee well-being. In A. Rossi, J. Meurs, and P. Perrewe (Eds*.), Improving employee health and well-being*, (pp. 65–81). Charlotte, NC: IAP Information Age Publishing.

Luthans, F. (2002). The need for and meaning of positive organizational behavioral. *Journal of Organizational Behavior*, *23*, 695–706. doi:10.1002/job.165.

Luthans, F., Avolio, B. J., Avey, J. B. & Norman, S. M. (2007). Positive psychological capital: Measurement and relationship with performance and satisfaction. *Personnel Psychology*, *60*(3), 541–572.

Maddi, S. R., Kahn, S. & Maddi, K. L. (1998). The effectiveness of hardiness training. *Consulting Psychology Journal: Practice and Research*, *50*, 78-86. doi: 10.1037/1061-4087.50.2.78

Markel, K. S. & Frone, M. R. (1998). Job characteristics, work-school conflict, and school outcomes among adolescents: Testing a structural model. *Journal of Applied Psychology*, *83*, 277–287.

Marks, S. R. (1977). Multiple roles and role strain some notes on human energy time and commitment. *American Sociological Review*, *2*, 921–936.

Masuda, A. D., McNall, L. A., Allen, T. D. & Nicklin, J. M. (2012). Examining the constructs of work-to-family enrichment and positive spillover. *Journal of Vocational Behavior*, *80*, 197–210. doi:10.1016/j.jvb.2011.06.002.

McNall, L. A., Masuda, A. D. & Nicklin, J. M. (2010). Flexible work arrangements, job satisfaction, and turnover intentions: The mediating role of work-to-family enrichment. *Journal of Psychology: Interdisciplinary and Applied*, *144*(1), 61–81. http://dx.doi.org/10.1080/00223980903356073.

McNall, L. A., Masuda, A. D., Shanock, L. R. & Nicklin, J. M. (2011). Interaction of core self-evaluations and perceived organizational support on work-to-family enrichment. *Journal of Psychology: Interdisciplinary and Applied*, *145*(2), 133–149. http://dx.doi.org/10.1080/00223980.2010.542506.

McNall, L. A. & Michel, J. S. (2011). A dispositional approach to work-school conflict and enrichment. *Journal of Business and Psychology*, *26*(3), 397–411. doi:10.1007/s10869-010-9187-0.

McNall, L. A. & Michel, J. S. (2016). The relationship between student core self-evaluations, support for school, and the work-school interface, *Community, Work and Family*, *20*(3), 253–272. doi:10.1080/13668803.2016.1249827.

McNall, L. A., Nicklin, J. M. & Masuda, A. (2010). A meta-analytic review of the consequences associated with work-family enrichment. *Journal of Business and Psychology*, *25*, 381– 396. doi:10.1007/s10869-009-9141-1.

Meachon, E., Nicklin, J. M., Varga, C., Healy, D. & Ewashkow, N. (2016, March). Exploring conflict and enrichment in academics, work, and personal life among graduate students. Poster presented at the annual Eastern Psychological Association Conference, Philadelphia, PA.

Michel, A., Bosch, C. & Rexroth, M. (2014). Mindfulness as a cognitive-emotional segmentation strategy: An intervention promoting work-life balance. *Journal of Occupational and Organizational Psychology*, *87*(4), 733–754.

Mosewich, A. D., Kowalski, K. C., Sabiston, C. M., Sedgwick, W. A. & Tracy, J. L. (2011). Self-compassion: A potential resource for young women athletes. *Journal of Sport and Exercise Psychology*, *33*(1), 103–123.

Myers, D. G. (2000). The funds, friends, and faith of happy people. *American Psychologist*, *55*, 56–67. doi:10.1037/0003-066X.55.1.56.

Neff, K. D. (2003). The development and validation of a scale to measure self-compassion. *Self and Identity*, *2*(3), 223–250.

Neff, K. D. (2009). Self-compassion. In M. R. Leary & R. H. Hoyle (Eds.), *Handbook of individual differences in social behavior*, (pp. 561–573). New York, NY: Guilford.

Neff, K. D. & Germer, C. K. (2013). A pilot study and randomized controlled trial of the mindful self-compassion program. *Journal of Clinical Psychology*, *69*(1), 28–44.

Neff, K. D., Rude, S. S. & Kirkpatrick, K. L. (2007). An examination of self-compassion in relation to positive psychological functioning and personality traits. *Journal of Research in Personality*, *41*(4), 908–916.

Nicklin, J. M. & McNall, L. A. (2013). Work-family enrichment, support, and satisfaction: A test of mediation. *European Journal of Work and Organizational Psychology*, *22*(1), 67–77. http://dx.doi.org/10.1080/1359432X.2011.616652.

Nicklin, J. M., Varga, C., Meachon, E., Healy, D., Ewashkow, N. & Gentles, K. (2015, March). Examining the balance among work, school, and personal life in college students: A positive psychology approach. Poster presented at the annual Eastern Psychological Association Conference, Philadelphia, PA.

Park, Y. & Sprung, J. M. (2013). Work-school conflict and health outcomes: Beneficial resources for working college students. *Journal of Occupational Health Psychology*, *18*(4), 384. doi:http://psycnet.apa.org/doi/10.1037/a0033614.

Park, Y. & Sprung, J. M. (2015). Weekly work-school conflict, sleep quality, and fatigue: Recovery self-efficacy as a cross-level moderator. *Journal of Organizational Behavior*, *36*(1), 112–127. doi:10.1002/job.1953.

Pedersen, V. B. & Lewis, S. (2012). Flexible friends? Flexible working time arrangements, blurred work-life boundaries and friendship. *Work, Employment and Society*, *26*(3), 464–480. doi:10.1177/0950017012438571.

Reivich, K. J., Seligman, M. P. & McBride, S. (2011). Master resilience training in the U.S. Army. *American Psychologist*, *66*(1), 25–34. doi:10.1037/a0021897.

Roche, M., Haar, J. M. & Luthans, F. (2014). The role of mindfulness and psychological capital on the well-being of leaders. *Journal of Occupational Health Psychology*, *19*(4), 476–489. doi:10.1037/a0037183.

Roeser, R. W., Schonert-Reichl, K. A., Jha, A., Cullen, M., Wallace, L., Wilensky, R. & Harrison, J. (2013). Mindfulness training and reductions in teacher stress and burnout: Results from two randomized, waitlist-control field trials. *Journal of Educational Psychology*, *105*(3), 787.

Rose, R. D. et al. (2013). A randomized controlled trial of a self-guided, multimedia, stress management and resilience training program. *Behaviour Research and Therapy*, *51*(2), 106–112. doi:10.1016/j.brat.2012.11.003.

Ruderman, M. N., Ohlott, P. J., Panzer, K. & King, S. N. (2002). Benefits of multiple roles for managerial women. *Academy of Management Journal*, *45*(2), 369–386. doi:10.2307/3069352.

Seligman, M. E. P. (1998). Building human strength: Psychology's forgotten mission. *APA Monitor*, *29*(1).

Seligman, M. E. P. & Csikszentmihalyi, M. (2000). Positive psychology: An introduction. *American Psychologist*, *55*, 5–14. doi:10.1037/0003-066X.56.1.89.

Shapira, L. B. & Mongrain, M. (2010). The benefits of self-compassion and optimism exercises for individuals vulnerable to depression. *Journal of Positive Psychology*, *5*(5), 377–389. doi:10.1080/17439760.2010.516763.

Sheldon, K. M. & Cooper, M. L. (2008). Goal striving within agentic and communal roles: Separate but functionally similar pathways to enhanced well-being. *Journal of Personality*, *76*(3), 415–448.

Shepherd, D. A. & Cardon, M. S. (2009). Negative emotional reactions to project failure and the self-compassion to learn from the experience. *Journal of Management Studies*, *46*(6), 923–949.

Shockley, K. M. & Singla, N. (2011). Reconsidering work-family interactions and satisfaction: A meta-analysis. *Journal of Management*, *37*(3), 861–886. doi:10.1177/0149206310394864.

SHRM Foundation. (2014). What's next: Future global trends affecting your organization; Evolution of work and the worker. *Economist Intelligence Unit*. Retrieved from http://whitepaper-admin.eiu.com/.

Sieber, S. D. (1974). Toward a theory of role accumulation. *American Sociological Review*, *39*, 567–578.

Singer, T. & Bolz, M. (Eds.). *Compassion: Bridging theory and practice; A multimedia book*, (pp. 291–312). Leipzig, Germany: Max-Planck Institute.

Singh, N. N., Singh, A. N., Lancioni, G. E., Singh, J., Winton, A. S. W., Singh, J., et al. (2010). Mindfulness training for parents and their children with ADHD increases the children's compliance. *Journal of Child and Family Studies*, *19*, 157–174. doi:10.1007/s10826-009-9272-z.

Siu, O. et al. (2010). Role resources and work-family enrichment: The role of work engagement. *Journal of Vocational Behavior*, *77*(3), 470–480. doi:10.1016/ j.jvb. 2010.06.007.

Smith, B. W., Dalen, J., Wiggins, K., Tooley, E., Christopher, P. & Bernard, J. (2008). The brief resilience scale: Assessing the ability to bounce back. *International Journal of Behavioral Medicine*, *15*, 194–200. doi:10.1080/10705500802222972.

Stein, S. J. & Book, H. E. (2011). *The EQ edge: Emotional intelligence and your success* (3rd ed.; pp. 134–137). Mississauga, ON: Jossey-Bass.

Vespa, J., Lewis, J. M. & Krieder, R. M. (2013). America's families and living arrangements: 2012. United States Census Bureau. Retrieved from https://www. census.gov/.

Wayne, J. H. (2009). Reducing conceptual confusion: Clarifying the positive side of work and family. In D. R. Crane & J. Hill (Eds.), Handbook of families and work: *Interdisciplinary perspectives*, (pp. 105–140). Lanham, MD: University Press of America.

Wayne, J. H., Musisca, N. & Fleeson, W. (2004). Considering the role of personality in the work-family experience: Relationships of the big five to work-family conflict and facilitation. *Journal of Vocational Behavior, 64*(1), 108–130. http://dx.doi.org/10.1016/S0001-8791(03)00035-6.

Wayne, J. H., Randel, A. E. & Stevens, J. (2006). The role of identity and work-family support in work-family enrichment and its work-related consequences. *Journal of Vocational Behavior, 69*(3), 445–461. http://dx.doi.org/10.1016/j.jvb.2006.07.002.

Wright, A. (2013). 5 trends changing the nature of work. *Society of Human Resource Management*. Retrieved from https://www.shrm.org/.

Yarnell, L. M. & Neff, K. D. (2013). Self-compassion, interpersonal conflict resolutions, and well-being. *Self and Identity, 12*(2), 146–159. doi:10.1080/ 15298868. 2011. 649545.

Zacchilli, T. L., Hendrick, C. & Hendrick, S. S. (2009). The romantic partner conflict scale: A new scale to measure relationship conflict. *Journal of Social and Personal Relationships, 26*(8), 1073–1096.

Zenner, C., Herrnleben-Kurz, S. & Walach, H. (2014). Mindfulness-based interventions in schools: A systematic review and meta-analysis. *Frontiers in Psychology, 5*, 1-20.

Zhang, J. W. & Chen, S. (2016). Self-compassion promotes personal improvement from regret experiences via acceptance. *Personality and Social Psychology Bulletin, 42*(2), 244–258.

In: Work-Life Balance in the 21st Century
Editor: Jessica M. Nicklin

ISBN: 978-1-53612-526-9
© 2018 Nova Science Publishers, Inc.

Chapter 9

STUDENT WORKERS' WORK-LIFE BALANCE: REVIEW, SYNTHESIS, AND RESEARCH AGENDA

YoungAh Park, PhD and Lucille Headrick*
School of Labor and Employment Relations,
University of Illinois at Urbana–Champaign,
Urbana-Champaign, IL, US

ABSTRACT

The number of college students employed while in school is increasing due to the rising cost of higher education. There are also working adults who are returning to school to obtain higher education or professional degrees while maintaining their paid jobs. This indicates that many working individuals have to manage work, school, and life demands, but little attention has been paid to their experiences in multirole conflict and facilitation. This chapter introduces student workers as an important yet underexplored population in the area of work-life balance. We first explain why this population is important to study in the contemporary world of work and briefly define the major concepts of work-school conflict and facilitation. Next, we provide a review of literature that summarizes and integrates what is known about the antecedents and consequences of the work-school interface. On the basis of identified gaps in the literature, we suggest directions for future research to better understand student workers' work-nonwork life balance, followed by a brief conclusion.

Most of the work-life research has focused on employees who strive to manage intersecting demands from work and family life, assuming that these are the two primary

---
* Corresponding Author Email: youngah.park.io@gmail.com.

life domains for many working individuals. There is, however, a working population that has been largely underrepresented in work-life research: individuals who are employed while pursuing higher education (hereafter, student employees or student workers). These student employees often struggle to manage their dual roles in work and school or even triple roles, including family. However, there is a lack of contextualized knowledge about their work-nonwork life balance (e.g., work-school, family-school) to guide and help student employees, educational institutions, and employers that support employees' higher education or hire students (Park & Sprung, 2013). Therefore, in this chapter, we shed light on this working population and provide a literature review on their work-nonwork life interface to integrate the findings, identify the literature's limitations, and generate a future research agenda. Before providing our literature review, we begin with a short introduction of student workers as an important working population, and the major concepts of their multirole conflict and facilitation to build a common ground.

STUDENT EMPLOYEES AS AN IMPORTANT WORKING POPULATION

According to recent statistics in the United States, about 42.5 percent of full-time college students and 80 percent of part-time college students have paid jobs (Bureau of Labor Statistics, 2015). The number of working students has also gone up with increasing tuition costs, which rose more than 200 percent in last 10 years (Mitchell, 2015). Considering full-time, year-round workers with a bachelor's degree earn about $30,000 more than those with a high school diploma (US Census Bureau, 2013), no one doubts that student employees' higher education is a priority. Accordingly, most traditional college students (i.e., those who enroll in college immediately after finishing high school) reported their school role as more important than their work role and would prefer to not work during the academic year, because they must fulfill school demands to earn their higher education degree (US Department of Education, 2012). However, from the perspective of employers, student workers are an integral part of the workforce in today's world of work as they fill many necessary and contingent jobs in various industries, such as retail, services, and universities and colleges (Hirschman & Voloshin, 2007). It is also important to consider that younger college students represent the future workforce. Their early experiences in navigating through multiple role domains shape and influence their attitudes, values, and approaches toward work and life (Arnett, 2000; Loughlin & Barling, 2001).

Furthermore, the number of working adults returning to school is on the rise (Willis, 2012). For example, in 2012, 56.6 percent of employers in the United States offered tuition reimbursement to employees, whereas only 34.9 percent did so in 2009. Unemployment rates in the United States from 2000 to 2013 showed that people (25 to 64 years old) with bachelor's or higher degrees had experienced much lower unemployment rates than those with lower levels of educational attainment (Kena et al., 2014). Likewise, working adults are coming back to school to advance or change their career through higher education. Considering prevalent economic stressors and uncertainties in the global economy (e.g., job insecurity and rapidly changing technologies), more working adults are likely to continue higher education to increase their career adaptability (Klehe, Zikic, van Vianen, Koen, & Buyken, 2012). Accordingly, online distance education is a popular option for many working adults who are juggling other life roles (Friedman, 2017; Ross-Gordon, 2011). About 32 percent of all two-year and four-year institutions reported providing distance-education programs for college degrees or certificates (Parsad & Lewis, 2008). These trends suggest there are an increasing number of people who need to deal with competing tensions among educational obligations, work obligations, and other life obligations (e.g., family). Unfortunately, work-life balance research has rarely focused on these adult students.

CONCEPTS OF WORK-SCHOOL LIFE CONFLICT AND FACILITATION

When it comes to work and school life, student employees can have both negative and positive experiences as they strive to manage work and school demands. *Work-school conflict* (WSC) refers to the extent to which student employees perceive that work interferes with their ability to meet school demands and responsibilities (Markel & Frone, 1998). For example, student workers may spend less time studying and doing homework because of their job, or they may go to school tired because of their job. On the other hand, *work-school facilitation* (WSF) refers to the extent to which a student worker perceives that participation in work improves the quality of the school role (Butler, 2007). For example, the things students do at work may help them deal with issues at school, or having a great day at work may make them better students at school. Note that these concepts can be applied to the other direction, from school to work. For instance, students' schoolwork may interfere with their ability to meet work demands (school-to-work conflict), and school experiences may help students deal with work demands (school-to-work facilitation). The literature has predominantly focused on student employees' *work-school* interface, although a few studies have examined other forms of bidirectional interface, including school-family conflict and facilitation (i.e., Hecht & McCarthy, 2010; Kremer, 2016; Xu & Song, 2013). Accordingly, our review centers on the work-school life, but we also incorporate the findings of school-family interface in our review and tables. With this in mind, we now turn to empirical studies on student employees' multirole conflict and facilitation to better understand the extant research findings.

REVIEW OF THE EMPIRICAL LITERATURE

Table 9.1 summarizes the published studies on WSC, while Table 9.2 summarizes the studies on WSF. Note that most of the studies in both tables are overlapping, but we separate the tables for ease of interpretation. In addition, although we refer to variables as predictors or outcomes of WSC and WSF, it is important to acknowledge that the majority of empirical studies have been cross-sectional in nature, and therefore, causal relations have not been established. We review the predictors and outcomes of WSC and WSF that come from three general sources: work domain, nonwork or school domain, and individual differences. We then discuss moderators and mediators that have been examined in the literature.

Antecedents of Work-School Conflict

Work Domain

The majority of empirical work on WSC has focused on the work role environment. This is in line with work-family research and its theoretical notion of domain specificity, that is, that work-role or work-domain variables tend to be the strongest predictors of work interference with another role domain (Byron, 2005). For example, spending more hours at work (i.e., work hours) has been associated with higher levels of WSC, which seems to be the most consistent correlate of WSC (Butler, 2007; Cinamon, 2016; Creed, French, & Hood, 2015; Hammer, Grigsby, & Woods, 1998; Markel & Frone, 1998; Meeuwisse, de Meijer, Born, & Severiens, 2017). Similarly, full-time employees reported greater school-to-work conflict than part-time employees among adult students in a weekend college program (Kirby, Biever, Martínez, & Gómez, 2004).

In addition, exposure to work stressors was positively associated with higher levels of WSC, such as workload or job demands (Adebayo, 2006; Butler, 2007; Markel & Frone, 1998; Meeuwisse et al., 2017) and job dissatisfaction (Markel & Frone, 1998). Of important note, both work hours and work demands had an independent relationship with WSC when they were tested together within a research model (i.e., Butler, 2007; Markel & Frone, 1998; Meeuwisse et al., 2017). In these studies, work hours and job demands were correlated each other to a small degree ($r = .24 - .30$, $p < .01$). This may suggest that on the one hand student workers should not work too many hours for pay to minimize WSC, but on the other hand their perceived work demands can still increase WSC regardless of actual hours worked. These findings are congruent with role scarcity theory, in that the time devoted to the work role may leave insufficient time to fulfill responsibilities in school life; furthermore, experiencing work stressors may also undermine student employees' ability or willingness to meet their school demands (cf. Greenhaus & Beutell, 1985).

On the contrary, other work-related factors may help to ease WSC. For example, greater social support from supervisors and coworkers was associated with lower levels of WSC (Adebayo, 2006). Also, Peter Kirby and colleagues (2004) found that social support at work was related to lower school-to-work conflict. Furthermore, Xu and Song (2013) showed that social support at work was negatively associated with work-school conflicts.[1] Similarly, McNall and Michel (2016) found that perceived organizational support (i.e., overall belief that organization values employees' contributions and cares about their well-being) was negatively associated with WSC. These findings suggest that support at work may alleviate WSC because it provides workers with resources (e.g., emotional and instrumental) that help them better manage work roles.

In addition, job control—one's autonomy over decisions regarding task conducts, work methods, timing, and scheduling (Hackman & Oldham, 1976; Karasek, 1979)—is a widely known resource, which can reduce strain directly or weaken the negative impact of work stressors on strain (see de Lange, Taris, Kompier, Houtman, & Bongers, 2003; Van der Doef & Maes, 1999, for a review). Accordingly, a couple of studies found job control to be negatively related to WSC among student employees (i.e., Butler, 2007; Meeuwisse et al., 2017). This suggests that job control allows student employees to address work demands with less stress experiences so they can conserve more psychological and time resources for their school role. Likewise, another study showed that psychological rewards gained at work (e.g., status enhancement and privileges) were negatively linked to WSC in a sample of college students in Australia (Creed et al., 2015).

Nonwork or School Domain

The nonwork or school environment factors were mostly shown to be negatively related to the interference between work and school as they may provide students with some form of support. For example, financial support from either school or family was negatively associated with WSC among Israeli working students (Cinamon, 2016). With supplementary financial resources, students may not have to work longer hours for pay and thereby are able to devote more time and energy to school. Furthermore, Hammer et al. (1998) examined nontraditional college students[2] in an urban university and their conflicts between work, school, and family life. They found that students' perceived effectiveness of the university's support services (i.e., tutorial, childcare, legal, computing, student/parent services, etc.) and general satisfaction with their educational experience had a negative relationship with WSC only; intriguingly, these school-based

---

[1] Xu and Song measured both directions of work-school conflict in one scale.
[2] Their sample reported working a mean of 29 hour per week and attending school for an average of 10 credit hours per quarter, and the mean age was 28.5 years.

support and educational satisfaction did not have significant relationships with other forms of role conflict (i.e., school-family and work-family). It should also be noted that credit hours were positively related to school-family conflict (Hammer et al., 1998). Similarly, Kirby and colleagues (2004) found that among students attending a weekend college program, general satisfaction with school was negatively related to school-to-work conflict. In addition, Xu and Song (2013) found that social support from family and school domains was negatively associated with interrole conflicts among work, school, and family life[3] among nurses in a master's, doctoral, or professional degree program. Adebayo (2006) examined social support that Nigerian nontraditional students received from their family and found its bivariate correlation with WSC ($r = -.49$, $p < .01$); however, the family support was not a significant predictor of WSC when it was entered into the regression model along with supervisor and coworker support. Given the high multicollinearity among family, supervisor, and coworker support in Adebayo's study (2006), relative weight analysis or dominance analysis (Tonidandel & LeBreton, 2011) should be helpful to fully understand the impact of family support relative to other types of support.

Individual Difference Factors

Individuals' personality characteristics can exacerbate WSC or protect against WSC. Hecht and McCarthy (2010) examined the hierarchical structure of interrole conflict and facilitation (work, family, and school based), using confirmatory factor analysis in two samples of student workers. They found that the interrole conflicts can be represented as a higher-order dispositional construct (i.e., higher order construct causing conflicts in work, school, and family). Their findings suggested that individuals do have propensities to experience interrole conflict and facilitation, irrespective of the enacted roles at any given time. In the second sample, unexpectedly, they found that problem-focused coping (i.e., aimed at reducing the cause of problems) was positively related to conflict tendencies and that avoidance coping (i.e., disengaging from stressful roles) was negatively related to conflict tendencies. As a post hoc reasoning, Hecht and McCarthy (2010) explained that individuals' additional efforts to solve problems might take even more time away from other roles, thereby increasing their tendency to experience conflicts. For the avoidance coping result, they explained that ignoring stressful conditions might help temporarily, as avoidance gives an opportunity to recover one's energy needed to address multiple roles over time.

As other personality variables, core self-evaluations (i.e., the fundamental assessments that individuals make about their worthiness, competence, and capabilities) and emotional stability were negatively linked to WSC (McNall & Michel, 2011; Olson, 2014, respectively). Relatedly, McNall and Michel (2016) discovered that students who

---

[3] Xu and Song (2013) measured multidimensional conflicts among work, school, and family roles.

had higher *school-specific* core self-evaluations tended to perceive lower WSC. They further found that this relationship was mediated by perceived organizational and family support, suggesting that school-specific core self-evaluations can be considered a desirable characteristic for obtaining organizational and family support for school to alleviate WSC. In sum, these positive personality traits allow individuals to seek for support in their environment to better cope with conflict between work and school.

Consequences of Work-School Conflict

Work Outcomes

In general, WSC has been shown to be linked with meaningful work-related outcomes. Notably, WSC can have a negative influence on affective reactions to one's job. For example, WSC has been associated with lower levels of job satisfaction (Cheng & McCarthy, 2013; Laughman, Boyd, & Rusbasan, 2016; Olson, 2014). In addition, Laughman et al. (2016) showed that higher WSC was related to greater turnover intentions. These findings are congruent with the work-family literature in that work-family conflict is also related to poor job attitudes (Allen, Herst, Bruck, & Sutton, 2000; Shockley & Singla, 2011). Also important, *school-to-work conflict* predicted student workers' poor task performance rated by their supervisors (Wyland, Lester, Ehrhardt, & Standifer, 2016). Thus, WSC may increase the negative attitudes student employees have toward their jobs as well as impair their job performance at work.

School Outcomes

Most of the empirical research on WSC outcomes has focused on school-related outcomes. In particular, scholars have been concerned with the effects on school performance, considering that student role is the primary life role among traditional college students. For example, several studies have found WSC to have a direct negative relationship with grades (Butler, 2007; Cinamon, 2016; McNall & Michel, 2011; Sy, 2006). Despite these previous findings, a recent study found no relationship between WSC and school performance (i.e., grade point average [GPA]; McNall & Michel, 2016). This nonsignificant relationship may have been due to the indirect effects of WSC on school outcomes. For example, Markel and Frone (1998) and Meeuwisse et al. (2017) suggested that WSC affects the effort students put into preparing for school (i.e., homework assignments and studying), and this school effort then predicts the grades students achieve. In addition, WSC was related to a host of negative feelings toward school, such as depressed, gloomy, and miserable (Creed et al., 2015), as well as to greater intention to quit school (Cinamon, 2016). The combined findings suggest that WSC causes stress in students' lives that may lead them to feel dissatisfied with their school roles.

Table 9.1. Summary of studies of the antecedents and consequences of WSC

Study	Research design	Antecedents of WSC	Consequences of WSC	Moderators	Key findings
Adebayo (2006)	125 graduate students in Nigeria, cross-sectional	- Workload - Social support: Supervisor Coworker Family			Workload was positively related to WSC. Social support (supervisor, coworker, and family) was negatively related to WSC.
Adebayo, Sunmola, and Udegbe (2008)	141 graduate students in Nigeria, cross-sectional		Subjective well-being	Proactive coping	WSC was negatively related to subjective well-being. This relationship was moderated by proactive coping, such that the relationship was stronger for individuals with low scores on proactive coping than those with high scores on proactive coping.
Butler (2007)	253 employed undergraduate students, cross-sectional	- Work hours - Job demands - Job control	School performance		Work hours and job demands were positively related to WSC, while job control was negatively related to WSC. WSC was negatively related to school performance. WSC mediated the relationships among work hours, job demands, and job control with school performance.
Butler, Dodge, and Faurote (2010)	106 employed undergraduate students, daily diary study for 14 consecutive days		Amount of alcohol consumed	Tension reduction expectancies	WSC was negatively related to alcohol consumption (contrary to what was predicted). In addition, they found that the negative relationship between WSC and alcohol consumption was stronger when tension reduction expectancies of alcohol were high.

Study	Research design	Antecedents of WSC	Consequences of WSC	Moderators	Key findings
Cheng and McCarthy (2013)	178 employed undergraduate students, two wave, measured both directions of WSC as separate constructs		- Work satisfaction - School satisfaction	- Escape avoidance coping - Psychological detachment - Cognitive avoidance coping	WSC was negatively related to work satisfaction. School-work conflict (SWC) was negatively associated with school satisfaction. Psychological detachment and cognitive avoidance did not independently moderate the negative relationship between the WSC and satisfaction. However, escape avoidance coping moderated the relationship. In addition, psychological detachment and cognitive avoidance coping jointly moderated the relationship between WSC and work satisfaction. Cognitive avoidance moderated the relationship between SWC and school satisfaction.
Cinamon (2016)	661 employed undergraduate students in Israel, cross-sectional, measured both directions of WSC as a combined construct	- Work hours - Financial support	- School performance - Academic planning (to stay in school) - Depression		Work hours were positively related to WSC. Financial support was negatively related to WSC. WSC was negatively related to grades and planning to stay in school and positively related to depression.
Creed, French, and Hood (2015)	185 employed undergraduate students in Australia, cross-sectional	- Time demands - Psychological rewards at work	School dissatisfaction		Time demands and fewer psychological rewards were related to WSC. WSC was positively related to negative feelings toward the university (school dissatisfaction).

Table 1. (Continued)

Study	Research design	Antecedents of WSC	Consequences of WSC	Moderators	Key findings
Hammer, Grigsby, and Woods (1998)	375 nontraditional employed undergraduate students, cross-sectional	- Work hours - Perceived effectiveness of school's supportive services - General satisfaction with educational experience			Work hours were positively related to WSC. Perceived effectiveness of the school's support services (i.e., tutorial, childcare, and legal) and general satisfaction with educational experience were negatively related to WSC.
Hecht and McCarthy (2010)	Study 1: 193 employed undergraduate students, cross-sectional, measured both directions of WSC as separate constructs Study 2: 284 employed undergraduate students, two wave, measured both directions of WSC as separate constructs	Disposition for role conflict	Life satisfaction		Support was found for the hierarchical structure of interrole conflict and facilitation in the first cross-sectional study. Then, they used a two-wave study to examine the nomological network around conflict and facilitation tendencies (coping styles and life satisfaction). Students have propensities to experience conflict and facilitation when they occupy multiple roles at any given time. WSC had a lagged effect on life satisfaction.
Kirby, Biever, Martínez, & Gómez (2004)	566 employed students attending a weekend college program, cross-sectional, measured the interference of school with work (i.e., school-to-work conflict)	- School satisfaction - Work status (full time versus part time) - Social support at work			Examined the impact of attending a weekend college program on adult students' work and family lives. They found that satisfaction with school and support at work predicted lower school-to-work conflict, while full-time employment predicted greater school-to-work conflict.

Study	Research design	Antecedents of WSC	Consequences of WSC	Moderators	Key findings
Kremer (2016)	100 nontraditional employed undergraduate students in Israel, cross-sectional, measured both directions of WSC as separate constructs		- Stress - Burnout		Examined family-work conflict (FWC), work-family conflict (WFC), work-school conflict (WSC), school-work conflict (SWC), school-family conflict (SFC), and family-school conflict (FSC) in a cross-sectional study. All forms were correlated to stress. But only SWC was significantly related to subjective stress and burnout in regression model.
Laughman, Boyd, and Rusbasan (2016)	304 employed undergraduate students, cross-sectional		- Job satisfaction - Burnout - Turnover intentions		WSC was negatively related to job satisfaction and positively related to turnover intentions and burnout. Burnout partially mediated the relationship between WSC and turnover intentions.
Markel and Frone (1998)	319 employed high school students, cross-sectional	- Workload - Work hours - Job satisfaction	- School readiness - School performance - School dissatisfaction		Job characteristics (workload, number of work hours, and job dissatisfaction) were positively related to WSC. WSC was negatively related to school readiness. School readiness was positively related to school performance, which was negatively associated with school dissatisfaction. In addition, results support a feedback relation, such that school dissatisfaction is negatively related to school readiness.
McNall and Michel (2011)	314 employed undergraduate students, cross-sectional	Core self-evaluations	School performance		Core self-evaluations were negatively related to WSC. WSC was negatively related to school performance.

Table 1. (Continued)

Study	Research design	Antecedents of WSC	Consequences of WSC	Moderators	Key findings
McNall and Michel (2016)	291 employed undergraduate students, two wave	- School-specific core self-evaluations - Perceived organizational support	- Psychological well-being - Burnout		Individuals with high school–specific core self-evaluations perceived greater organizational and family support, which was associated with decreased WSC. Also, both school-specific core self-evaluations and perceived organizational support directly predicted WSC. WSC was associated with increased psychological well-being and decreased burnout.
Meeuwisse, de Meijer, Born, and Severiens (2017)	167 non-Western ethnic minority employed undergraduate students and 666 ethnic majority employed undergraduate students in the Netherlands, cross-sectional	- Work hours - Job demands - Job control	- Study effort - School performance		Job control was negatively related to WSC while job demands and work hours were positively related to WSC. WSC was negatively associated with study effort, which resulted in lower school performance. Examination of ethnic-group differences revealed that ethnic majority students report higher levels of job demands than non-Western ethnic minority students and that non-Western ethnic minority students work more hours per week than ethnic majority students. Non-Western ethnic minority students also show higher levels of WSC, less study effort, and lower GPAs than ethnic majority students.

Study	Research design	Antecedents of WSC	Consequences of WSC	Moderators	Key findings
Olson (2014)	500 nontraditional employed undergraduate students, cross-sectional, measured both directions of WSC as separate constructs	- Emotional stability - Work demands - School demands	- Job satisfaction - School satisfaction		The author develops a measure of work-family-school-conflict (WFSC). There are four facets: work to school (WSC), school to work (SWC), family to school (FSC), and school to family (SFC). Work demands were positively related to WSC, and school demands positively related to SWC. Emotional stability was positively related to both WSC and SWC. Also, WSC and SWC were negatively related to job satisfaction and school satisfaction.
Park and Sprung (2013)	216 employed undergraduate students, two wave		Psychological well-being	- WSF - Supervisor work-school support - Personal fulfillment at work	WSC was negatively related to psychological well-being but not significantly related to physical health. WSF, supervisor work-school support, and personal fulfillment at work significantly reduced the negative relationship between WSC and psychological well-being. Personal fulfillment at work reduced the negative relationship between WSC and physical health.
Park and Sprung (2015)	74 employed undergraduate students, weekly diary study for five consecutive weeks		- Sleep quality - Fatigue		WSC was negatively related to sleep quality and positively related to fatigue. Sleep quality partially mediated the relation between sleep quality and fatigue. Also, recovery self-efficacy moderated the relationship between sleep quality and fatigue such that when recovery self-efficacy was low, sleep quality was negatively related to fatigue, and when recovery self-efficacy was high, this relation did not exist.

Table 1. (Continued)

Study	Research design	Antecedents of WSC	Consequences of WSC	Moderators	Key findings

Sy (2006)	117 Latina/o employed undergraduate students, cross-sectional		- School performance
			- Stress:
			   Work
			   School
					WSC was related to increased stress levels in work and school as well as lower school performance.

Wyland, Lester, Ehrhardt, & Standifer (2016)	170 employed undergraduate students, two wave, multisource, measured both directions of WSC as separate constructs	- Job demands - Social support at work - School demands - School control	Job performance		Job demands and support at work were positively related to WSC, while school demands and school control were positively related to SWC. SWC was negatively related to job performance. WSC was not significantly related to proposed outcomes. Collected information on performance from students' supervisors.
Xu and Song (2013)	201 students employed as registered nurses in South Korea, cross-sectional, measured work-family-school role conflicts	Social support: Work School Family	Depression		The purpose of this study was to develop measures of work-family-school role conflicts and role-related social support scales. They found acceptable validity and reliability for their scales. Also, work-school to family conflict, family-school to work conflict, and work-family to school conflict were all negatively related to social support from work, school, and family. Also, the role conflicts were positively associated with depression.

Note: All studies were conducted in the United States and measured only work-to-school conflict unless otherwise indicated.

Individual Outcomes

Some of the important individual outcomes of WSC include psychological and physical health and well-being. For example, Adebayo, Sunmola, and Udegbe (2008) found that WSC was negatively related to subjective well-being (i.e., life satisfaction and affective well-being). Similarly, both Park and Sprung (2013) and McNall and Michel (2016) consistently showed that WSC was related to poor psychological health, using the same measure (i.e., the General Health Questionnaire; Goldberg, 1978). Moreover, WSC has been found to be positively linked to several strain indicators, including stress perceptions (Sy, 2006), depression (Cinamon, 2016), and burnout (Laughman et al., 2016; McNall & Michel, 2016). In a weekly diary study (Park & Sprung, 2015), WSC during the week was related to greater end-of-week fatigue, in part because WSC led to poor sleep quality. Also, multirole conflicts among work, school, and family have been positively linked to depression (Xu & Song, 2013). These findings suggest that WSC can be conceptualized as a major stressor for student employees.

Unexpectedly, several studies have failed to support a direct relationship between WSC and strain indicators including life satisfaction, burnout, and physical symptoms (Cinamon, 2016; Creed et al., 2015; Kremer, 2016; Park & Sprung, 2013). Notably, a diary study (Butler, Dodge, & Faurote, 2010) found that daily WSC was negatively related to alcohol consumption, contrary to their hypothesis based on tension-reduction theory that views drinking as a behavioral reaction to high stressors (Conger, 1956; Frone, 2008). Butler et al. (2010) speculated that their participants may have thought drinking was aggravating their WSC experiences. However, under the same theoretical framework, Mo Wang, Songqi Liu, Yujie Zhan, and Junqi Shi (2010) found that daily *work-family conflict* was positively related to alcohol consumption after work. The incongruent findings point to the different nature of the role domains involved in the two studies. That is, both work and school domains are more oriented toward task achievement and performance, whereas family is primarily an intimate social domain that is more forgiving than work or school life. In other words, the opposing patterns suggest that work-school interface experiences do not always mirror the work-family interface experiences.

Antecedents of Work-School Facilitation

Work Domain

Most research on WSF has focused on workplace resources as potential antecedents to WSF. Most significant in this line of research is about the congruence between job requirements and collegiate study (Butler, 2007; Meeuwisse et al., 2017). Job-school congruence is perceived to be high when one's job requirements and school learning are complementary, such that the job requires knowledge or skills acquired in college. Job-school congruence was found to be positively related to WSF as it may generate relevant knowledge and skills that can be highly applicable to course programs at school (Butler, 2007). In the case of other work-related resources, Creed and colleagues (2015) showed that a combination of work-based benefits (e.g., skill development, rewards, and satisfaction from job involvement) was positively related to WSF. That is, the more psychologically and emotionally rewarding work is, the more this will facilitate one's school role. Furthermore, studies have found job control and perceived organizational support to be positively linked to WSF (Butler, 2007; McNall & Michel, 2016; Meeuwisse et al., 2017). A two-wave study also supported the positive link between job control and WSF; however, contrary to expectations, job demands (measured at an initial time point) predicted higher WSF about three to four weeks later (Wyland et al., 2016). Although it was not hypothesized, Butler (2007) also reported a positive bivariate correlation between job demands and WSF. Thus, the positive job demands–WSF relationship may be worthy of further investigation.

Nonwork or School Domain

Only a couple of studies that we are aware of have found nonwork-based correlates of WSF. Social support from family, friends, and significant others was positively related to WSF, which suggests that social support from personal life helps student employees better handle work and school roles (Cinamon, 2016). School-based resources (i.e., freedom to decide how to organize schoolwork activities, support from professors and classmates, and school relevance for one's job) predicted *school-to-work facilitation* (Wyland et al., 2016). However, unexpectedly, school demands (i.e., the extent to which school requires a great deal of work to be done) positively predicted *school-to-work facilitation* and *school-to-work conflict* at a later time point (after three to four weeks). Wyland and colleagues (2016) explained that this finding may have been due to the possibility that their participants viewed school and work demands as challenges rather than as hindrances, although their demand measures did not distinguish between the two.

Individual Difference Factors

Using working student samples who engaged in multiple roles in work, school, and family, Hecht and McCarthy (2010) demonstrated that individuals have a propensity for experiencing interrole facilitation among the three life domains. They further showed that problem- and emotion-focused coping styles were positively linked with individuals' propensity to experience facilitation among the work, school, and family roles. McNall and Michel (2011) found that core self-evaluations and proactive personality had a positive relationship with WSF. Similarly, school-specific core self-evaluations had a direct, positive relationship with WSF, and this relationship was mediated by perceived organizational support (McNall & Michel, 2016). In addition, Cinamon (2016) supported the positive relationship between work salience (i.e., perceived importance of work role to one's self-identity) and WSF, suggesting that work salience determines the extent to which student workers benefit from their work role to facilitate their school life. Similarly, Meeuwisse and colleagues (2017) found the positive association between job involvement (i.e., the extent to which individuals are involved in work role) and WSF. Taken together, the findings of individual differences suggest that people with certain characteristics feel more control over their lives and have greater opportunities for work and school roles to facilitate each other.

Consequences of Work-School Facilitation

Work Outcomes

WSF seems to benefit one's work-relevant outcomes. For example, WSF has been shown to have a positive relationship with work engagement (Creed et al., 2015) and job satisfaction (McNall & Michel, 2011, 2016; Wyland et al., 2016). Additionally, Wyland and colleagues (2016) demonstrated a positive link between WSF and supervisor-rated task performance and interpersonal facilitation at work (e.g., praising coworkers when they are successful). Despite the limited number of empirical research in WSF's outcomes, the findings suggest that the ability to integrate work and school roles should enhance one's positive emotional response to the work role, leading to important outcomes at work.

School Outcomes

The most significant benefits of WSF seem to be in the school domain. This makes sense as students with high WSF draw on resources at work to enhance their school life. WSF has been found to be positively related to school performance directly (Butler, 2007; Cinamon, 2016; McNall & Michel, 2011; Meeuwisse et al., 2017) and indirectly through its effect on study effort (Meeuwisse et al., 2017). In addition, WSF may also contribute to positive school attitudes as it was positively related to school satisfaction (Butler, 2007; McNall & Michel, 2011) and plans to stay in school and achieve higher education degrees (Cinamon, 2016).

Individual Outcomes

A few studies have examined the relationships between WSF and important individual outcomes. WSF had a positive relationship with well-being (Creed et al., 2015) and life satisfaction (Cinamon, 2016). Similar to the individual outcomes of WSC, there were some mixed findings in that WSF was not significantly related to depression (Cinamon, 2016), life satisfaction (Hecht & McCarthy, 2010), and psychological well-being and physical health (McNall & Michel, 2016; Park & Sprung, 2013). This issue will be further discussed in future research directions.

Table 9.2. Summary of studies of the antecedents and consequences of WSF

Study	Research design	Antecedents of WSF	Consequences of WSF	Moderators	Key findings
Butler (2007)	253 employed undergraduate students in the Midwest, cross-sectional	- Job control - Job-school congruence	-School performance -School satisfaction		Job control and job-school congruence were positively related to WSF. WSF was positively related to school performance and school satisfaction. WSF mediated the relationships of job-school congruence and job control with school performance and school satisfaction.
Cinamon (2016)	661 employed undergraduate students in Israel, cross-sectional, measured both directions of WSF as a combined construct	-Social support: Family Friends - Work salience - Financial support	-School performance -Academic planning (to stay in school) -Life satisfaction		Social support and work salience were positively related to WSF. WSF was positively related to school performance, planning to stay in school, and life satisfaction.
Creed, French, and Hood (2015)	185 employed undergraduate students in Australia, cross-sectional	-Work-based benefits -Enabling resources -Rewards Involvement	-Work engagement -Dedication -Psychological well-being		Work-based benefits (enabling resources, rewards, and involvement) were positively related to WSF. WSF was positively related to engagement (dedication) and well-being.
Hecht and McCarthy (2010)	Study 1: 193 employed undergraduate students, cross-sectional, measured both directions of WSF as separate constructs	Disposition for role facilitation			Support was found for the hierarchical structure of interrole conflict and facilitation in the first cross-sectional study. Then, they used a two-wave study to examine the nomological network around conflict and facilitation tendencies (coping styles and life satisfaction).

Study	Research design	Antecedents of WSF	Consequences of WSF	Moderators	Key findings
	Study 2: 284 employed undergraduate students, two wave, measured both directions of WSF as separate constructs				Students have propensities to experience conflict and facilitation when they occupy multiple roles at any given time. WSC had a lagged effect on life satisfaction but not WSF
McNall and Michel (2011)	314 employed undergraduate students, cross-sectional	-Core self-evaluations -Proactive personality	-Job satisfaction -School performance -School satisfaction		Core self-evaluations and proactive personality were positively related WSF. WSF was positively related to job satisfaction and school outcomes (performance and satisfaction).
McNall and Michel (2016)	291 employed undergraduate students, two wave	-School-specific core self-evaluations -Perceived organizational support	Job satisfaction		Individuals with high school-specific core self-evaluations perceived greater organizational support, which was associated with increased WSF. Also, both school-specific core self-evaluations and perceived organizational support were directly, positively related to WSF. WSF was positively related to job satisfaction.
Meeuwisse, de Meijer, Born, and Severiens (2017)	167 non-Western ethnic minority employed students and 666 ethnic majority employed students in the Netherlands, cross-sectional	-Job control -Job-school congruence -Social support: Coworker -Job involvement	-Study effort -School performance		Job-school congruence, job control, job involvement, and coworker support were positively related to WSF, which in turn was positively related to higher grades via study effort. Examination of ethnic-group differences revealed differences in the antecedents of WSC and the experience of WSC but no significant differences in WSF.

Table 2. (Continued)

Study	Research design	Antecedents of WSF	Consequences of WSF	Moderators	Key findings
Wyland, Lester, Ehrhardt, & Standifer (2016)	170 employed undergraduate students, two wave, multisource, measured both directions of WSF as separate constructs	-Job demands -Job control -Social support: Work School -School demands -School relevance	-Job satisfaction -Job performance -Interpersonal facilitation		Unexpectedly, job demands were positively related to WSF. In addition, job control and support at work positively related to WSF, while support at school, school demands, and school relevance were positively related to School-Work Facilitation (SWF). WSF was positively related to job satisfaction, job performance, and interpersonal facilitation. SWF was not significantly related to proposed outcomes. Collected information on performance from students' supervisors.

Note: All studies were conducted in the United States and measured only work-to-school facilitation unless otherwise indicated.

Mediation and Moderation Findings of Work-School Conflict and Facilitation

We have observed that only a handful of studies explored moderators and mediators in WSC and WSF research, although it is important to systematically search for intervening mechanisms and third factors that may change the nature of the relationships involving WSC and WSF.

Mediating Mechanisms

Markel and Frone (1998) found that WSC mediated the relationships among workload, work hours, and job satisfaction with school readiness. School readiness further predicted school performance. In addition, Butler (2007) showed that WSC mediated the relationships among work hours, job demands, and job control with school performance outcome. Also, WSF mediated the relationships of job-school congruence and job control with school performance and school satisfaction (Butler, 2007). In addition, McNall and Michel (2011) found that an individual's personality (i.e., core self-evaluations and proactive personality) is related to work and school outcomes, partially mediated by WSC and WSF. McNall and Michel (2016) also found that perceived organizational support and WSC partially mediated the effect of school-specific core self-evaluations on psychological health and burnout. In addition, perceived organizational support and WSF fully mediated the relationship between school-specific core self-evaluations and job satisfaction. Furthermore, Wyland and colleagues (2016) found that WSC and WSF mediated the effect of job demands and job resources on job satisfaction and performance, while school-to-work conflict and school-to-work facilitation mediated the effect of school demands and school resources on job satisfaction and performance.

Moderators

Using the stress framework, a couple of studies have explored the role of individuals' coping styles as moderators. For example, proactive coping—efforts taken in advance of a potential stressful event or prevent it before it occurs—moderated the negative relationship between WSC and subjective well-being, such that the relationship was stronger for individuals with low scores on proactive coping than those with high proactive coping (Adebayo et al., 2008). In a similar vein, Cheng and McCarthy (2013) examined three possible moderators: psychological detachment, cognitive avoidance coping, and escape avoidance coping. In their study, cognitive avoidance coping (e.g., "I refuse to think about it too much") mitigated the negative relationship between conflict originating in school and work and job satisfaction. However, psychological detachment—mental disengagement from work-related thoughts—did not show a buffering role in any of the work, school, and family domains. In addition, psychological detachment and cognitive avoidance coping jointly buffered the relationship between

WSC and work satisfaction. However, escape avoidance coping (e.g., "I hope a miracle will happen") aggravated the negative association between conflict and satisfaction.

Using the framework of job demands-resources theory (Bakker & Demerouti, 2007), Park and Sprung (2013) tested three resources student employees may possess to minimize the negative impacts of WSC. In particular, using two-time point measurements with a 10-week time lag, they found WSF as a moderator reducing the negative relationship between WSC and psychological health after controlling for baseline psychological health. Additionally, two other resources weakened the negative link between WSC and psychological health: supervisor's emotional support for work-school life and personal fulfillment as reasons for working. Personal fulfillment as reasons for working also reduced the positive link between WSC and physical symptoms, after baseline physical symptoms were controlled. This suggests that the negative impact of WSC on health outcomes was weaker for those students who chose to work for personal fulfillment reasons (e.g., obtaining experiences). In another study by Park and Sprung (2015), recovery self-efficacy (i.e., one's confidence in recovering from stress despite adverse circumstances) was supported as a meaningful individual difference factor to mitigate the weekly relationship between poor sleep quality stemming from WSC and end-of-week fatigue outcome (i.e., cross-level moderation effect). In other words, those student employees who had higher confidence in their ability to obtain recovery opportunities and actual recovery reported a nonsignificant link between sleep quality and end-of-week fatigue, whereas those with lower recovery self-efficacy reported the significant relationship.

Lastly, Butler and colleagues (2010) hypothesized that daily WSC would have a stronger positive relation with alcohol consumption, especially on days when student workers had stronger expectations that alcohol could reduce their feelings of tension (i.e., tension-reduction alcohol expectancy). Their results revealed a different interaction pattern: daily WSC was more negatively related to daily alcohol consumption, especially on days when students had higher tension-reduction alcohol expectancy. Butler and colleagues provided a post hoc explanation that those individuals might have thought, "I'd like to drink to reduce this tension, but I can't because it will make things worse." In addition, they did not find any evidence that sex moderated the day-level relationship between WSC and alcohol drinking in that the relationship did not differ for men and women.

AN INTEGRATED MODEL OF WORK-SCHOOL CONFLICT AND FACILITATION

To summarize and integrate the results of extant empirical work on student workers' work-school interface, we present Figure 9.1, an emergent model that captures what is known about the potential predictors and consequences of work-school life. With respect to potential predictors of WSC and WSF, three broad categories have emerged from the literature: work and nonwork (school and personal life) domain factors and individual differences. Our literature review also showed that work hours and job demands, which are typically considered work stressors, seem to be the primary cause of WSC, whereas job and personal resources (e.g., job-school congruence and proactive personality) mainly predict WSF. On the other hand, several resource factors are associated with both WSC and WSF, such as social support from work and nonwork, job control, and core self-evaluations.

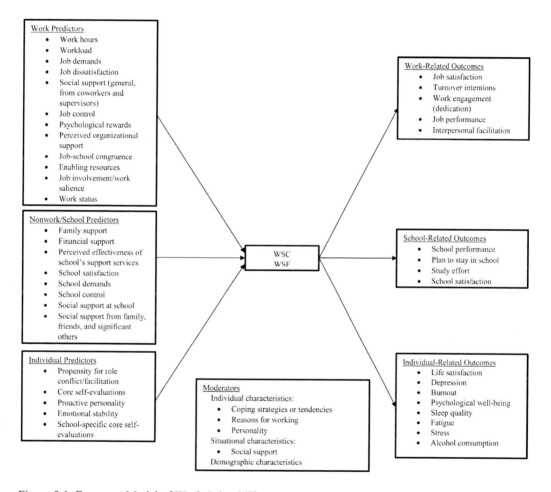

Figure 9.1. Emergent Model of Work-School life.

Parallel to the broad taxonomy of antecedents, possible consequences of WSC and WSF can include work-, school-, and individual-relevant outcomes. In particular, individual outcomes mainly include student workers' health and well-being, which were mostly linked with WSC rather than WSF. This pattern aligns with the work stress research in that stressors are examined as predicting important strain, well-being, and health outcomes. Conversely, compared to WSF, WSC was less frequently examined as a cause of important work outcomes (e.g., job satisfaction and turnover intention). This may be attributed to the nature of samples in the empirical work that mostly investigated traditional undergraduate students who were employed while attending school. In other words, the majority of the research has measured only *work-to-school* conflict (excluding the other direction from school to work), considering that those student workers mostly identify themselves as students who may value school or well-being outcomes more than work-relevant outcomes. In our review, only seven studies (refer to Tables 9.1 and 9.2) examined nontraditional students who are more concerned with their important work outcomes such as job performance that impact their financial resources (e.g., pay) to support their family and education.

Only a small number of studies have used path analyses to test WSC and WSF as mediating mechanisms to connect various antecedents and outcomes (i.e., Butler, 2007; Markel & Frone, 1998; McNall & Michel, 2011, 2016; Wyland et al., 2016). But when integrating the empirical findings, the causal linkages depicted in Figure 9.1 strongly suggest WSC and WSF as intervening mechanisms that explain relationships between the antecedents and consequences identified in the research. This is similar to the meta-analytic path analyses that have supported the mediating roles of work-family conflict between its predictors and outcomes (Ford, Heinen, & Langkamer, 2007; Michel & Hargis, 2008).

Although very little research has identified moderators, we classify the moderating variables into three broad categories: (a) individual characteristics of student employees (e.g., personality traits, reasons for working, and coping styles); (b) job- or family-based situational or contextual factors (e.g., social support); and (c) demographic characteristics, as shown in Figure 9.1. Scholars tested moderation effects on the path between WSC and well-being outcomes only, omitting the path from the antecedents to WSC and WSF. On the other hand, individual difference factors may also moderate the first causal path from work and nonwork predictors to WSC and WSF (Figure 9.1). For example, the person-situation interaction perspective (cf. Tett & Burnett, 2003) suggests that some personality traits are more activated under certain circumstances. As both the work and school life domains are task or performance oriented, the potential interrole conflict and facilitation can represent a unique context in which one's traits may interact with some of the antecedents of WSC and WSF.

FUTURE RESEARCH DIRECTIONS

As student employees' management of work-nonwork life is expected to lead to important work, school, and well-being outcomes, scholarly investigations on this working population is crucial. In this section, we frame a future research agenda that addresses identified limitations in the literature to advance knowledge about the intersections of work, school, and personal life among student workers.

Predictors and Consequences of Interrole Conflict and Facilitation

One of the most obvious limitations in the work-school literature is that much less is known about the positive interplay between work and school that can be a source of facilitation to one another (Butler, 2007). Considering the positive outcomes of WSF that were reviewed here (e.g., school and job performance, job and school satisfaction, and well-being), scholars should conduct more empirical research to better understand various work and nonwork domain factors that enable work-school facilitation in both directions (work to school and school to work). Moreover, some studies reported small, positive or negative correlations between WSC and WSF ($r = -.38$ to .23; Butler, 2007; Cinamon, 2016; McNall & Michel, 2011, 2016; Meeuwisse et al., 2017; Wyland et al., 2016), whereas others reported no significant relationships between the two (Creed et al., 2015; Hecht & McCarthy, 2010; Park & Sprung, 2013). This small or zero correlation may indicate that WSC and WSF are distinctive experiences and independent of each other, suggesting that they have different predictors. For example, stressors might better predict work-school conflict rather than work-school facilitation, whereas resource factors may contribute more to the facilitation than the conflict. Thus, greater research effort needs to be expended on examination of both work-school conflict and facilitation.

When it comes to work-based resources, we would like to note that some organizations have already implemented benefit packages specifically for employees who pursue higher education. For example, IKEA has a study leave policy that allows their employees to use two paid days for exam preparation, attendance, or assignment completion, and to extend unpaid leave up to two weeks for the same purpose (IKEA, 2014). No study, to our knowledge, has investigated formal policies or programs designed specifically for student employees, or flexible work programs that student employees can use as well. Thus, it would be fruitful to examine the effects of organizational policies or programs on employees' work-school conflict and facilitation and their job outcomes. As another important work-based resource, Park and Sprung (2013) borrowed the concept of family-supportive supervisors at work (Hammer, Kossek, Yragui, Bodner, & Hanson, 2009) and found that supervisors' emotional support for work-school life plays a stress-buffering role against WSC; however, they only investigated the emotional support dimension. Given that supervisors have much more power to make decisions on informal work-school life accommodations for student workers, future studies should extend examination of work-school supportive behaviors to other dimensions (e.g., instrumental support and creative work-nonwork life management). In a similar vein, a recent study has provided preliminary results that teachers are an important source of support for working students, such as teachers scheduling virtual office hours, utilizing software to assemble student work groups based on their schedules, and providing emotional support for WSC (Duperreault & Morganson, 2015). Thus, future research needs to explore specific work- and school-based resources that can be made available for student employees, and test their effectiveness in reducing work-school conflict and promoting work-school facilitation.

In addition, individuals may experience different combinations of interrole conflict and facilitation depending upon their role salience and situational factors. For example, a work-family study used latent profile analysis to show different typologies of work-family experiences: a group of people experiencing high work-family facilitation and low work-family conflict, another group of people experiencing both high conflict and facilitation, and so forth (Rantanen, Kinnunen, Mauno, & Tement, 2013). This latent profile analysis approach allows researchers to explore whether homogeneous subpopulations exist in a study sample (Wang & Hanges, 2011). For example, some groups of individuals might experience a dominant pattern of high work-school conflict and high family-school and family-work facilitation, whereas other groups of people might experience a combination of high work-school facilitation and high family-school and family-work conflict. From a practical point of view, this approach helps to identify individuals who share similar characteristics and attributes by connecting the group typologies with important outcomes. Therefore, future research may adopt this approach to explore and identify student employees' constellations of interrole conflict and facilitation among work, school, and family as it enables examining the concept of work-nonwork life balance in a more holistic, person-centric manner.

Overall, our review also revealed that job-relevant outcomes have received far less investigation than school outcomes. As students make up an important part of the workforce for many businesses, more research should examine the effects of work-school interface on the job-relevant outcomes (e.g., turnover, work engagement, job performance, accidents/injuries, etc.) to provide important organizational implications. That way, more organizational attention can be brought to work-school life balance issues, especially for employees who go back to school for career or degree enhancement. Also, importantly, we would like to note that research evidence on well-being and strain outcomes of WSC and WSF is fairly weak given the inconsistent findings on the hypothesized relationships that WSC and WSF have with well-being or strain indicators (i.e., Butler et al., 2010; Cinamon, 2016; Creed et al., 2015; Hecht & McCarthy, 2010; Kremer, 2016; Park & Sprung, 2013). The failure to support the relationships might have been due to methodological issues (see our methodological recommendations). Accordingly, future research should further clarify the negative and positive impacts of interrole conflict and facilitation on student employees' health and well-being, using longitudinal and objective indicators in particular.

Moderators

Considering that empirical evidence on moderating effects has been sparse, we call for more research on potential moderators. There is some evidence that individuals' coping strategies play an important role in alleviating or aggravating the negative effects of WSC (Adebayo et al., 2008; Cheng & McCarthy, 2013), but it still remains unclear whether those coping efforts can be used as an effective strategy in the long term. For example, one may cope with work-family conflict by sacrificing the family time or doing less than is ideal in the family domain as the family domain is more forgiving (e.g., delegating family duties to others and doing only good enough at home; Somech & Drach-Zahavy, 2007). These coping strategies, however, would not work well for school responsibilities because less dedication to or avoidance from school responsibilities would hinder academic performance for successful degree achievement. Also, the role of coping strategies has not been applied to work-school facilitation experiences in prior research, except Hecht and McCarthy (2010) who found a nonsignificant link between avoidance coping and interrole facilitation tendencies, and the significant positive link between adaptive coping and facilitation tendencies. Beyond testing the main effects of coping, it is necessary to systematically examine how different coping styles can interact with work-school interface to influence important outcomes.

Moreover, the two diary studies found that there are some meaningful factors that moderate the within-person links between WSC and important outcomes (Butler et al., 2010; Park & Sprung, 2015). Considering that we are far from understanding various factors that strengthen or weaken the within-person associations among predictors, work-school interface, and important outcomes, we call for a more systematic search for moderators in future research. While resources in various life domains are expected to reduce interrole conflict and increase interrole facilitation (i.e., main effects), they may also interact with potential causes of interrole conflict, or interact with interrole conflict to affect other outcomes. Conservation of resources theory proposed a concept of "resource caravans" that resources do not exist or operate in separation but rather come in bundles and work jointly (Hobfoll, 2002). Therefore, we recommend that future studies examine individual characteristics and situational factors that may drive the resource caravan for student workers.

Methodological Issues

Unraveling Causality

Most of the studies reviewed here used cross-sectional designs, which make causal inferences impossible. The major weakness of cross-sectional design combined with single-source report (e.g., self-reports) is widely known (Podsakoff, MacKenzie, Lee, &

Podsakoff, 2003). For example, such designs cannot rule out reverse causations in which poor health causes more WSC, or higher WSC causes greater perceptions of work and school demands. Although a few studies have utilized two measurement points (i.e., Cheng & McCarthy, 2013; Hecht & McCarthy, 2010; McNall & Michel, 2016; Park & Sprung, 2013; Wyland et al., 2016), they cannot establish causality. Moreover, to our knowledge, no study has used objective measures of health or strain outcomes in work-school research (e.g., heart rates, blood pressure, etc.), although some studies have used objective indicators of school outcomes (i.e., GPA; Butler, 2007; Cinamon, 2016; Markel & Frone, 1998; McNall & Michel, 2011, 2016; Meeuwisse et al., 2017; Sy, 2006). Reliance on self-report measures can be a concern because observed relationships between study variables may be driven by third factors that systematically bias reports (Podsakoff et al., 2003). Accordingly, future studies should use more rigorous designs with a combination of longitudinal measurements, objective indicators, and others' reports (e.g., supervisor rating; Wyland et al., 2016).

Of important note, a couple studies have used experience sampling methodology (ESM) to show that student workers' interrole conflict experiences fluctuate within individuals. Butler and colleagues (2010) showed that 57.5 percent of the variance in daily WSC was within persons, while Park and Sprung (2015) found that 39 percent of the variance in weekly WSC was within individuals. These findings suggest that the degree to which student workers experience WSC and its related consequences ebb and flow on a daily or weekly basis. ESM designs can even allow researchers to test the cross-level effects of important situational and individual difference factors on such fluctuations in work-school interface and well-being. Another benefit of ESM is to collect "real time" or "ecologically valid" data to minimize retrospective biases (Bolger, Davis, & Rafaeli, 2003). In sum, studies with ESM have potential to provide more insights about how short-term effects of interrole conflicts can be prevented or minimized so that interrole conflicts would not become a chronic stressor for student employees.

Lastly, we would like to point out that traditional college students are going through their early adulthood, so scholars may expect developmental changes in their interrole conflict and facilitation experiences during their time in school. Also, as universities and colleges have regular school breaks when school demands temporarily decrease, there may be some meaningful trends of their work-school interface in relation to their strain and well-being outcomes. Longitudinal measures can enhance causal inferences through estimating lagged or reciprocal relationships, or different forms of change effects, such as the effect of current changes in one variable on the subsequent changes in another variable (see Liu, Mo, Song, & Wang, 2015, for more details about different types of longitudinal modeling). Thus, we recommend that future research assesses various features of change in interrole conflict and facilitation over time (e.g., linear or nonlinear trends from freshman through senior, and across or within semesters and terms), which may be predicted by some individual and situational factors.

Diverse Samples

We would like to draw attention to the need for research on diverse samples, as the prior research findings were mostly based on traditional college students who were primarily white and female. Although we were glad to see that several studies have examined student workers with ethnic minority backgrounds or from outside of North America (i.e., Adebayo et al., 2008; Meeuwisse et al., 2017; Sy, 2006; Xu & Song, 2013), more investigations on diverse samples are necessary to enhance nuanced knowledge about different groups of student workers and their experiences with role conflict and facilitation in their important life domains. For example, student workers with lower socioeconomic status may experience greater challenges in managing interrole conflicts as they may not have sufficient, readily available resources (e.g., financial and informational support from family members with college degrees). Also, the status of full- and part-time attendance in school may reveal some differences in work-school interface and its outcomes, depending upon how the multiple roles are juggled.

Furthermore, recall that many working adults are returning to school, but there is little contextual knowledge about adult students' work-nonwork life balance in the literature. Thus, it is important to investigate nontraditional students' work-nonwork life interface. Although there is no precise definition of "nontraditional" students, they tend to be older and have other characteristics: delayed college enrollment, having dependents other than a spouse, being a single parent, or having a full- or part-time job (US Department of Education, 2002). In the educational field, some even argue that these students should no longer be viewed as nontraditional because of their growing presence on college campuses (Ross-Gordon, 2011). To better understand those nontraditional students' work-life balance issues, the existing focus on work-school interface is too narrow as they may have to juggle other life roles as a spouse or partner, parent, caregiver, and community member. In addition, nontraditional students may need more innovative educational structures and services to meet their multiple life roles while achieving educational goals. Accordingly, we recommend that future research should investigate nontraditional students and their work-nonwork life issues to increase knowledge about situational and individual factors that help them achieve the work-nonwork life balance that they want.

WSC and WSF Measurements

Last but not least, we would like to highlight measurement issues in the work-school literature. Markel and Frone's (1998) measure of WSC and Butler's measure of WSF have been most frequently used in the literature, and these scales were adapted from the work-family interface scales. Although nearly all studies showed acceptable levels of internal consistency reliabilities ($\alpha > .70$), no validation test has been conducted. Another limitation is the fact that studies mostly measured only one direction from work to school (e.g., "my job demands interfere with my schoolwork"). On the other hand, a few studies measured work-school conflict combining both directions (i.e., work to school and school to work; Adebayo, 2006; Cinamon, 2016) or adapted the measures to other life domains (i.e., school to family and family to school). As aforementioned, depending upon the nature of student workers (e.g., traditional or nontraditional students) and research questions, future studies may need to distinguish the bidirectionality of work-nonwork interface in order to investigate and clarify domain-specific predictors and outcomes. Thus, we strongly recommend conducting a full validation study to move the research forward in the area of student workers' work-nonwork life balance.

CONCLUSION

The growing number of working students has led to the emergence of research concerning the interface between work and school life. Despite the immaturity of this research, it has produced several consistent findings that highlight the potential importance of the work-school interface for working students and their organizations. We hope this chapter provides a foundation for an exciting new phase of research that helps us create work-life policies and interventions that benefit student workers, organizations, and educational institutions.

REFERENCES

Adebayo, D. O. (2006). Workload, social support, and work-school conflict among Nigerian nontraditional students. *Journal of Career Development, 33*, 125–141. doi:10.1177/0894845306289674.

Adebayo, D. O., Sunmola, A. M., & Udegbe, I. B. (2008). Subjective wellbeing, work-school conflict and proactive coping among Nigerian nontraditional students. *Career Development International, 13*, 440–455. doi:10.1108/13620430810891464.

Allen, T. T., Herst, D. E. L., Bruck, C. S., & Sutton, M. (2000). Consequences associated with work-to-family conflict: A review and agenda for future research. *Journal of Occupational Health Psychology, 5*, 278–308. doi:10.1037/1076-8998.5.2.278.

Arnett, J. J. (2000). Emerging adulthood: A theory of development from the late teens through the twenties. *American Psychologist, 55*, 469–480. doi:10.1037/0003-066X.55.5.469.

Bakker, A. B., & Demerouti, E. (2007). The job demands-resources model: State of the art. *Journal of Managerial Psychology, 22*(3), 309–328. doi:10.1108/02683940710733115.

Bolger, N., Davis, A., & Rafaeli, E. (2003). Diary methods: Capturing life as it is lived. *Annual Review of Psychology, 54*(1), 579–616.

Bureau of Labor Statistics. (2015). College enrollment and work activity of 2015 high school graduates. Retrieved from https://www.bls.gov/.

Butler, A. B. (2007). Job characteristics and college performance and attitudes: A model of work-school conflict and facilitation. *Journal of Applied Psychology, 92*, 500–510. doi:10.1037/0021-9010.92.2.500.

Butler, A. B., Dodge, K. D., & Faurote, E. J. (2010). College student employment and drinking: A daily study of work stressors, alcohol expectancies, and alcohol consumption. *Journal of Occupational Health Psychology, 15*, 291–303. doi:10.1037/a0019822.

Byron, K. (2005). A meta-analytic review of work-family conflict and its antecedents. *Journal of Vocational Behavior, 67*(2), 169–198. doi:10.1016/j.jvb.2004.08.009.

Cheng, B. H., & McCarthy, J. M. (2013). Managing work, family, and school roles: Disengagement strategies can help and hinder. *Journal of Occupational Health Psychology, 18*, 241–251. doi:10.1037/a0032507.

Cinamon, R. G. (2016). Integrating work and study among young adults: Testing an empirical model. *Journal of Career Assessment, 24*, 527–542. doi: 10.1177/1069072715599404.

Conger, J. J. (1956). Reinforcement theory and the dynamics of alcoholism. *Quarterly Journal of Studies on Alcohol, 17*, 296–305.

Creed, P. A., French, J., & Hood, M. (2015). Working while studying at university: The relationship between work benefits and demands and engagement and well-being. *Journal of Vocational Behavior, 86*, 48–57. http://dx.doi.org/10.1016/j.jvb.2014.11.002.

de Lange A. H., Taris T. W., Kompier, M. A. J., Houtman, I. L.D., & Bongers, P. M. (2003). "The very best of the millennium": Longitudinal research and the demands-control-(support) model. *Journal of Occupational Health Psychology, 8*, 282–305. doi:10.1037/1076-8998.8.4.282.

Duperreault, K. A., & Morganson, V. J. (2015). Teacher support: Expanding supportive supervision to the school domain. In V. J. Morganson & Y. Park (Chairs), *Resources for students in managing work, school, and family roles.* Symposium presented at the 30th annual meeting of the Society for Industrial and Organizational Psychology, Philadelphia, PA.

Ford, M. T., Heinen, B. A., & Langkamer, K. L. 2007. Work and family satisfaction and conflict: A meta-analysis of cross-domain relations. *Journal of Applied Psychology, 92*(1), 57–80. doi:10.1037/0021-9010.92.1.57.

Friedman, J. (2017). U.S. News releases 2017 Best online programs. Retrieved April 26, 2017, from https://www.usnews.com/.

Frone, M. R. (2008). Are work stressors related to employee substance use? The importance of temporal context assessments of alcohol and illicit drug use. *Journal of Applied Psychology, 93*, 199–206. doi:10.1037/0021-9010.93.1.199.

Goldberg, D. P. (1978). *Manual of the General Health Questionnaire.* Windsor, UK: NFER Nelson.

Greenhaus, J. H., & Beutell, N. J. (1985). Sources of conflict between work and family roles. *Academy of Management Review, 10*(1), 76–88. doi:10.5465/AMR.1985.4277352.

Grzywacz, J. G., & Bass, B. L. (2003). Work, family, and mental health: Testing different models of work-family fit. *Journal of Marriage and Family, 65*, 248–261. doi:10.1111/j.1741-3737.2003.00248.x.

Hackman, J. R., & Oldham, G. R. (1976). Motivation through the design of work: Test of a theory. *Organizational Behavior and Human Performance, 16*, 250–279. doi:10.1016/0030-5073(76)90016-7.

Hammer, L. B., Grigsby, T. D., & Woods, S. (1998). The conflicting demands of work, family, and school among students at an urban university. *Journal of Psychology, 132*, 220–226. doi:10.1080/00223989809599161.

Hammer, L. B., Kossek, E. E., Yragui, N. L., Bodner, T. E., & Hanson, G. C. (2009). Development and validation of a multidimensional measure of family supportive supervisor behaviors (FSSB). *Journal of Management, 35*, 837–856. doi:10.1177/0149206308328510.

Hecht, T. D., & McCarthy, J. M. (2010). Coping with employee, family, and student roles: Evidence of dispositional conflict and facilitation tendencies. *Journal of Applied Psychology, 95*, 631–647. doi:10.1037/a0019065.

Hirschman, C., & Voloshin, I. (2007). The structure of teenage employment. *Research in Social Stratification and Mobility, 25*, 189–203. doi:10.1016/j.rssm.2007.07.001.

Hobfoll, S. E. (2002). Social and psychological resources and adaptation. *Review of General Psychology, 6*(4), 307–324. doi:10.1037/1089-2680.6.4.307.

IKEA. (2014, January 24). *Not just a job* (benefits brochure). Retrieved from http://www.ikea.com/.

Karasek, R. A., Jr. (1979). Job demands, job decision latitude, and mental strain: Implications for job redesign. *Administrative Science Quarterly, 24*, 285–308. doi:10.2307/2392498.

Kena, G., Aud, S., Johnson, F., Wang, X., Zhang, J., Rathbun, A., Wilkinson-Flicker, S., & Kristapovich, P. (2014). The condition of education 2014 (*NCES* 2014-083). Retrieved from https://nces.ed.gov/pubs2014/2014083.pdf.

Kirby, P. G., Biever, J. L., Martínez, I. G., & Gómez, J. P. (2004). Adults returning to school: The impact on family and work. *Journal of Psychology, 138*, 65–76. doi:10.3200/JRLP.138.1.65-76.

Klehe, U-C., Zikic, J., van Vianen, A. E. M., Koen, J., Buyken, M. (2012). Coping proactively with economic stress: Career adaptability in the face of job insecurity, job loss, unemployment, and underemployment. In P. L. Perrewé, J. R. B. Halbesleben, & C. C. Rosen (Eds.), *Research in occupational stress and well-being* (Vol. 10; pp. 131–176). Bingley, UK: Emerald Group.

Kremer, I. (2016). The relationship between school-work-family conflict, subjective stress, and burnout. *Journal of Managerial Psychology, 31*, 805–819. doi: 10.1108/JMP-01-2015-0014.

Laughman, C., Boyd, E. M., & Rusbasan, D. (2016). Burnout as a mediator between work-school conflict and work outcomes. *Journal of Career Development, 43*, 413–425. doi:10.1177/0894845316633523.

Liu, Y., Mo, S., Song, Y., & Wang, M. (2015). Longitudinal analysis in occupational health psychology: A review and tutorial of three longitudinal modeling techniques. *Applied Psychology, 65*, 379–411. doi:10.1111/apps.12055.

Loughlin, C., & Barling, J. (2001). Young workers' work values, attitudes, and behaviours. *Journal of Occupational and Organizational Psychology, 74*, 543–558. doi:10.1348/096317901167514.

Markel, K. S., & Frone, M. R. (1998). Job characteristics, work-school conflict, and school outcomes among adolescents: Testing a structural model. *Journal of Applied Psychology, 83*, 277–287. doi:10.1037/0021-9010.83.2.277.

McNall, L. A., & Michel, J. S. (2011). A dispositional approach to work-school conflict and enrichment. *Journal of Business and Psychology, 26*(3), 397–411. doi:10.1007/s10869-010-9187-0.

McNall, L. A. & Michel, J. S. (2016). The relationship between student core self-evaluations, support for school, and the work-school interface, *Community, Work and Family, 20*(3), 253–272. doi:10.1080/13668803.2016.1249827.

Meeuwisse, M., de Meijer, L. A., Born, M. P., & Severiens, S. E. (2017). The work-study interface: Similarities and differences between ethnic minority and ethnic majority students. *Higher Education, 73*, 1–20. doi:10.1007/s10734-016-0012-1.

Michel, J. S., & Hargis, M. B. (2008). Linking mechanisms of work-family conflict and segmentation. *Journal of Vocational Behavior, 73*, 509–522. doi:10.1016/j.jvb.2008.09.005.

Mitchell, T. (2015, July 29). Chart: See 20 years of tuition growth at national universities. *U.S. News*. Retrieved from https://www.usnews.com/.

Olson, K. J. (2014). Development and initial validation of a measure of work, family, and school conflict. *Journal of Occupational Health Psychology, 19*, 46–59. doi:10.1037/a0034927.

Park, Y., & Sprung, J. M. (2013). Work-school conflict and health outcomes: Beneficial resources for working college students. *Journal of Occupational Health Psychology, 18*(4), 384. doi:10.1037/a0033614.

Park, Y., & Sprung, J. M. (2015). Weekly work-school conflict, sleep quality, and fatigue: Recovery self-efficacy as a cross-level moderator. *Journal of Organizational Behavior, 36*(1), 112–127. doi:10.1002/job.1953.

Parsad, B., & Lewis, L. (2008). Distance education at degree-granting postsecondary institutions: 2006–07. Retrieved from http://nces.ed.gov/.

Podsakoff, P. M., MacKenzie, S. B., Lee, J. Y., & Podsakoff, N. P. (2003). Common method biases in behavioral research: A critical review of the literature and recommended remedies. *Journal of Applied Psychology, 88*, 879–903. doi:10.1037/0021-9010.88.5.879.

Rantanen, J., Kinnunen, U., Mauno, S., & Tement, S. (2013). Patterns of conflict and enrichment in work-family balance: A three-dimensional typology. *Work and Stress, 27*, 141–163. doi:10.1080/02678373.2013.791074.

Ross-Gordon, J. M. (2011). Research on adult learners: Supporting the needs of a student population that is no longer nontraditional. *Peer Review, 13*, 26–29. Retrieved from https://www.aacu.org/.

Shockley, K. M., & Singla, N. (2011). Reconsidering work-family interactions and satisfaction: A meta-analysis. *Journal of Management, 37*(3), 861–886. doi: 10.1177/0149206310394864.

Somech, A., & Drach-Zahavy, A. (2007). Strategies for coping with work-family conflict: The distinctive relationships of gender role ideology. *Journal of Occupational Health Psychology, 12*, 1–19. doi:10.1037/1076-8998.12.1.1.

Sy, S. R. (2006). Family and work influences on the transition to college among Latina adolescents. *Hispanic Journal of Behavioral Sciences, 28*, 368–386. doi:10.1177/0739986306290372.

Tett, R. P., & Burnett, D. D. (2003). A personality trait-based interactionist model of job performance. *Journal of Applied Psychology, 88*, 500–517. doi:10.1037/0021-9010.88.3.500.

Tonidandel, S., & LeBreton, J. M. (2011). Relative importance analysis: A useful supplement to regression analysis. *Journal of Business Psychology, 26*, 1–9.

US Census Bureau. (2013). Income, poverty, and health insurance coverage in the United States (Series P60–245). Retrieved from https://www.census.gov/.

US Department of Education. (2012). Integrated postsecondary education data system completion survey. Retrieved from https://nces.ed.gov/ipeds.

US Department of Education, National Center for Education Statistics. (2002). Nontraditional undergraduates, *NCES* 2002-012. Retrieved from https://nces.ed.gov/.

Van der Doef, M., & Maes, S. (1999). The job demand-control(-support) model and psychological well-being: A review of 20 years of empirical research. *Work and Stress, 13*, 87–114. doi:10.1080/026783799296084.

Wang, M., & Hanges, P. J. (2011). Latent class procedures: Applications to organizational research. *Organizational Research Method, 14*, 24–31. doi:10.1177/1094428110383988.

Wang, M., Liu, S., Zhan, Y., & Shi, J. (2010). Daily work-family conflict and alcohol use: Testing the cross-level moderation effects of peer drinking norms and social support. *Journal of Applied Psychology, 95*, 377–386. doi:10.1037/a0018138.

Willis, M. (2012). Offering tuition reimbursement gives competitive edge. *Benefits USA 2012/2013*. Retrieved from http://www.compdatasurveys.com/.

Wyland, R., Lester, S. W., Ehrhardt, K., & Standifer, R. (2016). An examination of the relationship between the work-school interface, job satisfaction, and job performance. *Journal of Business and Psychology, 31*, 187–203. doi:10.1007/s10869-015-9415-8.

Xu, L., & Song, R. (2013). Development and validation of the work-family-school role conflicts and role-related social support scales among registered nurses with multiple roles. *International Journal of Nursing Studies, 50*, 1391–1398. doi:10.1016/j.ijnurstu.2013.01.003.

In: Work-Life Balance in the 21st Century   ISBN: 978-1-53612-526-9
Editor: Jessica M. Nicklin   © 2018 Nova Science Publishers, Inc.

Chapter 10

ENHANCING SELF-AWARENESS IN ORGANIZATIONS: A HOLISTIC APPROACH TO WORK-LIFE INTEGRATION

Elena O. Stepanova[1,], Lucía Ceja[2] and Félix Castillo[1]*

[1]Department of Psychiatry and Legal Medicine,
Autonomous University of Barcelona, Barcelona, Spain
[2]Family-Owned Business Chair, IESE Business School, Barcelona, Spain

ABSTRACT

Against the backdrop of positive organizational scholarship and work-life integration, the present study aims to explore the factors that lead to generative (capability/capacity enhancement, etc.) dynamics in organizations, and to study their effects on individuals' work-life integration.[1] Specifically, self-awareness, understood as one's awareness of, and trust in, one's own personal characteristics, values, motives, feelings, and cognition, is considered as one of the key factors that enhance generative dynamics such as individual and organizational strengths, vitality, and resilience, among others. The central question of the study was as follows: *How do practices enabling self-awareness affect the experience of one's work and personal environments?* To explore this research question, an intervention study was conducted in a nonprofit agricultural cooperative, located in the region of Catalonia, Spain. The study consisted of a series of training sessions, and a pre- and postcourse qualitative questionnaire. The training sessions focused on enhancing self-awareness, enabling human excellence, and capability

---

[*] Corresponding Author Email: elena.o.stepanova@gmail.com.
[1] Gratitude is extended to the Panakía Project Platform and the team of professionals who delivered the training course mentioned in this study, namely, Félix Castillo, Mónica Díaz, Rosa Garriga, Lu Rosales, and Elena Stepanova.
The authors would also like to express their thanks to Josep María Blanch and the KOFARIPS research group for the use of some of the questionnaire items.

building. The study comprised a total of 45 participants. Their testimonies revealed a heightened level of self-awareness and self-management, an improvement in relationships with colleagues and family members, and an enhancement of goal-setting subsequent to the training program. From an applied perspective, these findings point to the importance of developing training programs that enhance individuals' self-awareness, strengths, high-quality connections at work, and general work-life supportive environments.

Over the last several decades, the intensification of working life in both the public and private sectors (Blanch, Crespo, & Sahagún, 2012) and the higher level of stress and its adverse effects on employees' well-being (O'Driscoll, Poelmans, Spector, Cooper, Allen, & Sanchez, 2003) have drawn the research community's attention to the interaction between professional and personal areas of life. Initially considered conflicting spheres (Greenhaus & Beutell, 1985), work and family have been shown to be bidirectional, mutually beneficial, and enriching domains (Clark, 2000; Greenhaus & Powell, 2006). There has also been a shift of focus from family to life in general, acknowledging the importance of other realms of life besides those directly related to the family, thus allowing for the integration of employees' diverse roles and aspirations (Kalliath & Brough, 2008). The idea of balance between work and life has also been examined empirically (Greenhaus, Collins, & Shaw, 2003), and the term work-life integration is understood to encompass different aspects and stages of life, which do not necessarily require equal amounts of energy, resources, or time and hinge on individual circumstances and priorities (Rapoport, Bailyn, Fletcher, & Pruitt, 2002). Feldman and Hall (2013) took this idea even further by offering the whole person perspective: individuals, whether at home or at work, integrate various identities (e.g., professional, parent, writer, and community member) and coexist in various domains (e.g., work, family, self, and community) simultaneously. The precedence given to one of the identities or domains varies throughout people's lives. Hence, research argues that active participation in one field of life can provide access to resources and experiences that are conducive to individual development (Barnett & Hyde, 2001). Likewise, Greenhaus and Powell (2006) demonstrated that positive experiences generated in one role in life can serve to buffer the negative experiences (e.g., stress) faced in other roles (work-life enrichment). The authors define work-family enrichment as the extent to which experiences in one role improve the quality of life in the other. In this regard, the whole person perspective should be adopted when undertaking organizational efforts aimed at integrating work and life needs, in order to ensure that the practices and policies implemented reflect the actual needs and experiences of the workforce, thus benefiting both the individuals and the company as a whole.

The need to afford greater attention to employees, as an organization's most valuable asset, is also reverberated in the developing stream of research on positive organizational scholarship (e.g., Cameron, Dutton, & Quinn, 2003). Therefore, it is not surprising that one of the current interests of organizational psychologists is the relationship between organizational characteristics and employees' psychological well-being and performance (Macik-Frey, Quick, & Nelson, 2007). Companies put various structural support measures in place (initiatives that enhance employee control over their time, place, and amount of work), thereby providing employees with additional resources to integrate work, family, and personal life (Kossek, Lewis, & Hammer, 2010). Nevertheless, research has shown that these structural supports do not suffice, and cultural supports (informal policies and social and relational support as shown by supervisors, coworkers, and general organizational cultural norms supportive of one's personal demands) are prerequisites for work-life integration. Nevertheless, not all organizations are willing or prepared to offer cultural supports, or see the business case for doing so (Kossek & Friede, 2006), which does not prevent individuals from seeking and finding their own resources to integrate various aspects of life. In this regard, it seems pertinent to explore employees' work experiences in the organizational context where work-life enrichment is not directly addressed. The goal is to ascertain inherent resources at the individual and organizational levels that can be transferred to other realms of life, while providing information regarding key drivers of positive behavior in the workplace that can enable individuals to rise to new levels of achievement and flourishing in the integration of work-life spheres.

Positive organizational scholarship (POS) lays emphasis on positive organizational phenomena, resulting in enhanced human well-being. It is distinguished from traditional organizational studies in that it seeks to understand what represents the best of the human condition (Cameron et al., 2003). The fundamental idea of POS is that an understanding of the drivers of positive behavior in the workplace can enable individuals and organizations to rise to new levels of achievement and flourishing (Cameron & Spreitzer, 2011; Roberts, Spreitzer, Dutton, Quinn, Heaphy, & Barker, 2005). A key concept within the POS field is *self-awareness*, understood as one's awareness of, and trust in, one's own personal characteristics, values, motives, feelings, and cognition (May, Chan, Hodges, & Avolio, 2003). Self-awareness is considered one of the key factors that enhance generative dynamics, such as individual and organizational strengths, vitality, and resilience, among others (Forman, Herbert, Moitra, Yeomans, & Geller, 2007; Kashdan & Ciarrochi, 2013). It has also been propounded that self-awareness is critical to setting clear goals and priorities in life and acting accordingly, which may allow for better management of conflict between the work and life spheres (Friedman & Greenhaus, 2000). Acknowledging self-awareness also allows for a more holistic approach to work-life interaction (ibid.).

In the context of work-life enrichment and positive organizational scholarship, the present study aims to explore the factors that lead to generative (i.e., life-building, capability-enhancing, and capacity-creating) practices in organizations, and their effects on individuals' perception of work-life spheres. Specifically, the link between self-awareness practices and employees' work-life experiences is examined, and how these work-life experiences can produce generative dynamics for work-life integration.

Therefore, the central question of this chapter is as follows: *How do practices facilitating self-awareness affect the experience of one's work and work-life integration?* We hold a particular interest in observing individuals' perceptions of their own lives, working environment and sources of inspiration, the perceptions of a variety of life spheres, and experiences of social interactions and work practices. To answer this question, the holistic approach to work-life integration is first introduced. Subsequently, the existing link between work-life integration and positive organizational scholarship is delineated, as the basis for our research. This is followed by the presentation of an empirical exploratory study examining the perception of work-life integration experience prior and subsequent to a series of training sessions conducted as a personnel development effort in a nonprofit agricultural cooperative, located in the region of Catalonia, Spain. Finally, recommendations are put forward for future research and practice regarding ways organizations could contribute to their employees' well-being and work-life integration.

A HOLISTIC APPROACH TO WORK-LIFE INTEGRATION

Research exploring work-life balance originally focused on two life domains, namely, work and family. Over time, research has become more inclusive, expanding to the life domain, thus encompassing those with other needs or obligations besides family (Kalliath & Brough, 2008). For instance, single people without children, people with elderly care responsibilities, active community members, sportspeople, or those devoted to a particular hobby outside working hours (Casper, Marquardt, Roberto, & Buss, 2016) should also be taken into consideration. Attention was drawn to the fact that an individual's experience of work and life domains do not exist separately and are interrelated on a daily basis (e.g., one navigates through work and nonwork areas throughout the day) and reflect who people are (e.g., a professional, parent, soccer fan, etc.; Feldman & Hall, 2013). For this reason, Feldman and Hall (2013) suggested adding the "whole person" perspective to work-life research, which involves the interactions between three dimensions: domain, identity, and temporal integration (see Figure 10.1). They argue that different life settings or domains (e.g., work, family, community, and self) are not separate and therefore are not different identities or roles (e.g., employee, partner, and parent) (ibid.; Las Heras & Hall, 2008). Their cohesive interaction is key to positive functioning and general well-being. For example, an excelling employee absent from his parenting responsibilities might come up against challenges in his unattended family sphere, which depending on its scope, could eventually affect his performance.

The whole person approach, and specifically its domain facet, does not necessarily reflect people's boundary preferences for work-life integration (Nippert-Eng, 1996). It examines the person in the various contexts, acknowledging that shifting between domains does not mean switching off experiences that occurred therein. For instance, dual-career families with small children and eldercare responsibilities have demands that are permanent and spill over across various domains; these demands occupy an intense presence in people's lives. That is, an individual, while having different identities (e.g., woman, mother, and professional), depending on the specific context, activates one or another but integrates all of them, being one whole person (Feldman & Hall, 2013).

Finally, temporal integration reflects an individual's aspirations for the future, particularly linked to purpose and possibilities that generate vitality (Feldman & Hall, 2013), and entails continuous change as people evolve in their lives. For instance, understanding individuals' motivation and providing the context for their flourishing contributes to well-being and health that, through spillover effects, eventually contributes to better organizational performance. For instance, a longitudinal study on well-being in family, personal, and career spheres found that a high level of family and personal well-being predicted a high level of career success over time. Interestingly, the relationship did not hold in the opposite direction (Hall, Las Heras, Kossek, & Lee, 2007). In a nutshell, it is important to work alongside individuals at enhancing self-awareness of their own personal resources that arise in each of their different identities (depending on the context), with the aim of helping them integrate all of their different facets, acknowledging the wholeness of their being, and increasing their well-being and performance.

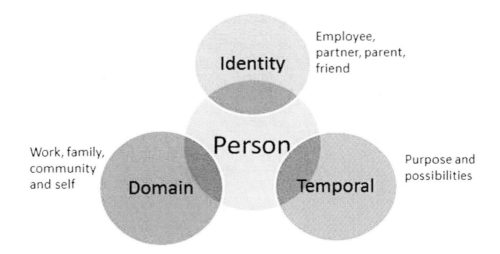

Figure 10.1. The whole person perspective (adapted from Feldman & Hall, 2013).

USING THE LENS OF POSITIVE ORGANIZATIONAL SCHOLARSHIP TO ENHANCE WORK-LIFE INTEGRATION

Positive organizational scholarship (POS) focuses on enriching organizational studies by exploring the positive, enabling characteristics (strengths, capabilities, possibilities, and challenges) in a context (individual, group, or organization) that leads to generative dynamics, allowing organizations and their members to flourish (Spreitzer, 2013). As in work-life enrichment, POS examines a variety of mechanisms that contribute to positive organizational dynamics: cognitive (meaning and sense making), affective (built on the theory of positive emotions), agentic (proactivity), and social structural (systems, job design, and structure).

One of the most widely used theories within POS, which argues that unlocking human potential and existing possibilities benefit organizational and human functioning (Spreitzer, 2013), is the Self-Determination Theory (SDT; Deci & Ryan, 2000). Self-Determination Theory indicates that self-determined motivation or intrinsic motivation (doing something because it is inherently interesting or enjoyable) flourishes in contexts that satisfy basic human needs for competence, autonomy, and relatedness. Clark Hull (1943) defined a basic need as an energizing state that, if satisfied, is conducive to health and well-being but, if not satisfied, contributes to pathology and ill-being.

Within SDT, a basic psychological need is described as a universal and innate nutrient for optimal functioning, personal growth, and work-life integration (Deci & Ryan, 2008). According to the SDT, self-determined motivation is based on the fulfillment of three basic psychological needs: (1) the need for autonomy; (2) the need for competency; and (3) the need for relatedness.

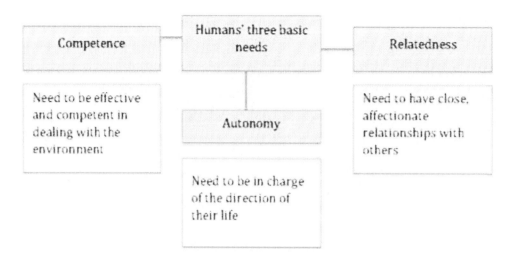

Figure 10.2. Three Psychological Needs adapted from Deci and Ryan (2000).

The need for autonomy is defined as individuals' desires to make their own choices, to express their feelings freely, and to initiate their own actions (Deci & Ryan, 2002). When the need for autonomy is fulfilled, individuals feel free to choose and organize their own actions (Deci & Ryan, 2000, 2002). The need for competence refers to individuals' desire to exert an effect on the environment and to achieve desired outcomes (Deci & Ryan, 2000). This need is expressed by individuals' propensity to engage in certain activities that will allow them to use their skills and to develop new competencies (Deci & Ryan, 2002). Thus, one's need for competence is satisfied when one feels sufficiently skilled to perform a task to the best of one's ability, and thus accomplish one's goals (Deci & Ryan, 2000, 2002). The need for relatedness refers to the desire to establish mutually caring bonds and positive alliances with others (Deci & Ryan, 2002). It refers to one's need to feel connected to others, to love and to care, as well as to be loved and cared for (Deci & Ryan, 2000).

Over the past two decades, much research has shown that self-determined motivation is a useful concept to understand human behavior in various life settings (see Deci & Ryan, 1985, 1991; Myavskaya & Koestner, 2011; Senécal, Vallerand, & Guay, 2001). Regarding the family context, Senécal and Vallerand (1999) demonstrated that individuals who show high levels of self-determined motivation toward family activities were more satisfied with their family life and experienced less work-family conflict. It is suggested that self-determined motivations toward both family and work activities are necessary to obtain psychological benefits derived from the full engagement in both domains in life. In this regard, several studies have found that individuals who show low levels of self-determined motivation at work are more likely to be aggressive in their families and to have poorer quality of family life (Senécal et al., 2001). Thus, it seems relevant to postulate that the higher the self-determined motivation of individuals, the higher their family well-being and vice versa.

Employees experience competence when challenged and given prompt feedback. Likewise, they experience autonomy when they feel supported to explore, take initiative and develop and implement solutions to their problems, and increase their personal resources. Furthermore, workers experience relatedness when they perceive others listening and responding to them. When these three needs are met, employees are more intrinsically motivated and actively engaged in their work-related activities. According to Deci and Ryan (2000), self-determined behavior requires a great deal of self-awareness and awareness of the organizational context. Training in self-awareness can therefore bear a positive impact on one's work and work-life integration, enhancing individual and organizational well-being and performance.

Therefore, adopting a holistic, whole person perspective means understanding the existence and interaction of the whole spectrum of resources and context-specific variables, related beyond work and family to life in general. Accordingly, we examined this idea in an organizational context following the delivery of a training program focused on enhancing self-awareness, enabling human excellence, and capability building.

Reiterating the central question of the present research study, on how practices facilitating self-awareness affect the experience of one's work and work-life integration, we explored the following: (a) What aspects in the personal and professional spheres are emphasized prior and subsequent to the training? (b) What sources of generative dynamics do employees produce themselves; perceive in the organization; and identify following the intervention? To answer these questions, an empirical study was conducted, which is described below.

EMPIRICAL FINDINGS

Background

To explore the research questions, an intervention study was carried out at the Dairy Company,[2] a nonprofit agricultural cooperative located in the region of Catalonia, Spain. The company offered a unique context for this research: it has a strong social cause, employing people with a varied level of mental and physical disabilities (180 out of the 280 staff members).

Methodology

The study entailed a series of training sessions, and pre- and postcourse questionnaires. The training sessions focused on self- and social awareness and management enhancement, enabling human excellence, and capability building. Such topics as strengths, emotional and cognitive awareness and management, mindfulness, interpersonal communication and relations, and organizational dynamics were covered. It was based on the advances of positive psychology, positive organizational scholarship, appreciative inquiry, the theory of complexity, and organizational psychology (see also Chapter 8 in this volume). It constituted a 40-hour course, delivered in five-hour biweekly training sessions with practical exercises during and in between the classes, and the distribution of reflection sheets following each session that appraised the participants' progress. The participants were divided into four groups—a total of 47 employees, representing almost half of the 100 company employees. The pre- and postquestionnaire assessed what employees valued in the organizational environment, their perception of the personal and the professional spheres, social climate, and interactions with their social

---

[2] Fictitious name.

network. To reiterate, the goal was to identify how the training course affected the perceptions of personal and organizational spheres.

Sample

A total of 45 questionnaires were collected: 18 before the course and 27 after. The sample comprised 71 percent women and 29 percent men, representing a variety of personal situations (single, married, living with relatives, and with and without childcare responsibilities), occupations (educator, gardener, psychologist, social worker, and manager), and different hierarchical levels within the organization.

Instrument

The original questionnaire consisted of seven open-ended questions and eight quantitative measures. The open-ended questions aimed to identify life experiences from a holistic perspective: perception of the work environment (sources of inspiration and motivation; adaptive behaviors at work; and organizational citizenship behaviors), life in general, and personal projects. Unfortunately, the quantitative part of the questionnaire, which assessed different aspects of quality of life and well-being, could not be analyzed due to the low number of participants. Therefore, only the qualitative results are presented.

Analysis

The analysis of the qualitative data was inspired by the Grounded Theory (Strauss & Corbin, 1998). The responses to open-ended questions were saved and separately entered and analyzed with the qualitative data analysis software Atlas.ti 6.2.27. First, all data was coded using a detailed open coding approach. Each code was defined and memos were written throughout the coding journey. This allowed codes to be refined, broken down, grouped, and compared. Second, axial coding was undertaken to allow the comparison of broader categories with their subcategories. Third, through the use of the Query Tool and the creation of supercodes, the themes and topics that arose before and after the intervention were explored, to help understand work-life experiences and whether changes had occurred. The topics that emerged were contrasted with the literature to allow further refinement and to enhance reliability (Creswell, 1994). The process of analysis entailed reading, reviewing, and documenting the process in memos throughout the analysis in order to determine overarching themes.

Results

This section is organized into three parts. First, key points related to the professional and personal spheres and their state of play prior and subsequent to the training course are presented (see Table 10.1). Second, the sources of generative dynamics are outlined; these are sources the employees (1) created themselves, (2) identified in their environment, and (3) incorporated as learning from the training course (see Table 10.2). Finally, the impact of self-awareness on the experience of work and personal environment is elucidated.

PROFESSIONAL AND PERSONAL LIFE PERCEPTION: KEY THEMES

The study aimed to ascertain the perception of the various facets of employees' lives (personal, professional, and personal) by asking respondents to define each life sphere using keywords and to elaborate on sources of motivation and inspiration at work and in life in general.

Perception of Professional Life

The myriad of words used by employees to describe their current experience at the Dairy Company both before and after the training course included gratifying and stimulating; development and growth; complex, challenging, and uncertain; and dedication, effort, and responsibility. This reflects the complex nature of employees' day-to-day working life, showing that different experiences can occur simultaneously, including both uplifting and challenging experiences.

In the postintervention phase, a number of differences were noted. For instance, a new category emerged, that is, collaboration, team, and belonging. The team and collaborative experiences were therefore rendered in a nuanced manner, describing not only the team members but also interactions: consolidated teams, solidarity, collaboration, colleagues, teamwork, people, team, companionship, capacity to listen and lend support, and empathy. This suggests a wider perception of professional experience, in which not only are the tasks and their effects on personal development mentioned but also the importance of the relational aspect of work is emphasized.

Table 10.1. Personal and professional life perceptions
before and after the intervention

Self-awareness	Training	Themes
Perception of own professional life	Before	Gratifying and stimulating Development, growth, surmounting of obstacles, change Complex, challenging, uncertain Dedication, effort, responsibility
	After	Development, growth, surmounting of obstacles, change Gratifying and stimulating Collaboration, team, belonging (*new*) Dedication, effort Complex, challenging, uncertain
Sources of motivation and inspiration at work	Before	Meaning derived from work Relationship with colleagues and interaction with challenged coworkers Satisfaction derived from doing a good job
	After	Creating a new or reinventing Finding meaning Learning Relational aspects
Life in general	No significant differences in the pre- and postphase	Aspects of life mentioned: 1. Positive emotions (freedom; excitement, energy, curiosity; love, hope) 2. Routines and obligations (planning; dedication, commitment, effort) 3. Relationships (family, maternity, partner; friends, relationships) 4. Personal development (growth, change; transcendence; self-awareness, enrichment) 5. Stress, loss, worry 6. Health
Personal projects	Before	1. Family related 2. Personal growth 3. Nature
	After	Transmitted a wider variety of projects: 1. Personal growth 2. Music, painting, leisure 3. Family related 4. Sports, dance 5. Learning 6. Traveling

Sources of Motivation and Inspiration at Work

Three subcategories emerged in the data:

1. *Generative aspects*, producing effects beyond the job itself: creating anew or reinventing, finding meaning, and learning;
2. *People-related sources*: collaboration, good working relationships with colleagues, and interaction with "challenged" colleagues; and,
3. *Work-related aspects*: environmental mastery, achieving objectives, or doing a good job.

Before the intervention, participants found motivation and inspiration directly in their work and in relationships with their various colleagues. For example:

> "I feel like I have done a good job." (administrative worker, woman)
> [What inspires me is] "to know that I can help a group of people contribute to a number of tasks that serve society." (gardener, man)

After the intervention, the generative sense-creating and reinvention aspects of work were highlighted. Participants referred to the relational aspect of their work, such as sharing experiences, knowledge, and collaboration with others, and to work-related aspects, such as autonomy, complementary work with colleagues, and doing a good job. For instance:

> "The meaning of my work lies in thinking that everything I do helps somebody find their place in society." (administrative worker, woman)
> "To know that many people and families depend on our decisions and actions." (operations, man)

Perception of Personal Life

Participants' perception of life through their choice of keywords covered a whole range of aspects, including the positive emotions experienced; routines and obligations; relationships and personal development issues; sources of concern; and preoccupation and health-related issues (see Table 10.2). The key themes in the pre- and post-training phase did not vary, reflecting the coexistence of various identities, domains, and their related experience in people's lives. The only perceived difference between the phases was a more detailed narrative of the life sphere in the postphase, in terms of both the individuals involved (in addition to the general description of family, it included children, friends, partner, mother, relationships, and maternity) and activities undertaken oriented toward personal growth (self-realization, achievement, transcendence, enrichment). This could be indicative of increased self-awareness and focus on specific aspects of one's daily life.

Personal Projects

Since the life sphere is conceptualized from a holistic perspective, participants were asked to define their personal projects using keywords. The emerged codes could be classified into various topics:

1. Specific projects: cooking, leisure, home, and traveling;
2. Relational: dialogue, sharing, family related, maternity, and friendship;
3. Based on self and personal growth, which also includes health and learning;
4. Based on the feelings they evoked: calmness, balance, sincerity, and love;
5. Work focused; and
6. Nature focused.

Before the intervention, the most emphasized topics were family related (children, partner, and family in general), personal growth (learning and personal skills), and nature. After the intervention, the topics encompassed a broader spectrum of activities: personal growth, leisure, and specific projects (reading and family-related activities; see Table 10.2).

Interestingly, in the postphase, such areas as maternity and friendship were referred to as a project. This could reflect their importance as standalone areas, which require specific time and energy allocation in order to nurture meaningful bonds. Therefore, the perceptions of personal and professional life before and after the training reflected the complexity and versatility of work and life. Themes revolving around meaningful work, empowering work-related aspects, social relations, and personal development, were emphasized in particular.

GENERATIVE DYNAMICS CREATED BY SELF, THE ENVIRONMENT, AND TRAINING

Several generative (capability-building) dynamics emerged in the data and covered three areas: created by employees themselves, related to the organizational context, and retained as takeaways following the intervention (see Table 10.2).

Table 10.2. Generative dynamics created by self, the environment, and training

Generative dynamics	Training	Themes
Self-created	Before	1. Connectedness to others 2. Own character traits
	After	1. Connectedness to others 2. Self-awareness, focus of attention, self-directedness 3. Get organized, get things done
Environmental factors	Before	1. Relational aspects 2. Company mission
	After	Both of these variables were given greater emphasis subsequent to the training course. 1. Relational aspects: agency focused 2. Company mission
Training factors		Main learning for professional and personal sphere: 1. Change of perception 2. Self-awareness 3. Self-management 4. Development of positive relationships

Self-Created Generative Aspects

Employees reported various actions they carried out to feel good about their day-to-day work. Both before and after the intervention, the relational aspect, specifically connectedness to colleagues by sharing conversations, experiences, and time, was highly emphasized as key to feeling good at work. For instance:

"Take the necessary time to respond and provide service to people, because if I do it in a hurry, I do not feel good about myself." (psychologist, woman)
"Have a good relationship with the people that surround me."(administrative worker, woman)

After the intervention, participants emphasized self-awareness (in terms of moods, emotions, and internal states) and the intentionality of focus of attention.

"Be aware that I feel comfortable at work." (woman)
"Start the day in a positive mood and with a smile." (administrative worker, woman)
"Enjoy each moment." (operations, man)

In addition, they expressed agency related to the work aspect and focus on productivity ("get things done"):

"Come to work prepared to accept changes." (woman)

"Be aware of the successes and results of the work done." (manager, man)
"Work with clear objectives in terms of production." (operations, man)

Generative Environmental Factors

Generative aspects identified in the professional environment focused on aspects revolving around meaning linked to the company mission and being part of the project (employment for differently challenged employees at risk of exclusion; care for the environment), the learning possibilities at work, and the feeling of having done a good job and of being useful by helping others. By way of example:

"It motivates me to work on such a human project, where people are put first and no day is the same." (finance, woman)

Aspects concerning reciprocity to the organization were linked to organizational citizenship behaviors (OCB). Before the training, in terms of OCB, participants emphasized the relationship aspect and collaboration with colleagues, as well as commitment to the company mission and its promotion. Both of these variables were emphasized after the training. In examination of the responses per phase, the prephase was found to focus on maintaining a good relationship with colleagues throughout the organization.

In the postphase, the focus was on the agentic aspect, that is, being proactive in the relationship. Helping relationships are emphasized, "lending a hand" and taking time to deliver good customer service, even if it implies longer working hours, and showing acts of kindness and patience.

[What I do is] "sometimes help challenged colleagues or people that encounter some form of difficulty in fulfilling their job, help others, when it is not my duty." (administrative worker, woman)

Therefore, the organization's mission provided individuals with a sense of purpose for their day-to-day activities and after the training. Being proactive in effecting change in one's day-to-day relationships was relevant.

Generative Training Factors

Subsequent to the training, we were interested in the aspects deemed most relevant for both personal and professional life (see Table 10.2). A variety of lessons learned and takeaways emerged, linked to general perception, self-awareness, self-management, and the building of positive relationships.

Respondents claimed the main takeaway from the course concerned the change of perception or focus of attention, that is, the ability to take perspective and adopt a new standpoint, show acknowledgment and appreciation of others and value oneself more, and be mindful of the present moment.

> "Although I recently suffered the death of a close family member, it helped me to learn to appreciate what I have and made me strong to keep going alone." (educator, woman)

Participants commented on an acquired introspection: the ability to listen to one's own feelings and intuition, to decide one's stance vis-à-vis different situations, to view things in a more positive manner, and to live with greater fulfillment.

> "The responsibility to listen to oneself and to others." (social worker, woman)
> "Have another view of reality, being able to reflect deeply without getting consumed by negative thinking." (caretaker, woman)

Self-awareness was reported as an important learning experience. It was conceptualized in terms of recognition and acceptance of one's emotions and reality in both the positive and negative senses, greater awareness of malaise, and its acceptance and empowerment to take action accordingly. Generally speaking, being more aware of life experiences and one's reality was considered to be an important takeaway.

> "Be aware of my reality and the power of responsibility and decision I have over it." (coordinator, woman)

In terms of self-management, participants acquired new skills with emotions and relationship management. They reported feeling more in charge of their lives and work by setting goals and objectives, and being equipped with tools to manage their day-to-day lives. One of the key lessons learned was that in order to build positive relationships, one must first address one's own view of the world, and manage one's own feelings and thoughts. Therefore, the generative dynamics of self-capability building, experienced in the organizational context and acquired thanks to the training course, rendered the enhancement of self-awareness an important aspect of personal well-being. Relatedness to other employees and meaningfulness derived from work generated meaning for participants' day-to-day activities and work interactions. This is discussed in greater detail below.

THE IMPACT OF SELF-AWARENESS ON WORK-LIFE EXPERIENCES

Participants' discourse regarding their personal and professional life was examined by means of the key training takeaways in an endeavor to understand how practices enabling self-awareness affect their work and life experiences. Three main topics emerged: (1) self and life perception, (2) work-related activities, and (3) relationship enhancement.

In line with the whole person perspective, self and life perception are inextricably linked. Participants specifically pointed out the benefits of more heightened self-awareness: being more aware of one's feelings and being equipped with the resources for self-care, being prepared to accept change, and not being consumed by negative thinking, all of which affects not only work but also life in general. Changes in terms of mood were also noted. The following characteristics were mentioned: focusing attention on the positive, starting the day on a positive note, lower expectations, being tolerant, showing empathy, communicating better and listening, being the one in charge of one's reality, and having the bigger picture in mind.

The experience of day-to-day life seemed to point to greater enrichment, namely, the enjoyment of everyday moments and enhanced awareness of life. Participants for whom self-awareness was the main takeaway described life in positive terms (hope, love, joy, projects, calmness, creativity, good mood, and energy) and also mentioned an awareness of their own decision-making power, awareness of life in general, and of their own emotions in particular.

"Particularly before certain situations, learn how to see the things from a positive standpoint and try to see the good side when faced with challenges." (administrative worker, woman)

"In order to take care of the network of our relationship, we first have to start with ourselves." (administrative worker, woman)

Enhanced self-awareness also bore an influence on the realm of work in terms of individual agency. In several instances, participants commented on having acquired clear objectives, becoming more organized on the whole, planning the day better, and endeavoring not to accumulate work, all of which could ease work-family conflict.

In terms of relationships, interconnectedness with others was underlined. Specifically, participants reported showing acts of kindness to colleagues and attempting to be in a general good mood and acting accordingly. Greater interrelatedness; sharing experiences and projects with colleagues, not necessarily work related; and learning from others were sources of motivation.

"I aim to do the job in the best possible manner. This implies helping others and letting others help me as well." (coordinator, social worker, woman)

Therefore, awareness of oneself and the social environment exerted a positive impact on one's everyday perception, life experiences, work, and interactions with others.

SUMMARY

To conclude, the present study revealed a number of interesting findings:

- Positive emotions can act as a source of enrichment in the workplace and other life spheres.
- Subsequent to the training sessions, participants highlighted the relational aspect of their work (sharing of experiences, knowledge, and collaboration); work-related aspects (autonomy and complementary work with colleagues); and doing a good job.
- In the postintervention phase, a new category emerged, that is, "collaboration, team, and belonging."
- In the post-training phase, keywords related to development, growth, surmounting of obstacles, putting in effort, navigating complexity, and having stimulating experiences were mentioned once again.
- The team's related and collaborative experiences were described in a more nuanced manner: consolidated teams, solidarity, collaboration, and colleagues.
- In the post-training phase, participants focused more on enhancing their relationships at work and at home.
- Support from the organizational environment bore a significant effect on employees' experience.
- Participants in the post-training phase made greater mention of life-related details, in terms of both the individuals involved and activities undertaken oriented toward personal growth.
- Everyday life experiences were also highlighted in the post-training phase: enjoyment of everyday moments and greater awareness of life.

The results suggest that the adoption of a holistic approach to work-life integration, not only taking individuals' specific work or family aspects into account but also considering their awareness of work-life experiences and consequent actions, facilitates more meaningful and positive experiences at work. Focusing on self-awareness prompts individuals to take a holistic view of their lives, establishing connections between its various domains. For instance, understanding how one's mood and emotional state affect interactions with family members or colleagues and reflecting on one's general life satisfaction reveals spillover effects between different spheres of social interaction. Integrating work and life therefore is not viewed as an exercise in combining seemingly separate spheres but rather draws one's attention to the existence of coexisting interrelated spheres in each individual's reality that may represent a source of enrichment and that may be enhanced through specific actions. These findings have implications for research and practice that are discussed below.

DISCUSSION

This chapter explored how enhanced self-awareness affects employees' perceptions of work and nonwork domains following a training course focused on personal development. The underlying goal was to gain an understanding of how organizations could support employees in their work-life integration efforts by bringing to light existing individual and organizational resources and providing self-development tools to handle day-to-day situations. The study suggests that life and work are inextricably linked and that experiences and resources learned at work (in this case by means of a training program designed to enhance self-awareness) can facilitate experiences in other realms of life. This advocates the holistic approach of work-life integration and inter-role enrichment. The results point to various areas for further study that are directly relevant to work-life researchers and practitioners: (1) enhance employee self-awareness; (2) promote high-quality connections; and (3) foster organizational support as catalysts for work-life integration in the 21st century. Each area is discussed in further detail below.

Enhance Employee Self-Awareness

"Know thyself" has been a popular aphorism since the time of ancient Greece. Awareness and knowledge of one's own emotions, cognition, and strengths allow individuals to develop new skills and more capacitating daily practices (Forman et al., 2007; Kashdan & Ciarrochi, 2013) to tackle obstacles related to work or personal life (Dallimore & Mickel, 2006), and should be considered as an integral part of work-life integration.

From the perspective of positive organizational scholarship, fostering self-determined motivation in employees can be regarded as a key generative mechanism that helps create spirals of positive emotions. The broaden-and-build theory of positive emotions (Fredrickson, 1998, 2009) holds that positive emotions momentarily expand people's attention and thinking, enabling individuals to draw flexibility on higher-level connections and wider-than-usual ranges of percepts or ideas. In turn, these broadened and flexible outlooks help people to discover and build survival-promoting personal resources. These resources can be cognitive, the ability to mindfully attend to the present moment or come up with multiple pathways toward a goal; psychological, such as the ability to maintain a sense of mastery over environmental challenges or be resilient in the face of adversity; social, such as the ability to give and receive love and social support; or physical, such as the ability to sleep well or ward off the common cold. According to several studies (see Fredrickson, 1998, 2009), frequent experiences of positive emotions can trigger upward spirals between positive affect and expansive, creative thinking, which lead to personal growth and flourishing. Overall, this study's findings reveal an association between positive emotions and life enrichment through the development of personal resources. This suggests that employees deem their lives to be richer, not because they experience more positive emotions, but because their greater positive emotions help them build resources for living successfully. Therefore, it is recommended that researchers further explore the link between positive emotions and life enrichment in different organizational contexts regarding a variety of role and domain-specific situations.

As shown in this research study, another important facet of self-awareness enhancement is finding meaning in the work performed, shown to be paramount to optimal functioning and growth (Ryan & Deci, 2001). Finding meaning in one's professional activity was associated with various work-related benefits, such as greater job satisfaction, motivation, and performance (Grant, 2007; Rosso, Dekas, & Wrzesniewski, 2010). In this study, the company mission and day-to-day activities were a source of meaningfulness and were reported as one of the drivers of employee motivation. It could be argued that not all companies have directly meaningful activities. Nevertheless, research has shown that meaning can be found in any kind of work, as it is personally constructed (Wrzesniewski, McCauley, Rozin, & Schwartz, 1997). In addition, there exist specific practices, such as job crafting, that organizations could implement (Berg, Dutton, & Wrzesniewski, 2013). Therefore, providing organizational support and opportunities for autonomy and mastery, and enhancing meaningfulness and enrichment between the professional and personal domains, are critical elements that foster self-determined behavior and ultimately affect employee well-being and perception of their quality of life.

Promote High-Quality Connections

The importance of relatedness, which is linked to self-determined motivation (Deci & Ryan, 2000), emerged as an important theme in this study. It is suggested that fostering high-quality connections could somewhat alleviate the possible inter-role strain often studied in research concerning work-family conflict (Greenhaus & Beutell, 1985). High-quality connections refer to the positive emotional experience of social interaction and the feeling of possible reciprocity (Dutton & Heaphy, 2003). They focus on personal growth and development resulting from the connection between individuals. In work-life related areas, high-quality connections refer to the feeling of trust between supervisors and employees that could lead to communicating specific needs on behalf of employees, for instance, the need for policy implementation or the introduction of informal arrangements, and supervisor's acceptance and trust that work demands are met (Spreitzer, 2013). In other words, high-quality connections provide a foundation for trusting other people's needs and motives when different domains conflict and represent a valuable source of social support in colleagues' interaction (ibid.; Ducharme & Martin, 2000). Likewise, Friedman and Greenhaus (2000) emphasized that more autonomy and networking with peers contribute to a quality working life. These suggestions for positive interpersonal interactions are in line with studies on the broadening effect of positive emotions.

Therefore, research would benefit particularly from examining how the enhancement of high-quality relations at work affects individuals' work-life integration and immediate working experience and, on a larger scale, from exploring how high-quality relations affect a company's day-to-day functioning, that is, social climate and level of creativity or performance. In applied terms, one way of promoting these high-quality interactions is by introducing gratitude practices, which were found to have an energizing effect at work, with the benefit of affording greater meaning to work (Fritz, Lam, & Spreitzer, 2011). Another means of building formal quality relationships at work is by introducing best practices, sharing, and mentoring activities that would not only contribute experiences from different domains but also help connect different generations at work (Feldman & Hall, 2013).

Foster Organizational Support

Other studies, similar to the present research, point to the importance of a general supportive environment as key to work-life integration (Kossek, Baltes, & Mathews, 2011). Nevertheless, though research reveals its benefits, such as increased work performance and well-being (Kossek, Colquitt, & Noe, 2001), the implementation of life-friendly practices is still an issue. Further research regarding implicit assumptions in the realm of work, family, life, and their interactions need to be considered, at both the organizational and the national levels (Lewis & Rajan-Rankin, 2013). Therefore, understanding the assumptions regarding the ideal worker, dedication, and effectiveness (Rapoport et al., 2002) could enhance organizational awareness of its functioning, own strengths, and stumbling blocks to optimal employee performance. One means of raising awareness at the organizational level, building on past successes and existing strengths, is through organizational development initiatives, appreciative inquiry being one of them (Cooperrider & Godwin, 2011). Engaging in strength-building initiatives among employees would allow the company to undergo a similar self-awareness process on a macro level and find new ways of functioning that are beneficial to both individuals and the business.

For those companies concerned over the introduction of flexibility or life-friendly practices, it should be noted that, in the eyes of employees, perceived organizational support relates not necessarily to the number of hours worked but rather to day-to-day professional experiences. For instance, in one study, a supportive organizational culture was indicative of less reported conflict among women professionals who worked 65-hour weeks, compared to women working 45 hours in a less supportive culture (Westring Friede et al., 2014). The perception of possibilities and resources available to the person are therefore valued by employees. Consequently, organizations should consider ways to foster enrichment by being more supportive of employees' needs, preferences, and aspirations (Feldman & Hall, 2013; McNall, Nicklin, & Masuda, 2010). Hence, it is necessary to provide customized policies, catering to individual needs at different stages of life and in the domains involved (Feldman & Hall, 2013). By supporting employees' work-life integration aspirations, needs, and personal strengths, companies could benefit from energy and resources flowing from one domain to another (Rothbard, 2001) and an increase in person-job fit (Kristof, 1996).

Finally, training and intervention initiatives are necessary. According to several scholars (e.g., Deci & Ryan, 2000; Hoffman & Field, 1995), training programs in areas such as increasing self-awareness; improving decision making, goal-setting and goal-attainment skills; enhancing communication and relationship skills; and developing the ability to celebrate success and learn from reflecting on experiences lead to greater employee self-determination. These programs can help employees learn how to participate more actively in organizational decision making by helping them become familiar with the planning process and identifying information they would like to share at planning meetings, and to develop skills to effectively communicate their needs and wants. Lastly, intervention initiatives could be one way of introducing new practices, showing their evidence-based benefits for employee well-being and satisfying companies' interest in return on investment (Hammer, Demsky, Kossek, & Bray, 2016).

STUDY LIMITATIONS

Due to the exploratory nature of the present study, several limitations should help to guide future research. The present study was conducted in a nonprofit agricultural cooperative, located in Catalonia, Spain. The company studied offered a unique context for this research, due to its strong social cause, employing people with a varied level of mental and physical disabilities (180 out of the 280 staff). Therefore, replicating the study in different organizational contexts could prove interesting to examine the effect of the organizational context on employees' work experience and family life.

Similarly, replication of the study with a larger sample of participants and comparison of the results with a controlled group of employees that do not participate in the training sessions could be relevant. The use of different types of objective measures may also prove beneficial, such as employee performance, turnover, or level of absenteeism as well as physiological measures such as heart rate, cortisol levels, and other measures to determine any changes at the neurophysiological level post-training.

Likewise, another consideration relates to the need to study the impact of the interventions used in the present study over time and to ascertain the effect of the flourishing individual in different life spheres on general organizational dynamics (systemic approach) and company performance. The use of the experience sampling method (ESM) could be an interesting option to explore such dynamics. More specifically, the ESM refers to data collection regarding both the context and content of individuals' daily life. This purpose is shared by other methods; however, the advantage of ESM lies in its ability to capture daily life as it is directly perceived from one moment to the next, affording the opportunity to examine the spillover effect from one life domain to another (Hektner, Schmidt, & Csikszentmihalyi, 2007). The method is capable of achieving this aim by asking individuals to provide written responses to both open- and closed-ended questions at several random times over each day of an average week in their life, whenever a personal digital assistant (PDA or email alarm) prompts them to respond. The ESM notably reduces the likelihood of retrospection, as it minimizes the amount of time elapsed between the experience during and after the intervention and the account of the experience, making it a highly powerful method for capturing the temporal and dynamic aspects of the development of self-awareness and work-life integration.

Similarly, it may be interesting to examine further contextual information regarding each participant's job characteristics in order to gain a more thorough understanding of how the fulfillment of the three basic psychological needs (i.e., the need for autonomy, the need for competency, and the need for relatedness proposed by the SDT) bears an impact on work-life integration and organizational performance, and how gaining self-awareness of the three psychological needs and their fulfillment is integrated into the narratives of the study's participants regarding work-life integration.

To conclude, work-life integration is a complex undertaking both for individuals and organizations. Promoting self-awareness and enhancing resources and strengths inherent to individuals and their professional environment, and promoting meaningfulness in daily activities and high-quality relationships seems like a promising path to explore for research and practice in the field of work-life integration.

REFERENCES

Barnett, R. C. & Hyde, J. S. (2001). Women, men, work, and family: An expansionist theory. *American Psychologist*, *56*, 781–796.

Berg, J. M., Dutton, J. E. & Wrzesniewski, A. (2013). Job crafting and meaningful work. In B. J. Dik, Z. S. Byrne, & M. F. Steger (Eds.), Purpose and meaning in the workplace, (pp. 81–104). Washington, DC: *American Psychological Association*.

Blanch, J. M., Crespo, F. J. & Sahagún, M. A. (2012). Sobrecarga de trabajo, tiempo asistencial y bienestar psicosocial en la medicina mercantilizada [Work overload of work, duration of medical assistance and psychosocial well-being in commodified medicine]. In E. Ansoleaga, O. Artaza, & J. Suárez, J. (Eds.), Personas que cuidan personas: Dimensión humana y trabajo en salud [People that care for others: The human dimension and work in the healthcare sector], (pp. 176–182). Santiago, Chile: *Pan American Health Organization/World Health Organization*.

Cameron, K. S., Dutton, J. E. & Quinn, R. E. (2003). Foundations of positive organizational scholarship. In K. S. Cameron, J. E. Dutton, & R. E. Quinn (Eds.), *Positive organizational scholarship*, (pp. 3–13). San Francisco: Berrett-Koehler.

Cameron, K. S. & Spreitzer, G. M. (2011). *The Oxford handbook of positive organizational scholarship*. New York, NY: Oxford University Press.

Casper, W. J., Marquardt, D. J., Roberto, K. J. & Buss, C. (2016). The hidden family lives of single adults without dependent children. In T. D. Allen & L. T. Eby (Eds.), *The Oxford handbook of work and family*. New York, NY: Oxford University Press.

Clark, S. C. (2000). Work/family border theory: A new theory of work/family balance. *Human Relations*, *53*, 747–770.

Cooperrider, D. & Godwin, L. (2011). Positive organizational development: Innovation inspired change in an economy and ecology of strengths. In K. S. Cameron & G. M. Spreitzer (Eds.), *The Oxford handbook of positive organizational scholarship*, (pp. 737–750). New York, NY: Oxford University Press.

Creswell, J. W. (1994). Research design: *Qualitative and quantitative approaches*. Thousand Oaks, CA: Sage.

Dallimore, E. & Mickel, A. (2006). Quality of life: Obstacles, advice, and employer assistance. *Human Relations*, *59*(1), 61–103.

Deci, E. L. & Ryan, R. M. (1985*). Intrinsic motivation and self-determination in human behavior*. New York, NY: Plenum.

Deci, E. L. & Ryan, R. M. (1991). A motivational approach to self: Integration in personality. In R. Dienstbier (Ed.), *Nebraska symposium on motivation: Perspectives on motivation*, (Vol. *38*, pp. 237–288). Lincoln, NE: University of Nebraska Press.

Deci, E. L. & Ryan, R. M. (2000). The 'what' and 'why' of goal pursuits: Human needs and the self-determination of behavior. *Psychological Inquiry*, *11*, 227–268.

Deci, E. L. & Ryan, R. M. (2002). *Handbook of self-determination research*. Rochester, NY: University of Rochester Press.

Deci, E. L. & Ryan, R. M. (2008). Self-determination theory: A macrotheory of human motivation, development and health. *Canadian Psychology*, *49*, 182–185.

Ducharme, L. J. & Martin, J. K. (2000). Unrewarding work, coworker support, and job satisfaction. *Work and Occupations*, *27*(2), 223–243.

Dutton, J. E. & Heaphy, E. (2003). The power of high-quality connections. In K. S. Cameron, J. E. Dutton, & R. E. Quinn (Eds.), *Positive organizational scholarships: Foundations of a new discipline*, (pp. 263–278). San Francisco: Berrett-Koehler.

Feldman, E. R. & Hall, D. T. (2013). Work-family research and practice: What if the whole person mattered? In S. A. Y. Poelmans, J. H. Greenhaus, & M. Las Heras Maestro (Eds.), *Expanding the boundaries of work-family research: A vision for the future*, (pp. 91–106). London: Palgrave Macmillan.

Forman, E. M., Herbert, J. D., Moitra, E., Yeomans, P. D. & Geller, P. A. (2007). A randomized controlled effectiveness trial of acceptance and commitment therapy and cognitive therapy for anxiety and depression. *Behavior Modification*, *31*, 772–799.

Fredrickson B. L. (1998). What good are positive emotions? *Review of General Psychology*, *2*, 300–319.

Fredrickson, B. L. (2009). *Positivity*. New York, NY: Three Rivers Press.

Friedman, S. D. & Greenhaus, J. H. (2000). *Work and family: Allies or enemies? What happens when business professionals confront life choices*. Oxford, UK: Oxford University Press.

Fritz, C., Lam, C. F. & Spreitzer, G. M. (2011). It's the little things that matter: An examination of knowledge workers' energy management. *Academy of Management Perspectives*, *25*(3), 28–39.

Grant, A. M. (2007). Relational job design and the motivation to make a prosocial difference. *Academy of Management Review*, *32*(2), 393–417.

Greenhaus, J. H. & Beutell, N. J. (1985). Sources of conflict between work and family roles. *Academy of Management Review*, *10*(1), 76–88.

Greenhaus, J. H., Collins, K. & Shaw, J. (2003). The relation between work-family balance and quality of life. *Journal of Vocational Behavior*, *63*, 510–531.

Greenhaus, J. H. & Powell, G. N. (2006). When work and family are allies: A theory of work-family enrichment. *Academy of Management Review*, *31*(1), 72–92.

Hall, D. T., Las Heras, M., Kossek, E. E. & Lee, M. D. (2007, July). Success in work, family, and personal life: Fixed, fanciful, or fleeting? *II International conference of work and family harmonizing work, family, and personal life: Strategies for crossing boundaries*. Barcelona, Spain.

Hammer, L. B., Demsky, C. A., Kossek, E. E. & Bray, J. W. (2016). Work-family intervention research. In T. D. Allen & L. T. Eby (Eds.), *The Oxford handbook of work and family*, (pp. 349–361). New York, NY: Oxford University Press.

Hektner, J. M., Schmidt, J. A. & Csikszentmihalyi, M. (2007). *Experience sampling method measuring the quality of everyday life*. London: Sage.

Hoffman, A. & Field, S. (1995). Promoting self-determination through effective curriculum development. *Intervention in School and Clinic, 30*, 134–141.

Hull, C. L. (1943). *Principles of behavior: An introduction to behavior theory*. New York, NY: Appleton Century Crofits.

Kalliath, T. & Brough, P. (2008). Work-life balance: A review of the meaning of the balance construct. *Journal of Management and Organization, 14*(3), 323–327.

Kashdan, T. B. & Ciarrochi, J. (2013). *Mindfulness, acceptance, and positive psychology: The seven foundations of well-being*. Oakland, CA: New Harbinger.

Kossek, E. E., Baltes, B. & Mathews, R. (2011). How work family research and finally have an impact in the workplace. *Industrial and Organizational Psychology: Perspectives on Science and Practice, 4*, 3.

Kossek, E. E., Colquitt, J. A. & Noe, R. A. (2001). Caregiving decisions, well-being, and performance: The effects of place and provider as a function of dependent type and work-family climates. *Academy of Management Journal, 44*, 29–44.

Kossek, E. E. & Friede, A. (2006). The business case: Managerial perspectives on work and family. In M. Pitt-Catsouphes, E. E. Kossek, & S. Sweet (Eds.), *The work and family handbook: Multi-disciplinary perspectives and approaches* (pp. 611–626). Mahwah, NJ: Erlbaum.

Kossek, E. E., Lewis, S. & Hammer, L. B. (2010). Work-life initiatives and organizational change: Overcoming mixed messages to move from the margin to the mainstream. *Human Relations, 63*(1), 3–19.

Kristof, A. L. (1996). Person-organization fit: An integrative review of its conceptualizations, measurement, and implications. *Personnel Psychology, 49*, 1–49.

Las Heras, M. & Hall, D. T. (2008). Integration of career and life. In D. Billimoria & S. K. Piderit (Eds.), *Handbook on women in business and management*, (pp. 178–205). Northampton, MA: Edward Elgar.

Lewis, S. & Rajan-Rankin, S. (2013). Deconstructing 'family supportive cultures': A vision for the future. In S. Poelmans, J. Greenhaus, & M. las Heras, *New frontiers in work-family research: A vision for the future in a global world*, (pp. 53–69). Basingstoke, UK: Palgrave Macmillan.

Macik-Frey, M., Quick, J. C. & Nelson, D. L. (2007). Advances in occupational health: From a stressful beginning to a positive future. *Journal of Management, 33*(6), 809–840.

May, D. R., Chan, A., Hodges, T. & Avolio, B. J. (2003). Developing the moral component of authentic leadership. *Organizational Dynamics, 32*, 247–260.

McNall, L. A., Nicklin, J. M. & Masuda, A. D. (2010). A meta-analytic review of the consequences associated with work-family enrichment. *Journal of Business and Psychology, 25*, 381–396.

Myavskaya, M. & Koestner, R. (2011). Psychological needs, motivation, and well-being: A test of self-determination theory across multiple domains. *Personality and Individual Differences*, *50*, 387–391.

Nelson, D. W. (2009). Feeling good and open minded: The impact on positive affect on cross-cultural emphatic responding. *Journal of Positive Psychology*, *4*, 53–63.

Nippert-Eng, C. E. (1996). *Home and work: Negotiating boundaries through everyday life*. Chicago: University Chicago Press.

O'Driscoll, M., Poelmans, S., Spector, P. E., Cooper, C. L., Allen, T. D. & Sanchez, J. (2003). Family-responsive interventions, perceived organizational and supervisor support in the work-family conflict-strain relationship. *International Journal of Stress Management*, *10*(4), 326–344.

Rapoport, R., Bailyn, L., Fletcher, J. & Pruitt, B. (2002). *Beyond work-family balance: Advancing gender equity and workplace performance*. San Francisco: Jossey-Bass.

Roberts, L. M., Spreitzer, G., Dutton, J., Quinn, R., Heaphy, E. & Barker, B. (2005). How to play to your strengths. *Harvard Business Review*, *83*, 74–80.

Rosso, B. D., Dekas, K. H. & Wrzesniewski, A. (2010). On the meaning of work: A theoretical integration and review. *Research in Organizational Behavior*, *30*, 91–127.

Ryan, R. M. & Deci, E. L. (2001). On happiness and human potentials: A review of research on hedonic and eudaimonic well-being. In S. Fiske (Ed), *Annual review of psychology*, (Vol *52*, pp. 141-166). Palo Alto, CA: Annual Reviews, Inc.

Rothbard, N. P. (2001). Enriching or depleting? The dynamics of engagement in work and family roles. *Administrative Science Quarterly*, *46*, 655–684.

Senécal, C. & Vallerand, R. J. (1999). Construction et validation de l'Échelle de Motivation envers les Activités Familiales (ÉMAF) [Construction and validation of the Motivation toward Family Activities Scale]. *Revue Européenne de Psychologie Appliquée* [*European Journal of Applied Psychology*], *49*, 261–274.

Senécal, C., Vallerand, R. J. & Guay, F. (2001). Antecedents and outcomes of work-family conflict: Toward a motivational model. *Journal of Personality and Social Psychology*, *27*, 176–186.

Spreitzer, G. M. (2013). Using a positive organizational scholarship lens to enrich research on work-family relationships. In J. G. Grzywacz & E. Demerouti (Eds.), *New frontiers in work and family research*, (pp. 1–17). New York, NY: Routledge.

Strauss, A. L. & Corbin, J. (1998). *Basics of qualitative research: techniques and procedures for developing grounded theory*. Sage Publication.

Waugh, C. E. & Fredrickson, B. L. (2006). Nice to know you: Positive emotions, self-other overlap and complex understanding in the formation of a new relationship. *Journal of Positive Psychology*, *1*, 93–106.

Westring Friede, A., Speck, R., Dupuis Sammel, M., Conant, E., Tuton, L., Abbuhl, S. & Grisso, J. (2014). Culture matters: The pivotal role of culture for women's careers in academic medicine. *Academic Medicine, 89*(4), 658–663.

Wrzesniewski, A., McCauley, C. R., Rozin, P. & Schwartz, B. (1997). Jobs, careers, and callings: People's relations to their work. *Journal of Research in Personality, 31*, 21–33.

In: Work-Life Balance in the 21st Century
Editor: Jessica M. Nicklin

ISBN: 978-1-53612-526-9
© 2018 Nova Science Publishers, Inc.

Chapter 11

REIMAGINING WORK-LIFE BALANCE: LESSONS IN BRINGING WORK TO LIFE AND BRINGING LIFE TO WORK

Tracy Brower*, PhD
Holland, MI, US

ABSTRACT

Today, both the popular press and the academic literature are rife with articles about stress, time poverty, and challenges with "having it all." The typical solution is "work-life balance," but what if we have it all wrong? This chapter suggests that the very paradigm of work-life balance is limiting. It suggests evidence-based alternatives of work-life integration, fulfillment, and a life-course perspective in order to reframe the challenges and reimagine the solutions, not just for women with children but also for those in all situations, including men and those without children. Based on primary qualitative research with individuals and corporations, this chapter recommends creative approaches to providing work-life supports in the form of benefits, policies, practices, and organizational cultural norms. In addition, it makes the business case for work-life integration and work-life supports—demonstrating the positive quantitative impacts of work-life harmony for both people and organizations.

Most of us work for a living, and work is an important part of life. Rather than a clean separation between "work" and "life," a *full life* is characterized by work that is fulfilling, uses our gifts, and is fundamentally social. In the same way that work is a part of life, life should be a part of work. Organizations will be most successful when they embrace employees as full people with families and when they recognize employees'

---
* Corresponding Author Email: tbrower108@gmail.com.

importance beyond the doors of the workplace and beyond the hours they spend contributing to the company's goals.

Based on my accumulated research and my findings from my study exploring executive perspectives on work-life and business outcomes (described fully in *Bring Work to Life by Bringing Life to Work: A Guide for Leaders and Organizations*),[1] I suggest that when companies prioritize employees and their welfare, the companies also perform better. In addition, leveraging work-life supports—benefits, policies, practices, and organizational cultural norms—helps bring work to life and bring life to work. When they bring work to life, employees express their talents and passions in careers that fulfill them and in turn produce better results for organizations.

The lines between work and life are becoming less clear. They are fuzzy and fading. This is thanks to multiple demands, technology, and the speed at which change is occurring. Because work and life are coming together, our collective challenge is to determine how to create the conditions for work and life to be positive experiences— work in which people want to bring discretionary time and effort, and personal lives where people have enough energy at the end of the day or the end of the shift to bring their best to their families, friends, and community.

In our blurred world, leaders and organizations have responsibilities to help meet employee needs, and one way they can do so is by attending to and providing work-life supports. What are work-life supports more specifically? They are the benefits, policies, practices, and organizational cultural norms that help employees navigate demands. They are benefits such as maternity, paternity, and adoption leaves. They are policies that allow telecommuting and leaders who focus on results and outcomes rather than simply time in the office. They are programs that allow for ongoing education and community outreach. Work-life supports go beyond benefits, policies, and programs, however. They also include organizational cultures in which it is possible for them to be fully utilized by employees—without the stigma commonly associated with taking advantage of some work-life policies. The endgame is not for companies to get as much as they can from employees or vice versa. Instead, the goal is for employees to find fulfillment in a way that advantages both them and the organization. Fundamental to this equation is the provision of plenty of choice for employees.

Our current paradigm is limiting though. Specifically, work-life balance is the wrong notion. Balance suggests an either/or and a mutual exclusivity between work and life. It suggests that work and life are part of a zero-sum relationship in which it is impossible to have both. The concept of bringing work to life requires a broader view that provides for the integration and connection between work and life. Accomplishing this integration and connection is not a prescriptive approach, nor does it have one right answer. Instead,

---

[1] For a full description of the research, see my book Bring Work to Life by Bringing Life to Work: A Guide for Leaders and Organizations (Brookline, MA: Bibliomotion, 2014).

there are multiple right answers depending on individual needs and company-unique situations.

In addition, work-life integration and fulfillment are for everyone. They are not just for those who are married or those with children. They are not just issues for women. As a matter of fact, in 2010, 20 percent of women did not have children and 49 percent of those were voluntarily without children (Sandler, 2013). Work-life integration must embrace all aspects of life—those associated with raising children and those that go beyond children. Work-life integration and fulfillment are relevant and important for men and women, for those with and without children, and for those in multiple types of life situations. As a society, we benefit when we include our whole population in our dialogue about work-life solutions.

Therefore, the purpose of this chapter is to describe new perspectives in considering the "work-life balance" challenge and to provide a solution set as well as rationale for the adoption of new solutions. I begin by recommending three alternative perspectives because the approach to a problem or challenge inherently affects the ways in which it can be solved. I lay out these new perspectives as important starting points for framing the challenge of work-life. Then, I provide possibilities for work-life supports (benefits, policies, and practices) and examples of companies that are incorporating them for their employees. I close by discussing the rationale for companies to provide work-life supports. From cost savings to attraction and retention, there is agreement on the positive impacts of work-life supports, and I reflect on those toward the close of the chapter.

A NEW PERSPECTIVE

The ability to find creative solutions for a fulfilling work-life experience is rooted in the definition of the challenge. Rather than a focus on work-life balance, I recommend three alternatives: work-life integration, a life-course perspective, and a paradigm of fulfillment.

Integration

Rather than balance, an alternative view is to consider the extent to which employees must *integrate* life and work—coordinating, blending, and bringing elements of work and life into a unified whole. There is both connection and fluidity between work and family, and the relationship between the two is an ongoing navigation. In my extensive discussions with both employees and companies, some have expressed resistance to the concept of integration, arguing that employees would rather keep work and life separate than to integrate them. However, the question is really one of boundaries. It is both appropriate and critical that people are able to set boundaries between their work and life, but ideally they should be able to manage the boundary themselves in the way that is best for them. For some, this means a greater amount of mixing related to the time they spend on work and life throughout a typical day. For others, it means more separation between the activities of work and life. Choice is key. Employees must have the opportunity to manage work and life—and the demands of each—in the ways they most prefer. The notion of integration versus segmentation is further discussed in Chapters 3 and 4 of this volume.

The Life Course

Throughout their lives, workers require varying levels of work-life support. Through days, months, seasons, and years, needs change and must be accommodated differently. On a day-to-day basis, employees need flexible working hours for appointments, health, and even volunteer work. In periods of months, workers need varying supports through the seasons. This is especially true for workers with children in school and the extent to which the school calendar dictates requirements for childcare. Over the course of years, needs vary based on whether employees are new to their career, have a partner, have children, or need to support elderly parents or family members.

The point here is that a longer-term nonstatic perspective is most helpful. As needs change, so must the work-life supports that employees have and the ways they are able to manage the boundaries between work and life. Managing boundaries between work and life assumes a porosity: that work and life are a fluid whole that evolves over time. Again, it isn't a trade-off between work and life (as a balance paradigm would connote) but rather a perspective that embraces a whole person model in which needs change over time and in which it is possible to "have it all" in both work and life.

Creating Fulfillment

In addition to perspectives of integration and life course, a perspective of fulfillment is also a critical alternative to the idea of balance. A fulfillment paradigm starts with the assumption that every employee can achieve a high degree of satisfaction and success with regard to their work-life. It is a starting point that leads to more creative solutions. If we assume we can find fulfillment, this necessarily leads to a more emphatic belief in the capacity to find ways to accommodate work-life demands and requirements—and reach a positive level of satisfaction in each.

The conditions for fulfillment can be significantly affected by leaders. Recognition for a job well done, fostering plenty of employee autonomy, and providing multiple technology solutions for working away from the office are examples where work-life supports can provide for work-life fulfillment. A sense of fulfillment encourages employees to bring themselves to work and to fully contribute their passions, creativity, and talents in the workplace. This fulfillment can be created in a variety of ways:

- when employees have the chance to engage in work that inspires them;
- when workers are able to align their talents with the tasks that the organization needs them to perform;
- when people feel their work contributes to a broader sense of purpose; and
- when people have time to contribute to the community of which their organization is a part.

In situations where people perceive their work as just another burdensome demand, they may not be able to access their best. Alternatively, when work is more fully an opportunity to express creativity, contribute talents, and connect with others, it becomes a source of fulfillment.

All kinds of work can provide for a sense of purpose and fulfillment. The cable installer isn't just hooking up equipment, he is providing a connection to the outside world for the elderly widow who watches television. The bus driver isn't just driving kids around, she is contributing to educational opportunities for children. The manufacturing associate isn't just making a widget, he is fabricating the part that goes into a hospital bed that helps patients heal more quickly and return home to their families. The accounts-receivable clerk isn't just ensuring invoices are paid; she is helping to keep her company viable and thus contributing to the employment opportunities for others in her community. In all these cases and more, the opportunity is for companies to raise the level of awareness and importance of people's work. All work is inherently valuable, and organizations can help employees become more aware of the value they bring.

All of these perspectives, work-life integration, the life course, and work-life fulfillment, are starting points to frame the challenge of work-life. Keeping these in mind provides an important way of thinking as leaders and companies seek to ensure that employees are attracted to join companies, stay with companies, and bring their best through their work.

Beyond these perspectives, certain mechanisms are also helpful in creating the conditions for work-life fulfillment. I call these work-life supports. They are factors such as benefits, policies, practices, and organizational cultural norms. Companies that start with the assumption that work-life integration is possible, that embrace a fluid view of work-life over the life course, and that seek to provide a fulfilling work experience for employees use work-life supports as the mechanisms that provide options, possibilities, and alternatives for employees. In turn, organizations that successfully offer work-life supports glean the payoff of employees who are more satisfied, and this in turn results in more motivated, more engaged employees. These are positive for both people and organizations in which they work. Next we turn to a discussion of what these work-life supports are and how they are beneficial to people and companies.

THE POWER OF WORK-LIFE SUPPORTS

Work-life supports are mechanisms to achieve the vision of bringing work to life and living a new paradigm of integration, fulfillment, and support over the life course. My research with multiple organizations and senior leaders since 2008 has suggested there are a significant amount of options for providing work-life supports. They are as varied and individual as workers themselves. My definition of work-life supports is as follows: benefits, formal policies, and informal practices and organizational cultural norms that help employees integrate work and life. Examples of benefits include workers' compensation, disability, insurance coverage, pet-care benefits, education and training, and sick leave. Policies are the rules that guide a company's operations. Examples are flex time, caregiving leaves, telecommuting, and employee assistance programs. Organizational practices are perhaps the most nuanced category of work-life supports and include organizational cultural norms and other patterns of behavior regarding the way the organization runs. These often include practices that allow work team leaders and other company officials discretion, such as whether to let an employee leave early in order to meet a family obligation or how much free time to offer employees to work on projects outside of their formal job responsibilities.

MULTIPLE OPTIONS FOR WORK-LIFE SUPPORTS

There is a plethora of options that support work-life, and while these are categorized in Table 1, there are gray areas between them. Overall, it is helpful to consider work-life supports as broadly as possible—and not underestimate the power of any of these to contribute to a fulfilling work-life culture.

Those items associated with alternative working hours are most commonly identified as work-life approaches, but in truth, work-life supports are much broader than just those that are most commonly identified, as evidenced by the variety in the above listing. Thinking broadly about work-life supports and defining options expansively is fundamental to creating work-life fulfillment. More options lead to more creativity in problem solving and also give employees more choice in the alternatives that work best for them.

Table 1. Summary of work-life supports

Insurance and benefits	Leaves
Adoption assistance	Caregiving leaves
Adoption leaves	Parental leaves
Health and dental benefits	Family leave
Eldercare benefits	Maternity leave
Gender reassignment benefits	Extended maternity leave
Rehab benefits	Paternity leaves
Vision benefits	Long-term leave
Pet-care benefits	Short-term leave
Workers compensation	Job-back guarantees
Disability	Sabbaticals
Wellness and mental health	**Retirement**
Corporate counseling services	Staged retirement
Corporate medical services (e.g., flu shots)	Retirement planning assistance/education
Employee assistance programs (EAP)	Pension plans and/or defined contribution
Wellness benefits	plans
Healthy food education	
On-site health/fitness classes	
Care-related solutions	**Education**
Online referral service for childcare	Time off to attend classes
Kindergarten on-site	Tuition reimbursement
Summer program for children	On-site classes
Emergency backup childcare	Permission to attend non-work-related
Near-site or on-site childcare	classes
Eldercare and/or financial assistance for eldercare	
Hours of work	**Work location**
Option to leave early	Work at home
Flex time	Telecommuting policy
Core hours	Provision of telecommuting office
Compressed workweek	equipment/furniture
Time tracking	IT support at home
Reduced summer hours	Education regarding how to work at home
Seasonal medium-term options	successfully
Scheduled working hours same as school days	Company-provided 3rd or 4th places
Limited overtime requirements	
Alternative hours (e.g., four 10-hour days)	
Part-time work	
Job sharing	
Option to not work weekends	
Extended breaks during the day	
Vacation pools for time off	
Core hours	

Table 1. (Continued)

Physical environment	Amenities
On-site lactation rooms	Pretax dollars for public transportation
Food, coffee, lunches	Cab service when working late
Free afternoon snacks	Takeout dinners
Places for people to meet and connect	Order-in dinners at the office
Stimulating interiors	Shuttle to/from work
Constantly refreshed/updated interiors	Dry-cleaning services
Light, ambient noise, moderate traffic/activity	On-site dental services
Wi-Fi, telepresence, sharing technologies	Car detailing services
Navigation and way-finding	Car snow-removal services
Lower height walls, more glass, transparency	On-site car detailing
Private spaces	On-site greeting card printing/envelopes
Phone booths	Discounts for area entertainment
Protocols for use of the space	Parking apps to assist in finding nearby
Flexibility—user-controlled changes	parking spots
Proximity of leaders	Athletic club memberships
	On-site fitness center
	On-site farm-to-table services

Technology	Job content, job design, leadership, management
Support/education for new technology skills	Control the content of one's work/projects
Social networking	Choice of roles in a rotation program
IT help hub	Standards of work for consistency
IT policies	Independent agent model
Choice of device and/or BYOD	Multiple people doing same job
Best available technology	Work aligned with talents, creativity, passion
Technology kiosks for non-white-collar access	Prioritization of assignments
Borrow-a-laptop program	Mentoring; reverse mentoring
	Career development
	Recognition
	Managing based on performance, not presence
	Providing appropriate autonomy and choice
	Reinforcing a broader purpose for each employee's work

Community	
Community program for area children	
Time off to volunteer	
On-site activities	
On-site activities to benefit the community	

One especially effective form of work-life support is flexible working, which allows employees to choose where, when, and how they work. In my research (Brower, 2014), I found that companies that make flexible working options available find their employees to be more engaged and more likely to stay with the company for longer periods of time. They also find that the costs of providing such policies are outweighed by the benefits of happier employees who are more likely to contribute discretionary effort. As an example, workers may have choice about the project on which they work or the ways in which they solve work-related problems.

Flexible working approaches provide people with control and autonomy over their work and therefore help them manage the boundaries between work and life in the ways that work best for them. Some companies, such as two different oil and gas companies in the south, offer the option for employees to work a compressed workweek in which they work a lesser number of days but more hours in each day, thus providing them with flexibility within which to meet family obligations. They allow this option for both their white-collar and their blue-collar workers. Other companies, such as a human services organization in the northeast and a utility company in the west, offer creative options such as sabbaticals or stricter policies against working on weekends, respectively. These too are offered to both white- and blue-collar employees. From managers to gas-line technicians and from human service counselors to maintenance employees, these companies are finding ways to creatively provide options for their people.

Flexible working options and the control that employees are able to exercise over their own schedules require high levels of trust and accountability. The increased ownership and choice over work are intended to help employees integrate the demands of work and home and reduce the negative spillover that can result from work to home or vice versa. None of these kinds of benefits, policies, or practices suggest that companies provide free rides to employees. Rather, these kinds of approaches are successful when people are highly productive and responsible for their work and when companies manage to achieve objectives and results rather than simply presence in the workplace.

A Disconnect: Using Work-Life Supports

One challenge of work-life supports is the preponderance of benefits, policies, and practices that are available but the relatively few numbers of employees that take advantage of them. This is also discussed in Chapters 2 and 6 of this volume. The extent to which employees often don't take advantage of work-life supports is sometimes attributed to personal preference, but in reality it is often because of a concern about the social stigma attached to the work-life supports. With business financial pressures and regular reductions in employee jobs in the news, some employees have levels of job insecurity that cause them to want to be in the workplace regularly. Even if they don't feel job insecurity, they may believe their opportunities for advancement in the organization could be limited if they are perceived as working less or using work-life options to a great extent.

Both employees and companies have a role to play in increasing the extent to which employees take advantage of work-life supports. First, companies can actively encourage workers to take advantage of work-life practices and communicate explicitly about their desire for a culture that embraces employees' full lives both inside and outside of work. It is to the company's advantage to do this because, when employees feel valued and when they have a sense of fulfillment beyond just their work, they are more likely to contribute their best (this is discussed further later in this chapter).

In one example, a manufacturing company adopted a practice of sharing employee success stories of work-life integration. Each month, an employee was featured on the company intranet site sharing a bit about his or her life outside of work, his or her family, and his or her beyond-work interests. Where it was appropriate, the stories included examples of how the employee was working alternative hours or ways the employee was finding ways to integrate work and life via policies or practices. The employees that were featured were in all kinds of life situations. They were both men and women, both with partners and single, both with and without children, representing multiple generations, and in various positions with the company. This approach helped the company reinforce their respect for people and their view of employees as whole people. It also encouraged others to take advantage of work-life benefits, policies, and practices.

Second, employees can consciously choose to take advantage of work-life practices and set the tone for others. A critical way that people learn how to behave is through watching others, and organizational culture is fundamentally about social norms and "the ways things get done around here." Given this, each worker has a powerful role to play in setting the tone for others and influencing the culture. There is strength in numbers, and as more workers take advantage of work-life practices, it becomes easier for additional workers to take part—thus creating positive momentum. As an example, there is a consumer packaged goods company in which employees wanted to work more from home. The marketing team got together and decided that the whole team would work from home on alternating Fridays. This removed the stigma for individual employees in the group who wanted to work from home in addition to removing the pressure to be in the office for team meetings on that day. It also sent a signal to other groups and individuals about the viability of working differently. In another example, an employee had been leaving the office early about once a week in order to attend his grandson's soccer games. At his coworkers' urging, he began to be more transparent about why he was leaving early on those days, thus setting a tone for others to flex their hours as well. Importantly, he was also transparent about where he was making up the time—he was working in the evenings in order to complete his work.

In any of these situations, the key is performance. Taking advantage of work-life supports provides employees with freedom, choice, and the opportunity for more flexibility, but it must also include hard work and the achievement of results.

The Need to Benchmark

When companies seek to improve their approaches to supporting employees through work-life, they often want to benchmark against other companies. When they do, they learn that *more* companies are offering *more* options for work-life supports to *more* employees all the time, so companies are wise to focus in this area if they want to successfully compete for talent and engagement among employees. Employees of all generations are increasingly demanding work-life supports and actively choosing companies in which they experience more of these and in which they believe they will find more fulfilling work. In addition, companies vary widely in the amount and types of work-life supports they are offering. For instance, an oil and gas company in Texas allows employees to work from home in special circumstances once in a while. When they do, they must agree with their manager up front about their alternative working, and they must demonstrate the results of their work when they are back in the office. In another example, a manufacturing company in the Midwest allows summer hours in which employees may choose to work half days on Fridays June through August. In addition, there is another manufacturing company that keeps a vacation pool that is "funded" by employees who donate vacation to the pool. When line employees need time off, they are able to tap into the vacation pool. In another example, a professional services firm established core hours for their employees in which everyone must be in the office Tuesdays through Thursdays 10:00 a.m. until 3:00 p.m., but outside of those hours, employees may choose whether they work within the office or from other locations. Finally, a pharma company allows its employees to work whenever and wherever they choose as long as they complete their work effectively. Work is managed purely by outcomes, and employees have extensive freedom about where, how, and when they work.

Most critical is that organizations match their work-life approaches to their cultures (or their desired cultures), rather than implementing a one-size-fits-all blueprint based on a superficial comparison to other companies. In addition, I recommend what I call the *Goldilocks Rule*: companies must have the "just right" amount of work-life supports—not too many and not too few—based on the organization's culture and goals. I also recommend that they have *as many as necessary but as few as possible*, when it comes to their work-life supports. The goal is to support employees and create the conditions for great corporate results while avoiding a complex bureaucracy of policies and practices that have the unintended consequence of limiting flexibility.

MAKING A BUSINESS CASE FOR WORK-LIFE SUPPORTS

For some, the benefits of work-life supports seem intuitively obvious, but not all companies are convinced. My research with senior executives at a variety of companies suggests a strong business case for implementing work-life supports and for positive organizational results such as engagement, productivity, cost savings, and enhanced attraction and retention of employees. The logic is fairly simple: work-life supports are good for people, which in turn leads to their greater engagement and contribution, which in turn leads to more positive business outcomes (for example, lower costs, greater productivity, and improved customer satisfaction), which in turn leads to better overall organizational outcomes such as profitability and financial performance (see Figure 1). When organizations serve people, they serve their own business results.

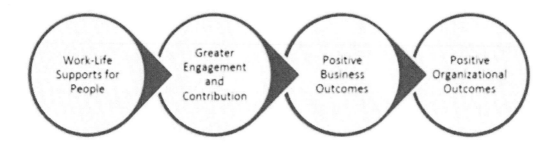

Figure 1. Model of work-life supports.

Executives in my study (Brower, 2014) strongly believe that work-life supports result in positive outcomes for companies. While they have differing perspectives on which outcomes are most positively affected, they are united in their belief that they are positive in that effect. Kyle,[2] a longtime executive at one of the nation's largest oil and gas companies, describes a situation in which a member of his staff was dealing with her husband's Lou Gehrig's disease and the significant time off of work that necessitated. The company accommodated her absences for many months. As a result, her commitment to the company was cemented because she was so appreciative of the company's support. Some situations are not as extreme, of course, but the point remains. Another executive from a manufacturing company says, "When employees don't have to worry about health care or financial issues, they can focus on success and growing our business. They have the mental clarity . . . to take the initiative and implement new ideas." The chief people officer for a leading global technology company agrees that employee engagement and contributions are maximized when distractions are reduced: "Having an engaged workforce is essential to success. We understand that people who are able to focus on their work with minimal distraction are going to have the highest

---

[2] Names are pseudonyms.

chance to help the company grow and succeed." Her company invests heavily in programs such as day care, on-site health care, athletic club memberships, dry-cleaning services, sabbaticals, and many other programs that help employees feel important, appreciated, and supported in both their work and their life.

The Dynamic of Reciprocity

One element of our human condition is the concept of reciprocity. People tend to choose to respond to those around them in a way that is consistent with the way others treat them (Gouldner, 1960; Settoon, Bennett, & Liden, 1996). When employers help employees, the employees in turn want to help the company. They want to respond in a way that mirrors the benefits they've received from the company. This reality works to the benefit of both parties, and work-life supports are a "give" for the company in turn to "get" from employees. When people feel valued, it typically enhances their commitment to the organization.

Organizations have both opportunities and obligations to serve employees. Barbara is with a banking institution and says that people in her company work many hours, and as a result, the company should provide them with flexibility. It is the reciprocity argument turned toward the company. Barbara also makes an argument for the positive effects on results. She says that within her organization flexibility leads to engagement, which in turn leads to productivity and positive results. Michelle, an executive at a manufacturing company, also links work-life supports to productivity. She believes that companies keep costs down when they increase engagement and retention in employees because the company is meeting them halfway. In her comments, she demonstrates our deeply felt human desire for reciprocity. Her comments are also a reflection of how perceived organizational supports (Eisenberger & Stinglhamber, 2011) tend to foster enthusiastic and productive behaviors among employees. Ultimately, there is a mutually beneficial relationship set up between the company and the employee. A company that leverages work-life supports creates conditions for work-life integration and fulfillment and in turn positively influences its business results.

There is also a tie to happiness. Livia, from a media company, says that people perform better when they are happier at their jobs and have flexibility. Ross, from an oil and gas company, says ensuring that employee needs and business needs are met translates into winning employees' hearts and minds. In this situation, he believes, employees are more likely to give their best because they feel respected and appreciated. They contribute enthusiastically rather than simply demonstrating compliance or submission. This dynamic of reciprocity is most compelling when it is both emotional and cognitive. Companies that win both hearts and minds achieve the highest levels of engagement and commitment from employees.

Powerful Messages

Work-life supports send strong messages about the extent to which a company values an employee. Michelle, an executive at a manufacturing firm, says that work-life supports communicate to employees they are valued as people, not just for the tasks they perform. She says that this affects their engagement because they in turn feel better toward the company even if they do not personally take advantage of the programs and policies available. Diane, from a media company, believes that bonding and enthusiasm are positively affected by providing work-life support programs. She says that people will "go the extra mile" when they believe the company cares about them as a whole person.

Cost Savings

Saving money is also at the top of leaders' lists regarding the positive outcomes of work-life supports. Frank, from a manufacturing company, and for whom a portion of his responsibilities include real estate and facilities, calculates that he saves $100,000 in facility costs by giving one employee flexibility and allowing him or her to work from home. Isaiah and Lee also lead real estate and facilities departments at international technology companies. They each agree that they save money through work-life supports because absenteeism is reduced in all parts of their workforce. As an example, more flexibility usually results in workers who work from home when their child is sick rather than missing work entirely.

Talent Attraction and Retention

Employee experience is also critical to attracting and retaining talent, and work-life supports can be a powerful differentiating factor. Ross, from an oil and gas company, says that work-life supports are more important than ever today. In his view, they create the kind of workplace that is differentiated from other kinds of companies because employees are becoming more astute and demanding. Employees are raising the bar on their own expectations for a full range of work-life options.

The generally accepted cost of turnover is three times an employee's salary. This includes costs for lost productivity as well as recruiting and training. It does not include costs for the loss of organizational memory, nor the costs for loss of the best and brightest employees. Work-life supports provide a reason for employees to join and stay with a company. A 2013 study of workplaces by the American Psychological Association found that when companies promote well-being and performance, their turnover was only 6 percent. In comparison, the national average turnover rate is 38 percent (APA, 2013).

Creating an environment of work-life support and fulfillment pays off for employees and for companies.

Isaiah, from a technology company, says that his company competes fiercely for talent. Work-life supports are a critical component for him. Barbara, an executive at a bank, agrees. She says that autonomy and flexibility are crucial to positive employee experience, and repeatedly, flexibility is a real factor for people in making decisions about where they want to work and how much discretionary time they choose to give. Ross, an executive from an oil and gas company, sees this in a similar way. He says that top talent will not be attracted to a business unless there is an atmosphere of work-life support and an opportunity for fulfillment in both work and life. Recent research corroborates that flexibility in the workplace is attractive. Specifically it found that when workplaces offer flexible options, they are more attractive to 90 percent of workers (Morgan, 2013).

Measuring the Impact

Sometimes leaders make the point that work-life supports are too difficult to measure, and indeed measuring the impact is challenging. Work-life supports are always part of a system and a holistic experience of work. It can be very difficult to isolate the variables of work-life supports. Lisa, head of HR from a leading global technology company, says that leaders can become overly focused on the costs of an activity because the costs are tangible. However, she recommends listing costs and benefits side by side in order to determine where satisfaction can be created for employees and the extent to which happiness and engagement provide intangible positive returns. Despite the challenges in measuring work-life supports' impacts, it is still important to provide them based on the competitive marketplace for talent and the preponderance of anecdotal and quantitative support for the strategy.

Multiple Options

There are multiple right answers as to how leaders and organizations implement work-life supports. Rather than a prescriptive or formulaic approach, companies are right to create a cocktail of work-life supports that help employees to integrate work and life and create the conditions for fulfillment. Leaders are right to implement benefits, policies, practices, and cultural norms that are in alignment with the company's current and desired goals and culture. They are also right to ensure that work-life supports are part of the business rather than a program-of-the-month or a short-term solution.

Companies must be explicit in making the case for how work-life supports fit into the overall framework within which an organization operates.

SUMMING IT UP

Rather than an approach of "work-life balance," I recommend taking a different perspective on work-life, which includes work-life integration over the life course and the assumption that work and life can both be part of a fulfilling whole. These perspectives set the stage for a more expansive and creative view of how we solve problems and reimagine options for all kinds of employees who are seeking fulfillment through both work and life. A holistic and broad view of work-life supports includes benefits, policies, practices, and cultural norms that a company provides in order to help employees to integrate work and life. Perhaps most importantly, the provision of work-life supports is good for people and also good for companies. The business case is powerful, and multiple senior executives reinforce that from cost savings to attraction and retention of the best talent, the benefits of work-life supports are worth the effort to implement. Work-life supports serve both people and organizations, and when they operate effectively, they help bring work to life and life to work.

REFERENCES

American Psychological Association (*APA*). (2013). Stress in America. Retrieved July 16, 2013, from http://www.apa.org/.

Brower, T. (2014). *Bring Work to Life by Bringing Life to Work: A Guide for Leaders and Organizations*. Brookline, MA: Bibliomotion.

Gouldner, A. (1960). The norm of social reciprocity: A preliminary statement. *American Sociological Review, 25*, 161–178.

Eisenberger, R., & Stinglhamber, F. (2011). *Perceived organizational support: Fostering enthusiastic and productive employees*. Washington, DC: American Psychological Association.

Morgan, J. (2013). 8 indisputable reasons for why we don't need offices. *Forbes*. Retrieved October 1, 2013, from http://www.forbes.com/.

Sandler, L. (2013, August 12). None is enough. *Time*.

Settoon, R. P., Bennett, N., & Liden, R. C. (1996). Social exchange in organizations: Perceived organizational support, leader-member exchange, and employee reciprocity. *Journal of Applied Psychology, 81*, 2019–227.

INDEX

P

R

Z